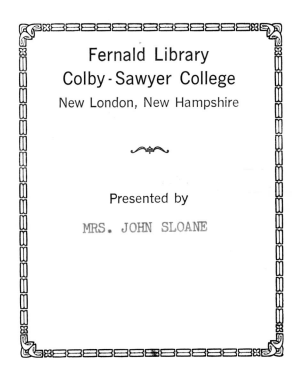

BLACK AMERICANS AND THE POLITICAL SYSTEM

Lucius J. Barker
Jesse J. McCorry, Jr.

Washington University, St. Louis

Winthrop Publishers, Inc.
Cambridge, Massachusetts

Library of Congress Cataloging in Publication Data

E
185. 61
B23

Barker, Lucius Jefferson
   Black Americans and the political system.

   Bibliography: p.
   Includes index.
   1. Afro-Americans — Politics and suffrage.   2. Uni-
ted States — Politics and government — 1945-
I. McCorry, Jesse J. joint author.   II. Title.
E185.61.B23   323.1′19′6073   75-33043
ISBN 0-87626-080-6
ISBN 0-87626-079-2 pbk.

© *1976 by Winthrop Publishers, Inc.*
   17 Dunster Street, Cambridge, Massachusetts 02138

CONTENTS

Preface / vii

1 Black Americans and the Political System: Politics of Uncertainty / 1

The Black Population: A Political-Social Profile / 2
Political Status / 9
The Political System: What Place for Blacks? / 11
Topics for Discussion / 22

2 The Nature of the Problem / 25

Poverty Set Conditions for Black Political Behavior / 26
Beginnings of Economic Inequality / 28
War Increases Black Opportunities / 30
The Political Education of Black Americans / 31
Income Gains and Losses Since World War II / 33
Income is Not the Only Problem: Patterns in Public Schools
    and Black Education / 40
The Housing Problem and the "Ghettoization" of the Black
    Middle Class / 47
Black Affluence Does Not Produce Security / 51
Class Insecurity is Part of the Problem / 55
Blacks and Whites Do Not See the Same Reality / 57
The Problem: Black and White Attitudes / 62
Topics for Discussion / 67
Suggested Readings / 68

3 The Nature of the System / 69

Introduction / 69
American Political Values / 70

iii

Features of the System / 75
On Elites and Political Participation / 78
Topics for Discussion / 88
Suggested Readings / 89

4   The Quest for Political Resources / 91

Voting is a Limited Political Resource / 92
The Development of Habits of Nonparticipation / 94
Political Education / 96
Institutional Structure as Protection and Political
    Depressant / 97
Black Urbanization and the Entry into Politics / 100
Black Upper Classes and Political Leadership Roles / 102
Surge and Decline of the Black Organizational Base / 107
Citizenship is More than Legal Rights / 109
Resource Use and Political Outcomes / 113
Rewards from Political Activism / 120
One Man — One Vote / 122
Bureaucracy as a Representative Institution / 123
Topics for Discussion / 130
Suggested Readings / 132

**5   Change Through Law: Courts, Politics, and the Legal
Process / 133**

Courts, Politics, and the Legal Process / 135
Participants in the Legal Process: An Overview / 139
Lawyers and the Legal Profession / 140
Courts and Judges / 149
Topics for Discussion / 161
Suggested Readings / 162

6   Change Through Law: Courts and Policy-Making / 165

Introduction / 166
Courts, Policy-Making, and Civil Rights / 166
Constitutionalizing Racism: Its Birth and Decline / 168
The Supreme Court from Warren to Burger: Implications
    for Black Americans and the Political System / 171

The Warren Court and Racial Discrimination / 172
Crime and Poverty: Old Problems, New Law / 175
The Warren Court and Civil Rights: An Overview / 176
New Judges, New Trends: The Burger Court / 177
A Setback to Busing: The Detroit Case / 182
The Burger Court and the Rights of the Poor / 185
"Law and Order": The Nixon Pledge and the Court
    Performance / 189
Continuity and Change: From Warren to Burger / 191
Implications for Black Americans / 192
Importance of Judicial Support / 195
Impact on Lower Courts / 197
The Role of the Supreme Court: A Summary View / 198
But Not by Judges Alone: Impact and Compliance / 199
Topics for Discussion / 202
Suggested Readings / 203

7 **Change Through Politics: Interest Groups and Political
Parties / 205**

Introduction / 206
Interest Groups: Nature and Operation / 207
Black Interest Groups: Problems Old and New / 215
"Coalitions in the Civil Rights Movement," Lucius J.
    Barker and Donald Jansiewicz / 216
The Civil Rights Movement: New Groups, New
    Directions, New Problems / 235
Political Parties / 240
Interest Groups and Political Parties: Some Concluding
    Observations / 255
Topics for Discussion / 258
Suggested Readings / 259

8 **Change Through Politics: The President and Congress / 261**

Introduction / 262
The President / 262
The Congressional Arena / 266
The President, Congress, and Black Americans: Some
    General Observations / 276
From Protest to Politics: The Congressional Black
    Caucus / 285

"The Black Caucus: Five Years Later," Alex Poinsett / 285
Topics for Discussion / 301
Suggested Readings / 302

9   Policy-Making and the Need for Political Resources / 304

Introduction / 305
The Policy Process — An Overview / 305
Agenda Setting and Initiation / 307
Initial Outcome: The Legislative Product / 313
Secondary Outcome: Administration and Impact / 322
Response, Feedback and Future Prospects / 324
Topics for Discussion / 327
Suggested Readings / 328

10   The Problem Restated / 330

Introduction / 332
The Problem in General Perspective / 332
The Problem in Topical Perspective / 346
A Concluding Note / 351
Topics for Discussion / 352
Suggested Readings / 353

The Constitution of the United States / 355

Glossary / 370

Index / 378

PREFACE

This is a book about how black people fare in the American political system. But it is more than just another book on black politics. It may also be viewed as an "introduction" to American national government. Indeed, this volume attempts to combine the salient features of black politics with those of American politics generally. The effort, however, has been trying and exhausting, and we know that much more can be done. Nonetheless, it does represent a beginning which we hope will allow our readers to gain more insight into the nature of black politics and the workings of our political system.

In many ways the story of blacks provides one of the most penetrating yet seldom used vantage points from which to view the nature and operation of the American political system. This vantage point allows us to see quite vividly that some of our most cherished political values do not necessarily operate to the benefit of all Americans. We sometimes need to be reminded, for example, that "majority rule" for whites has too often meant "minority oppression" for blacks. In addition, the story of blacks in American politics allows us to relate the constitutional theory and structure of our political institutions to their everyday practice and operation. It is interesting to note, for example, *how and in what ways* the structures and functions of the presidency, the Congress, and the Supreme Court affect the aspirations of blacks and other minorities. In a similar vein, we view the role that interest groups and political parties perform in the political system. And though we only summarize the nature and functions of these various institutions, we are nonetheless struck with what even this brief summary reveals about the nature of our governmental operation. Herein lies the major purpose of this volume. It is not that the system favors the rich and powerful, that blacks remain an oppressed people, and that racism lurks in the hearts of many white Americans — although there is some truth in each of these things.

Rather our major purpose here is to show that in large measure the structures of the political system and their present operation seriously disadvantage blacks and other minorities as they attempt to gain the full benefits of American society. As such, it follows that the major strides which blacks have made came only with uncommon sacrifices. That the nation's political institutions and processes have been able to endure might speak well for the system, but can hardly be encouraging to blacks who view that system with something less than Olympian detachment. In this volume we attempt to assess the situation of black Americans in fair but realistic terms.

Some additional comments. The reader should note that words in **boldface** type are included in a Glossary at the end of the volume. We trust that this brief explanation of terms will prove helpful. Additionally, at the conclusion of each chapter there are several Topics for Discussion. The Topics are designed to stimulate discussion on problems related to materials in the particular chapter. Also, a *Teachers Manual* is available for instructors who wish to use it with the text. For each chapter, the *Manual* includes lecture suggestions, behavioral objectives, and a variety of essay and objective questions.

Many persons have helped us in many ways and we wish to thank them all. However, as in any endeavor of this kind, there are those whose assistance and encouragement merit special mention. First of all, we wish to acknowledge our professional colleagues who read the entire manuscript and offered valuable criticisms and suggestions. Among these are Professor E. Wally Miles of San Diego State University, Professor Jewell Prestage of Southern University of Baton Rouge, Professor Nolan Jones of the University of Michigan, and Professor Robert Salisbury of Washington University, St. Louis. We also profited greatly from the comments of several professional colleagues who refereed the manuscript for the publishers and who, as usual, remain anonymous.

We happily acknowledge a debt of gratitude to our colleagues in the Department of Political Science here at Washington University. They provide what must be the optimum in terms of a pleasant and stimulating intellectual environment. The debt to our present (and former) graduate assistants is great and we acknowledge their help, knowing full well that in naming some we run the risk of omitting others. Nonetheless, among those who helped are: Marc Schnall, Peggy Heilig, Michael Mulkey, Kenneth Wald, David Ahl, Lawrence Callum, Michael Combs, Thomas Likens, and Wayne McIntosh. We also wish to express our appreciation for the untiring and cheerful assistance of our secretarial staff, Ms. Natalie Sekuler and Ms. Lillian Ehrlich. By working the usual miracles, they saw the manuscript through several revisions while keeping the Department afloat.

Our publishers have been more than professional publishers; they have been friends as well. James J. Murray III, president of Winthrop, must be given credit for seeing that an idea which was casually raised in conversation did not die prematurely. Nancy Benjamin, our production editor, did one of the most kindly jobs of "pestering" us with questions and deadlines that we have ever experienced. Others at Winthrop, including William Sernett, helped considerably to make our task much easier. We must also thank those who granted us permission to use materials and photographs to enhance the richness of this volume. Specific acknowledgment to them is made elsewhere.

As is usually the case, some of the suggestions which were given to us have been declined at our own peril. And, for the resulting errors of omission and commission we accept full responsibility. We trust that our readers will call them to our attention.

For
Maude, Tracey, and Heidi
and
Tracey, Erica, and Leah

1

BLACK AMERICANS
AND THE POLITICAL SYSTEM:
POLITICS OF UNCERTAINTY

In the process of [a] hundred years of waiting, black people . . . have developed a split personality. The supreme law of the land establishes their freedom and guarantees them equality of treatment; but they accept and act upon this guarantee at their peril. And this is so because each day the men who are charged with interpreting and applying the law equally give the lie to this guarantee. So the black man even now is in doubt from day to day and from community to community what the law of the day, as applied to him, really is.

Judge George W. Crockett, Jr. *

Black Americans make up about 11 percent or 23,000,000 of the approximately 214,000,000 in the United States. During the 1960's the black population increased by almost 4 million. Though the rate of increase has slowed, it nevertheless shows the difference in growth rates between whites and blacks in this country. And in a **political system** where population and votes contribute to political power, a minority of such size has considerable weight.

But we need to know more before we can assess the influence of black Americans and their role(s) in American politics. For example, how is the black population distributed? What is the socioeconomic status of black Americans? What is the attitude of blacks toward politics and the political system? What is the structure of the American political system?

* *Science and Society*, Sp., 1969, 33:225. Reprinted with permission.

How does this structure relate to black hopes and political efforts? Answers to these and similar questions, especially the latter two, are undoubtedly shaped by many factors. However, it is particularly important to understand the experience of blacks in the political system. What that experience can tell us about the present and what it suggests for the future status of blacks in the system are among the principal reasons for this volume. This chapter examines the characteristics of the black population. It also describes generally how this minority has fared in the American political system.

The Black Population: A Political-Social Profile

Black Americans are strikingly big-city oriented.[1] This urbanization began just before World War I. It continues today although at a slower rate. The black population has remained virtually constant. Yet there has been a sharp drop in the white population in the nation's central cities. (See Figure 1-1; see also Table 1-1.)

At first, the increase among blacks was mainly due to the rapid migration of blacks from the South. The people who migrated hoped to profit from "war" jobs in the industrializing and **urban** North. At the same time, of course, they too had heard of — or imagined — the "good life" in the "free" North as compared to the "slave" South. This desire was reinforced by the daily indignities and legal restrictions that blacks suffered in the South. The "good life" stories coming from the son or cousin who returned home briefly and told of finding a "new" life in the North also was a factor.

Since the late 1960's this general south to north migration among blacks has considerably slowed. There are some indications that a reverse trend southward might be developing.[2] This situation may be because the "good life" of the North is contrasted daily to the stark realities of existence there. Also, the real and symbolic changes in the legal, economic, and political status of blacks in the South has affected the trend. The reverse migration shows blacks moving into fast-growing cities such as Atlanta, Georgia, and Houston, Texas. The geographer Harold Rose has described this central city concentration of blacks as a **"national ghetto system."**[3] As the ghetto spreads whites continue their exodus to suburbia. Figure 1-1 shows that the pace of white **suburbanization** slowed between 1960 and 1970. But it did not signal the start of a

---

[1] For an interesting and innovative account of black population patterns, see Harold Rose, *The Black Ghetto: A Spatial Behavioral Perspective* (New York: McGraw-Hill, 1971).

[2] *Ebony Magazine*, "Blacks Returning South."

[3] Rose, *The Black Ghetto*, p. 15ff.

Millions of Persons

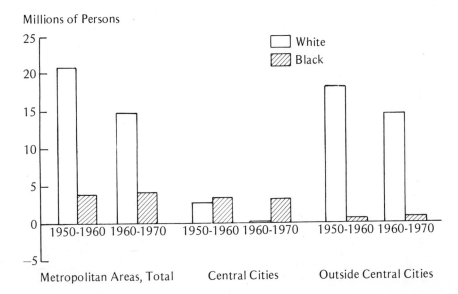

FIGURE 1-1
Population Changes in Metropolitan Areas, By Race: 1950–1960 and 1960–1970

SOURCE: Reprinted from *Statistical Abstract of the U.S.,* 1974, p. 4.

cityward migration. As a consequence, many of the nation's largest urban areas either have, or will soon have, black majorities.

The magnitude and potential impact on the nation of this movement of black Americans were beginning to be recognized as early as the late 1950's. In a 1957 essay entitled "The New America," *Newsweek* wrote:

> The Negroes are on the move. More and more of them are swarming from the farms of the South into the cities of the North. In 1900, only 10 percent of the Negro population lived outside the South; today, 40 percent do. . . . This vast movement is creating equally vast changes in the social, cultural, economic, and political complexion of the nation, and particularly of the North, creating tensions and problems that never existed before.[4]

The magazine's readers might have been startled by the figures in some of the largest cities (see Table 1-2). Clearly, blacks were becoming numerically important. *Newsweek* made the inevitable political connection, saying that "with migration swelling ranks of the Negro voters in

---

[4] *Newsweek,* December 23, 1957.

TABLE 1-1
Population, by Race — States: 1950 to 1970 [As of April 1, Resident population]

STATE	1950 WHITE	NEGRO	OTHER RACES	1960 WHITE	NEGRO	OTHER RACES	1970 WHITE	NEGRO NUMBER	NEGRO PERCENT OF ALL CLASSES	OTHER RACES
U.S. ------	135,149,629	15,044,937	1,131,232	158,831,732	18,871,831	1,619,612	177,748,975	22,580,289	11.1	2,882,662
N.E. ----	9,161,156	142,941	10,356	10,242,389	243,363	23,615	11,388,774	388,398	3.3	64,491
Maine --	910,846	1,221	1,707	963,291	3,318	2,656	985,276	2,800	0.3	3,972
N.H. ----	532,275	731	236	604,334	1,903	684	733,106	2,505	0.3	2,070
Vt. ------	377,188	443	116	389,092	519	270	442,553	761	0.2	1,016
Mass. --	4,611,503	73,171	5,840	5,023,144	111,842	13,592	5,477,624	175,817	3.1	35,729
R.I. -----	777,015	13,903	978	838,712	18,332	2,444	914,757	25,338	2.7	6,630
Conn. --	1,952,329	53,472	1,479	2,423,816	107,449	3,969	2,835,458	181,177	6.0	15,074
M.A. ----	28,237,528	1,875,241	50,764	31,280,078	2,785,136	103,238	32,921,730	3,955,755	10.6	321,555
N.Y. ----	13,872,095	918,191	39,906	15,287,071	1,417,511	77,722	15,834,090	2,168,949	11.9	233,928
N.J. ----	4,511,585	318,565	5,179	5,539,003	514,875	12,904	6,349,908	770,292	10.7	47,964
Pa. ------	9,853,848	638,485	5,679	10,454,004	852,750	12,612	10,737,732	1,016,514	8.6	39,663
E.N.C. --	28,543,307	1,803,698	52,363	33,253,272	2,884,969	86,783	36,160,135	3,872,905	9.6	219,436
Ohio ----	7,428,222	513,072	5,333	8,909,698	786,097	10,602	9,646,997	970,477	9.1	34,543
Ind. -----	3,758,512	174,168	1,544	4,388,554	269,275	4,669	4,820,324	357,464	6.9	15,881
Ill. -------	8,046,058	645,980	20,138	9,010,252	1,037,470	33,436	9,600,381	1,425,674	12.8	87,921
Mich. --	5,917,825	442,296	11,645	7,085,865	717,581	19,748	7,833,474	991,066	11.2	50,543
Wis. ----	3,392,690	28,182	13,703	3,858,903	74,546	18,328	4,258,959	128,224	2.9	30,548
W.N.C. --	13,576,077	424,178	61,139	14,749,345	561,068	83,702	15,481,048	698,645	4.3	139,494
Minn. --	2,953,697	14,022	14,764	3,371,603	22,263	19,998	3,736,038	34,868	0.9	34,065
Iowa ----	2,599,546	19,692	1,835	2,728,709	25,354	3,474	2,782,762	32,596	1.2	9,018

State	1950 White	1950 Negro	1950 Other Races	1960 White	1960 Negro	1960 Other Races	1970 White	1970 Negro Number	1970 Negro Percent of all Classes	1970 Other Races
Mo.	3,655,593	297,088	1,972	3,922,967	390,853	5,993	4,177,495	480,172	10.3	18,834
N. Dak.	608,448	257	10,931	619,538	777	12,131	599,485	2,494	0.4	15,782
S. Dak.	628,504	727	23,509	653,098	1,114	26,302	630,333	1,627	0.2	33,547
Nebr.	1,301,328	19,234	4,948	1,374,764	29,262	7,304	1,432,867	39,911	2.7	10,715
Kans.	1,828,961	73,158	3,180	2,078,666	91,445	8,500	2,122,068	106,977	4.8	17,533
S.A.	16,041,709	5,094,744	45,882	20,047,496	5,844,565	79,671	24,112,395	6,388,496	20.8	170,446
Del.	273,878	43,598	609	384,327	60,688	1,277	466,459	78,276	14.3	3,369
Md.	1,954,975	385,972	2,054	2,573,919	518,410	8,360	3,194,888	699,479	17.8	28,032
D.C.	517,865	280,803	3,510	345,263	411,737	6,956	209,272	537,712	71.1	9,526
Va.	2,581,555	734,211	2,914	3,142,443	816,258	8,248	3,761,514	861,368	18.5	25,612
W. Va.	1,890,282	114,867	403	1,770,133	89,378	910	1,673,480	67,342	3.9	3,415
N.C.	2,983,121	1,047,353	31,455	3,399,285	1,116,021	40,849	3,901,767	1,126,478	22.2	53,814
S.C.	1,293,405	822,077	1,545	1,551,022	829,291	2,281	1,794,430	789,041	30.5	7,045
Ga.	2,380,577	1,062,762	1,239	2,817,223	1,122,596	3,297	3,391,242	1,187,149	25.9	11,184
Fla.	2,166,051	603,101	2,153	4,063,881	880,186	7,493	5,179,343	1,041,651	15.3	28,449
E.S.C.	8,770,570	2,698,635	7,976	9,338,991	2,698,839	12,296	10,202,810	2,571,291	20.1	29,369
Ky.	2,742,090	201,921	795	2,820,083	215,949	2,124	2,981,766	230,793	7.2	6,147
Tenn.	2,760,257	530,603	858	2,977,753	586,876	2,460	3,293,930	621,261	15.8	8,496
Ala.	2,079,591	979,617	2,535	2,283,609	980,271	2,860	2,533,831	903,467	26.2	6,867
Miss.	1,188,632	986,494	3,788	1,257,546	915,743	4,852	1,393,283	815,770	36.8	7,859
W.S.C.	12,037,250	2,432,028	68,294	14,090,149	2,768,203	92,903	16,104,903	3,010,174	15.6	205,483
Ark.	1,481,507	426,639	1,365	1,395,703	388,787	1,782	1,565,915	352,445	18.3	4,935
La.	1,796,683	882,428	4,405	2,211,715	1,039,207	6,100	2,541,498	1,086,832	29.8	12,976

TABLE 1-1
Population, by Race — States: 1950 to 1970 [As of April 1, Resident population]

STATE	1950			1960			1970			
	WHITE	NEGRO	OTHER RACES	WHITE	NEGRO	OTHER RACES	WHITE	NEGRO NUMBER	NEGRO PERCENT OF ALL CLASSES	OTHER RACES
Okla. ----	2,032,526	145,503	55,322	2,107,900	153,084	67,300	2,280,362	171,892	6.7	106,975
Tex. ----	6,726,534	977,458	7,202	8,374,831	1,187,125	17,721	9,717,128	1,399,005	12.5	80,597
Mt. ------	**4,845,634**	**66,429**	**162,935**	**6,514,294**	**123,242**	**217,524**	**7,798,087**	**180,382**	**2.2**	**303,093**
Mont. --	572,038	1,232	17,754	650,738	1,467	22,562	663,043	1,995	0.3	29,371
Idaho --	581,395	1,050	6,192	657,383	1,502	8,306	698,802	2,130	0.3	11,635
Wyo. ----	284,009	2,557	3,963	322,922	2,183	4,961	323,024	2,568	0.8	6,824
Colo. ----	1,296,653	20,177	8,259	1,700,700	39,992	13,255	2,112,352	66,411	3.0	28,496
N.Mex.--	630,211	8,408	42,568	875,763	17,063	58,197	915,815	19,555	1.9	80,630
Ariz. ----	654,511	25,974	69,102	1,169,517	43,403	89,241	1,604,948	53,344	3.0	112,608
Utah ----	676,909	2,729	9,224	873,828	4,148	12,651	1,031,926	6,617	0.6	20,730
Nev. ----	149,908	4,302	5,873	263,443	13,484	8,351	448,177	27,762	5.7	12,799
Pac. -------	**13,936,398**	**507,043**	**671,523**	**19,315,718**	**962,446**	**919,880**	**23,579,093**	**1,514,243**	**5.7**	**1,429,295**
Wash. --	2,316,496	30,691	31,776	2,751,675	48,738	52,801	3,251,055	71,308	2.1	86,806
Oreg. --	1,497,128	11,529	12,684	1,732,037	18,133	18,517	2,032,079	26,308	1.3	32,998
Calif. ----	9,915,173	462,172	208,878	14,455,230	883,861	378,113	17,761,032	1,400,143	7.0	791,959
Alaska --	92,808	(1)	35,835	174,546	6,771	44,850	236,767	8,911	3.0	54,704
Hawaii --	114,793	2,651	382,350	202,230	4,943	425,599	298,160	7,573	1.0	462,828

[1] Not identified separately.
SOURCE: U.S. Bureau of the Census, *U.S. Census of Population: 1950,* vol. II, part 1; *1960,* vol. I; and *1970,* vol. I, part B. Reprinted from *Statistical Abstract of the U.S.,* 1974, p. 29.

TABLE 1-2
Black Population Growth: Selected U.S. Cities (in thousands)

	Detroit	St. Louis	Baltimore	Chicago	N.Y.C.	Phila.	Los Angeles	D.C.
Total (1957)	1,910	863	974	3,790	7,800	2,200	2,240	855
1900	4	36	79	30	61	63	2	87
1940	149	109	166	278	458	251	64	187
1957	475	225	280	633	948	462	255	375
1967 est.	600	300	390	870	1,100	522	800	475

the central cities, changes are due."[5] The article continued by asking, "Could the migrants turn Northern cities into predominantly colored communities run by colored officials?" "Not in the foreseeable future," answered *Newsweek*, "except conceivably in Washington. . . ." "But," concluded the magazine, "Negro influence will gain steadily."[6]

Newsweek's prediction has not come true fully. Some of these northern cities, including Washington, D.C., have indeed come under "colored" officials. In 1967 blacks won several mayoral elections: Carl Stokes in Cleveland, Richard Hatcher in Gary, Indiana, and Kenneth Gibson in Newark. Blacks have continued to win prominent urban political offices. More recently, of course, Maynard Jackson became Mayor in Atlanta, Coleman Young in Detroit, and Thomas Bradley in Los Angeles. For the most part, however, these political gains are closely connected to the shrinking white populations of the central cities. But though whites continue to abandon central cities as places of residence, they continue to influence what happens in "downtown."

The distribution and trends in the black population have brought with them certain consequences that affect the socioeconomic conditions of blacks. When whites flee the central city, they take more than personal possessions. Business and industry soon follow, intensifying the tax losses that result from declines in property tax revenues. This seriously lessens job opportunities for blacks remaining in the cities. It also lessens the city's financial ability to carry on functions which make a city livable. These phenomena add to the bleak unemployment picture for blacks. (Black unemployment continues to be double that of whites.) They also contribute to the self-fulfilling prophecy of "how blacks live in the ghetto."[7]

The eroding economic base of central cities, and its corresponding effects on blacks, is indicated in several ways. The extent of unemployment and **underemployment** among blacks, for example, is starkly reflected in Census Bureau reports. These reports show that *one out of every three blacks* (33 percent) in the United States have income below the "low income level" — in short, below the **poverty level**. On the contrary, fewer than *one out of ten* (or about 9 percent) white Americans are below this level. In addition, the black ghetto is characterized by poor, run-down, and overcrowded housing, dirty streets and generally poor sanitary conditions, a high level of crime, and poor and overcrowded schools. It is true that there has been improvement in the socioeconomic status of blacks. For example, the number of black families with incomes

---

⁵ Ibid.

⁶ Ibid.

⁷ For a penetrating analysis of ghetto conditions, see Rose, esp. chapters 2, 3, and 5. Also see Kenneth Clark, *Dark Ghetto* (New York: Harper & Row, 1965).

of $10,000 or more has increased. But there has also been improvement in the socioeconomic status of whites: this means that the inequality gap between whites and blacks has not changed very much in the last decade. The change that has occurred tends to broaden rather than to narrow the difference in income between whites and blacks. One possible exception is in the area of education, where the gap seems to be narrowing. But the quality of that education is another matter. A more detailed analysis of these and other factors is reserved for the next chapter. For our purposes here, it is sufficient to say that essentially the socioeconomic status of blacks, when compared to that of whites, has improved little — if at all — in the last ten years. Blacks remain disadvantaged and deprived of the things which make a good life.

Political Status

More blacks are engaged in traditional modes of political participation than ever before. The last ten years has indeed seen a turning away from "protest to politics." But for blacks, protest was the only effective form of political action until quite recently. There are more blacks voting, engaged in political party activity, campaigning for national, state, and local offices, and winning such offices than ever before. By 1975, for example, more than 3,500 blacks held local elective office. But political status goes beyond electoral politics. A crucial measure is how much given interests find representation in administrative and appointive public service positions. Such positions might include high-level administrative posts in the government bureaucracy (for example, cabinet positions and upper level political appointments in cabinet departments); top-level civil service positions; and ranking positions in state and local bureaucracies (for instance, state commissioner of education, director of streets and parks). Also important is representation in the legal profession and public safety fields. Perhaps our suggestion here appears to go "against the grain" of the ideal of neutral competence in the public service sector. But we find little to cheer about noting that Washington, D.C., got its first black uniformed police sergeant in 1957, or that only in that year did fire departments in big cities begin to recognize that blacks made satisfactory employees.[8]

Black representation in such administrative areas, in comparison to elective offices, is woefully sparse.[9] Black representation in elective and

---

[8] Fire departments are notoriously closed in their recruitment practices. In some ways they resembled the craft unions in the way they passed jobs from generation to generation within families.

[9] See chapter 4, for more data in this area.

appointive administrative positions and its implications for the political system is reserved for later discussion. A few preliminary comments are in order.[10]

The absence of blacks in high administrative positions suggests one explanation for the lack of improvement in the overall political status of blacks. For it is at this stage of the policy-making process where actual distribution (allocation) of resources takes place. Accordingly, the political advances symbolized by increased black voter registration and office-holding is perhaps more apparent than real. Moreover, the highly visible political activities — such as voter registration drives, election of big-city black mayors — conceal as much as they reveal about American politics. Such activities do not tell us very much about the overall process by which the actual allocation of values takes place in the political system. This lack creates tension between the image and the reality of change in the political status of blacks. It may also help to explain that while signs of change are all around, the lives of most blacks remain unchanged.

To be sure, the Civil Rights Act of 1964 and following legislation have brought about and indicate important changes in the legal, social, and economic status of blacks and other minorities. Moreover, much evidence shows that black political participation through voting was greatly strengthened and secured by the Voting Rights Act of 1965 and its amendments. Blacks now could register and vote in the South and did so in record numbers. This was indeed a significant accomplishment. These votes meant the election of a record number of blacks to public office. And this also showed the effectiveness of the legislation and the belief which it furthered that "the system worked." Many Americans, black and white, were understandably proud of these accomplishments. This, perhaps more than anything else, gave rise to the slogan "from Protest to Politics." The phrase seems to have caught on and is quite fashionable among white and black intellectuals and leadership groups. As far as blacks are concerned, the apparent change from "protests to politics" may be viewed as a strategy for survival, as a way of at least trying to *conserve* gains already made. This is especially plausible in view of the broad popular support for "law and order" in the 1968 presidential election. "Law and order" was widely interpreted as a euphemism for putting blacks back in their "place." Possibly, then, blacks had more to lose than gain by continued protests. It is not at all certain that blacks have discarded protests as a political resource. Neither is it certain, despite signs of progress, that blacks are convinced that the kinds of change needed to deal with their grievances can come through current political processes.

---

[10] See chapter 4.

Indeed, one conclusion from data on black attitudes toward the political system is that the gains made by blacks in the 1960's did not increase black trust in government.[11] In fact, that trust, when compared to whites, has declined significantly since 1968. Obviously, changes in the national political mood, reflected in the election and reelection of President Richard Nixon, sparked this decline in trust. Thus, black politicians and other leaders are in a difficult position. They, more than others, recognize the day-to-day problems of survival that their constituents have. And, they feel the constant pressures for immediate relief. At the same time, however, black officials understand, though many of their constituents do not, that to overcome these problems through the political process of bargaining and compromise is no easy, short-time job. That job is made more difficult because blacks generally lack the traditional resources needed to win victories and gain favorable policies in the political process. For example, blacks in Congress do not have the numbers or standing to wield significant influence there. Nor do they have a sufficiently broad and stable base from which to engage in day-to-day hard bargaining with congressional and administrative leaders.

Thus, as far as working through normal processes of the system are concerned, blacks in America do really face a problem. Indeed, in view of the basic inequalities that still exist, it is clear that many white Americans have not firmly concluded that blacks *should* be accorded a place, position, and status in American society the *same* as whites. Simply put, there is much evidence that some doubt remains in the white mind as to *whether blacks really are as good as whites* and hence *deserving* of the same treatment. In saying this, we are keenly aware that modern interpretations of the racial problem seldom surface as boldly as we have stated it here. But it is all too apparent that efforts to minimize or submerge the problem do not advance the cause of human rights or domestic tranquility. Consequently, and in view of history, the matter of race poses as much of a problem for white Americans as it does for blacks. Let us take a brief look at this history as we attempt to place the problem in broader perspective.

The Political System: What Place for Blacks?

Blacks have always had a place in American political life. But it has always differed from that of most Americans. When the Constitution was drafted, and later in the Constitution itself, democratic

---

[11] For a concise summary of racial attitudes toward government based on data from the Survey Research Center of the University of Michigan see Richard Dawson, *Public Opinion and Contemporary Disarray* (New York: Harper & Row, 1973), pp. 116–124, esp. 121.

values approved by the emerging United States were not intended to apply to the blacks in slavery. In fact, specific constitutional provisions, such as the **"three-fifths" compromise**,[12] were explicitly designed to keep blacks in a disadvantaged position from the nation's birth.

Any doubts about this were put to rest by the Supreme Court itself in the now famous (or infamous) *Dred Scott* case.[13] At issue was the attempt by Congress through the Missouri Compromise of 1820 to overcome the division in the nation over the expansion and existence of slavery. However, the Compromise was not to hold. Chief Justice Taney, who spoke for the Court in the *Dred Scott* decision, said in effect that Congress was without power and acted unconstitutionally in depriving a citizen "from holding and owning property of this kind [slaves] in the territory mentioned in the Compromise or in any place in the United States. Congress had no authority to confer the rights and privileges of citizenship on slaves or their descendants." One writer has put the matter succinctly and in broader perspective: the case "which gratuitously deprived blacks even in free states of rights of citizenship, is an example — often repeated — of how blacks become little more than pawns in litigation nominally concerning civil rights, but actually providing a forum for the resolution of competing interests of the white majority."[14]

More important for our purposes here, however, is Chief Justice Taney's detailed opinion of the actual and intended meaning of the Constitution and other historical documents and practices concerning the status of blacks in the early history of the country. Taney's opinion is quoted at length.[15]

> The question is simply this: can a negro, whose ancestors were imported into this country and sold as slaves, become a member of the political community formed and brought into existence by the Constitution of the United States, and as such become entitled to all the rights, and privileges, and immunities, guarantied by that instrument to the citizen. . . .
> . . .The only matter in issue before the court, therefore, is, whether the descendants of such slaves, when they shall be emancipated, or who are

---

[12] See Article I, sec. 2 which provided that "Representatives . . . shall be apportioned among the several States . . . by adding to the whole number of Free Persons . . . three fifths of all other Persons." This provision was later overcome by the Fourteenth Amendment. For other provisions in original Constitution that disadvantaged blacks see Article I, sec. 9; and Article IV, sec. 2.

[13] *Dred Scott* v. *Sandford* (60 U.S. 393, 19 How. 393, 1857). Of course, federal courts prior to *Dred Scott* had rendered pro-slavery decisions. See, for example, Bell, "The Judicial Response to Slavery Issues," note 12, *infra,* p. 22ff.

[14] Derrick A. Bell, Jr., *Race, Racism and American Law* (Boston: Little, Brown and Co., 1973), p. 2.

[15] 60 U.S. 393, 1857.

born of parents who had become free before their birth, are citizens of a state in the sense in which the word "citizen" is used in the Constitution of the United States. . . .

. . .We think they are not, and that they are not included, and were not intended to be included, under the word "citizens" in the Constitution and can, therefore, claim none of the rights and privileges which that instrument provides for and secures to citizens of the United States. On the contrary, they were at that time considered as a subordinate and inferior class of beings, who had been subjugated by the dominant race, and whether emancipated or not, yet remained subject to their authority, and had no rights or privileges but such as those who held the power and the government might choose to grant them.

The question then arises, whether the provisions of the Constitution, in relation to the personal rights and privileges to which the citizens of a state should be entitled, embraced the negro African race, at that time in this country, or who might afterwards be imported, who had then or should afterwards be made free in any State; and to put it in the power of a single State to make him a citizen of the United States, and endue him with the full rights of citizenship in every other State without their consent. Does the Constitution of the United States act upon him whenever he shall be made free under the laws of the State, and raised there to the rank of a citizen, and immediately clothe him with all the privileges of a citizen in every other state, and in its own courts?

In the opinion of the court, the legislation and histories of the times, and the language used in the Declaration of Independence, show that neither the class of persons who had been imported as slaves, nor their descendants, whether they had become free or not, were then acknowledged as a part of the people, nor intended to be included in the general words used in that memorable instrument.

It is difficult at this day to realize the state of public opinion in relation to that unfortunate race, which prevailed in the civilized and enlightened portions of the world at the time of the Declaration of Independence, and when the Constitution of the United States was framed and adopted. But the public history of every European nation displays it, in a manner too plain to be mistaken.

They had for more than a century before been regarded as being of an inferior order; and altogether unfit to associate with the white race, either in social or political relations; and so far inferior, that they had no rights which the white man was bound to respect; and that the negro might justly and lawfully be reduced to slavery for his benefit. He was bought and sold, and treated as an ordinary article of merchandise and traffic, whenever a profit could be made by it. This opinion was at that time fixed and universal in the civilized portion of the white race. It was regarded as an axiom in morals as well as in politics, which no one thought of disputing, or supposed to be open to dispute; and men in every grade and position in society daily and habitually acted upon it in their private pursuits, as well as in matters of public concern, without doubting for a moment the correctness of this opinion. . . .

The language of the Declaration of Independence is equally conclusive. It begins by declaring that, "When in the course of human events it becomes necessary for one people to dissolve the political bands which have connected them with another, and to assume among the powers of the earth the separate and equal station to which the laws of nature and nature's God entitle them, a decent respect for the opinions of mankind requires that they should declare the causes which impel them to the separation."

It then proceeds to say: "We hold these truths to be self-evident: that all men are created equal; that they are endowed by their Creator with certain unalienable rights; that among these are life, liberty, and the pursuit of happiness; that to secure these rights, governments are instituted, deriving their just powers from the consent of the governed."

The general words above quoted would seem to embrace the whole human family, and if they were used in a similar instrument at this day, would be so understood. But it is too clear for dispute, that the enslaved African race were not intended to be included, and formed no part of the people who framed and adopted this Declaration; for if the language, as understood in that day, would embrace them, the conduct of the distinguished men who framed the Declaration of Independence would have been utterly and flagrantly inconsistent with the principles they asserted; and instead of the sympathy of mankind, to which they so confidently appealed, they would have deserved and received universal rebuke and reprobation.

. . . They perfectly understood the meaning of the language they used, and how it would be understood by others; and they knew that it would not, in any part of the civilized world, be supposed to embrace the negro race, which, by common consent, had been excluded from civilized governments and the family of nations, and doomed to slavery. They spoke and acted according to the then established doctrines and principles, and in the ordinary language of the day, and no one misunderstood them. The unhappy black race were separated from the white by indeliable marks, and laws long before established, and were never thought of or spoken of except as property, and when the claims of the owner or the profit of the trader were supposed to need protection. . . .

No one of that race had ever migrated to the United States voluntarily; all of them had been brought here as articles of merchandise. The number that had been emancipated . . . were but few in comparison with those held in slavery; and they were identified in the public mind with the race to which they belonged, and regarded as a part of the slave population rather than the free. It is obvious that they were not even in the minds of the framers of the Constitution when they were conferring special rights and privileges upon the citizens of a State in every other part of the Union. . . .

The legislation of the States . . . shows, in a manner not to be mistaken, the inferior and subject condition of that race at the time the Constitution was adopted. . . .

The conduct of the Executive Department of the government has been in perfect harmony upon this subject with this course of legislation. . . .

No one, we presume, supposes that any change in public opinion or feeling, in relation to this unfortunate race, in the civilized nations of Europe or in this country, should induce the court to give to the words of the Constitution a more liberal construction in their favor than they were intended to bear when the instrument was framed and adopted.

What the construction was at that time we can hardly admit of doubt. We have the language of the Declaration of Independence and of the Articles of Confederation, in addition to the plain words of the Constitution itself; we have the legislation of the different States, before, about the time, and since the Constitution was adopted; we have the legislation of Congress, from the time of its adoption to a recent period; and we have the constant and uniform action of the Executive Department, all concurring together, and leading to the same result. And if anything in relation to the construction of the Constitution can be regarded as settled, it is that which we now give to the word "citizen" and the word "people."

But *Dred Scott* did not settle the slavery issue. If anything, it made the situation worse and eventually led to the Civil War. That war is considered the great divide in the position of blacks. And in many ways it was. As a result of that conflict, blacks did gain the legal status of freedmen through presidential proclamation and congressional statutes. More importantly, the **Civil War Amendments** (Thirteenth, Fourteenth, and Fifteenth) were added to the Constitution. These amendments sought to put this newly gained freedom for blacks on sound constitutional footing.

But the constitutional status of blacks was anything but basic. A presidential election (Hayes-Tilden, 1876) once again sacrificed the status of blacks under the guise of national reunification.[16] The politicking that put Hayes in the White House further subjected blacks to the mercy (and caprice) of their former masters and whites generally. Of at least equal importance were decisions of the U.S. Supreme Court that acted to erode and narrow the protections given blacks in congressional statutes as well as in the newly enacted constitutional amendments. Take, for example, the Court decision involving the Civil Rights Act of 1875. The Act sought to guarantee "that all persons within the jurisdiction of the United States shall be entitled to the full and equal enjoyment of the accommodations, advantages, theaters and other places of public amusement; subject only to the conditions and limitations established by law, and applicable alike to citizens of every race and color, regardless of any previous condition of servitude." Here then was a congressional attempt to give meaning to the newly enacted Civil War Amendments,

---

[16] The literature on this election is extensive. See the accounts in W. H. Dunning, *Reconstruction, Political and Economic: 1865-1877* (New York: Harper Torchbooks, 1962), pp.281ff.; and Herbert Agar, *The Price of Union* (Boston: Houghton Mifflin Co., 1967).

especially the Fourteenth. This amendment forbids states from making or enforcing laws that abridge the "privileges and immunities" of United States citizens, depriving "any person of life, liberty or property without due process of law," or from denying to "any person within [their] jurisdiction of equal protection of the laws."

But in the *Civil Rights Cases* (1883)[17] the Court held that the Fourteenth Amendment (or any other provision of the Constitution) did not confer on Congress the authority to pass the Act of 1875. The Fourteenth Amendment, said the Court, was intended to apply to "state action of a particular character. . . . Individual invasion of individual rights is not the subject-matter of the amendment." In short, the Court said that the Amendment prohibited *state* action, not *private* action. For the ex-slaves, this decision was a step back to *Dred Scott*. It permitted systematic exploitation of the freedmen. The precedent of the *Civil Rights Cases* even today haunts the effective realization of constitutional rights for black Americans.

The Court further eroded the status of blacks in *Plessy* v. *Ferguson* (1896).[18] Here the Court gave judicial (and constitutional) sanction to the "separate but equal" doctrine. The Court held that Louisiana possessed ample legislative authority through its police powers (promotion of comfort and public peace and good order) to require segregation of the two races on passenger trains. Said the Court:

> The object of the amendment [Fourteenth] was undoubtedly to enforce the absolute equality of the two races before the law, but in the nature of things it could not have been intended to abolish distinctions based upon color, or to enforce social, as distinguished from political, equality, or a comingling of the two races upon terms unsatisfactory to either. Laws permitting, and even requiring, their separation in places where they are liable to be brought into contact do not necessarily imply the inferiority of either race to the other, and have been generally, if not universally, recognized as within the competency of the state legislatures in the exercise of their police power.

In addition, the Court brushed aside the plaintiff's (Plessy) contention that the Louisiana statute would stamp "the colored race with a badge of inferiority." To enforce its position that "social prejudices" cannot be overcome by legislation, the Court said:

> Legislation is powerless to eradicate racial instincts or to abolish distinctions based upon the physical differences, and the attempt to do so can only result in accentuating the difficulties of the present situation. If the

---

[17] 109 U.S. 3.
[18] 163 U.S. 537.

civil and political rights of both races be equal, one cannot be inferior to the other civilly or politically. If one race be inferior to the other socially, the Constitution of the United States cannot put them upon the same plane.

It is worthwhile to observe in passing that while law was rejected as a means of changing behavior, there was no hesitation in its use to create and maintain an elaborate system based upon racial divisions. Perhaps the only ray of hope for blacks in this otherwise dismal Court decision could be found in Justice Harlan's powerful dissent. Said Harlan:

> . . . in view of the Constitution, in the eye of the law, there is in this country no superior, dominant, ruling class of citizens. There is no caste here. Our Constitution is color-blind, and neither knows nor tolerates classes among its citizens. In respect of civil rights, all citizens are equal before the law. The humblest is the peer of the most powerful. The law regards man as man, and takes no account of his surroundings or of his color when his civil rights as guaranteed by the supreme law of the land are involved. It is therefore to be regretted that this high tribunal, the final expositor of the fundamental law of the land, has reached the conclusion that it is competent for a state to regulate the enjoyment by citizens of their civil rights solely upon the basis of race.

Blacks, however, got small satisfaction from Harlan's "color-blind" concept. Indeed, with the Constitution and politics against them, the status of blacks at the turn of the century was very definitely at the mercy of the states and the private whims of white society. The physical costs (for example, lynchings) to the few blacks who violated their status were sufficient to keep most blacks in their places.

The status of blacks was also affected by **industrialization**, urbanization, economic **depression** and war during the first decades of this century. These phenomena affected all Americans, but blacks perhaps most of all. During the Depression of the 1930's, for example, blacks were the "last hired, first fired." Even so, however, Franklin Delano Roosevelt's New Deal led blacks to abandon their Republican leanings (and the ghost of Lincoln) and to join Roosevelt's emerging Democratic coalition.[19]

But Roosevelt's developing coalition did little to help racial equality. In fact, the government even promoted racism during the Depression and post-Depression era. Consider some of the Democratic programs developed during the New Deal. One of the first major programs was in the area of housing. The Federal Housing Administration (FHA), estab-

---

[19] A little noted but insightful critique of the New Deal's impact upon blacks is presented in Ralph J. Bunche's "A Critique of New Deal Social Planning as it Affects Negroes." *Journal of Negro Education* 5 (January 1936): 59-65.

lished in 1934, proposed to help Americans purchase their own homes through governmental underwritings of loans. Many blacks were not able to take advantage of this program because (1) they could not meet the minimum financial standard of the program, and (2) they were only extended credit if they built homes within their own racial group.[20] Indeed, in a section labelled "Protection from Adverse Influences," the FHA Underwriting Manual discussed how "properly enforced zoning regulations" and "effective restrictive covenants . . . provide the surest protection against undesirable encroachment and inharmonious use" of property locations. The Manual stated:

> To be most effective, deed restrictions should be imposed upon all land in the immediate environment of the subject location.
> Carefully compiled and fully enforced zoning regulations are effective because they not only exercise control over the subject property, but also over the surrounding area. However, they are seldom complete enough within themselves to assure a homogeneous and harmonious neighborhood.
> Recorded restrictive covenants should strengthen and supplement zoning ordinances. . . . Recommended restrictions should include provision for the following:
> . . . Prohibition of the occupancy of properties except by the race for which they are intended.[21]

The overall effect of FHA policy was to limit black ownership of housing in any area, black or white. Gunnar Myrdal noted this in his famous study of *An American Dilemma*:

> The damage done to the Negroes is not only that the FHA encourages segregation. There is also the fact *that this segregation is predominantly negative*. It would work much less hardship on the Negro people if it were merely a question of keeping Negroes and whites apart, and not, predominantly, of keeping the Negro out. In other words, if the policy of segregation were coupled with large-scale positive effort to give the Negro additional living space, it would be much less harmful.[22] [Emphasis in original.]

The government received much criticism for promoting racial segregation in the housing industry. Yet the FHA policies described above

---

[20] For a succinct discussion of public housing policies as related to the New Deal see Gunnar Myrdal, *An American Dilemma* (New York: Harper & Row, 1944), pp. 348–53. Also see National Committee Against Discrimination in Housing, *How the Federal Government Builds Ghettoes* (New York: NCADH, 1967).

[21] U.S. Federal Housing Administration, *Underwriting Manual*, sec. 980. (Revised Feb. 1938)

[22] Myrdal, *An American Dilemma*, pp. 349–50.

continued for more than a decade before they were dropped. In any event, it is quite clear that such policies served to continue many of the problems of racial segregation that we still face today.

Consider, moreover, the effects of war, such as those of World War II. The war held important consequences for blacks, especially in terms of jobs and population mobility. Blacks learned skills in wartime that increased both their job opportunities and their expectations in peacetime. Black soldiers fortunate enough to return home had a chance to receive support to continue or to begin their education, segregated though it was. And perhaps even more important, for black Americans to fight in a war for democracy and freedom overseas could not help but cause concern and sympathy for them to enjoy "democracy and freedom" at home.[23] President Truman's appointment of a Committee on Civil Rights, which came forth with its 1947 report *To Secure These Rights*,[24] indicated this concern and sympathy. At least the report focused attention on civil rights as a *national* issue.

However, much more was needed to alter the status of blacks. There were some blacks and others who dared to improve that status. (Of course, history is filled with examples to show that even during slavery blacks fought for freedom.) In large part, this action to change the status of blacks was engineered by the National Association for the Advancement of Colored People (NAACP), an organization founded in 1909. The NAACP chose to pursue change through courts and law. Despite earlier judicial setbacks, and in terms of its objectives and resources, this NAACP strategy appeared more plausible than other courses of action, such as seeking change through Congress or state legislatures.

The litigation onslaught of the NAACP and blacks began to meet with success. A high point of this success came in the famous 1954 *Brown* decision.[25] In this decision the Supreme Court ruled racial segregation in public schools unconstitutional. It is hard to overestimate the importance of *Brown* to civil rights interest and the civil rights movement. Mostly, it served to *nationalize* and *publicize* the problem of race. Throughout much of our history, the tendency was to submerge, minimize, and localize the problem. In effect, the states were allowed to

---

[23] Black gains during World War II came, however, only after a strong threat of massive black protests were made to President Roosevelt by A. Phillip Randolph and other prominent blacks who were angry over the lack of governmental actions against lynchings in the South and of continued discrimination. Of particular concern was the lack of integration in the Armed Services. The extent to which such threats had an effect can be inferred from the creation of a special government office to investigate "The Negroes' Morale."

[24] *To Secure These Rights,* The Report of the President's Committee on Civil Rights (New York: Simon and Schuster, 1947).

[25] *Brown* v. *Board of Education of Topeka* (347 U.S. 483, 1954).

Wide World Photos

Shown just following the announcement of the 1954 Supreme Court *Brown* decision, from left: George E. C. Hayes, Thurgood Marshall, James M. Nabrit.

handle the matter pretty much as they pleased. But in the 1950's, certain forces were coming together which would no longer allow the issue to be so handled. These forces included: the broadening distribution of the black population throughout the nation, especially in urban areas; the increasing role of the federal government in areas of social welfare, education, and the economy; changing sociological and moral concepts with respect to race; and a growing social and political consciousness among blacks to rid the nation of racism. The latter two forces, of course, were sparked and nourished by the emergence of Martin Luther King and the civil rights movement. What the Supreme Court did by its *Brown* ruling, however, was to stimulate these forces and provide the legal framework within which they could work to deal with the problem of race. To be sure, the Court decision encouraged blacks to fight for their rights with greater determination and with greater resources. For the first time since Reconstruction blacks had the valuable resource of "the law." Moreover, the position of the Court, plus the increasing demonstrations and protests of the civil rights movement, spurred the elective-political branches to join the battle and to pass remedial legislation.

In addition, the election of John F. Kennedy in 1960 and the overwhelming reelection of President Johnson in 1964 gave promise that a new position and status for blacks was becoming accepted, although gradually. But this hope was not realized. The gap between hope and reality dramatically exploded in the urban unrest and violence of the 1960's. Apparently many white Americans, along with some blacks, failed to recognize that legal statutes were a poor substitute for many hopes that had been hidden by several centuries of slavery and oppression. Moreover, the style of political action that blacks had successfully used in the moral and quasi-religious crusade for civil rights proved unequal to the task of political conflict.

We have seen quite clearly that the status of blacks in American society has largely been determined, as Chief Justice Taney said in *Dred Scott*, by the "indelible marks" of race and color. And for the most part, these are the same "indelible marks" that continue to shape the everyday life of blacks (and other minorities) in this country. For example, whites have no worry about whether they will be harassed by police. Longhairs as longhairs might be, but not whites as whites. Whites have no worry as to whether they can buy a house where they choose, or whether they dare apply in person for a job or apartment they really want. Whites seldom question whether a judge will treat them with respect. Whites in America take such things for granted. It does not occupy their minds — or if it does, it's just a matter of a few dollars, a new suit of clothes, or a haircut. Nor do whites have to worry that they will be reminded of their "place."

But blacks in America in the 1970's have to be very much aware and alert to these indignities or outright insults. The black American can never be sure. It does not matter, with few exceptions, what one's educational background or economic status is. The cutting edge in America remains very much one of *race* and *color*. And unfortunately, yesterday's hopes (the Warren Court, the Johnson presidency) are seemingly always dashed by today's realities (Nixon presidency, Burger Court). Given this situation, there is little wonder that blacks remain a disadvantaged and frustrated people.

In short, the history of blacks in America is not at all encouraging. There has been some progress. But basically blacks still do not enjoy the same rights and privileges as white Americans do. Thus, as the nation celebrates its bicentennial, there remains a certainty and an uncertainty about black life in this country. The certainty is that blacks, in widely unequal numbers, are at the lower ends of just about every part of American life. The uncertainty is whether this certainty can be overcome within the existing framework of the political system.

Topics for Discussion

1. Demographic data suggest that black Americans may be returning to the old South. Discuss the political, social, and economic implications of this North to South migration.

2. Black Americans in the last ten years have generally been turning away from "protests to politics." Why do you think this change has occurred? Do you agree with this turn to "politics"? Why or why not? In your discussion, be sure to comment on the potential costs and benefits of following the "protests" strategy in comparison to following the "politics" strategy. Are there other strategies you would suggest? Explain and defend your suggestion.

3. Do you agree (or disagree) that the status of blacks in American society has largely been determined, and continues to be determined, by the "indelible marks" of race and color? What evidence can you cite to support your position? Discuss.

4. The U.S. Supreme Court has been instrumental in the denial and procurement of rights for black Americans. For instance, during slavery and Reconstruction the Court was in the forefront of sanctioning policies that promoted a legal and social system which destined blacks to second-class citizenship. On the other hand, the Warren Court was in the forefront in developing policies to eliminate racial segregation. What long-term effects do you think the early role of the Supreme Court, dating roughly from the *Dred Scott* decision (1857) through *Plessy* v. *Ferguson* (1896) has had (or continues to have) on the legal, political, and social status of blacks? Discuss.

Suggested Readings

Beard, Charles A. *An Economic Interpretation of the Constitution of the United States.* New York: Macmillan Company, 1954.

A work concerning the constitutional history of the nation with emphasis on the economic basis of the Constitution.

Bell, Derrick. *Race, Racism and Law.* Boston: Little, Brown, 1973.

A collection of cases and materials that portray the racism in American law.

Bennett, Lerone. *Black Power U.S.A.: The Human Side of Reconstruction, 1867-1877.* Chicago: Johnson Publisher and Co., 1967.

A humanistic interpretation of Reconstruction.

Clark, Kenneth B. *Dark Ghetto: Dilemmas of Social Power.* New York: Harper & Row, 1965.

A penetrating analysis of the social and political problems of the ghetto which, for the most part, result from poverty.

Dubois, W.E.B. *Black Reconstruction.* New York: Harcourt Brace Jovanovich, 1935.

A forceful essay devoted to analyzing the role of blacks in the attempt to reconstruct democracy in America, 1860-1880.

Franklin, John Hope. *From Slavery to Freedom: A History of Negro Americans.* New York: Alfred A. Knopf, 1974.

The seminal study on the history of black Americans in the United States which analyzes slavery, Reconstruction, the New Deal, the Civil Rights movement, and the present.

Franklin, John Hope. *Reconstruction After the Civil War.* Chicago: University of Chicago Press, 1961.

A penetrating discussion of the plight of blacks immediately following the Civil War.

Frazier, E. Franklin. *The Negro in the United States.* New York: Macmillan Company, 1957.

An assessment of the status of blacks in America.

Hamilton, Charles. *The Black Experience in American Politics.* New York: Capricorn Books, 1973.

A collection of readings that analyzes the plight of blacks in America.

Harrington, Michael. *The Other America.* Baltimore, Md.: Penguin Books, 1962.

A seminal work on the problems of being poor in America.

Henderson, Lenneal J., Jr., ed. *Black Political Life in the United States.* San Francisco: Chandler Publishing Co., 1973.

Articles that deal with various aspects of black political experiences. Includes a detailed bibliographical essay by editor.

Kilson, Martin. "Political Change in the Negro Ghetto, 1900-1940's," in Nathan I. Huggins, Martin Kilson, and Daniel M. Fox, eds., *Key Issues in the Afro-American Experience.* New York: Harcourt Brace Jovanovich, 1971.

This work, like those in the entire volume, examines the changing status of black Americans.

Logan, Rayford W. *The Betrayal of the Negro.* New York: Collier Books, 1965.

A comprehensive analysis of the status of blacks in America between 1877 and 1901.

Myrdal, Gunnar. *An American Dilemma.* New York: Harper & Row, 1964.

A classic study analyzing the status of blacks in America.

McPherson, James M., Laurence B. Holland, James M. Banner, Jr., Nancy J. Weiss, Michael D. Bell, *Blacks in America: Bibliographical Essays.* Garden City, N.Y.: Doubleday & Co., 1972.

Detailed bibliographical essays organized around important topics and periods in black history. A useful tool for research on black history.

Parsons, Talcott, and Kenneth Clark. *The Negro American.* Boston: Houghton Mifflin, 1965.

A collection of essays on the status of blacks in America.

Rainwater, Lee. *Behind Ghetto Walls.* Chicago: Aldine Publishing Co., 1970.

An examination of the dynamics of the socioeconomic inequality of the American political system with emphasis on the ghetto.

Rose, Harold. *The Black Ghetto: A Spatial Behavioral Perspective.* New York: McGraw-Hill, 1971.

An examination of America's urban black communities from a geographic perspective.

Taeuber, Karl E., and Alma F. Taeuber, *Negroes in Cities: Residential Segregation and Neighborhood change.* Chicago: Aldine Publishing Co., 1965.

A penetrating comparative analysis of the pattern as well as the process of residential segregation over time.

Wirt, Frederick M., Benjamin Walters, Francine Rabinowitz, and Deborah R. Hensler, *On the City's Rim: Politics and Policy in Suburbia.* London: D. C. Heath and Co., 1972.

A study of the political consequences of suburbanization.

2

THE NATURE
OF THE PROBLEM

White people may have thought little about Negroes until recently, but most Negroes cannot ignore the white man. The white man holds the key to freedom, comforts and pleasures they aspire to, Negroes feel, and it is also the white man who has prevented them from achieving these things. How the Negro views whites is important since white society must eventually come to grips with Negro demands.

William Brink and Louis Harris, *The Negro Revolution in America**

The principal measure of progress toward equality will be that of employment. It is the primary source of individual or group identity. In America what you do is what you are: to do nothing is to be nothing; to do little is to be little. The equations are implacable and blunt, and ruthlessly public. . . .

It is the measure of white bona fides. It is the measure of Negro competence, *and also of the competence of American society.* Most importantly, the linkage between problems of employment and the range of social pathology that afflicts the Negro community is unmistakable. Employment not only controls the present for the Negro American but, in a most profound way, it is creating the future as well.

Daniel P. Moynihan**

---

* Copyright © 1963 by Simon and Schuster, Inc. Reprinted with permission of Simon and Schuster.

** Daniel Moynihan, quoted in *The Report of the National Advisory Commission on Civil Disorders* (Washington, D.C.: U.S. Government Printing Office, 1967).

The problem, stated simply, is that blacks still do not enjoy the privileges and benefits of the American society as fully as do whites. As a consequence, blacks bear more of the deprivations and costs that society puts on all citizens. The problem can be seen in every sphere of American life — in politics, in socioeconomic status, and in the legal and judicial processes.

This chapter examines the inequality gap that exists between blacks and whites along many socioeconomic lines. We review some socio-economic data which show gross inequities between blacks and whites in such basic areas as education, jobs, housing, unemployment, and income. We will also discuss the impact of racism and the **class** structure on black American life. We close this chapter with a look at some of the differences in black and white attitudes toward each other, and toward the political system generally.

Poverty Set Conditions for Black Political Behavior

One of the most ironic aspects of the unequal and uncertain status of blacks is the degree to which the white majority has come to blame black Americans for many of the problems that blacks face. This is particularly so when one attempts to find causes for the economic differences between blacks and whites. The explanations have been numerous. They have ranged from the characterization of blacks as essentially "childlike" in need of adult guidance and supervision to the modern view which finds the major problem in family disorganization. And, when blacks began their great northward migration in the early part of this century it was claimed that they were naturally the victims of their "newcomer" status in urban life. From this perspective some observers, black and white, saw the position of urban blacks from rural backgrounds as comparable to that of the East and Central European peasants of the late nineteenth and early twentieth centuries.[1]

The "modern" explanation is presented in perhaps its most sophisti-

---

[1] Early conceptions of black slaves as children received elaborate justifications. Among the many works which discuss perceptions and attitudes see: John Hope Franklin, *From Slavery to Freedom* (New York: Alfred A. Knopf, Inc. 1967); Winthrop Jordan, *White Over Black* (Chapel Hill: University of North Carolina, 1968); and David Brion Davis, *The Problem of Slavery in Western Culture* (Ithaca: Cornell University Press, 1966). Although the "newcomer" theme is not specifically treated as such, early twentieth century efforts to grapple with the problems of blacks in urban America suggest this orientation. See, for example, St. Clair Drake and Horace Clayton, *Black Metropolis* (New York: Harcourt Brace Jovanovich, 1945), esp. pp. 69–76. More recently we find evidence of the persistence of this "newcomer" characterization in the "Gray Areas Projects" of the Ford Foundation, a forerunner to the government-funded War on Poverty.

cated form in Daniel Moynihan's *The Negro Family: A Case for National Action*.[2] Moynihan assigned to a "weak" black family structure much of the blame for economic instability and general social disorganization in black communities. There is much evidence that a woman-headed household is more vulnerable to economic stress than is one headed by a man. Of course, a woman-headed household differs from the accepted American norm of a male-headed home. But to imply, as the Moynihan report did, that strengthening black family structures would solve the problems of underemployment, unemployment, illegitimacy, welfare dependency, and a wide range of other social problems is both poor guidance for policy and one-sided. No one, least of all blacks, contends that the women-headed household is not a problem. Yet, between black and white Americans when the causes of political and economic insecurity are discussed, agreement ends there.[3]

To make the plight of blacks understandable to most whites is a difficult task. In addition to economic explanations, there are also differing attitudes about poverty between black and white Americans. Perhaps because of the large number of blacks who receive various types of public assistance, much of the white opinion tends to characterize the black recipient as "the undeserving poor." In this view the black citizen is seen variously as lazy, criminal, or at best incompetent. A slightly less harsh view holds that those who must depend upon public aid are simply the victims of unfortunate circumstances. Personal problems which cannot be effectively managed are thought to merit sympathetic consideration and private charity. The organization of the society or the economic system is seldom regarded as a causal factor in the depressed conditions of the black poor.

Many, perhaps most, white Americans today would deny any guilt in the injustices done to blacks by their ancestors. Yet they have to recognize that those experiences form a very intimate history for black citizens. Ex-slaves in the South were forced into what amounted to a feudal relationship with their former masters. The political repression which maintained this feudalism was a constant reminder to both blacks and whites of black inferiority and inequality. Moreover, the numerous barriers to full participation in American life have only served to heighten the blacks' feelings of difference from their fellow citizens.

---

[2] Washington, D.C.: U.S. Government Printing Office, 1965.

[3] Since the War on Poverty the examination of the problems of black (and white) poverty has received unusual attention. As a result the literature on the subject is vast and diverse. See, for example: William K. Tabb, *The Political Economy of the Black Ghetto* (New York: Norton, 1970); S. M. Miller and Frank Reissman, *Social Class and Social Policy* (New York: Basic Books, 1968); Kenneth Clark, *Dark Ghetto* (New York: Harper & Row, 1965); Kenneth Clark and Jeannette Hopkins, *A Relevant War on Poverty* (New York: Harper & Row, 1970).

Deprivation in their public and private lives became a principal part of black **political socialization.**

For a long time many Americans believed in the melting pot thesis. This stressed the view that race did not matter. The United States, it was said, was a color-blind society in which people were evaluated on the basis of individual merit. If indeed the melting pot thesis were ever true, a general exception was made for blacks. It was possible for the European immigrant to be "melted"; in many cases all that was necessary was anglicizing a name and learning to speak English. The public education system performed this latter task quite well. Shades of white did not generally matter, leading blacks to coin the phrase, "If you're white, you're all right; if you're black, get back." The expression sums up the black's belief about his position in American life.

For many white Americans *the problem* cannot be explained. Their difficulty, however, is easily understood. One need only look to the failure of educators, until quite recently, to make even an effort to portray accurately black life in the context of America's development. All too frequently, historians paid little attention to blacks except as they figured in the Abolition movement and the Civil War. Some passing references were made to supposed black corruption during a brief experiment with black politicians during Reconstruction. But then there was virtually complete silence. It was not merely a case of the "invisible man"; rather, blacks were an invisible people. So long as this condition remained, the plight of black people was not likely to become a part of the policy agenda.

One explanation for the omission can be found in the lack of political resources under black control. However, to say that blacks do not possess political resources hides more than it reveals. For the gain and use of political resources, even ones as limited as the vote, depends in large measure upon satisfying other requirements. Among these prerequisites, we now recognize that economic status is of significant importance. Of the various aspects of the problem of black status, economic deficiency is easiest to demonstrate. But it is perhaps the most difficult to solve.

Beginnings of Economic Inequality

Poverty among black Americans is the simplest indicator of their status in society. This economic inequality, of course, has been a constant feature of the black experience. Slavery in the South explains the position of blacks for that region until late in the nineteenth century. After emancipation, southern governments devised other means to exclude the former slaves from economic, social, and political forms of participation in American life. In the so-called "free states" the situation was not significantly better, as Litwack has pointed out:

> Prevailing racial **stereotypes,** white vanity and the widely held conviction that God had made the black man to perform disagreeable tasks combined to fix the Negro's economic status and bar him from most "respectable" jobs. White workers refused to accept the Negro as an apprentice; businessmen rejected his application for credit; and educational restrictions severely hampered his training for the professions.[4]

Although seemingly free, blacks in the North were as effectively excluded from the socioeconomic and political participation as were the slaves in the South. (Litwack points out, for example, that after Maine's statehood in 1819, every state admitted before the end of the Civil War restricted suffrage to whites. [p. 31]) Nor did urbanization and industrial development help to improve the lot of free blacks outside the South. Until about 1830 blacks at least could gain employment in various menial and service occupations. But with the spectacular surge in European immigration between 1830 and 1860 free blacks found themselves competing with whites. The competition for low status and low paying jobs all too often led to interracial violence between blacks and white immigrants in the cities. It also tended to result in further economic displacement for blacks.

However, after the Civil War most serious black economic problems began to emerge. Emancipation came suddenly in the midst of civil war. The economic problems of the former slaves were made worse by the depressed economic conditions of the region and by the lack of planning which came before President Lincoln's decision to emancipate the slaves.

Although no longer slaves, the freedmen found themselves bound by a new relationship that strongly resembled feudalism. Through sharecropping and tenant farming arrangements enforced by a repressive political system blacks were often as firmly tied to their former masters as they had been in the antebellum period. There seemed to be little likelihood of substantial economic improvement in black life for there were few opportunities available. For blacks, the opportunity to move up the economic ladder was provided by a major change in the national and international environments. Just as the Civil War created the conditions for emancipation, so did World War I produce the circumstances for large-scale black entry into the labor force.

---

[4] Leon F. Litwack, *North of Slavery: The Negro in the Free States 1790–1860* (Chicago: University of Chicago Press, 1961), p. 157.

War Increases Black Opportunities

World War I created an increased need for labor in the industrializing North. The European immigrants could no longer fill the need because congressional *restrictions* had reduced their flow to the United States. However, a supply of labor was available in the South. Northern industries got many blacks to leave by promising them higher and steady earnings. The attractiveness of the "free North" also encouraged blacks to leave the area of their birth. The historian Allan Spear has described the situation with regard to Chicago:

> First, southern Negroes heard only vague rumors of a better life in the North. Soon, however, they were confronted with concrete alternatives to their . . . plight. Labor agents, sent south first by the railroads and later by the steel companies, met Negroes on street corners, at churches, in barber shops, and in pool rooms. They offered free transportation . . . to any laborer who agreed to migrate.[5]

Southern politicians tried to block these recruitment efforts. They enacted legislation to prevent black migration from the South. Supposedly the objective of these political actions was to protect contracts and other agreements between sharecroppers and landowners. The practical consequence, however, was to control the movement of blacks, thus ensuring a constant labor supply for southern agricultural neeas.[6] This restrictive legislation was not widely adopted in the South and the black migration grew. On arrival at their destinations, these newcomers did not find the streets of Chicago, Philadelphia, and Detroit "paved with gold." They had traded a miserable rural situation for an equally miserable, and quite different, urban life style. And, though they judged themselves to be better off, black workers had few prospects of moving from their concentration at the lower end of the occupational ladder. Moreover, the American labor movement, which had shown considerable **ambivalence** on the question of race since the late nineteenth century, carefully ignored the conditions of black workers. Admittedly some of the hostility may have been based on some employers' use of blacks as strike-breakers. But union discrimination against black labor had been practiced before this was done. And, of course, once the strikes were settled blacks were once again unemployed or underemployed. The pattern of black employment in low paying, low skilled, and menial jobs was well-established during the early years of the twentieth century. It was not to undergo much change until after the Depression.

---

[5] *Black Chicago: The Making of A Negro Ghetto (1890–1920)* (Chicago: University of Chicago Press, 1967), p. 133.

[6] John S. Ezell, *The South Since 1865* (New York: Macmillan, 1965) points out that the state of Florida "in 1916 . . . enacted a penalty of $1,000.00 for any person convicted of enticing a Negro to leave the state" (p. 193).

Even then, continued discrimination and exclusion would have serious consequences for black participation in American life.

In common with other citizens black Americans suffered through the national economic problems that followed World War I. Quite naturally, those at the lowest end of the economic spectrum felt the effects of the Depression most keenly. And, in view of the general state of the economy, blacks could expect few positive changes in their circumstances.

However, with the initiation of the various social programs in the New Deal Administration of Franklin D. Roosevelt black hopes for broad changes in their circumstances rose.

The Political Education of Black Americans

The Depression in a sense set the stage for a black political style which was to last three decades. During these thirty years, as had previously been the case, the presidency was the focal point of black attention. Unlike other citizens who had recourse to lower levels of the political system — that is, the parties at the local or state levels — black exclusion from participation at these intermediate levels forced them to turn to the one office which symbolized the entire nation. Even the president, they soon learned, could not act on their demands without due consideration of what he considered to be "politically feasible." Questions of justice and right were subordinated to considerations of expediency. Or, to put it most kindly, a positive response to black concerns could be set aside "in the national interest." Thus during the New Deal blacks tried to eliminate the doctrine of "separate but equal." Many people believed that this slogan applied only in the South. But in practice it was a national policy, because the federal government acted slowly, or not at all, on black grievances. Political demands were expressed to President Roosevelt, but he was reluctant to begin responsive measures. He feared that southern members of Congress would block his legislative proposals to deal with national economic problems following the Depression. And, when World War II broke out in Europe, with America's direct involvement increasingly more likely as German forces advanced, black concerns loomed even less important on the presidential agenda. Moreover, Roosevelt apparently believed that any government action to meet demands for better treatment of blacks in the South would set off a wave of interracial violence. Closing the inequality gap between blacks and whites, as had been the case with ending Reconstruction, was suspended for the sake of national unity. Blacks, though still lacking political resources, refused to accept the president's reasoning.

Discrimination in employment in the defense industries was strongly resented. In addition, job discrimination had another highly symbolic aspect which the masses of black Americans could not understand; the record of the military services was in many respects worse than that of private industry. National appeals for unity in common cause against a common enemy had a hollow ring for black Americans. After all, they were not wanted in the Air Corps and Marines. The Navy would accept black enlistees, but only as messmen. And the Army accepted blacks only in traditionally all-black units. That blacks couldn't freely defend the nation in the military effort heightened their sense of injustice.

Recognizing an opportunity in the president's need for domestic unity to strengthen the morale of the nation's European allies, black leaders acted.

To be sure, there was a history of black protest against job discrimination. Mostly it had been localized — that is, confined to one community — and frequently the demonstrators focused upon specific employers. It was hoped that success would have a domino effect. Such, for example, were the expectations during the Chicago boycotts against job discrimination in the 1930's. And, since its founding, the Urban League had tried with limited success to open opportunities for black workers through private negotiations. But neither the League nor the NAACP had initiated political demonstrations to press black demands.

However, by 1941 black Americans began to think in terms of the mass demonstration, and political mobilization of black Americans with a specific objective, the nation's capital, in mind. For this effort, blacks revealed a stronger organizational sense of purpose and cohesion than they had shown before. The movement was led by men such as A. Phillip Randolph, head of the Brotherhood of Sleeping Car Porters, and Walter White of the NAACP. The March on Washington Movement, as it came to be known, had substantial support from the black masses. The black church, which often stayed away from secular involvements, also gave its support. Randolph, White, and other leaders talked of 50 to 100 thousand black Americans descending on the seat of government. Whether these numbers would have in fact appeared is unknown. The march did not take place. But to President Roosevelt and other government officials the Movement was a believable threat. Reluctantly President Roosevelt granted some of the demands that the Movement organizers wanted.

Employment in war industries did produce some economic gains. However, black income levels did not immediately match those of whites. This is confirmed when we note the income data from the war years, 1939-1946, shown in Table 2-1. These figures do show some change in the relative positions of blacks. But it is ironic that such movement appeared to have been dependent upon the general economic mobilization for World War II. Along with the modest economic improvements shown in Table 2-1, blacks also saw some gains in the political realm. Political developments are treated in more detail in Chapter 4. But it should be noted here that the question of race began to get more attention after the New Deal. This was in part a consequence of its value to the deliberate efforts of the Democratic Party to build an effective national voter coalition in support of its programs and candidates in the urban states of the North.

Income Gains and Losses Since World War II

Figures 2-1 and 2-2 show that black incomes have risen since World War II. And while these figures show income data for families rather than individuals, it is strikingly clear that the relative income position of black Americans has moved only slightly since the end of World War II. Moreover, the stagnation which is shown for 1969 and 1970 was followed by a decline. Current (1975) economic conditions suggest that this decline will continue. The optimistic conclusions drawn from the data just presented must be changed when one looks at the situation of the black southerner. (See Figure 2-3.)

These figures also indicate that despite the recent increase in the numbers of blacks who are returning to the South, economic potential alone does not appear to be the most important consideration. The 1970-1972 figures for blacks in the South are approximately equal to those of other blacks a decade earlier. If the existence of a reverse black migration is to be believed, the explanation must be sought in non-economic areas. We will return to this subject in a later chapter.

The picture so far presented is bleak enough it might seem. But there is one further issue to be discussed in the matter of socioeconomic inequality. Black unemployment reveals, perhaps better than similar figures for whites, a structural weakness in the American economic system. The constant high unemployment rate among blacks has led

TABLE 2-1
Median Annual Income of White and Nonwhite Males 1939–1946

YEAR	WHITE MALES	NONWHITE MALES	WHITE/ NONWHITE DIFFERENCE	PERCENT OF NONWHITE TO WHITE
1939	$1112	$ 460	$ 652	41
1945	2176	1158	1018	53
1946	2223	1367	856	61

SOURCE: Adapted from Raymond S. Franklin and Solomon Resnik, *The Political Economy of Racism* (New York: Holt, Rinehart and Winston, 1973), p. 38.

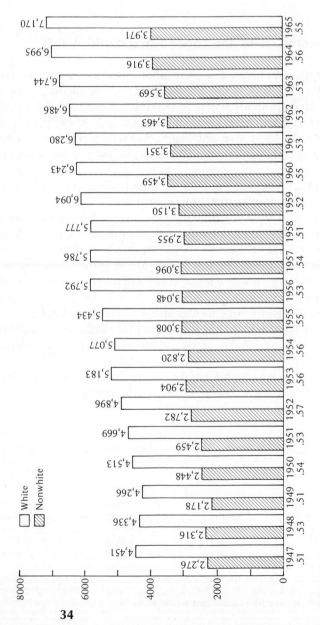

FIGURE 2-1
Median Family Income by Color, 1947–1965

SOURCE: Table " Median Family Income in Constant (1962) . . .1947–1962" from "Occupation and Income" in *Transformation of the Negro American* by Leonard Broom and Norval Glenn. Copyright © 1965 by Leonard Broom and Norval Glenn. By permission of Harper & Row, Publishers.

34

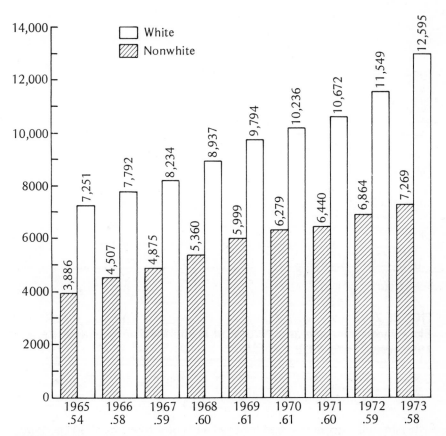

FIGURE 2-2
Median Family Income by Color, 1965–1972 (in current dollars)

SOURCE: *Social and Economic Characteristics of the Black Population*, 1972 —
Bureau of the Census, CPR, series P-60, no. 85 (Dec. 1972) and series P-60, no.
87 (June 1973).

some analysts to conclude that there exists a "dual labor market." Of
this phenomenon Michael Piore has written:

> The poor are . . . separated from the non-poor in the . . . sense that they
> have economic value where they are and hence that there are groups
> interested, not only in resisting the elimination of poverty, but in actively
> seeking its perpetuation.[7]

The facts of job discrimination certainly lend force to the implication in
Piore's assertion. But, even if one does not wish to accept such a harsh

---

[7] Michael J. Piore, "Jobs and Training," in Samuel Beer and Richard Barringer, eds.,
The State and the Poor (Cambridge: Winthrop Publishers, 1970).

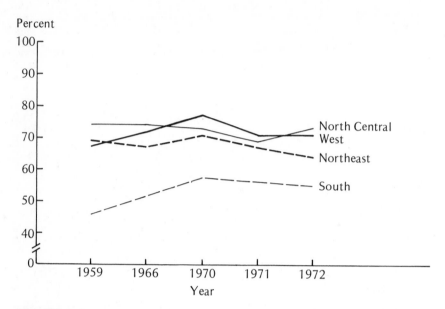

FIGURE 2-3
Black Median Income as a Percent of White Median Income by Region: 1959, 1966, 1970–1972

SOURCE: Bureau of the Census 1959–71, Current Population Reports, series P-23, no. 42. 1972, series P-60, no. 87.

criticism of the economic system one fact is of interest here. In economic planning and projections it is assumed that there will always be some level of unemployment. That is, not everyone who wants a job will have one. For blacks in particular discrimination is further complicated by a condition which economists have termed **structural unemployment.** This concept is defined by economist Paul Samuelson as

> unemployment which cannot be cured by expansion of overall monetary demand, but which is attributable to lack of proper skills, location and attitudes among youth, the aged, the illiterate, minorities, . . . and the technologically displaced.[8]

Traditionally, black unemployment rates have been much larger than those of whites but only in part as a result of these structural characteristics. In the past decade the nation has begun to acknowledge the contribution of racism in chronically high black unemployment.

Of course, it is also possible to argue that the extent of structural unemployment is exaggerated because jobs are always available. How-

---

[8] Paul Samuelson, *Economics,* 6th ed. (New York: McGraw-Hill, 1964), p. 572.

ever, in many instances these jobs are unattractive because of low wages. And in comparison with other sources of income — for example, unemployment benefits, public assistance, or simple leisure — the employment opportunity may be unattractive.[9] Moreover, one's attitude influences job-seeking. Since the mid-sixties there has been increased emphasis placed on the quality of one's work. Many black males, even those with low skills, have apparently turned down jobs which were regarded as "dead-end." As a result of these factors, black unemployment figures for the past decade do not reflect much progress. Figures 2-4 and 2-5 show unemployment figures for blacks as compared to

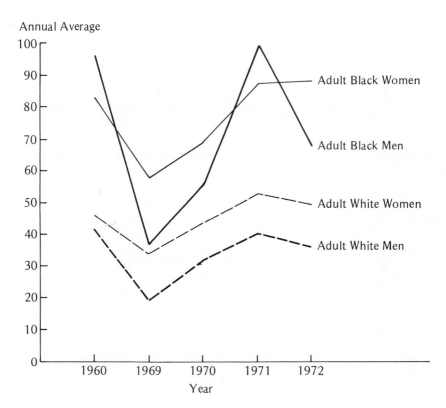

FIGURE 2-4
Unemployment Rates by Race and Sex: 1960, 1969–1972

Source: U.S. Bureau of the Census 1960–61, Current Population Reports, series P-23, no. 42 and U.S. Department of Labor, Bureau of Labor Statistics 1972, *Employment and Earnings.*

---

[9] Cf. The insightful treatment of this issue in Eliot Liebow, *Tally's Corner* (Boston: Little, Brown, 1967).

Annual Average

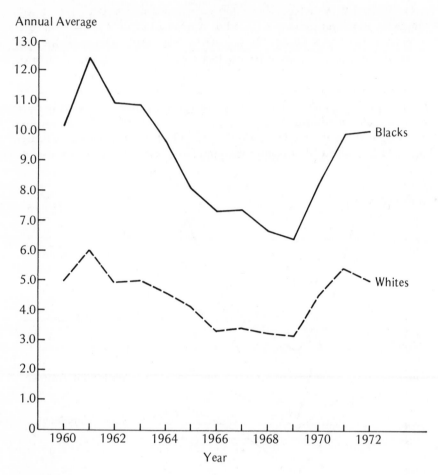

FIGURE 2–5
Unemployment Rates: 1960–1972

SOURCE: U.S. Bureau of the Census 1960–71, series P-23, no. 42. U.S. Department of Labor, Bureau of Labor Statistics, 1972, *Employment and Earnings,* 1973.

whites. There is a tragic and almost predictable character to the unemployment picture for blacks: the rate, for the periods shown, is almost uniformly twice the figures for whites. In spite of the large increases in total black employment — for example, 1970–1971 — there is no indication of a "catch-up" effect. Nor is there any evidence that the highly praised job-training programs of the Johnson and Nixon administrations were able to break this pattern. A more detailed look at the employment picture for blacks is provided in Figure 2-4. The rates for black men vary considerably; one sees peaks and valleys of extreme proportions. When we examine the rates for black women, however, the lowest figures do not match those of the men. And what is even more interesting is that the employment picture for black women appears more optimistic. In contrast, the evidence for white women shows a consistent relationship to the rates for white men: the difference does not exceed 1.5 percent for the 12-year period shown. Of course, part of the explanation for the better outlook for black women's employment is related to the kinds of jobs available to them. It is also important to recognize that the black women in the labor force are more likely to be employed full-time than white women.

These are some of the bare economic facts of life with which the black community must contend. In the face of such limitations, and especially their seemingly unchanging character, it is small wonder that many blacks seem to have changed back to their earlier pattern of resignation.

The employment figures for the black American relate strongly to the overall state of the national economy. None of the specific federal efforts to help have been able to break this relationship in any meaningful and lasting way. Some legal instruments such as Fair Employment Practices (FEPC) were enacted during the Truman administration. In addition, the Nixon administration proposed a system of quotas aimed at craft unions in particular. But such measures apparently have little effect in the face of economic forces. For when the nation's economic health is strong and vigorous, blacks get relatively more jobs. But if the economy slows, black men are most likely to be the first to feel its effects, and in disproportionate numbers.

We can also compare economic status by examining the data for the period 1960-1972. During this period, blacks were making their most widely publicized political gains in this century. The figures in Figure 2-6 reflect family, as opposed to individual incomes. The conclusion found in these data is inescapable: blacks are not catching up. Indeed, after a steady rise between 1965 and 1970, a period of decline is apparent. It should be kept in mind that family income for blacks is more frequently based upon both husband and wife working than in white households. Figure 2-7 compares labor force participation for the year 1972. Oddly enough, the figures in Figure 2-7 reveal that the difference in participation rates between black women and white women (49 percent vs. 43 percent) is almost identical to that between white men and black men (80 percent vs. 75 percent).

Because more black than white women are in the labor force we can see that their contribution to the middle-class income standard of $10,000 is greater. Similarly, if we were to remove that contribution, the gap between blacks and whites would be even wider than is shown. Moynihan in his ''benign neglect'' recommendation to former President

Percent

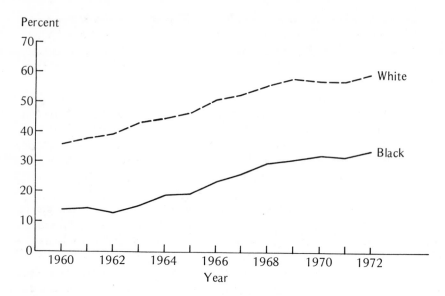

FIGURE 2-6
Families With Incomes of $10,000 or More: 1960-1972

SOURCE: U.S. Bureau of the Census, Current Population Reports, series P-60, no. 87, June 1973.

Nixon, and others as well, found reason for considerable optimism in the size of this black middle class. Yet Moynihan, who only a few years earlier had been concerned about the status of the black family, seemed unconcerned that black husband and wife both had to work to get even *this close* to whites. Moreover, Moynihan overlooked the fact that there were more black women in the labor force; also they were more likely to be employed on a full-time basis.* And, the implications of working black women on the patterns of child-rearing are obvious.

Income is Not the Only Problem: Patterns in Public Schools and Black Education

Closely related to economic opportunity and mobility is education. Education also measures the extent to which blacks were excluded from participation in American life. In the former Confederate states, especially, the doctrine for "separate but equal" education had

---

* See, for example, "Differences Between Incomes of White and Negro Families By Work Experience of Wife and Region: 1970, 1969, 1959," Special Studies, Series P-23 #39

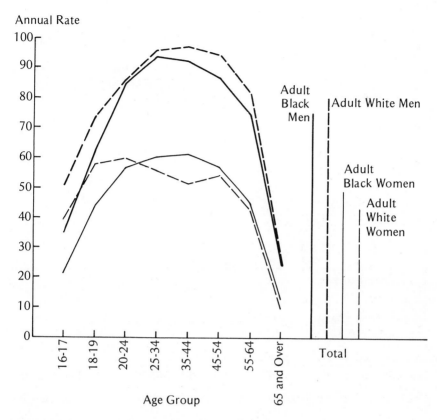

FIGURE 2-7
Labor Force Participation Rate, by Sex and Race: 1972

SOURCE: U.S. Department of Labor, Bureau of Labor Statistics, *Employment and Earnings*, 1973.

become a mockery. Black schools were indeed separate, but far from equal. Despite the problems involved with defining an equal education, it became increasingly clear that what black children received in southern schools fell short of basic education standards. The minimal standards of equality for blacks which the Supreme Court announced in *Plessy* v. *Ferguson* were seldom met. As political scientist Thomas Dye wryly noted, the South emphasized separate and virtually ignored

---

(December 1971) Bureau of the Census; and also see the discussion in a *New York Times* article after this report was issued. The *Times* began their story with this comment:

A much heralded indication of black economic progress in the nineteen-sixties was thrown into doubt by a special Census Bureau report . . . [*New York Times*, December 20, 1971, p. 40-C].

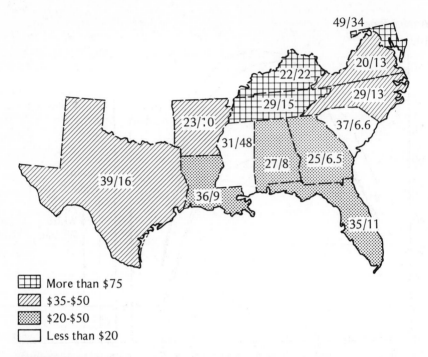

	More than $75
	$35-$50
	$20-$50
	Less than $20

FIGURE 2-8
Expenditures per Pupil for Black and White Students under "Separate but Equal," 1930

SOURCE: From George A. Davis and O. Fred Donaldson, *Blacks in the United States: A Geographic Perspective*, p. 164. Copyright © 1975 by Houghton Mifflin Company. Reprinted with permission of the publisher.

equal.[10] Ironically, this doctrine was apparently first applied to primary schools in Boston prior to the Civil War.[11] But it was in the South following the Civil War that the doctrine took its most harmful form. Significant changes in this pattern did not take place until after the Supreme Court's 1954 ruling.

Briefly, we wish to point out that this legal victory was regarded by some as a vindication of the black political strategy of litigation. The use of the courts by the NAACP was the principal means by which black Americans could supplement their otherwise limited access to the political system.*

---

[10] Thomas R. Dye, *The Politics of Equality* (Indianapolis: Bobbs-Merrill, 1971), p. 39.

[11] George A. Davis and O. Fred Donaldson, *Blacks in the United States: A Geographic Perspective* (Boston: Houghton Mifflin, 1975), p. 171; and see also Litwack, *North of Slavery*.

* See Chapters 5 and 6.

Despite impressive gains it should be remembered that those gains have come only since 1954. For a substantial portion of the current adult black population, therefore, the *Brown* decision had little effect. Moreover, to the extent that this 1954 decision led to better educational opportunities (a point which is in some dispute) its effects were primarily felt in the South. As the black protest moved into the North in the early 1960's it was to be expected that schools would again become an object of black attention. In part, questions of segregated education continued to be important. But, segregation north of the Mason-Dixon Line was less a problem of specific legal statutes than one based upon apparently *natural forces,* that is, where people wanted to live. It was quickly seen that "natural forces" was but a euphemism for residential segregation. Black Americans were less able to exercise free choice in finding homes. Also, the habit of the neighborhood school concept continued. Thus, many large northern urban school districts were "discovered" to be quite as segregated **de facto** as those in the South were **de jure.**[12]

With their greater economic resources, many white families have been able to leave large cities for surrounding suburban areas. As these white families left the cities, the school vacancies created have been filled by nonwhite students. And as the number of nonwhite students rose, it led to further decreases in white student enrollment. This all too familiar pattern in urban education inevitably seems to produce a sharp decline in the ability of urban public school systems to teach effectively the remaining nonwhite students.

To improve the education chances for black children, northern black parents began to press both for integration and for a more equal distribution of public school resources. There appeared to be much evidence that integration would raise the level of black childrens' achievement. This was the distinct impression created by the 1966 Coleman Report. This government-financed study documented the existence of unequal educational opportunities. The Coleman Report has been controversial since its release. It raised many more questions than answers about public education.[13] Released during the early years of the War on Poverty the Coleman study was initially viewed by blacks as support for their demands for better education. But as black militancy and activism spread integration seemed to lose much of its appeal to blacks. Moreover, some black critics began to see an implication of racial in-

---

[12] One of the earliest systematic investigations of this problem is the study of Patricia Cayo Sexton, *Education and Income* (New York: Compass Books, 1961).

[13] An interesting set of secondary analyses of this report are contained in Frederick Mostetter and Daniel Moynihan, eds., *On Equality of Educational Opportunity* (New York: Vintage, 1972), especially Chapters 1-2.

feriority in the Coleman Report. It appeared to show that black educational achievement was related to the presence of white children in the schools. Many blacks took exception to that implication. It should be kept in mind that the criticisms received by the Coleman study came in the midst of a period when black Americans were undergoing the most intense self-examination in their history. In addition, the mid-1960's were witness to expressions of community and racial solidarity among blacks which had not been evident during previous attempts to achieve equality in American society. This nationalism, or ethnocentrism, was commonly referred to as "black power."

We do not claim that there has been no improvement in the quality of education received by black children. Indeed, the data presented in Figure 2–9 indicate the degree of advance which has taken place in the

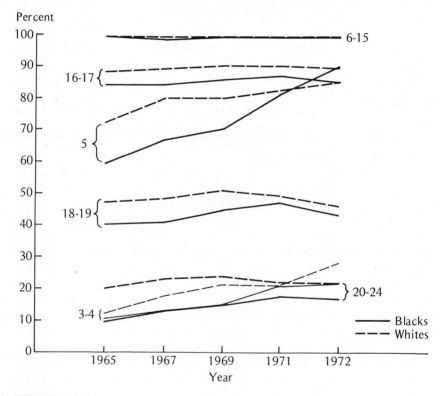

FIGURE 2–9
Percent Enrolled in School By Age: 1965, 1967, 1969, 1971, 1972

SOURCE: U.S. Bureau of the Census 1965–71, Current Population Reports, series P-23, no. 42, 1972.

Wide World Photos

Little Rock, Arkansas — 1957. Nine black students gather in front of Central High School surrounded by troops who escorted them into the schools.

past few years. In terms of enrollments, the educational gap between blacks and whites is closing. To the extent that greater mobility results from increased education, the narrower gap could be a good sign for the future. But from the black perspective it is a measure of the problem that such a gap exists at all.[14] Despite the improvements in enrollment figures, some widely heralded experiments to increase parental involvement, increased numbers of black teachers and school administrators, and changes in curricula to make them more relevant to the black experience, learning problems of black children remain.

---

[14] In addition to the black disenchantment just noted with the persistence of this gap some studies have begun to suggest that the relationship between education and income, or mobility, may not be as strong as many have previously believed. A useful discussion of this view is contained in Christoper Jencks et al., *Inequality: A Reassessment of the Effect of Family and Schooling in America* (New York: Basic Books, 1972).

Ellis Herwig, Stock, Boston

Boston, Massachusetts — 1975. Policemen escort school buses to South Boston High School through that racially troubled area.

In 1954, and again in the 1960's, many Americans believed that if the schools were integrated these learning problems would be corrected. But, as we have noted above the connections between integration and learning are not as clear-cut as was first supposed. And while integration proceeded in the South, when this approach to the same problems was applied in northern cities it was met with violence which equalled that of Little Rock, Arkansas, in 1957 and several Southern universities in the early 1960's. Boston, Massachusetts, and Pontiac, Michigan, have been the scenes of substantial white protests. There were bus burnings in Pontiac and mob violence against blacks in Boston.

For some blacks the price of integration, whether in the schools or other parts of the society, is seen as too high. Nevertheless, a majority of blacks continue to give support to the idea of an integrated society. And, as might be expected, black support for the idea of integration declined most sharply during the 1960's. Nevertheless, a majority of black Americans maintain their belief in the value of the idea. It is not quite so clear, however, that they continue to give that support without reservations. One of the sources of this hesitancy can be found in the inability of black Americans to secure adequate housing. In some ways the difficulties in the area of housing bring together the different aspects of black inequality. For, despite the improvements in income, educational attainment, and jobs, black Americans continue to face serious problems in the housing market. This often means that they cannot exercise the freedom of choice in finding desirable communities which might lead to better educational facilities and opportunities for their children even when they have the ability to pay. The attempts by some northern cities to achieve racial balance by busing has also brought into sharp focus the ways in which the separate inequalities which we have discussed up to this point combine in affecting the quality of black life. In particular, it is worth noting that the need for busing shows why the ghetto continues as a dreary fact of urban American society. In a very real sense, black Americans, no matter what their income class, have restricted opportunities to leave traditional black communities.

The Housing Problem and the "Ghettoization" of the Black Middle Class

In the first instance, of course, housing is a question of income. And with the rise in black incomes there have been increases in the number of owner-occupied housing among blacks. Figure 2–10 reveals the pattern of this increase since 1930.[15] However, these gains in black ability to own their homes are not solely a consequence of improved economic circumstances. They are also the results of specific government rulings compelling public officials and private citizens to behave in nondiscriminatory ways toward black citizens. Moreover, government actions, generally in the form of legal rulings, have followed intensive and persistent litigation initiated by blacks. This frequent use of the judicial branch of government is another measure of the inequality gap of blacks. We shall examine the courts in greater detail in chapters 4 and 5. But their value to blacks in attempting to reduce the gap needs to be mentioned. Thus, in the area of housing, despite having enough income in many instances, blacks were unable to purchase homes in many American communities. Most of the excluding practices were private, "gentleman's agreements," or restrictions. (These discriminated against Jews and other minority group members as well.)

---

[15] For further details see Bureau of the Census, "Negro Population 1790–1915" (Washington, D.C.: United States Government Printing Office, 1918); and "Negroes in the United States: 1920–32" (Washington D.C.: United States Government Printing Office, 1935).

Percentage

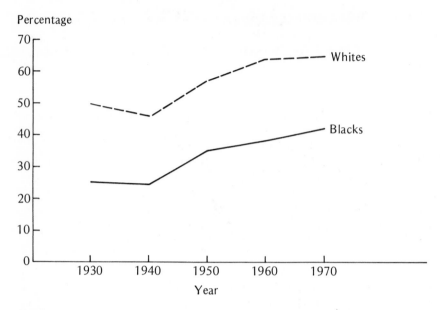

FIGURE 2-10
Owner-Occupied Housing Units: 1930, 1940, 1950, 1960, 1970

SOURCE: U.S. Bureau of the Census.

However, when the government entered the housing field through the practice of federally insured mortgages (Federal Housing Administration, Veterans' Administration mortgages, and the like), it followed the discriminatory practices which were used by private sellers in maintaining the character of a given community. If blacks or other minorities did not already reside in the area, the U.S. government was not going to start a change in that pattern. As a result, some of the violence which came with black efforts to leave the ghettos was the government's fault. In the area of housing, blacks were not able to get the government to act meaningfully until 1948 when the Supreme Court struck down restrictive covenants in its ruling in *Shelley* v. *Kramer*.

Government reluctance to act in the field of housing opportunities had the predictable effect of restricting blacks, regardless of income or other socioeconomic characteristics, to the city proper. Prior to the Korean War, the few black Americans who lived outside the central cities were often domestic employees for whites. However, though the suburban growth which began after World War I largely ignored blacks many sought better housing conditions. The ideal of home ownership was as strong among racial minorities as among the white population.

SUBURBANIZATION OF THE PROBLEM

The pressures on the housing market were greatest in the years immediately following World War II. Competition was keen because the home construction industry was slow to recover from the necessities of a wartime economy. For those blacks who sought available housing outside the traditional ghettos, violent white resistance frequently attended their efforts. Gradually, however, as black incomes rose (See Table 2-1.) and with the help of legal and legislative actions after World War II black Americans joined the movement from the central cities.[16] The figures given in Table 2-2 show tremendous increase in this movement for the decade 1960–1970. As we might expect, this change coincided with the dramatic rise in political activity among black Americans. The data presented in Table 2-2 are of course selective. But they indicate some lessening in the racial exclusivity of the suburban rings around the city. Black rates of suburbanization do not approach those of urban migration before World War I or after World War II. For example, in 1950 approximately 4.5 percent of the total suburban population was black; by 1970 they constituted just 4.9 percent of the total. For the central cities and suburbs shown in Table 2-2 the rate of black increase was uncommon. Indeed, Connolly pointed out that he chose to look at

> suburban communities that more than doubled the number of their black inhabitants during the 1960's such that blacks constituted at least 10 percent of the total population in 1970.[17]

A good deal of the movement of blacks outside central cities is because of the growth of the ghetto rather than significant removal of racial barriers. Black population increases in the cities expanded the traditional ghettos to the cities' boundaries. Thus, for a number of the suburban areas shown, their proportion of blacks resulted from location in the paths of ghetto growth. University City, Missouri, next to St. Louis, and Takoma Park, Maryland, next door to Washington, D.C., as well as Wilkinsburg, Pennsylvania, near Pittsburgh are examples of this phenomenon. Nevertheless, it is worth noting that the black suburbanites were differentiated from central city blacks. One of the most

---

[16] See the discussion of black suburbanization in Harold X. Connolly, "Black Movement Into the Suburbs," *Urban Affairs Quarterly* 9:1 (Sept. 1973) and also see the sources cited there.

[17] Connolly, p. 93. A slightly different perspective on black suburbanization, suggesting the ghettoization of blacks outside central cities can be found in Reynolds Farley, "The Changing Distribution of Negroes Within Metropolitan Areas: The Emergence of Black Suburbs," *American Journal of Sociology* 74:4, pt. 1 (January 1970): 512–29.

TABLE 2-2
Population of Suburban Communities by Central City and Race

Central City	Suburb	1960			1970			Percentage Negro Increase 1960–1970
		Total	Negro	% Negro	Total	Negro	% Negro	
Hartford	Bloomfield	13,613	812	6.0	18,301	2,450	13.4	202
N.Y. City	Freeport	34,419	2,407	7.0	40,374	7,467	18.5	210
	Roosevelt	12,883	2,241	17.4	15,008	10,135	67.5	352
	Spring Valley	6,538	636	9.7	18,112	4,147	22.9	552
Newark	East Orange	77,259	19,220	24.9	75,471	40,099	53.1	109
	Linden	39,931	2,602	6.5	41,409	5,320	12.8	105
Wash., D.C.	Hillcrest Hts.	15,295	60	a	24,037	3,357	14.0	5,495
	Takoma Park	16,799	437	2.6	18,455	2,297	12.4	426
Pittsburgh	Wilkinsburg	30,066	726	2.4	26,780	5,315	19.8	632
Cleveland	East Cleveland	37,991	804	2.1	39,600	23,196	58.6	2,785
	Shaker Heights	36,460	357	1.0	36,306	5,250	14.5	1,371
	Warrensville Hts.	10,609	20	a	18,925	4,007	21.2	19,935
Detroit	Highland Park	38,063	7,947	20.9	35,444	19,609	55.3	147
Chicago	Harvey	29,071	1,986	6.8	34,636	10,711	30.9	442
	Joliet	66,780	4,638	6.9	80,378	9,507	11.8	105
	Markham	11,704	2,505	21.4	15,987	7,981	49.9	219
	Maywood	27,330	5,229	19.1	30,036	12,416	41.3	137
	Zion	11,941	564	4.7	17,268	2,345	13.6	316
St. Louis	Univ. City	51,249	88	a	46,309	9,281	20.0	10,447
Las Vegas	North Las Vegas	18,442	33	a	36,216	8,785	24.3	26,521
Los Angeles	Altadena	40,658	1,484	3.6	42,380	11,496	27.1	675
	Carson	38,059	50	a	71,150	8,752	12.3	17,404
	Inglewood	63,390	29	a	89,985	10,066	11.2	34,610
	Pomona	67,157	880	1.3	87,384	10,648	12.2	1,110

a. Less than 1.0%.

Source: U.S. Bureau of the Census (1971b, 1963). Adapted from Table I in Harold Connolly, "Black Movement into the Suburbs," *Urban Affairs Quarterly* 9:1 (September 1973): 94.

interesting pieces of information is shown in Table 2-3 which compares suburban and central city black family income. In only three of the communities does the median income of suburban blacks fall below that of blacks in the central cities. But the income differential reappears, again with three exceptions, when the income comparison is made across racial lines. (See Table 2-4.) Although in a better situation than blacks in the central cities, blacks in the suburbs do not do as well as whites. And with regard to the suburban black median income we see that it requires a greater labor force participation rate among black women to achieve the levels indicated. (See Table 2-5.)

It is interesting to find that the rate of home ownership among the black suburbanites is higher in just over half (13) of the communities included in Table 2-5. This fact strengthens our belief that the ideal of home owning is at least as strong among blacks as among whites. Indeed, given the relative inequality of blacks in society such property may represent their most tangible demonstration of security and status.

Black Affluence Does Not Produce Security

While it is frequently believed that money income leads to relatively secure status positions in American society, this belief has to be qualified when applied to the situations of black Americans. Neither income nor professional occupations can ensure members of this minor-

TABLE 2-3

Index of Suburban Negro Median Family Income Compared to Central City Negro Median Family Income[a]

Carson	187.5	Maywood	133.9
Shaker Heights	181.1	Harvey	129.5
Bloomfield	172.8	Spring Valley	127.0
Inglewood	171.0	East Cleveland	123.8
Warrensville Heights	168.6	Hillcrest Heights	122.4
University City	157.8	Freeport	120.5
Roosevelt	153.0	Zion	108.5
Markham	147.2	Pomona	107.3
Linden	144.3	Joliet	101.5
Wilkinsburg	138.0	North Las Vegas	95.8
Altadena	136.2	Highland Park	94.0
East Orange	134.0	Takoma Park	94.0

a. Central city Negro median family income = 100.
SOURCE: U.S. Bureau of the Census (1972b). Adapted from Connolly, p. 104.

TABLE 2-4

Index of Suburban Negro Family Income Compared to Suburban White Median Family Income[a]

BLACK MEDIAN INCOME ($)			
Carson $13,474	114.7	Maywood 10,552	84.4
Inglewood 12,291	114.5	Linden 9,732	84.1
Warrensville Heights 12,841	110.4	Zion 8,554	81.4
Roosevelt 10,940	95.8	East Orange 9,036	79.9
Markham 11,600	93.1	Spring Valley 9,080	79.8
East Cleveland 9,432	91.2	Altadena 9,785	76.6
Harvey 10,211	89.9	Pomona 7,708	75.5
Wilkinsburg 8,412	89.4	North Las Vegas 6,534	71.5
Highland Park 8,126	86.5	Joliet 8,000	68.9
Bloomfield 12,161	85.7	Shaker Heights 13,793	66.1
Hillcrest Heights 10,393	85.6	Takoma Park 7,977	65.5
University City 10,313	85.2	Freeport 8,613	64.1

a. Suburban white median family income = 100.
SOURCE: U.S. Bureau of the Census (1972b). Adapted from Connolly, p. 105.

ity that they can freely exercise their freedoms. In such conditions of uncertainty we question the benign implications of views like the following from the political scientist Thomas Dye in his work *The Politics of Equality:*

> Whites feel that they can communicate with the black middle class, but not with the black masses. They regard blacks at the top of the social pyramid as living examples of what the determined or talented Negro can accomplish in a democratic capitalist society.[18]

Our reluctance to accept assessments that treat the problems of race in the United States solely as a problem of class is based on the continued occurrence of incidents such as that described in the following account. The situation seems simple enough; a black physician and his wife with secure professional standings and a high income occupation wanted to find new housing. However, "the determined or talented Negro" must still bear the stigma of being black, regardless of the objective indicators of class.

"I Can Never Be Sure" — The Maxwell Case.*

It came as a surprise to everyone. Well, almost everyone except Mrs. Maxwell herself, and perhaps two other people.
Real estate broker Pat O'Grady was handling the sale between Dr. and

---

[18] Dye, p. 92.
* Adapted with permission from the *Milwaukee Journal*, April 28, 1974. Emphasis added.

TABLE 2-5
Suburbs Ranked by Negro Median Family Income with Proportion of Married Women (husband present) in Labor Force. Proportion of Home Ownership by Race (in percentages)

SUBURB	INCOME ($)	MARRIED WOMEN (HUSBAND (PRESENT) IN LABOR FORCE		HOME OWNERSHIP	
		NEGRO	WHITE	NEGRO	WHITE
Shaker Heights	13,793	65.2	25.5	73.4	60.2
Carson	13,474	66.9	39.8	81.7	72.7
Warrensville Heights	12,841	65.4	40.2	88.9	39.8
Inglewood	12,291	71.8	44.7	74.3	33.2
Bloomfield	12,161	65.4	38.9	86.7	78.5
Markham	11,600	59.6	39.7	93.3	89.4
Roosevelt	10,940	52.3	35.0	73.9	80.0
Maywood	10,552	66.9	42.9	55.9	66.3
Hillcrest Heights	10,393	72.5	44.8	34.9	40.6
University City	10,313	70.5	37.8	79.7	58.5
Harvey	10,211	53.5	37.4	54.2	61.1
Altadena	9,785	61.1	39.9	70.0	75.2
Linden	9,732	59.3	39.7	52.6	66.0
East Cleveland	9,432	61.7	42.2	40.1	28.0
Spring Valley	9,080	60.8	40.1	14.5	30.1
East Orange	9,036	61.9	42.8	30.0	20.3
Freeport	8,613	56.3	37.7	50.3	62.4
Zion	8,554	74.2	48.0	55.6	55.0
Wilkinsburg	8,412	55.4	34.8	56.9	42.3
Highland Park	8,126	45.9	38.3	51.8	32.0
Joliet	8,000	59.0	34.5	39.2	64.5
Takoma Park	7,977	65.9	50.0	23.2	39.6
Pomona	7,708	51.1	40.4	63.0	56.2
North Las Vegas	6,534	55.8	35.7	59.2	60.6

SOURCE: Adapted from Connolly, Table 3, p. 103.

Mrs. John W. Maxwell, of the 21st floor at Prospect Towers, and the owner of an eighth floor apartment next door at the Newport, 1610 N. Prospect Ave.

It wasn't the first time the Maxwells had considered the Newport, but this time they were serious. And less easily frightened off.

Five years of Prospect Towers had taught them to like apartment living. But this time they wanted to buy a condominium apartment, citing the tax advantages and the building of equity.

Although neighboring buildings are integrated, the Newport, with its apartments ranging from $40,000 to $100,000, had remained white.

The Maxwells are people who are accustomed to "firsts."

Maxwell, at 77 limiting his medical practice to three or four afternoons a week, is the first black to have been named chief of staff of a Wisconsin hospital — St. Anthony's in 1954.

On Thursday, the Maxwells became the first blacks to move into the Newport, but only after being the first blacks to file suit in Federal Court alleging that racial discrimination prevented their buying an apartment there.

Their real estate salesman Pat O'Grady said, "I still can't believe that this happened in this day and age. I thought we had progressed a little further than this."

Their attorney Seymour Pikofsky said, "After having worked with the Milwaukee Legal Services and dealing with the problems of the poor, it takes a great deal to surprise me.

"But I guess I was surprised that it happened to someone of Dr. Maxwell's stature. I'm not surprised, though, that there are some people and some places around here that discriminate."

One of their new neighbors at the Newport is Ben Barkin, head of a public relations firm and, by his own description, one of the leaders in the fight for open housing here.

"In our day, we've seen some progress — in employment, in housing," Barkin said. "That's why I think I was startled when they were turned down."

As Barkin and others explained, only two members of the Newport's board of directors voted against the Maxwells.

The twist was this: In the Maxwell's case, for some reason, it was decided that a unanimous vote was needed to buy into this all-white community.

As the story goes, according to Newport residents and friends, when the Newport board of directors was faced with a suit, they decided to have their attorney review the bylaws. The attorney advised the board that a unanimous vote was not necessary.

Atty. Elwin A. Andrus, president of the Newport Corp., refused to answer questions about the Maxwells, saying: "It seems to me it doesn't need to be further aired." He did say, however, that "there was no change in the vote" and that the board's reversal "was not based on the suit."

Even though Mrs. Maxwell functions clearly within the mainstream of Milwaukee society, she said she was not surprised by the Newport's decision.

"Being a black person, I can never by sure," she said. "I've learned to expect discrimination, and I had a feeling about this."

"Now you see," Mrs. Maxwell said, "it doesn't matter. You do all the things you're supposed to do, and it still doesn't matter. That's the tragedy of it all.

"It's not that I expect more for myself than I expect for any other person. I certainly don't go around thinking 'I'm Mrs. Maxwell, I expect extra treatment.'

"My point is, if they do this against us, what do they do against the less fortunate people?"

It is perhaps a measure of social progress that cases such as the Maxwell's have become less frequent. But, then, Dr. and Mrs. Maxwell were not part of the black masses except by virtue of their race. For many whites that alone is sufficient basis for discrimination. Black Americans can never be sure, even now after so many positive changes have taken place, of what to expect from whites.

Class Insecurity Is Part of the Problem

The uncertainty which is described in the *Maxwell Case* is a part of the problem because it has been the broad middle class which carries a major burden in transmitting the values of American society.[19] Moreover, a considerable portion of the political leadership comes from this class. While blacks, like other Americans, have long recognized the need for leadership if their status were to be improved, the obstacles to its emergence in the black sub-culture have been numerous and un-commonly difficult to overcome. The fact that the ghetto residential system has contributed to the inability of the black middle class to take on this role is a major point in understanding the slowness which has characterized the black rise to a position of political effectiveness.

Black communities have typically contained all income and social classes within a defined geographic area of the city. Not only did this mean there was little or no separation between classes, but differentiated social interaction was also limited. As a result, class distinctions (such as they were) in the ghetto increasingly came to be almost exclusively a function of income. The black "middle class" imitated the white model based upon movies, the media, and impressions gained from the contacts between white families and their domestic help. The "black bourgeoisie" began to behave with what they believed was a middle or upper middle class life style. However, the values which help to define a class could not be adapted to their lives. Nor could the political roles that are played by the white middle class develop in the black communities.

As previously noted, free blacks in the North managed to acquire a degree of stability and secure income in various service trades and as domestic workers for wealthy white families. This handful of the total black population made up the bulk of the northern black middleclass in the early part of this century.[20] There were, however, few opportunities for black communities to increase significantly the size of this class due

---

[19] A useful discussion of this point is contained in Arthur N. Holcombe, *The Middle Classes in American Politics* (Cambridge: Harvard University Press, 1940). But see the criticism of the black middle class political style in Nathan Hale, *Black Anglo-Saxons* (New York: Macmillan, 1970).

[20] Cf. Spear, *Black Chicago* and Drake and Cayton, *Black Metropolis*.

to outside restrictions. As a consequence, the black class structure re-sembled a pyramid instead of a diamond.* That is, the black **stratifica-tion** system rested on a very broad lower class and rapidly rose to the point, whereas the white stratification system has a bulge at the middle, narrowing to points at either ends. In both instances the narrowing represents smaller population sizes. (See Figure 2–11.)

In part because of its small size, the black middle class was at the same time victimized by the common problem of the race which was shared by all blacks in the society. The black middle class had tried to show its conformity to the values of society. It had also shown its loyalty to the political system over several generations. Still, the black middle class took a more direct approach in an effort to achieve equal citizenship rights. In the civil rights demonstrations in the South and later in the antipoverty protests of the North, middleclass and lowerclass blacks could unite for they had common problems. In the past decade black Americans seemed to be fighting against the likelihood that they would become a permanent minority.[21] In this regard, the black rebellions of

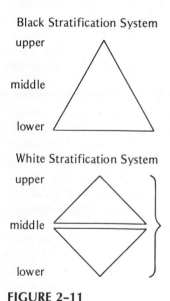

FIGURE 2–11

---

* This pyramidal arrangement was presented by Drake and Cayton in their work *Black Metropolis,* and later adapted by Dye in *The Politics of Equality.*

[21] Robert A. Dahl, although certainly not the first to discuss this problem, presents an excellent statement of the implications of a permanent minority for democratic governance in his *Preface to Democratic Theory* (Chicago: University of Chicago Press, 1956); see espe-cially chapter 5.

the past decade can be seen as an effort to escape the dependence upon governmental *largesse* in their efforts to create a real political identity. The problem, of course, is that racial solidarity became a key part of these movements. And, as long as blacks use race in what they consider to be positive ways, the white majority is free to see such activities as unfriendly to *their* idea of the liberal American tradition.

There is a degree of irony in this white response. Most blacks have believed that white racial solidarity is responsible for their inequalities. Ample evidence supports the view that whites have closed ranks, literally and figuratively, to stop black advancement in the past. And, it should be emphasized that white solidarity (or its appearance) against black efforts is an integral part of the American liberal tradition.

Some people might argue that rebellious actions by blacks during the sixties were "bad." Yet, we should realize that those acts revealed an apparent inability of the government to solve social problems which are a major reason for any government's creation. The point is not that blacks acted badly; in any case, by what standard could one judge? Rather, after two centuries of white evasion on *the problem* black Americans showed a new political assertiveness. After all, violence is as much a political resource as income, status, occupation, position, and so forth. Admittedly, violence is an extreme measure and thus cannot be used consistently. But, without traditional resources, and under appropriate circumstances, "a despised minority" may resort to extremes to relieve its inferior status. Thus, violence was directed against the status quo, against a social order that prizes order and stability. For the black minority the gradual process of change which had become an accepted part of the political culture would not be enough. It was much too slow to meet their needs and political demands.

The nature of *the problem* then, is more than the socioeconomic inequality of blacks. For as we have seen, successful achievement along social and economic lines has not led to the kind of freedom that black Americans believe is due.

Blacks and Whites Do Not See the Same Reality

"Our nation is moving toward two societies, one black, one white — separate and unequal," charged the Kerner Commission Report in 1968. The Commission placed the major responsibility for this development on white racism.

Yet the extent of white recognition accorded the Kerner Commission's findings was limited, at best. One month following the Report's release, a *Newsweek* story showed that blacks and whites still disagreed over the causes of the violence, and white willingness to share responsibility for finding solutions.[22] There is reason to believe that this disagreement stems from a different understanding of the term "white racism" between the black and white publics. As Skolnick suggested, "The average [white] person is likely to reserve the emotionally loaded term 'racism' for only the most extreme assertions of white supremacy and innate Negro inferiority."[23] Even if we accept Skolnick's explanation, the finding that follows for blacks indicates a perceptual gap based upon race. In the same data noted above the black response supported the contention of white racism's responsibility by a 58 to 17 percent margin.[24] Perhaps a clearer picture of this difference in perceptions can be gained from data provided by the Kerner Commission. It was reported that "one out of eight Negroes perceives a world where almost all white people dislike Negroes."[25] They go on to say that this represents "nearly two million Negro adults from 16–69 [who] see themselves as a widely disliked minority." And among black college graduates almost two-thirds believed that most whites don't care whether blacks advance or not.[26] From other data we could be led to view these feelings as nothing more than a collective misreading of white sentiment; when white people are asked to respond to the (abstract) concept of the right of Negroes to equal treatment, they come down strongly against discrimination.[27] There is persuasive support for this generalization in Table 2–6.

However, white feelings on questions of equality for blacks are not consistent in specific areas. We can see this inconsistency in the lesser amounts of support for equality as the concept touches upon social nearness. No more than half of the white population would "favor letting as many Negroes as want move into a neighborhood." However, there are some problems in attempting to grasp the real significance of these responses when we compare them with the figures in Table 2–7.

There is a more serious problem in black-white relations. This arises from the white position of assumed moral superiority. As Campbell and Schuman put it:

> While admitting the presence of discrimination, white people show a strong tendency to blame the disadvantaged circumstances of Negro life

[22] Newsweek, April 22, 1968, p. 24.

[23] Jerome H. Skolnick, *The Politics of Protest* (New York: Ballantine Books, 1969), p. 169.

[24] Ibid., p. 180.

[25] Angus Campbell and Howard Schuman, *Racial Attitudes in Fifteen American Cities* (Ann Arbor, Mich.: Institution of Social Research, University of Michigan, 1968), p. 25.

[26] Ibid.

[27] Ibid., p. 36.

TABLE 2-6
White Male Attitudes Toward Integration and Segregation by Age Group*: I

	16–19	20–29	30–39	40–49	50–59	60–69
Negroes have a right to live where they choose	70%	67%	68%	60%	65%	55%
Favor laws preventing job discrimination against Negroes	68	78	73	65	60	64
Would not mind at all having a Negro supervisor	89	89	85	83	88	86

*Adapted with permission from Angus Campbell and Howard Schuman, *Racial Attitudes in Fifteen American Cities* (Ann Arbor, Mich.: Institution for Social Research, University of Michigan, 1968), p. 36, Table III-9.

TABLE 2-7
White Male Attitudes Toward Integration and Segregation by Age Group: II

	16–19	20–29	30–39	40–49	50–59	60–69
Wouldn't mind at all having a Negro family next door	55%	59%	55%	42%	45%	60%
Would like to see their children have Negro friends	27	24	24	16	14	14
Oppose idea of all Negro employment in Negro neighborhoods	70	62	72	61	63	74
Would vote for a qualified Negro mayor	NA	70	74	58	59	66

Source: Campbell and Schuman, Ibid.

on Negroes themselves. Although they do not subscribe to genetic theories of racial inferiority, they find much to criticize in the attitudes and behavior patterns they see as characteristic of Negroes and apparently feel that it is within the power of Negroes to improve their own situation.[28]

The possibility that whites would move from such a position to one favoring special efforts on behalf of blacks might be expected as blacks

---

[28] Ibid.

moved into the American mainstream. Yet, the data do not support such an expectation, for as Campbell and Schuman noted:

> The prospect of passing laws to protect Negro rights to equal treatment is less . . . supported . . . than the abstract right itself.[29]

It is not difficult for blacks to move from the position of regarding themselves as members of a "widely disliked minority" to a view of distrust of whites. This is possible even when whites portray themselves as sympathetic to the goals sought by the minority.

Some objective basis for this distrust is provided by Free and Cantril.[30] Whites were asked (in 1964) if Negroes should "have more influence in government and political matters than they have now, or less influence than they have now." One-fifth of the authors' "complete liberals" and one-third of the "predominantly liberal" answered "less influence." Keeping in mind that nonviolence had recently reached its height, this is a discouraging finding, for black influence on government was low. It may well have been that the recently passed Civil Rights Act of 1964 influenced these responses. That makes the findings even more ironic from the viewpoint of the black minority.

By 1969 Brink and Harris found that substantial numbers of blacks expected white attitudes toward them to change following the political violence.[31] Their data indicated that most blacks, including middle and upper income southerners, expected these attitudes to be better. Among middle and upper income blacks there was a decrease of 26 percent among those who expected attitudes to be "better." At the same time there is an almost equal increase in this category among low-income non-southerners. The information in Table 2-8 from surveys conducted by Louis Harris suggest the continuing extent of the problem of attitudes. Indeed, it is interesting to observe that black stereotypic thinking about whites seems to have increased while for whites there have been some significant decreases. Note, however, that white attitudes have changed least in two areas with policy implications for black Americans: "blacks have less native intelligence" and "blacks want to live off the hand-out." These opinions are relevant to what the nation does, or does not do on the questions of equal education and economic opportunity.

---

[29] Ibid.

[30] Lloyd A. Free and Hadley Cantril, *The Political Beliefs of Americans: A Study of Public Opinion* (New York: Simon and Schuster, 1968), pp. 123–34.

[31] W. Brink and L. Harris, *The Negro Revolution in America* (New York: Simon and Schuster, 1969), p. 258.

TABLE 2-8
Black Stereotypes of Whites

	1971			1970		
	Agree %	Dis-agree %	Not Sure %	Agree %	Dis-agree %	Not Sure %
Whites feel that blacks are inferior	81	11	8	81	11	8
Whites give blacks a break only when forced to	79	13	8	77	15	8
White men secretly want black women	76	7	17	74	7	17
Whites are really sorry slavery for blacks was abolished	70	14	6	63	18	19
Whites have a mean and selfish streak in them	68	18	14	65	20	15
Whites are physically weaker than blacks	65	15	20	55	21	24
Whites are scared that blacks are better people than they are	62	23	15	66	21	13
Whites are less honest than blacks	58	19	23	50	23	27
White people need to have somebody like blacks to lord it over	52	28	20	49	31	20
Whites are more apt to catch diseases	49	18	33	44	21	35

White Stereotypes of Blacks

	1971	1963
Whites Who Agree That:	%	%
Blacks are less ambitious than whites	52	66
Blacks laugh a lot	48	68
Blacks smell different	48	60
Blacks have lower morals than whites	40	55
Blacks want to live off the hand-out	39	41
Blacks have less native intelligence	37	39
Blacks keep untidy homes	35	46
Blacks breed crime	27	35
Blacks care less for their families	26	31
Blacks are inferior to whites	22	31

Source: Reprinted with permission from Louis Harris, *The Anguish of Change* (New York: W. W. Norton, 1973), pp. 233, 236–237

The Problem: Black and White Attitudes

White ambivalence and hostility on racial matters has necessarily contributed to the importance of race for black Americans. The white American, North and South, still has not confronted the dilemma so forcefully presented in Gunnar Myrdal's work some three decades ago. While public opinion surveys confirm the existence of a widespread belief in equality as an abstract principle, white Americans are less supportive of the specific and operational measures which give day to day meaning to these equalitarian concepts.

Black efforts to exercise the political and social rights which they believe are embodied in these liberal principles have met with too many rebuffs. In the face of such rejections black Americans are understandably hampered as they try to find a viable social place and political role. Race and color still matter.

Yet, blacks have endured their second-class status with the hope that the dominant majority would relinquish their role as "keepers of the gate" to full citizenship status. Perhaps as a consequence of the long black insistence on legal rights, the white community and its leaders believed that the various Civil Rights Acts of the post–World War II period had met all the outstanding black demands. This belief was shattered by the outbreak of violent political protest in late 1964.

Throughout the nonviolent phase of black political protest (1960–1964) white attitudes were consistently negative in what they thought of the mass demonstrations. For example, nearly two-thirds (64 percent) of whites held unfavorable attitudes toward the "Freedom Riders." (These individuals, black and white, with sponsorship from CORE and other civil rights groups, deliberately challenged the segregationist practices in public accommodations throughout the South during the early 1960's.) But this figure came from the only 63 percent who had some idea of what Freedom Riders were. By December of 1963 white attitudes toward Negro actions to achieve civil rights showed that 59 percent of white northerners were opposed to such actions; in the South the figure opposed stood at 78 percent.[32]

An example of a gap between blacks and whites on matters of race can be seen in the data reported in Table 2-9. When asked to rate the effectiveness of black actions for civil rights, the opinions vary widely.

These differences persisted through the 1960's. Quite naturally, white evaluations became even more negative after the first wave of civil violence occurred in the middle sixties. Nevertheless, after the violent urban conflicts between 1964 and 1968, black Americans continued to believe strongly in an integrated society. As we shall see, these different

---

[32] Hazel Erskine, "The Polls," *Public Opinion Quarterly* 31:2 (1968) 656.

TABLE 2-9
Have Demonstrations Helped or Hurt the Negro Cause

1. Whites nationwide:

	Helped	Hurt	Other No Opinion
June, 1963	36%	45%	19%
July, 1965	27	58	15

2. When the race of respondents is controlled we find:

	Helped	Hurt	Other No Opinion
1965 Whites	24%	62%	14%
1965 Blacks	63	14	23

Source: Hazel Erskine, "The Polls," *Public Opinion Quarterly*, 31:2, p. 659 (no totals given). Reprinted with permission.

attitudes also reflected a difference in understanding why blacks engage in political violence or "unconventional" political acts.

Perhaps the most useful concept in attempting to explain social and political activity among blacks is the continued strength of blacks' belief in integration. Table 2-10 indicates attitudes of blacks toward integration. It should also be understood that differing opinions on the pace of integration were a crucial factor in black attitudes. Indeed, a 1969 study

TABLE 2-10
The Goal: An Open Society

Would rather send children to an integrated school	Yes	78%	No	9%
Would rather live in an integrated neighborhood	Yes	74%	No	16%
Blacks should have a separate nation in the U.S.	Yes	21%	No	69%
Blacks will make more progress by running their own schools, businesses, and living in their own neighborhoods rather than by integrating	Yes	13%	No	78%

Undecided omitted

Source: Copyright 1969 by Newsweek, Inc. All rights reserved. Reprinted by permission.

by Conant et al. suggested that on the pace of integration in the society, the most liberal whites are not as dissatisfied as the most conservative blacks.[33]

However, if the Conant findings are at all valid, a black sense of improved social relations becomes even more difficult to explain. An example of this sense of improvement is found in a study conducted in Buffalo, New York.[34] The authors suggested that "most blacks see their lives and their future . . . tied to that of their community and nation, and that by and large they have a strong sense of affect for the political system that persists. . . ."[35] The strength of black affect partially explains the differences seen in Tables 2-11 and 2-12. Here blacks and whites were asked to rate the "progress of the nation" in the area of black-white relations, and their sense of optimism for the future.

TABLE 2-11
"Sense of Progress" of the Nation*

	WHITES	BLACKS
Worse	44%	28%
Same	33	26
Better	18	29
Much Better	5	17

* Sample size over 1,000.
SOURCE: Adapted from Everett F. Cataldo et al., "Political Attitudes of the Urban Poor" (paper prepared for delivery at the APS Association Annual Meeting, Washington, D.C., September, 1968), p. 5, Table 5. Reprinted with permission from the American Political Science Association.

TABLE 2-12
"Sense of Optimism" for the Future

	WHITES	BLACKS
Worse	18%	19%
Same	38	38
Better	28	31
Much Better	16	12

SOURCE: Cataldo. Reprinted with permission from the American Political Science Association.

---

[33] R. W. Conant et al., "Mass Polarization: Negro and White Attitudes on the Pace of Integration," in *American Behavioral Scientist* 13:2 (November-December, 1969): 254.

[34] Everett F. Cataldo et al., "Political Attitudes of the Urban Poor" (a paper prepared for delivery at the APS Association Annual Meeting, Washington, D.C., September, 1968), p. 12.

[35] Ibid.

The authors found that:

> both racial groups were virtually identical in their sense of optimism: 44 percent of the whites viewed the future optimistically, as did 43 percent of the blacks. The authors concluded on the basis of their findings, "We do not see . . . a black community despairing of how far it has come and where it is going. . . ."[36]

The optimism reported in Table 2-12 is, however, tempered by the rather pessimistic views reflected in Table 2-11. Here, sizable majorities of blacks and whites believed that the nation as a whole had made little headway in dealing with racial matters. Indeed, the whites interviewed by Cataldo and his co-workers were found to be decidedly more pessimistic in this area than blacks.[37]

In view of the general white tendency to regard the civil violence of the past decade as little more than race riots and looting episodes, it is not difficult to understand why they would be more negative than blacks in their evaluations. Reenforcing this limited evaluation is a rather consistent white American belief that black problems, to the extent that they even agreed that there were any, did not justify the resort to political violence. This may help to explain why whites in the Cataldo study so strongly saw little progress in the nation's handling of the problem of race. Some additional findings in the Cataldo study highlight some significant differences in the conception of roles and functions government is expected to assume by blacks and whites. (See Tables 2-13 and 2-14.) Because blacks and whites agreed that the government s role in the areas of justice and civil rights was important it is worthwhile to note that twice as many blacks as whites believed government to be ineffective in these crucial areas.

Nor are the findings for Buffalo unique. In their study of the Detroit riots, Aberbach and Walker's findings were quite similar to those found in Buffalo. They reported that "whites [were] much more satisfied with their past and present lives [than blacks]." However, they also found "both racial groups . . . strongly optimistic about the future."[38] This study also gives further evidence of the importance of integration to blacks; it noted that blacks talked "almost exclusively in terms of integration, better personal relationships with whites and respect and dignity for all, while more than 30 percent of the whites spontaneously en-

---

[36] Ibid., p. 7.

[37] The reader might want to compare these findings with the black-white perceptions of the "Opportunity Structure" in Joan H. Rytina et al., "Income Stratification Ideology: Beliefs About the American Opportunity Structure," *American Journal of Sociology* 75:4, pt. 2 (January 1970): 703–15.

[38] Joel D. Aberbach and Jack L. Walker, *Political Trust and Racial Ideology,* Institute of Public Policy Studies Discussion Paper #8 (Ann Arbor: University of Michigan, Institute of Public Policy Studies, n.d.), p. 19.

TABLE 2-13
Blacks Believe in Active Government

ITEM	RACE	IMPORTANT	OF SOME IMPORTANCE	SHOULD NOT DO AT ALL
(1) Provide a chance to make a good living.	Blacks	94%	5%	1%
	Whites	79	17	4
(2) Insure equal opportunity to participate in political decisions	Blacks	88	10	2
	Whites	78	17	5
(3) Provide welfare services	Blacks	85	13	2
	Whites	72	24	4
(4) Facilitate social mobility	Blacks	64	28	8
	Whites	56	29	15
(5) Redistribution of wealth and prestige	Blacks	51	29	20
	Whites	39	30	31

White N = 697–718
Black N = 225–266

SOURCE: Cataldo, p. 9. Reprinted with permission of the American Political Science Association.

TABLE 2-14
Governmental Role and Function and Effectiveness

	RACE	IMPORTANT	EFFECTIVE	INEFFECTIVE
(1) Providing justice for all	Blacks	98%	60%	40%
	Whites	97	79	21
(2) Securing civil rights and liberties	Blacks	97	55	45
	Whites	91	78	22

SOURCE: Cataldo, pp. 9–10. Reprinted with permission of the American Political Science Association.

dorse[d] segregation or separation of some kind."[39] The authors also point out that

> The white community, not the black, is divided over the desirability of integration and whites are more depressed than blacks about the prospects for future race relations.[40]

And a study conducted after the Watts riots reported that blacks expected the riots to have important positive effects on white attitudes.

[39] Ibid.
[40] Ibid., p. 20.

And they expected such changes at relatively superficial levels.[41] The authors also noted an undercurrent of despair in their Los Angeles sample. They noted that "Negroes did not expect fundamental changes in the social distance between the races." The strong belief in integration which has sustained much of the black protest seems to have lessened. After the civil rights and voting rights acts were passed blacks developed a sense of pride that many whites found to be disturbing.

Taken together, these findings did not show any closing of the gap in perceptions between the races. While these data are not current, little has happened to suggest that the authors of the study were overly pessimistic. Indeed, the notion of two societies put forth in the Kerner Commission Report confirmed many of the important realities of black life in America. And in a (1969) report entitled *One Year Later*, prepared a year after the Kerner Report, some of the Commission members concluded that little had changed.[42] That conclusion, unfortunately, seems equally valid in 1975.[43] The problem, in its most basic form, remains one of white racism.

But blacks have continued, although by less violent means, to seek change in the nation's political, social, and economic institutions. Because these institutions are slow to respond — that is, because the society is still unwilling to acknowledge black claims — change is difficult and slow. However, as we shall see in the next chapter, the difficulty in bringing about change is a salient feature of our political institutions and the political system generally.

Topics For Discussion

1. Try to define "rational behavior." To what extent does the behavior of whites, in their interaction with blacks, qualify as rational behavior?

2. Why have the attempts by the federal government to assist blacks economically largely failed to produce the desired results? How could these programs be made more effective?

3. Discuss what is meant by "equality." What kinds of equality are possible in a modern society? Are all forms of equality desirable, or are some types of equality incompatible?

---

[41] T. M. Tomlinson and David D. Sears, "Negro Attitudes Toward the Riot" in Nathan Cohen, ed., *The Los Angeles Riots: A Socio-Psychological Study* (New York: Praeger, 1970).

[42] Urban America, Inc. and the Urban Location. *One Year Later* (New York: Praeger, 1969). And see the retrospective on Watts by Jon Nordheimer in The *New York Times* (August 7, 1975), p. 1. Also see the story on Watts in the *San Francisco Sunday Examiner and Chronicle* (August 10, 1975), pp. 1, E.

[43] See, for example, a 1975 report of the U.S. Commission on Civil Rights, *Twenty Years After Brown: Equality of Economic Opportunity* (Washington, D.C.: U.S. Government Printing Office, 1975).

Suggested Readings

Blackstone, William T., ed. *The Concept of Equality*. Minneapolis, 1969.

An exploration of different aspects of human equality, justice, and opportunity.

Bullock, Charles S. and Harrell R. Rodgers, Jr., eds. *Black Political Attitudes: Implications for Political Support*. Chicago: Rand-McNally, 1972.

Investigations of the political beliefs, attitudes, and stereotypes of blacks; political socialization of black children; and policy outputs and black political influence.

Campbell, Angus et. al. *The American Voter*. New York: John Wiley & Sons, 1964.

Classic study of voting behavior in the 1950's.

Clark, Kenneth. *Dark Ghetto: Dilemmas of Social Power*. New York: Harper & Row, 1965.

A strong picture of life among ghetto dwellers; sharpens one's awareness of the problems facing many black Americans today.

Dye, Thomas. *The Politics of Inequality*. Indianapolis: Bobbs-Merrill, 1971.

Deals with the social and political inequities of the American political system.

Harlan, Louis R. *Separate but Unequal*. New York: Atheneum, 1969.

A study of public school campaigns and southern racism from 1901 to 1915.

Lenski, Gerhard. *Power and Privilege: A Theory of Social Stratification*. New York: McGraw-Hill, 1966. Chapters 1, 2, 4.

An examination of the structure and dynamics of distributive systems in agrarian and industrial societies.

Liebow, Eliot. *Tally's Corner*. Boston: Little, Brown, 1967.

Another descriptive account of the black situation, in this case the story of black streetcorner men.

Samuelson, Paul A. *Economics*. New York: McGraw-Hill, 1974. Chapters 18, 19.

A straightforward examination of unemployment, its causes and correction through macroeconomic changes.

3

THE NATURE
OF THE SYSTEM

. . . when we talk about black politics we are not talking about ordinary politics. And we are not talking about ordinary politics because the American political system has not created a single social community in which the reciprocal rules of politics would apply. Conventional politics cannot solve this problem, because conventional politics is a part of the problem. It is part of the problem because the political system is the major bulwark of racism in America. It is part of the problem in the sense that the political system is structured to repel fundamental social and economic change.

We hear a great deal about the deficiencies, real or imagined, of certain black leaders, but not enough attention, it seems to me, is paid to the framework within which they operate. That framework prevents radical growth and innovation — as it was *designed* to prevent radical growth and innovation.

Mervyn M. Dymally, "The Black Outsider and the American Political System"*

Introduction

Why do blacks and others talk about the "system," the "establishment"? What are the values of the system and what are its basic features? What are its biases? Who runs the system, who are the

---

* Second Part, in Mervyn M. Dymally, ed., *The Black Politician: His Struggle for Power*, (Scituate, Mass.: Duxbury Press, 1971), p. 120. Reprinted with permission.

"political actives," who are the "élites," and why? How do blacks view the system? How are they affected by the system's values, features, and structures? These and related questions comprise the focus of the present chapter. In a larger sense, however, dealing with such matters is what this volume is all about. Our immediate purpose here, however, is to get an overall view of the system, its values, its features, and its nature. To these we now turn.

American Political Values

INDIVIDUALISM

Individualism is the one value that penetrates the entire American political value system. Undoubtedly this is because there are many interpretations of individualism. In one sense, it means a basic commitment to democratic principles that emphasize the importance and worth of each individual, the essential equality of all people, and the necessity of freedom for the full development of the individual. Rather than the state or government, it is the individual who occupies the central stage in the American value system. This emphasis upon the importance and worth of the individual is certainly one of the main currents throughout the history of democratic thought.

The Declaration of Independence provides one of the earliest and most vivid expressions of this doctrine in the American experience. Here Thomas Jefferson wrote that "all men are created equal and are endowed by their Creator with certain inalienable rights, . . . and among these are life, liberty and the pursuit of happiness." Government, according to Jefferson, was instituted to secure these ends. Whenever any government destroys them — that is, life, liberty, or property — it is the *right* of the people to throw off such governments and institute others that would secure these ends.

Here was the base for the notion that though all people may not have the same talents, intellect, and so on, each and every person nonetheless should be treated as equal to any others. All people have the same right to life, to freedom, to property. No person was to be slave of another. Each should be treated as an individual. Each should be able to develop to full potential. This, in turn, requires that all individuals should have maximum freedom to do what they choose to chart their lives and their future. Individualism, in this sense, means a strong commitment to the equality of *all* persons.

Equality, in the American experience, has come to mean political, legal, and social equality. Political equality is perhaps best expressed, at least in more recent times, through the "one man, one vote" principle.

Each person's vote or voice in public affairs — elections — should be the same as that of any other person. By legal equality is meant that no person is above the law, all are subject to the law. Put another way, every individual is equal before the law. Social equality indicates that there should be no caste or class, that people should not be treated badly because of their station in life or the circumstances of their birth.

The interpretations of these basic political values, however, were not initially meant for blacks. This seems to be so of at least Jefferson's Declaration of Independence and other early American pronouncements. That these pronouncements were not meant to apply to blacks was forcefully shown, as we have seen, by Chief Justice Taney in *Dred Scott*. Likewise, this position had also been reflected in earlier decisions of federal courts. Nonetheless, the importance of America's democratic values did not start with Jefferson. Nor of course, has it ended with him. These basic principles are very evident for democratic government. Those who deny these values to others tread on perilous grounds indeed.

As the history of blacks in this country shows, denial or attempted denial of these principles may lead (and have led) to persistent frustrations. And it can lead to disruptive behavior that can affect the individual as well as society. Yet for many Americans, especially blacks but others as well, these principles are more ideal than real. Take equality, for example. Political, social, and legal equality are so closely related that it is difficult if not impossible to enjoy one type of equality if denied the other types. Or put another way, to deny equality in one area affects the realization of equality in other areas. Many blacks, because of *social* inequities — for example, poverty — do not enjoy *political* or *legal* equality and vice versa.

There are those, of course, who hold that it is not equality that the American political value of individualism means but rather something called "equality of opportunity." But our view is that this doctrine, "equality of opportunity," has become a fashionable way by which many white liberals and others, whether they mean to or not, continue the status quo in American society. The doctrine does indeed ring hollow when it is so often used to rationalize why blacks and other minorities are denied jobs and other advantages. Thus, "equality of opportunity" becomes a cruel hoax as those who support the doctrine refuse to do what is necessary to remove inequalities that have been and are fostered by the *system*, not by the individual. Consequently, we strongly hold that there remains the necessity to achieve a basic equality in the legal, social, and political sense before "equality of opportunity" takes on any real meaning.

There is yet another interpretation that many Americans give to individualism. This is the view that individualism also means that government should *leave* individuals free, leave them *alone* to develop their capacities to their full potential. This is the economic notion of laissez-faire with sociopolitical implications. It also involves the so-called Protestant Ethic — those who work hard and have initiative will make it. And given the state's (government's) hands-off attitude, it is the individual's own fault and no one else's if he does not succeed. However, many people feel that government assistance is needed to give many individuals an equal and fair chance. In short, the key question is: is it a proper function of government to help those who are socially and economically disadvantaged? The most visible symbols of this controversy are government welfare programs, especially those identified with aid to individuals. And the most visible of the individuals receiving such aid are blacks. But it should be clearly stated that in actual numbers more whites than blacks are on welfare. That blacks are the most visible welfare recipients, however, is in part due to their concentration in the nation's cities. And these are the areas that are today the focus of much attention. In any event, blacks and others contend that their low socioeconomic status is beyond their control — beyond the control of the "individual" — and is due primarily to biases in the system. The overwhelming evidence presented in Chapter 2 and throughout this volume supports this view — the view that "system biases" more likely than not explain the low socioeconomic status of blacks in American life. Nonetheless, the battle continues to be joined by those who hold strongly to the Protestant Ethic (the work ethic) and who strongly oppose government support to the disadvantaged. Such government benefits, they argue, impede individualism and individual initiative.

Most Americans, black and white, believe that individualism is a very important value. Yet, it is readily apparent that they disagree on the meaning of this concept and how it should be put into practice. But it does little good to hold to *individualism* in terms of freedom and equality when some individuals are in fact denied the *means* necessary to realize such freedom and equality, and to realize their full potential as individuals. Yet this seems to be the result of how the system's attachment to individualism as a political value has been translated into practice. And this is the problem facing many black Americans today.

MAJORITY RULE AND MINORITY RIGHTS

In large measure the concept of minority rights is contained in our discussion of individualism. But we compare it here with **majority rule** to indicate how Americans hold to two values that seem contradictory or at least in conflict. The idea that political decisions should be made by majority rule is based on the premise that individuals have equal voice and free choice in making such decisions. The argument is made that since one individual is equal to the next, both votes count the same. Thus, there is a strong preference (and necessity) that decisions of the majority should prevail over any minority or smaller group of individuals. Certainly we have often heard the view that we should all do what the majority says, including those in the minority. In fact, having majority rule work as a way of making decisions rests as much on acquiescence of the minority as it does on the sheer weight of numbers of the majority. But, as we have indicated, Americans hold to both majority rule and minority rights. Therefore, there is a built-in tension between the two values. This tension involves the *content* of the decision as well as the *process* of the decision. In short, by holding to minority rights we do put some limits on majority rule. For majority rule to be accepted as legitimate and for it to prevail, it must respect minority rights. A professor who taught one of the authors in an introductory American government course put the matter this way: the majority should not do anything to the minority that would keep the minority from becoming the majority in the way in which the majority became the majority. For example, to the extent that the majority deprives minorities of the right to vote (or other rights), to that extent is the legitimacy of majority rule diminished. By the same token, appeals or obligations of minorities to go along with such majority decisions are also lessened.

LEGALISM

We have heard many times the expression that America has a "government of laws and not of men." The phrase symbolizes the legalistic mold of the American political system. The chief symbol of this American attachment to legalism is the written Constitution which is the fundamental law. From the town or city council to the county board, to the state and national governments, the citizen is overwhelmed with legalism. It flows from laws enacted by legislative bodies, with orders of executives, and with rules and regulations coming from many bureaucratic structures. In this sort of situation, the symbols of **legalism**, of strict obedience to law and rules, assume an importance of their own, aside from the actual impact of particular laws on individuals. This strong attachment to the idea of written law is accompanied by the view that it is not only practical but also *desirable* to have such regulations. This idea is so widespread in American thinking that it goes beyond government policies and actions and extends into private life and organizations. Consequently, it is not unusual for a new organization or club to argue about "by-laws" which will govern the group's activities.

To be sure, the attachment to legal forms is important to the functions of the political system. The *law* is used to shape major directions or changes in social policy. And it is called into play in distributing benefits and costs, policies and programs to various groups. But laws, no matter how well written, are neither self-enforcing, nor self-interpreting. Moreover, the law is not always what the statute says it is. Frequently one can find gaps or room for maneuver within the legal boundaries. It is this characteristic of American law, the *un*written law, which can be as important to individual citizens as that which is written. In any event, this preoccupation with law and legalism gives importance to those who are trained in law. It gives lawyers generally a dominant role in politics and government far beyond their sheer numbers. It also points up the importance of courts as policy-making arenas in allocating benefits and values in the political system. This subject is explored more fully in a later chapter.

CONFLICT BUT COMPROMISE

Given their heterogeneous population mix, Americans have come to expect conflict. But we have also come to expect that conflict can be managed. Conflicts cover many issues in American life. They may be drawn along a number of lines: racial, ethnic, social, economic, political, or more likely over a combination of these. And, as we shall discuss later, some of this conflict is built into the system itself. In any event, the racial conflict (or problem) cuts across all these lines. It promotes sharp divisions and provokes strong emotions from the parties involved. To many Americans, mainly white Americans, it is a conflict (to some just another conflict) that not only has to be managed by the system, but one that *can* be managed through restraint and reason. Essentially this means that both sides must give a little and compromise their differences. This willingness to compromise is perhaps the most important characteristic of American politics. Neither side can expect the other side to give in completely; the *American* way is the *middle* way. To hold fast to your position, no matter what the cause, is viewed as hostile, unsportsmanlike, uncooperative.

The strong belief in managing conflict through compromise has without question influenced settlements or progress (as distinguished from solutions) of many problems, including those related to race. This leads to the commonly accepted and related assumptions (1) that all problems can be settled; and (2) that the system provides for adequate correction of these problems. These assumptions are so strongly fixed in American political life that they require little discussion. Consequently, Americans are reluctant to voice contrary views. For example, it certainly seems plausible to suggest that all problems cannot be settled or that the system is unable to correct particular grievances. However, so strong is the belief that all problems can be settled within the system that even those who doubt these assumptions either directly or indirectly act as if such doubts do not exist.

Equally as strong is the belief that such problems or conflicts can (and should) be settled peacefully and without violence. Americans have such faith in the system that it matters little that violence has occurred and was necessary to achieve certain objectives in the past. The fact is, they hold, that such violence or disruptive actions are unnecessary today. All conflicts (problems) can be settled within the system *peacefully*.

Features of the System

The values of the system are so tied to its main features that it is difficult to say whether such values have more influence on the system or vice versa. What we can say is that both the values and the features of the system reinforce one another. Take, for example, the main aspects of the constitutional–legal system. Consider **popular sovereignty, limited government,** *individual rights*. The idea that the people are sovereign, that they are supreme, is firmly implanted in the Constitution and its amendments. This supremacy is voiced by the people through regular and periodic elections. They select representatives (a representative government) to translate this sovereign will into everyday governing. The people, however, retain sovereignty. Through a written constitution they limit what the representatives as governors can do. Here is the idea of *limited government*. It finds expression in the Constitution through such provisions as the delegated powers of the Congress and the Bill of Rights. The Bill of Rights, for example, is designed to limit governments from intruding upon rights of the individual. But, as with many features of American government, when we go below the surface a number of factors emerge. The problem of defining the people (and hence making the concept of popular sovereignty work) has been a continuing one for democratic governments generally and American government in particular. The problem is one of inclusion and exclusion.[1] Blacks, women, 18-year-olds, as well as malapportioned urban residents, readily come to mind. And while all of these groups are now formally included as part of the people, their actual inclusion may be another matter. This suggests, as black Americans well know, that constitutional–legal inclusion does not necessarily guarantee inclusion in practice.

Let us explore this idea a bit further. Elections are a main way to translate popular sovereignty into a working, **representative govern-**

---

[1] Frank J. Sorauf, *Party Politics in America* (Boston: Little, Brown, 1972), 2nd ed., p. 3.

ment. But this raises a number of questions. For example, what are the dynamics of American elections? What are the structures of elections? What consequences flow from these structures, such as single-member districts, or the frequency of elections? Who is advantaged by these structures? Who is disadvantaged? In the single-member district, for instance, the winner takes all. This means that the majority (even if a coalition of minorities) rules and the minority loses. But elections, as we know, afford a way of managing conflict, quieting issues, and promoting compromises.

In any event, the election winner is pictured as representing all of the people of his constituency, even though he may not be of a particular group or faction. And he may indeed try very hard to reflect the views of all his constituents up to the point that it tends to disturb his potential for reelection. But can he *really* represent the group when he is not *of* that group? This, of course, raises an age old question about representation. We only repeat it here to emphasize its continuing importance to blacks and others insofar as it pertains to the structure of elections and the nature of representative government.

Of course, other constitutional–legal features such as **federalism** and **separation of powers** also shape our political landscape. With respect to federalism, the Constitution provides for a division of powers (authority) between a national (some call it federal) government and states. This division of powers between national and state governments certainly has consequences for how we deal with problems and how we manage conflict. For one thing, it means in a basic sense that the number of forums to deal with conflict is fifty-one rather than one as would be the case of a single central government. This increase in number of forums to deal with conflict may also and often does bring about an *increase* in conflict itself. And, of course, some people see benefits in using states as experimental laboratories. Others see the need for unified action, for a single national policy. The point here is that federalism is not without its advantages and disadvantages in given situations. Federalism, for example, permitted southern states to "handle" the racial problem as they saw fit; this worked to the advantage of whites but to the serious disadvantage of blacks. In any event, that federalism is so much a part of the political system often requires negotiations, bargaining, and compromise among various controlling interests in state and national governments.

The Constitution also incorporates the doctrine of *separation of powers*. Under this doctrine, the authority of the national government is divided among three branches: legislative, executive, and judicial. The functions are allocated accordingly: the legislature is to make laws, the executive to enforce laws, and the judiciary to interpret laws. But the lines of separation are not this neatly drawn. Indeed, under another arrangement — **checks and balances** — the Constitution also gives each branch some say in how the other branches carry on their functions. For example, Congress can pass legislation, but the president may veto it. However, the legislation can still become law if Congress can muster enough votes (two-thirds of both houses) to re-pass it over the president's veto. And, of course, the Supreme Court can invalidate laws passed by Congress, even those approved by the president. But the Constitution provides the Supreme Court with neither the "sword nor the purse" to enforce its rulings. It must depend on the president and others to do so. Thus, while the Constitution provides for three independent branches, it at the same time so intermingles their authority as to make it necessary for the branches to be *interdependent* rather than *independent* of each other. In short, one purpose of separation of powers and checks and balances is to keep government officials from becoming too powerful.

These constitutional features are also designed to keep any group, not even a majority, from a complete domination of government at any one time. The Constitution provides that officials of the three branches are to be selected for different terms of office and by different constituencies. For example, all members of the House of Representatives are elected every two years from essentially local constituencies, the congressional districts. Presumably, they represent different interests and have different loyalties from U.S. senators, one-third of whom are elected every two years for six-year terms with the entire state as the unit of election. The president may represent still different interests from congressmen and senators. He is elected for a four-year term with the entire nation as his constituency. And members of the federal judiciary, including the Supreme Court, are appointed by the president with the approval of the Senate. They hold office for life and are not subject to popular election. Overall then, the manner in which the Constitution provides for the selection and tenure of public officials poses formidable barriers to the complete domination of government by any group or interest at a given time.

Just as with federalism, the actual operation of separation of powers and checks and balances fosters both conflict and cooperation. Different constituencies and overlapping terms of office tend to cause conflict. But the fact that the three branches share in each other's powers — as, for example, the president and Congress do in law-making — tends to compel cooperation and compromise. In short, federalism, separation of powers, and checks and balances reflect the diversity of interests in American politics. They also *institutionalize* and *preserve* the *prevailing* rather than *aspiring* interests. They promote **incremental and marginal change** rather than **decisive and fundamental change**. And no matter what their virtues, these features of American politics pose built-in disadvantages to the kind of decisive, fundamental change needed to deal with problems facing blacks and other minorities.

The two-party system also stands out as a striking feature of American politics. Our parties have developed as the political system has developed and vice versa. Indeed so interwoven are political parties with the political system that many Americans perhaps assume that such organizations are expressly provided for in the Constitution. They are not. Understandably, then, the two-party system both influences and promotes the dominant political values of the system. Consider, for example, the role of parties in forming majorities and promoting the majority-rule principle. Consider, moreover, the extent to which the need to form majorities leads to an attempt to get diverse interests and individuals to work together, and to the necessity of conflict management through moderation and compromise. As Sorauf put it:

> At the most fundamental level the American parties, and those of the other democracies, serve democracy by reaffirming and promoting its basic values. The very activities of the two gigantic and diversified American parties promote a commitment to the values of compromise, moderation, and the pursuit of limited goals. They also encourage the political activity and participation that a democracy depends on. And they reinforce the basic democratic rules of the game: the methods and procedures of orderly criticism and opposition, change by the regular electoral processes, and deference to the will of the majority.[2]

Political parties certainly reinforce the basic values of American politics. These organizations operate on and promote the assumption that *all* problems can be settled and settled *peacefully within* the political system. That parties are large and diversified organizations also means that they handle problems so as to promote the values of "compromise, moderation, and the pursuit of limited goals." As such, our party system serves to reinforce the type of "incremental and marginal change" that is so characteristic of American politics.

On Elites and Political Participation

Black Americans, perhaps more than other citizens, have reason to show more concern for élites and "the tyranny of the majority." They are, despite increased participation in the political process, almost a "permanent minority" in American politics. Many blacks still

---

[2] Ibid., p. 54.

see discriminatory practices against them as individuals and as a group. The existence of such practices in broad segments of white society almost makes a discussion of élites unnecessary. Similarly, the notions of majority rule and agreement on values combines with the élite presence to make up a political system which black Americans view as inevitably hostile to their interests. From the perspective of the black minority, the middle-class "politically actives," "amateur democrats," as well as the upper class, constitute an establishment. Because the consensus on American values heavily depends on the actions and attitudes of such groups the black minority tends to regard them as essentially the same with respect to black concerns.

In the late 1950's social scientists such as Floyd Hunter and C. Wright Mills produced books which seemed to show that there existed what has come to be known as a **"power élite"** in most American communities. These élites were said to exercise much influence on the shaping of public policy. Seldom were the members of these élite groups elected officials. Their activities were frequently out of the public view. The work of these two scholars touched off an academic debate which continues to the present.[3]

In this chapter we do not directly enter the power élite discussion. However, we do take the position that some members of American society possess more political resources than others. And, as a consequence of this difference, those who have such advantages will use them in ways that further their ideas of the "public interest." In the United States this interest has increasingly come to be defined by a large and growing middle class. Moreover, the strength of the middle class position in defining the general interest is enhanced by the general acceptance of its sociopolitical values by members of the lower classes. Accepting the values of the middle class is made easier by the widespread belief that upward mobility is both desirable and possible for members of lower socioeconomic groups.

In a political system that has long proclaimed its notion of equality, it may appear strange that American society has a class structure. However, the opportunities for social mobility available to most white Americans reduces the perception of rigidity along class lines in the American

---

[3] For the original statements of these views see Floyd Hunter et al., *Community Power Structure* (Chapel Hill: University of North Carolina Press, 1953); and C. Wright Mills, *The Power Elite* (New York: Oxford University Press, 1956). Perhaps the most notable critiques of the positions set forth in these works are contained in Robert A. Dahl, *Who Governs* (New Haven: Yale University Press, 1960); and Nelson W. Polsby, *Community Power and Political Theory* (New Haven: Yale University Press, 1963). The writings of Peter Bachrach and Mortons Baratz provide a contrasting interpretation to that presented by Dahl and Polsby; the reader should carefully examine the arguments put forth in their essay "The Two Faces of Power," *APSR* (1962): 947-52.

class system. It is this relative openness and the pressures to "better oneself" which have led to a growing middle class. Of course, this effect is also aided by the general wealth and productivity of the nation.

The existence of class distinctions does not often become an issue of wide public concern. But this does not mean that the American citizen is unaware of these differences. Indeed this awareness can be seen in the extent to which expressions such as "power structure" and "power élite" have entered everyday conversation. Moreover, the American public also recognizes the existence of an unequal distribution of power as another example of the way in which wealth is distributed. An indication of this perception can be gained by looking at Table 3-1.

It is no surprise to find that the poor (white and black) selected big business and the rich as most powerful. But in view of the historical circumstances of black poverty it is interesting to find that the black poor differed from the white poor by only 5 percentage points. However, the 13 point spread between poor blacks and middle income blacks is unexpected. Form and Rytina suggest that the explanation for this finding may be found in the amount of education. "While the relationship of income strata to perception of 'big businessmen' and 'the rich' as most powerful is curvilinear, . . . a greater percentage of the middle educational strata see [these categories] as most powerful."[4] The absence of widely different views between blacks and whites might suggest that race by itself does not exert a strong influence on judgments about the distribution of power.

Such a view is challenged by the data presented in Table 3-2. Table 3-2 shows the presence of a racial effect regarding the "economic dominance," that is, control by a unified wealthy élite model and the "pluralistic" — dispersed and competitive interests — model. The black poor are consistently distinctive from whites regardless of class. Interestingly, they are also more likely to interpret the distribution of power in pluralistic terms than the black middle class. It may be the case that because the pluralist conception is prominently taught in the civics curriculum it is an easy explanation for the less well educated and poor among blacks as well as low income whites.

The previous tables have revealed some differences in black opinion which follow income/class lines. These data suggest a lack of racial solidarity in black communities. However, the black poor and black middle class do exhibit closer identity of opinion on the lack of power exercised by blacks. (See Table 3-3.) But by a substantial margin only the black poor support the idea of equality in the distribution of societal power (Table 3-4). Equality in the distribution of political influence is a

---

[4] William H. Form and Joan Rytina, "Ideological Beliefs on the Distribution of Power in the U.S.," *ASR* 34 (February 1969):19–31. Reprinted in Charles F. Andrain, ed., *Political Life and Social Change* (Belmont, California: Duxbury Press, 1971), p. 124.

TABLE 3-1
Interest Group Selected as Most Powerful, by Income and Race (Percents)

INCOME	RACE	UNIONS	BIG BUSINESS AND RICH	MILITARY	ALL OTHERS	DON'T KNOW	TOTAL %	(N)
Poor	Negro	32	41	11	14	3	101	(37)
	White	14	46	10	17	12	99	(59)
Middle	Negro	17	54	13	8	8	100	(48)
	White	33	52	8	5	3	101	(150)
Rich	White	54	28	4	13	0	99	(46)
Total, analytic sample	%	30	47	9	10	5	101	
	(N)	(104)	(164)	(31)	(34)	(17)		(350)
Total, systematic sample*	%	26	52	6	10	6	100	
	(N)	(48)	(97)	(13)	(17)	(12)		(183)

* For unions vs. big business and rich vs. all others run against poor vs. middle and rich, x^2 = 8.28, d.f. = 2, P = <.02.
SOURCE: William H. Form and Joan Rytina, "Ideological Beliefs on the Distribution of Power in the U.S.," fn. ASR 34 (February 1969), 19–31. Reprinted in Charles F. Andrain, ed., *Political Life and Social Change* (Belmont, California: Duxbury Press, 1971). Reprinted with permission.

TABLE 3-2
Selection of Societal Models of Power Distribution, by Income and Race (Percents)

INCOME	RACE	MODELS OF POWER DISTRIBUTION MARX (ECONOMIC DOMINANCE)	MILLS (ELITIST)	RIESMAN (PLURALISTIC)	TOTAL %	(N)
Poor	Negro	33	6	61	100	(36)
	White	23	22	55	100	(64)
Middle	Negro	40	16	44	100	(45)
	White	17	20	63	100	(143)
Rich	White	12	23	65	100	(43)
Total, analytic sample	%	22	19	59	100	
	(N)	(74)	(62)	(195)		(331)
Total, systematic sample*	%	18	19	63	100	
	(N)	(32)	(33)	(109)		(174)

* For poor vs. middle and rich, x^2 = 1.80, d.f. = 2, P = <.50.
* For Negro vs. white, x^2 = 13.08, d.f. = 2, P = <.01.
SOURCE: Form and Rytina.

TABLE 3-3
Interest Group Selected as Least Powerful, by Income and Race (Percents)

INCOME	RACE	POOR	SMALL BUSINESS	FARMERS	NEGROES	JEWS	UNIVERSITY PROFESSORS	ALL OTHERS	DON'T KNOW	TOTAL %	TOTAL (N)
Poor	Negro	46	11	11	19	8	0	3	3	101	(37)
	White	37	11	13	6	11	1	3	17	99	(70)
Middle	Negro	35	6	19	23	4	0	2	10	99	(48)
	White	35	17	12	9	4	6	7	10	100	(151)
Rich	White	20	26	7	9	4	11	24	0	101	(46)
Total,	%	35	15	12	11	6	4	7	9	99	
analytic sample	(N)	(122)	(53)	(42)	(39)	(22)	(15)	(25)	(33)		(352)
Total,	%	36	14	15	7	4	5	6	13	100	
systematic sample	(N)	(67)	(26)	(27)	(13)	(8)	(9)	(11)	(25)		(186)

SOURCE: Form and Rytina, p. 126.

82

TABLE 3-4
Interest Groups Which Ought to Be Most Powerful, by Income and Race (Percents)

INCOME	RACE	ALL SHOULD BE EQUAL	BIG BUSI- NESSMEN	LABOR UNIONS	ALL OTHERS	DON'T KNOW	TOTAL %	(N)
Poor	Negro	64	0	14	8	14	100	(36)
	White	43	6	6	28	17	100	(65)
Middle	Negro	47	4	9	25	15	100	(47)
	White	40	9	13	29	9	100	(149)
Rich	White	39	30	0	27	4	100	(46)
Total, analytic sample	%	44	10	9	26	11	100	
	(N)	(150)	(34)	(32)	(88)	(39)		(343)
Total, systematic sample*	%	41	8	12	29	10	100	
	(N)	(76)	(15)	(22)	(55)	(18)		(186)

* For "all should be equal" vs. all others, and poor vs. middle and rich, $x^2 = 30.94$, d.f. = 1, P = <.001.
SOURCE: Form and Rytina, p. 127.

difficult task to achieve in any society. The founders of the American government knew that perfect equality, as a practical matter, was beyond their capacities. Moreover, they were aware that the work before them was not an exercise in building Utopia. But, while the framers sought to assure at least formal legal and political equality of all citizens, the development of inequities in the possession and use of political resources was another matter.

The real problem of élites in the American democracy is not that they exist; rather, the difficulty stems from what the masses of people believe they do and for whom they do it. Theoretically, one could argue that the idea of an élite is at odds with the meaning of democracy. But most Americans have been relatively satisfied with this arrangement. They accepted the method, the process by which the governors are given power to decide. That is, most citizens regard the electoral procedures of the system as legitimate. This practice follows the democratic methods as defined by Joseph Schumpeter: "the democratic method is that institutional arrangement for arriving at political decisions in which individuals acquire the power to decide by means of a competitive struggle for the people's vote."[5] Those who vote in the majority for a particular

[5] Joseph A. Schumpeter, *Capitalism, Socialism and Democracy* (New York: Harper & Row, 1950), p. 269.

candidate have, in effect, given the office-holder their proxies to act on their behalf during his or her term in office. Even the voters who cast their ballots for the defeated candidate accept the results as binding because they had the opportunity to register a different viewpoint. The outcome is regarded as fair in most cases. It is treated as a binding result, because the procedures leading to a given electoral outcome have legitimacy. That is, the *process* by which a given outcome was reached was open to participation by all citizens. The American political system is regarded by most observers as continually open to the citizenry. Thus, those who for whatever reasons fail to exercise their franchise are thought to have other opportunities to attempt to influence the conduct and policies of government. That "other" opportunities exist to influence government and secure more preferred policy outcomes may suggest that electoral results are less binding than is sometimes thought. But, this only means that despite suffering defeat on a given issue or in a particular policy area opportunities to overcome such setbacks are available to *some* members of the political system. This type of flexibility is most apparent in the policy-making process. The election of public officials is less subject to changes except at regularly scheduled times. And, *élites* — that is, white Americans who have many resources compared to blacks — are more likely to use these resources to influence policy decisions than to elect individual candidates to public office.

This should not be taken to mean that influence is absent in such electoral campaigns. For one finds that those who put themselves forward for public offices frequently do so at the urging of groups who can command significant political power.[6] This feature of the recruitment process suggests that the consensus on political values is not likely to be radically disturbed by the electoral outcome. Persons who are too dissimilar from those most concerned with potential office-holders are unlikely to be put forth as candidates. The resulting *sameness* of opposing candidates may help to explain why a large portion of the citizenry does not have a participant orientation to political affairs.

For many Americans the idea of "civic duty" (that is, responsibility to participate in government) starts and stops at the point of voting (see Table 3-5). Despite the belief in a "duty" to vote, the American electorate has shown less willingness to do so (see Table 3-6). The data presented in tables 3-5 and 3-6 show the limited role played by the general public in their governance. Politically active members of the society — that is, those for whom politics is an important concern — make

---

[6] Examinations of the political recruitment process are numerous. One of the most rewarding investigations is reported in James David Barber, *The Lawmakers* (New Haven: Yale University Press, 1965); Donald R. Matthews also looks at questions of recruitment in his *U.S. Senators and Their World* (New York: Vintage, 1960).

TABLE 3-5
Sense of Civic Duty among Party Actives and the General Citizenry[a]

I THINK THAT EVERYONE HAS A DUTY TO BE ACTIVE IN POLITICS	GENERAL CITIZENRY		PARTY ACTIVES		TOTAL	
Disagree	31	(24%)	2	(4%)	33	(19%)
Agree	96	(76%)	44	(96%)	140	(81%)
Total	127	(100%)	46	(100%)	173	(100%)
correlation significant at .01						

I THINK THAT ONE FULFILLS HIS CIVIC DUTY IF HE VOTES REGULARLY						
Disagree	26	(21%)	18	(39%)	44	(26%)
Agree	100	(79%)	28	(61%)	128	(74%)
Total	126	(100%)	46	(100%)	172	(100%)
correlation significant at .05						

a. Data are from a survey in Evanston, Illinois, conducted by a graduate seminar at Northwestern University (Jenson, 1960).
SOURCE: Lester W. Milbraith, *Political Participation* (Chicago: Rand McNally, 1965), p. 62; and also see the examination of citizenship responsibilities in Gabriel Almond and Sidney Verba, *The Civic Culture* (Boston: Little, Brown, 1965).

TABLE 3-6
Percent of Voting Age Population that Voted

YEAR	NATIONAL	WHITE	BLACK
1952	61.6%	79 %	33 %
1956	59.3	76	36
1960	63.1		
1964	61.8	70.7	57.5
1968	67.8	69.1	57.6
1972	63.0	64.5	52.1

SOURCES: National, 1952–68: U.S. Bureau of the Census, *Statistical Abstract of the United States: 1972*, 93rd ed., Washington, D.C.: GPO, 1972, p. 373. National, 1972: U.S. Bureau of the Census, *Current Population Reports — Population Characteristics*, "Voter Participation in November, 1972," Series P-20, No. 244, December, 1972, p. 1.

up a small minority, 5 to 7 percent, according to Milbraith, of the total population. Political involvement results from other things acting in combination — for example, race, socioeconomic status (SES), education, religion, and so forth — upon the individual citizen. One of the strongest of these influences is SES. Relative material security is usually found to be positively associated with political activity beyond voting. In this sense, then, material security provides time to give attention to other areas of life. Members of lower socioeconomic classes do not have this resource. The politically active role goes to those with means almost by default. But this unequal distribution seems to be both cause and consequence of the attitudes about political life held by substantial parts of the public. The lack of material security in the black population partly explains their low political participation.

Another factor is the black belief that government pays them little attention (see Figure 3-1). Even at a time when the national government was most responsive to black concerns the information presented in Figure 3-1 is not encouraging. Between 1964 and 1968 the percentage of blacks agreeing with the statement "public officials don't care what we think" was over 50 percent. And these four years include the enactment of civil rights legislation and the initiation of the War on Poverty. As we can see, by 1972 the proportion of blacks in agreement had reached almost 70 percent. Significantly, few black Americans were in the "don't know" or uncertain categories.

Figure 3-2 offers a different perspective on this question. In Figure 3-1 the question related to public officials; in Figure 3-2 the concern is

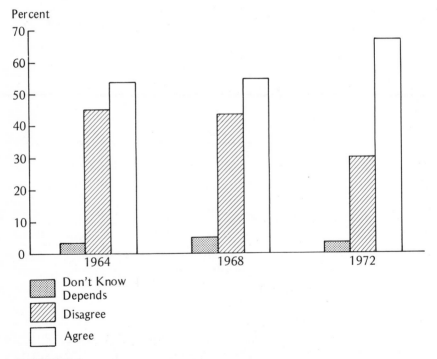

FIGURE 3-1
Black Views: "Public Officials Don't Care What We Think"

SOURCE: Data from Inter University Consortium for Political Research, Survey Research Center, University of Michigan, *American National Election Study* (1964, 1968, 1972).

with government responsiveness. It would appear that black Americans make a distinction which is based upon a perception of the president as the government and his individual role in meeting the political demands of blacks. Such a linkage helps to explain the sharp decline between 1968 and 1972 when a Republican occupied the White House. Moreover, the cynicism reflected in Figures 3-1 and 3-2 suggests much unhappiness with the pace of progress on black concerns. Despite some gains in the political area of civil rights, socioeconomic improvement for the mass of black Americans was limited. And it should be remembered that black urban communities had, by 1968, gone through a period of violence unequaled in American history. But that period of profound upheaval produced little change. Assessing the national response to its report of

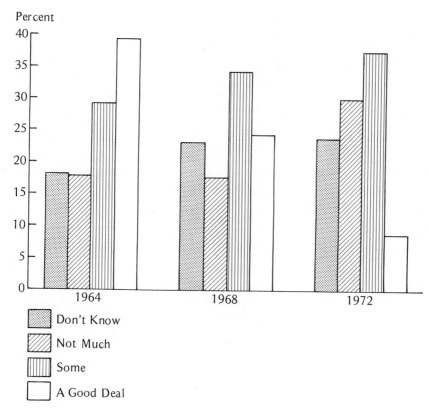

FIGURE 3-2
Black Views: "How Much Attention Government Pays to People"

SOURCE: Data from Inter University Consortium for Political Research, Survey Research Center, University of Michigan, *American National Election Study* (1964, 1968, 1972).

1968, the National Advisory Commission on Civil Disorders observed in
One Year Later

> Blacks and whites remain deeply divided in their perceptions and experi-
> ences of American society. The deepening of concern about conditions in
> the slums and ghettos on the part of some white persons and institutions
> has been counterbalanced — perhaps overbalanced — by a deepening of
> aversion and resistance on the part of others.[7]

However, to a degree which may appear surprising to some, black
Americans agree with the values which support the political system.
Despite their historical experience, blacks have shown little weakening
in their attachment to American government and society. The cynicism
discussed earlier in this chapter was based upon specific conditions or
institutions. Low rates of voter turnout do not necessarily reflect an-
tigovernment attitudes. Rather, they can be seen as a rational response
to circumstances in which racial concerns are unlikely to be effectively
met.

Of course, black Americans would like to change the system. But
most do not support revolutionary means of doing so. **Political socialization** has worked to maintain "diffuse support" for the system among
the minority citizenry. And, there have been enough specific rewards
and responses to black concerns and demands to maintain that support.
At the same time, the black minority has struggled to acquire a greater
measure of rewards to agree with their conception of the meaning of
citizenship. The following chapter examines some attempts by blacks to
gain the necessary resources for bringing about change in the distribution of political rewards.

Topics For Discussion

1. The political value system in America contains values
that appear (at certain times at least) to be contradictory. For example,
some of the connotations of "individualism" (and "minority rights")
seem contradictory or in opposition to the value of "majority rule."
Discuss how these values — individualism (minority rights) and majority rule — work to the advantage and disadvantage of blacks and other
minorities in their struggle for equality.

2. Within America, there are basically two competing concepts describing how the American political system actually functions:
how decisions are made and by whom. These two concepts are referred
to as the "élitist model" and the "pluralist model." Discuss the sig-

---

[7] Urban America, Inc. and The Urban Coalition, *One Year Later* (Washington, D.C.: The
Urban Coalition, 1969), p. 116.

nificance and implications of these two models as they relate to: (1) the distribution of power in American politics; and (2) the attempts by blacks and other minorities to overcome the problems that face them.

3. Do you agree with the authors that "no matter what their virtues, these features of American politics (for example, separation of powers, two-party system) pose built-in disadvantages to the kind of *decisive, fundamental change* needed to deal with problems facing blacks and other minorities"? Justify your position.

Suggested Readings

Bachrach, Peter. *The Theory of Democratic Elitism.* Boston: Little, Brown, 1967

A critique of the democratic creed in America.

Commager, Henry S. *Majority Rule and Minority Rights.* New York: Peter Smith, 1950.

Looks at democracy, judicial review, and how they affect majority rule and rights of minority.

Dahl, Robert A. *Pluralist Democracy in the United States: Conflict and Consent.* Chicago: McNally & Co., 1967.

An analysis of the American political system by one of the leading exponents of pluralism.

Dahl, Robert A. *Who Governs? Democracy and Power in an American City.* New Haven: Yale University Press, 1961.

A description of decision-making in New Haven, Connecticut, exemplifies how pluralist democracy operates in that city.

Dye, Thomas R. and Harmon Ziegler. *The Irony of Democracy: An Uncommon Introduction to American Politics.* Belmont, California: Wadsworth Publishing Co., 1970.

Examines the American political system as an "elitist" democracy and challenges the prevailing pluralistic-democratic view of the American political system.

Elazar, Daniel. *American Federalism: A View from the States.* New York: Crowell, 1966.

A study in American federalism concentrating on the states' perception of the increased expansion of the federal government.

Hartz, Louis. *The Liberal Tradition in America: An Interpretation of American Political Thought Since the Revolution.* New York: Harcourt Brace Jovanovich, 1955.

An examination of political thought in America since the American Revolution.

Holden, Matthew, Jr. *The White Man's Burden.* New York: Chandler Publishing Co., 1973.

An examination of the possibilities of the American republic to reconcile racial conflict.

Kariel, Henry S. *The Decline of American Pluralism.* Stanford: Stanford University Press, 1961.

A critique and challenge to pluralism in the American political system.

Knowles, Louis L., and Kenneth Prewitt, eds. *Institutional Racism in America.* Englewood Cliffs, N.J.: Prentice-Hall, 1969.

A collection of essays and articles that argue that racism is ingrained in the structuralized institutional fiber of the United States.

Mills, C. Wright. *The Power Elite.* New York: Oxford University Press, 1956.

A study of the dominance of the "power elite" in the American social system.

Parenti, Michael. *Democracy for the Few.* New York: St. Martin's Press, 1974.

Focuses on the theme that the American political system functions to serve the interests of corporate wealth at the expense of the majority of the people.

Polsby, Nelson W. *Community Power and Political Theory.* New Haven: Yale University Press, 1966.

A review from a pluralist perspective of the literature on community power structures and policy-making in local communities in hope of developing a theory on power distribution in America.

Riker, William H. *Federalism: Origin, Operation, Significance.* Boston: Little, Brown, 1964.

Considers the development, the workings, and the consequences of federalism.

4

THE QUEST
FOR POLITICAL RESOURCES

In allocating income, wealth, status, knowledge, occupation, organizational position, popularity, and a variety of
other values every society also allocates resources with
which an actor can influence the behavior of other actors
in at least some circumstances. . . . Extreme inequalities in
the distribution of such key values as income, wealth,
status, knowledge and military prowess are equivalent to
extreme inequalities in political resources.

Robert A. Dahl, *Polyarchy**

Those who seek change through politics must have the
resources necessary to bring about that change. This chapter examines
more closely the extent to which blacks possess those resources that
determine whether a group can accomplish its objectives through the
political process; that is, through legislative and administrative policy-
making. Political resources include more than the right to vote. Public
policy in the United States is also influenced and shaped by forces other
than electoral majorities. Broadly, the concept of political resources does
cover such things as the number and position of blacks in public office,
including elective and appointive positions. Public office is used in this
context to mean government **bureaucracy.** We take the position that
these organizations are political instruments; as such, they can be used
by political officials as well as by strong groups in their environments.
These points are treated in detail in Chapter 9. They are also relevant to
our discussion of black political resources.

Organized **interest groups** provide additional resources needed to
bring about change through politics. Here we look at black interest
groups, their strengths and weaknesses, and how they relate to the
political process.

* New Haven: Yale University Press, 1971, p. 82.

We conclude the chapter by looking at leadership as a political resource. In the end, leaders must garner the resources needed, and use them to achieve the desired result. Leaders determine, for example, whether, how, and when to forge coalitions and for what ends. But success in dealing with *the problem* does not rest on the shoulders of black leaders alone. They operate in the larger world of politics that is principally white.

Thus far, black Americans have had to depend upon substantial white support, either numerical majorities or a small number of white political actors with significant political power — for example, presidents or the Supreme Court — to make any progress toward solving the dilemma of their status. By themselves, of course, blacks do not have the votes to resolve the issue. But the vote poses some more general problems as well.

Voting Is A Limited Political Resource

For the most part, Americans have been taught to believe that their vote is an almost sacred possession. They are also taught that it is the most powerful political instrument under the direct control of the individual citizen. We agree that the vote is an important resource in political affairs. However, the political process responds to more than votes. In the first place, it should be noted that opportunities to cast votes are infrequent, while decisions affecting the public welfare (or some portion thereof) are made on a daily basis. Yet these routine actions are not put before the general public. Secondly, the vote of any individual citizen has a significant effect on the political process only when it is combined with that of others.[1]

Despite the limits of the vote the losing interests in American politics seldom take "no" for the answer. Thus, other means to influence the political process have been sought and developed. Most political scientists refer to those means as political resources. Among the most prominent and easily recognized of political resources we follow Robert Dahl in listing the following:[2]

1. income
2. wealth
3. status
4. knowledge
5. military prowess

---

[1] An excellent discussion of the vote and the need for majorities can be found in Robert A. Dahl, *A Preface to Democratic Theory* (Chicago: University of Chicago Press, 1956); and also see the volume entitled *Why Vote?* by Joyce Mitchell (Chicago: Markham, 1971).

[2] Dahl, *Polyarchy*, p. 82.

Each of these resources can be used to political advantage by those who possess them. And, of course, they can be harmful to politics, as the Watergate scandals of the Nixon administration so clearly revealed.

Political resources will be employed by those who possess them and who also regard political activity as an effective way to achieve their desired ends. In addition, those who lack the necessary resources but have strong preferences for particular political objectives will work to obtain sufficient political power to secure and maintain or protect those objectives. We believe that seeking resources implies their possession by others. Thus, the political process should be seen as covering more than the regularly scheduled occasions when the general citizenry registers its preferences. It is the way in which political systems work out questions of distributing power in satisfying the demands made of government.

Despite the limitations of the vote as a political resource, securing this right dominated the black political agenda from emancipation until the middle 1960's. But measured by voting turnout blacks have not been as politically active as white Americans. In part, the lower voting rates for blacks are a result of low income and education.[3]

However, we believe that low income and education do not adequately explain this phenomenon, especially when one notes the increases in socioeconomic standing of the black minority. A more satisfactory explanation can be found if one looks at the political socialization of the black American. What they learned about politics and their political roles virtually assured them that blacks were outside American life in all meaningful senses. In this sense Dahl's observation seems especially appropriate:

> An individual is unlikely to get involved in politics if he thinks that the probability of his influencing the outcome of events, of changing the balance of rewards by means of his political involvement, is low.[4]

Because political involvement was forbidden for such a long time and for such large numbers of black Americans, it should come as no surprise that they would place a low value on involvement even after the right to vote was achieved. It should be useful, therefore, to take a brief look at black socialization. It is particularly valuable to examine those experiences in the South. It was there that the majority of black Americans

---

[3] Angus Campbell, Donald Stokes, and Warren Miller, *The American Voter* (New York: Wiley, 1960); Gabriel Almond and Sidney Verba, *The Civic Culture* (Boston: Little, Brown, 1965); Sidney Verba and Norman Nie, *Participation in America* (New York: Harper & Row, 1972). The literature on participation is vast; these citations are merely illustrative.

[4] Robert A. Dahl, *Modern Political Analysis* (Englewood Cliffs, N.J.: Prentice-Hall, 1963), p. 61.

began to learn about politics. We should also keep in mind that political habit can be a resource or an obstacle to political involvement.

The Development of Habits of Nonparticipation

Black slavery ended in the United States as a tactical move by President Lincoln in the context of the Civil War. Since that time black political activity has been principally concerned with changing the institutions and practices of society. In addition, blacks, at least until the middle 1960's, have also sought to change the attitudes of the white majority in America. That is, changing the stereotyped attitudes about blacks held by many white Americans was a prominent goal sought by the former slaves, their descendants, and blacks in general.

Formal political actions to secure these changes seemed likely during the early phase of Reconstruction. A number of blacks, with the help of the Republican party, secured local, state and national political offices. Moreover, the federal government appeared to be willing to assist through agencies such as the Freedmen's Bureau. The bureau was given a considerable responsibility to help the former slaves' transition to freedom through land grants, "technical assistance," and education. But these activities and black experience in government were effectively ended after the Hayes-Tilden presidential campaign of 1876. As part of the price for his victory, President Hayes ended the period of federal Reconstruction by withdrawing Union military personnel from the Confederacy. This ushered into American history the period which W. E. B. DuBois has called "black reconstruction." Others have described it as near-feudalism.

To some, the compromise which resulted in a Democratic president taking office in 1876 was a necessary step to reunifying the nation. It also meant that the problems of new black citizens would be dealt with by their former masters. Thus, race was reduced to a regional problem. The South dealt with "their" black problem by creating an oppressive legal system. This system has come to be known as the *black codes*. The institution of "Jim Crow," a rigid system of discrimination, supported by Ku Klux Klan terrorism and white supremacist social attitudes, was the New South's way of dealing with the race problem. Blacks who held political office were very quickly removed. The halting government efforts to give the freedmen a firmer economic footing came to a virtual standstill. Although they were no longer slaves, neither were black Americans free. A distant government in Washington, D.C., seemed uninterested. Blacks once more could only dream about equal standing with other American citizens. In general terms then, black consciousness about the potential uses of political action to achieve equality as citizens began to form in the latter part of the nineteenth century.

For the first half of this century a major part of black political energies was spent in attempting to obtain the free right to vote on local, state, or national questions. That this form of political expression should almost become an obsession for black Americans shows the power of **political symbols.** Since emancipation, blacks were taught to believe that the franchise held the key to gaining true citizenship. The naive faith in the vote was created and reinforced by the public education system. For it was this agent of political socialization which taught blacks, and other citizens, that voting was a principal requirement for the good citizen.

The political process had been used by other depressed groups in American life to improve their state, so why not for blacks? In part the answer to that question is based upon the geographic distribution of the black American. Not until the massive northward migration in the early twentieth century did political action become a viable instrument for black use. However, the effectiveness of black political action was limited due to the weak socioeconomic base of northern black communities. In addition, the early arrivals in the North lacked any tradition of political participation. As a result of practices that had excluded blacks in southern politics, there had been few opportunities to develop such a tradition. When blacks arrived in the North there were still few incentives to participation. Access to politics was effectively blocked by firmly established political organizations. The few blacks who could get into the machine politics of such places as Chicago seldom exerted influence beyond the city's boundaries. As long as black Americans were regarded as a southern problem, there was little likelihood that any forms of political organization and activity would emerge. Nor did blacks in the North lend much assistance. Except for the NAACP there were no organized political groups which might press for the rights of blacks. And, despite a growing allegiance to the Democratic party after 1933, and a cautiously sympathetic president in Franklin D. Roosevelt, party politics was of little use.

However, a significant weakness in black political hopes was the absence of a sense of identity between blacks in the North and those who remained in the South. Black Americans, unlike the white ethnic communities of the urban North, were unable to exploit their common origins, the shared experience of slavery, for a form of communal politics. In addition, there are other important sources of political orientations. To gain a better understanding of these sources we have to look at two key institutions that influenced black political development: the black church and the school. The schools effectively reinforced the basic symbols and rituals of the political system. At the same time the black church, with its conservative Protestantism, advised acceptance of inferior status as a test of spiritual strength.

Political Education

The schools for black children in the South of the post-Civil War period and early twentieth century performed their tasks well. The school children were effectively Americanized by learning the basic symbols and rituals of the nation. These were important in instilling loyalty. But the black public schools of the South were poor places to learn a participant political role. Nor would these youths, or even those of immigrant families in the North, learn much about the mixed makeup of the society. With regard to the education of the immigrant children, Dahl wrote:

> The public school is the greatest and most effective of all Americanization agencies. This is the one place where all children in a community or district, regardless of nationality, religion, politics or social status, meet and work together in a cooperative and harmonious spirit. . . . The children work and play together, they catch the school spirit, they live the democratic life, American heroes become their own, American history wins their loyalty, the Stars and Stripes, always before their eyes in the school room, receives their daily salute.[5]

We now know more clearly that this optimistic description is less than accurate. The statement is especially weak when Dahl asserts that children "live the democratic life" in the schools, as though those institutions bore no relationship to the society which created them. Moreover, the kind of education provided for southern blacks stressed such things as "intelligent management of farms, ownership of land, habits of thrift, patience, and perseverance, and the cultivation of high morals and good manners. . . ."[6] This emphasis was due largely to the influence of Booker T. Washington. Rather than providing for liberal education the few black colleges and the lower schools followed his advice that

> for years to come the education of . . . my race should be so directed that the greatest proportion of the mental strength of the masses will be brought to bear upon the everyday practical things of life. . . .[7]

---

[5] Robert A. Dahl, *Who Governs* (New Haven: Yale University Press, 1960), pp. 316–17. But see Oscar Handlin, *The Uprooted* (Cambridge: Harvard University Press, 1951) for a different treatment of this experience for white immigrants.

[6] John Hope Franklin, *From Slavery to Freedom*, 3rd ed. (New York: Alfred A. Knopf, 1967), p. 391.

[7] Ibid., pp. 391–92.

It was enough if the schools taught loyalty. The kind of educational experience that the majority of blacks received was not likely to lead to a sense of political consciousness. In our view black Americans developed an orientation to political life that has since been designated as a "subject orientation";[8] that is, the citizen was a passive figure, inactive in political and social affairs and for whom such affairs had little if any importance. But still, blacks remained loyal. Despite the obvious gaps between the promises and performances of the government, black Americans conformed to the rituals and paid respect to the symbols of citizenship.

To be sure, this subject orientation was not solely a consequence of the education received by blacks. Much of the education which was made available to the ex-slaves and their children was church-related. Northern missionaries taught in the institutions that they created. Especially in the private colleges for blacks, the religious influence on their instruction was undoubtedly strong. Because northern Protestant churches provided substantial funds for college construction this relationship is not surprising. It is worth noting, however, that education came to be seen by blacks as a way to mobility. But such mobility was not taken to imply a challenge to the various controls that whites exerted over black lives. The instructional emphasis on the three R's and moral strength was strongly reinforced by other institutions in southern black life.

Institutional Structure As Protection and Political Depressant

Political passivity in black communities, especially in the South, was also reinforced by the dominant institution of the sub-culture: the black church. This single institution occupied a considerable amount of the time which black families had after work. Church attendance was not simply a Sunday morning affair. Services were also held in the evening during the week and many had Sunday evening services as well. Often these latter, such as the Baptist Young People's Union (B.Y.P.U.), had a semi-social purpose for teenage youths. The black church was also a community center. It had many purposes in much of the South as long as these purposes did not conflict with the church's principal activities. Through the performance of its several roles the church came to occupy a prominent place in the lives of black communities.

With few exceptions black ministers exercised a defensive brand of leadership. That is, they accepted the status quo and generally guided

---

[8] Almond and Verba, *The Civic Culture.*

the attention of their congregations in otherworldly directions. Gayraud Wilmore has described the black clergy as depressing any **nationalistic** or radical tendencies in their communities. "[M]ost . . .," he writes, "drew back from the hard-line, self-defense position of men like Robert Charles and Bishop Turner"[9] against Ku Klux Klan terrorism. Black religion, until after World War II, was cautious in its treatment of secular issues. Of course, they were outspoken in their criticisms of individual and group transgressions of Christian principles but always in the context of religious values.[10] As far as possible, southern black church members avoided explicit references to the political and social issues that contributed to the black problems. Black southerners were, after all, excluded from participation in the affairs of the wider society. Thus, there was little to be gained from their discussion.

The black church, which formed the core of most southern black communities, served to keep their membership from active political expression. Openly engaging in political action in the South carried with it the dangers of physical punishment. For this reason the church's position can be viewed as protective. To the extent that black communities in the South, especially prior to the late 1940's, had any political activities, they tended to be "intramural." Of course, the leadership positions which the ministers assumed were in part a consequence of possessing *time* to be involved. In addition, it should be recalled that from the point of view of whites in the South, it was efficient to use black ministers in their dealings with black communities. Black ministers had ready access to larger numbers of blacks than did most white southerners. Thus, the "authoritative allocation of values" interpreted and prescribed by the dominant class could be quickly communicated to the black population.

Black church leaders accepted being used as agents of the politically powerful. But they believed they were also carrying out a valuable purpose in so doing. As Lomax and others have pointed out:

> Violence [against blacks] was always in the air. Seldom a week passed that we didn't get word of some Negro who had been beaten or lynched by white mobs. (Some four thousand Negroes were lynched between 1889 and 1922, . . .).[11]

---

[9] Turner and Charles were early exponents of a belief in black separation from the United States. Charles was an "avid" follower of Turner who worked for a black colonization group called the International Migration Society. He was killed by New Orleans police after having killed six white men. See Gayraud Wilmore, *Black Religion and Black Radicalism* (New York: Doubleday Anchor, 1973), pp. 190–95.

[10] See the insightful discussion of this point in Louis E. Lomax, *The Negro Revolt* (New York: Harper & Row, 1962), p. 47.

[11] Ibid., p. 51.

Little wonder then, that blacks, following the philosophy of Booker T. Washington, might learn the three R's, "but their great aim was to become well-trained construction workers, cooks, farmers and mechanics."[12] And, to the students who passed through Tuskagee Institute, Washington also taught them to keep their place, respect and obey the law, and respect the white race.

The late nineteenth century experiment in black political participation in the South came to an end before 1900. Acceptance of the blacks' place at the bottom of the social order, separate and unequal, became the rule. And, by the very brevity of that experience, underscored by the inability of black communities to offer any resistance and the unwillingness of others to intervene on their behalf, blacks were compelled to submit to white domination.

The one-party Democratic tradition of southern politics which began in the late nineteenth century provided no incentives to Republicans to challenge these practices of exclusion. Thus, the handful of blacks who had voted for the Republican party during Reconstruction found themselves without supporters in the region and virtually ignored nationally. For example, there were some Republicans who wanted President Theodore Roosevelt to utilize the power of the Fourteenth Amendment against southern disfranchisement of blacks. This amendment provides for reducing a state's congressional representation when a portion of the eligible electorate is prevented from voting.[13] Roosevelt refused, however,

> to entertain any project of the kind advocated by Senator Platt, by Senator Crumpacker, and others because as is so often the case in politics I am confronted, not with the question of doing what is ideally right (which would of course be at once to reduce the representation in those states. . .) but of doing what is mostly expedient and practical although not ideally right; that is to decline to start an agitation from which, as far as I can see, no good will come.[14]

For blacks, the easy answer on the part of presidents has always reduced the likelihood of government actions in their behalf. The Roosevelt example just cited is part of a consistent pattern of presidential behavior. This behavior has confounded black efforts to acquire the political strength needed since emancipation. Under such circumstances one should not wonder that blacks adopted rational withdrawal as their most prudent course of action. These are some of the conditioning

---

[12] Ibid., p. 33.

[13] See section 2, Amendment 14. It may be noted that this penalty still exists.

[14] Quoted in George Sinkler, *The Racial Attitudes of American Presidents* (Garden City, N.Y.: Doubleday, 1972), pp. 425-26.

factors which blacks brought with them in their migration northward as World War I opened in Europe. In addition, the habits of nonparticipation which were products of these factors were also to become a part of the new black communities.

Black Urbanization and the Entry Into Politics

As the nation became more urban so too did its black citizens. Shortly before World War I the rural blacks began moving to the industrializing North. Politically, blacks, like the earlier illiterate and poverty-stricken immigrants, came under the sway of the established urban political organizations. These gave the new migrants limited access to the political process. Nevertheless, the political machines valued their votes. In return for their ballots the black newcomers, like the ethnics before them, received personal services and material assistance. In a few northern cities, such as Chicago, a subordinate, black political organization could emerge with sufficient strength to gain elected offices. Chicago, however, was only one city; blacks did not do as well in places like Detroit or New York City.[15] Part of the reason for black inability to use the machine route to political power rests upon the reform movements which swept through urban America in the early twentieth century.

Urban reform was an essentially middle and upper middle class reaction to political corruption associated with big-city politics. The political corruption of the period rested, in part, upon the willingness of businessmen to cooperate with the urban political machines in order to advance and protect their economic interests. The reform movement also contained an "anti-bigness" element which sought to prevent the domination of the economy by monopolistic practices by a few strong business interests.

Reform of urban governments was partially achieved by the introduction of civil service procedures for municipal employment. In so doing, **patronage,** one of the principal sources of power for the political machines, was severely limited. And, for the political ambitions of blacks, this meant that the machine would not serve as the vehicle for economic and social mobility which it had been for white ethnic communities. Moreover, in those cities where well-organized political machines continued to function, other practices inhibited the development of effective political strength among blacks.

---

[15] See, for example, Melvin Holli, *Reform in Detroit: Hazen S. Pingree and Urban Politics* (New York: Oxford University Press, 1969); and Theodore Lowi, *At the Pleasure of the Mayor* (New York: The Free Press, 1964).

The widely used northern practice of using indirect leadership for black communities limited black political strength. For example, the Tammany organization in New York City agreed to allow a black to head its Harlem contingent. However, he remained subordinate to a white member of the regular organization when it came time to discuss the black community in Tammany affairs. [16] Many of the reformers saw little difference between immigrants newly arrived from Europe and black migrants from the South. [17] The theorists of urban reform entertained measures comparable to the "black codes" of the South as a way to eliminate corruption and other "evils" of urban government. Disfranchisement was discussed by men like Frank Goodnow who bemoaned the withdrawal of the middle classes from city governance. In spite of the handicaps created by urban reform movements, the political machines and other urban political organizations brought a few blacks a measure of political strength. As Lowi pointed out for New York City, this recognition took the form of appointment. However, the black appointees did not, perhaps could not, exploit their positions for general black community advantage. [18] In part, of course, these individuals were handicapped by the low levels of political consciousness among their black constituents. The political habits which these southern migrants brought North would take time to change.

In the meantime, the migrants, who had come North primarily for economic rather than for political or social reasons, were struggling to establish themselves in a new and somewhat bewildering environment. The new migrants also became aware that, at least in some sectors of urban black communities, political activity was encouraged. Moreover, the goal of black equality with white Americans — that is, integration — became a black ideology.

The blacks who were in a position to be picked for appointive political positions came, for the most part, from the black middle and upper classes. And members of these classes often held themselves aloof from the masses. In addition, middle and upper class blacks in the early part of this century (1900–1930) tended to maintain their loyalties to the Republican party while the black masses were moving more and more to the Democratic side. Also, the orientation to political activity which these classes reflected was undoubtedly derived from the behavior of white Americans with whom they compared themselves. And, especially among the professional and business members of the black classes,

---

[16] See Claude McKay, *Harlem* (New York: Harcourt Brace Jovanovich, 1972).

[17] Cf. Melvin G. Holli, *Reform in Detroit*, Ch. 8, and also see the discussion of the negative impact of immigration upon city government in James Bryce, *The American Commonwealth* (abridged; New York: Capricorn, 1964).

[18] Cf. Lowi, *At the Pleasure of the Mayor*, pp. 37, 42–43.

copying white middle and upper class withdrawal from the "nitty-gritty" of politics was almost inevitable. Blacks political actors came from the black minority, but they have not, in most senses of the term, been *representatives* of that minority group in class and value outlooks. Black urbanization, then, did not immediately produce a unified black political community.

Black Upper Classes and Political Leadership Roles

Class distinctions have played a consistent part in American political life since the adoption of the Constitution. In particular, we know that wealth is related to political participation. That is, those who possess wealth are more likely to vote and involve themselves in other forms of political activity such as working in a campaign. Since American society has such a large and growing middle class, it is no surprise to find that members of this class consistently show up as more active than either lower or upper classes. Because social mobility has been much easier for white Americans than for blacks, it stands to reason that expansion of the middle class has meant growing political strength for that class. And whites who move up into the middle class soon learn to play their expected political roles. In this fashion older members of the middle class serve as models for the ethnic immigrants. However, the black middle class, to the extent that one exists, has been handicapped in its political growth. The racism which hindered black mobility generally made infrequent distinctions within black communities. It is necessary then to keep in mind that all social strata of the black minority were, for the most part, outside the mainstream of the society's development.

But, the black middle class has served useful purposes. They have been, for example, the first points of contact between blacks and whites when it was necessary or desirable for the total black population to be aware of some broad social or political issue. This kind of usage of the black **élite** has been practiced for generations. Thus, in 1862 President Lincoln

> called a group of blacks to the White House and told them about the hard realities of American life concerning the future of black men in the United States. . . . Lincoln told them that Congress had made an appropriation to colonize their kind outside the country, that he had long been in favor of the idea and that he wanted to tell them why this step was necessary.[19]

Black spokesmen such as Frederick Douglass, Booker T. Washington, and Mary McLeod Bethune are examples of the use to which élites were

---

[19] Sinkler, *The Racial Attitudes of American Presidents,* p. 51.

put by high officials. Unfortunately, the limited access which these individuals enjoyed did not lead to broader political power for the majority of blacks. Within the black élite there are obviously some who maintain a degree of contact with the broad ranges of the white élite in the society. Whenever there is talk of improving interracial understanding, or programs of *social uplift* for the black masses, it is from this élite that the "showcase" blacks have been recruited. Although having the outward signs of relatively high status, the black élite still meet racial bias in many of their cross-racial dealings. As St. Clair Drake put it:

> Their victimization flows primarily from the fact that the social system keeps them "half in and half out," preventing the free and easy contact with their occupational peers which they need; and it often keeps them from making the kind of significant intellectual and social contributions to the national welfare that they might make if they were white.[20]

That a black élite exists is not in dispute. Nor do we argue that they are not given a measure of prestige by non-élite members of black communities. In part, of course, such distinction within the community results from wealth. But it also results from the recognition given to this class by the dominant society. In terms of converting this *symbolic* resource into social and political power we have seen that the black élite was victimized in much the same way as the less well placed masses. The extent of political power held by this élite group or its ability to define goals for the entire black population is difficult to assess.[21] To the extent that prestige was useful to the black élite, it served only to preserve social distinctions as reflected in differences in life styles. As the black population moved North, however, and under the influence of the political organizations which they found upon arrival, the élite group did begin to develop a political orientation. That orientation was generally consistent with the political culture which they entered. And the reader should recall that the urban migrants usually became members of established black communities in which social and political relations were more or less stable.

However, as more job opportunities became available a larger black middle class began to emerge. This class began to take a more active interest in local political affairs after 1910. The extent of their participation continued to be limited by the victimization process, however.

---

[20] St. Clair Drake, "The Social and Economic Status of the Negro in the United States," *Daedalus* 94,4 (Fall, 1965): 781.

[21] On the use of prestige as a basis for social stratification and conversion into other resources, see S. N. Eisenstadt, "Continuities and Changes in Systems of Stratification" in Bernard Barber and Alex Inkeles, eds., *Stability and Social Change* (Boston: Little, Brown, 1971), pp. 61–81.

Opportunities were still restricted in the political arena as they were in other areas of American life. We have seen, nevertheless, that the middle class was able to make some political inroads through the machine structures of Chicago. Similar advances were also being made in New York City although its first black congressman, Adam C. Powell, did not take office until 1945.

The black élite tends to be found among that group to which Wilson has referred as the "prestige leaders."[22] Wilson observes:

> . . . prestige leaders' most common characteristic is that they tend to avoid controversy. In the past, they may have been active on the boards of the NAACP or the Urban League, but now they have risen above that. . . . [They] confine their efforts largely to noncontroversial civic enterprises, such as settlement houses, the Red Cross or Community Fund, the United Negro College Fund, [or] the Joint Negro Appeal. . . ."[23]

These blacks with prestige may avoid controversy and clearly partisan political activities. However, their real support for black community interests can be seen in the degree to which they give money to black groups with controversial political purposes. Such support, however, is given quietly and with very little public display. The prestige leader of the North is comparable to the conservative leader of the South described by Ladd:

> . . . Conservative leaders are more frequently associated with projects in which Negro political objectives are *not* involved. . . . They have sought to be known as prominent educators, businessmen, civic leaders, and so on, rather than as race leaders. Conservatives frequently play leading roles in Negro businessmen's groupings, in parent-teachers associations, in United Fund drives, and the like.[24]

As we have seen, the attitudes of the black élite are somewhat related to their economic positions and their desires to maintain that life style. Although this is not a full explanation of the development of these attitudes, it is, perhaps, a more powerful reason for blacks than for whites. Yet it is still the case that the political attitudes of the black élite, like those of the white élite, are a product of several forces. Gabriel Almond made the point well in an essay written some years ago:

---

[22] James Q. Wilson, *Negro Politics: The Search for Leadership* (New York: The Free Press, 1960), pp. 256–61; and see Drake, "The Social and Economic Status of the Negro in the United States."

[23] Wilson, *Negro Politics*, pp. 256–57.

[24] Everett Carll Ladd, Jr., *Negro Political Leadership in the South* (New York: Atheneum, 1969), pp. 160–61.

. . . political attitudes are not the defenses of any particular value such as economic interest, but rather are a part of a total system of values and attitudes characteristic of individual persons, living in particular cultures, at specific historic periods. Attitudes and actions on questions of public policy may in part be understood as instruments of defense or aggrandizement of these value systems.[25]

Seen in this light, it is possible to understand the behavior of the black élite as product of the complex forces of political socialization. This would be especially the case for those successful blacks who had achieved their success under the late nineteenth century influence of the "Gospel of Wealth."

With its emphasis upon good manners and behavior during the first half of this century, the black middle class was also constrained in its political activity. Again, we can see the influence of a desire to preserve a particular style of life as a force against political action within the black community. And the presence of numerous voluntary associations did little to reorient middle class interests to politics for redress of black grievances. Outside the area of machine politics the black middle class was unable to develop a consistent political role. Thus, the club movement in American politics was not a congenial setting for efforts to develop political power for the black community. A good deal of the reason, excluding racial prejudice, had to do with the nature of the incentives for political participation. In part, the problem has been a lack of commitment to middle class notions of "good government" vs. politics. Wilson observed:

. . . amateur club leaders have been disheartened by their attempts to bring Negroes into the movement. Except for a handful with an intellectual orientation or professional background, most potential Negro leaders seem (to the amateur Democrat) to be primarily interested either in the conventional rewards of the professional politician or in "racist" slogans and extreme positions. Few seem to share the white liberal's concern for "integration" and "equal opportunity". . . .[26]

The inability of white Americans to comprehend was understandable. Black Americans were examining the goals which should be sought and the means which would be appropriate to their achievement. Support for political gains by blacks because they were black was criticized by a number of liberal whites in the clubs as racist and extreme. Even before

---

[25] Gabriel A. Almond, "The Political Attitudes of Wealth," reprinted in Nelson W. Polsby et al., eds., *Politics and Social Life* (Boston: Houghton Mifflin Co., 1963), p. 278.

[26] James Q. Wilson, *The Amateur Democrat* (Chicago: University of Chicago Press, 1962), p. 280.

the outbreak of black political violence some blacks had become disenchanted with notions of integration and equal opportunity as the following passage from *The Amateur Democrat* suggests:

> We're beginning to feel that this attitude among white liberals is never going to get us anywhere and what we need is not opportunity but power. The only way we're going to get that is by drawing [the district] lines to give it to us. You're never going to have a Negro elected anywhere from a district that isn't all-Negro. We're just kidding ourselves if we think we can get it on any other basis.[27]

This comment restates the black uncertainty about white intentions concerning the distribution of power and the black desire for a larger share of that power. What political and social strength blacks could get prior to and after the Depression was, for the most part, confined to cities like Chicago and New York. With the exception of Chicago's southside, none of the northern black ghettos were able to send a representative to national office. Of course, it is obvious that this weakness resulted in part from the electoral limits of black communities. But few observers looked for explanations of the low participation rates. Moreover, to the extent that blacks did get involved in politics, the broad payoffs for the black masses were few. However, the New Deal programs of Roosevelt renewed black political optimism for a short time.

After World War I the upper level of black society did not provide the leadership of political activity that one might have expected given the American political tradition. This is not surprising, however, for two reasons. For the most part, the upper class black population has tended to maintain its identification with the Republican party over the years. This class continues to be composed of professionals and businessmen and their party allegiance resembled that found among the white population. But a more important reason was the shift in party allegiance among blacks of the lower and middle classes. Partisan changes from overwhelming black Republicanism to the Democratic party began with the election in 1916 of Woodrow Wilson. It was given added impetus by the Depression and the election of Franklin Roosevelt in 1932. However, the solid Democratic vote from blacks did not really emerge until the 1940's. And then it was only after the national government had specifically responded to some intensely held policy preferences of the black Americans. Roosevelt's executive order banning discrimination in hiring in the World War II defense industries was followed by President Truman's elimination of segregation in the Armed Services.

---

[27] Ibid., 283.

Surge and Decline of the Black Organizational Base

It is of interest to point out that black support for the NAACP and the Urban League was principally from those groups which could afford the time and money to do so — that is, the middle and upper classes. Because of the social barriers which members of these classes encountered, in common with members of the black lower class, they were gradually drawn back into political actions. However, they did not become active partisans in urban politics. As with the organizations that they helped to create, there emerged a division of political labor in America's black communities.

Without responsive representatives in the various state legislatures and in Congress, blacks turned to the courts in an effort to achieve a measure of political equality. W. E. B. DuBois signaled this move in his "The Immediate Program of the American Negro" which was published in 1915, thus,

> . . . we must fight obstructions; by continual and increasing effort we must first make American courts either build up a body of decisions which will protect the plain legal rights of American citizens or else make them tear down the civil and political rights of all citizens in order to oppress a few.[28]

We noted earlier that black efforts to form a national organization concerned with equal political and social rights had suffered setbacks. Yet the need for such an organization was not ignored. By the opening of World War I two such organizations had been formed: the NAACP and the National Urban League. There was an agreed upon division of labor concerning black problems. The Urban League concentrated on the social and economic problems of the black newcomers to the cities. It tended to take a moderate position on racial questions and to avoid open political controversy. The NAACP, on the other hand, was definitely political. It was the militant (for the time) protest organization and watchdog of political rights for black Americans.

The NAACP has been, and continues to be, the most respected organization of black civil rights interests. Yet it has not been a mass mobilization organization. Developing an activist membership, except for financial support, was not one of its national purposes. Public activity in the sense of protest demonstrations that involved many parts of the black community was not regarded as an appropriate strategy for an

---

[28] Reprinted in *Black Protest Thought in the Twentieth Century,* 2nd ed., pp. 67-74; the passage cited is at p. 70.

essentially litigation-oriented organization. However, local chapters could engage in such demonstrations. This was seen in Chicago during the 1920's and 1930's boycotts over job discrimination. There was always a degree of tension between the national organization and the local chapters. This was because of the risk of losing needed white financial support to pursue legal objectives if the local organizations pressed their demands too aggressively.

The victories were slow in coming. But at least blacks, with substantial support from white legal experts including Clarence Darrow, found an important resource. But the limitations of the law to correct social problems that affected black Americans were obvious to some black scholars prior to World War II. For example, Ralph J. Bunche expressed his reservations in explicit terms, arguing that

> Extreme faith is placed in the ability of [votes and the courts] . . . to free the minority from social proscription and civic inequality.[29]

Bunche believed that in spite of victories achieved along these lines, the NAACP's approach was not the right one for the problem. Corrections for the problems of the black American's status were not likely to come through either increased voting or favorable court actions. "The inherent fallacy of this belief," Bunche maintained,

> rests in the failure to appreciate the fact that the instruments of the state are merely the reflections of the political and economic ideology of the dominant group, . . . the political arm of the state cannot be divorced from its prevailing economic structure, whose servant it must inevitably be.[30]

Arguments such as those made by Bunche were not likely to have much effect on black thought. He was writing at a time when few blacks had the education to critically appreciate such a scholarly analysis of their problems. Critiques of this type were also unlikely to be widely noted in black higher education. These colleges and universities depended upon white philanthropy or upon the several southern state legislatures which financed the segregated educational systems. In the abstract, of course, one could argue that blacks might have adopted a more radical stance, especially in their colleges and universities. For blacks still in the South, however, it was necessary to establish priorities. Voting and other forms of "social agitation" were low on that scale. Acceptance of disfranchisement of the black citizen was part of the

---

[29] Ralph J. Bunche, "A Critical Analysis of the Tactics and Programs of Minority Groups," *Journal of Negro Education* 4,3 (July, 1935): 315.
[30] Ibid.

price to be paid for educational opportunity, and indeed for physical well-being.[31]

The NAACP and the League have at various times been joined by other organizations that have more specialized concerns. However, all of the black organizations with any significant national impact have depended upon whites for some portion of their financial support. This dependence has, in the eyes of some blacks, weakened the legitimacy of their claims to be "black" organizations. The two older organizations were joined by others as blacks increased their pressures for changes in the American system. Of the newer organizations, three have played an important role as instruments of black political action: The Congress of Racial Equality (CORE), founded in Chicago in 1942 by James Farmer; the Southern Christian Leadership Conference (SCLC) founded by Martin Luther King, Jr. in 1957 in Birmingham; and the Student Nonviolent Coordinating Committee (SNCC) formed in 1960 just after the first black student sit-ins in North Carolina.

Citizenship Is More Than Legal Rights

Almost exactly two decades after black Americans had demonstrated a surprising solidarity on questions of equality and justice (the March on Washington Movement of 1941) the three organizations mentioned above joined together to press many of the same demands. Although black protest agendas show a high degree of consistency over time, after 1960 these issues were made part of the national political agenda. This nationalization was in large part a result of the change in tactics used by black organizations. Instead of relying on the private and legal approaches of the League and the NAACP, the SCLC, CORE, and SNCC pursued their objectives in full public view. Of course, the media played an important role in directing public attention to black protests. The tactic was direct action and confrontation. Strong political action was the common means of the three newer black groups. While the older organizations were supportive, and in fact many of their members were involved in these new forms of political expression, the NAACP and Urban League as such did not mobilize their memberships. The participation of these two organizations was essentially symbolic. But it did contribute to the sense of unity among blacks, as well as to the perception of black unity among white Americans.

To a significant extent black political action of the sixties drew partici-

---

[31] Cf. Paul Lewinson, *Race, Class and Party* (New York: Grosset & Dunlap, 1965), pp. 129–31.

Wide World Photos

The price of the vote: As late as March, 1965, white Alabama state troopers swing clubs to break up voter demonstration march by blacks in Selma.

pants from a wide range. The younger and most courageous were involved in direct action, such as the sit-ins, the "freedom rides," and the like. These small groups were most active in conducting voter registration drives and challenging segregation in public accommodations. Courage was an important requirement because southern hostility was not passive. Physical assaults and murder were recognized as real possibilities. It was partially in recognition of such risks that blacks and their white supporters adopted the strategies of nonviolence and passive resistance to their political purposes. By these means it was hoped that provocations to personal attacks would be avoided, or at least minimized. Moreover, it was believed that this strategy would enhance the morality of the protest demonstrations.

In general, protest proved to be nonviolent as far as the black participants were concerned. Southern whites, however, started enough brutal assaults and caused enough deaths among the activists to keep the elements of drama high. The murders of Ms. Viola Liuzzo and Rev. James Reeb, both white, the bombing of a black church in Birmingham during Sunday services, causing the deaths of three children, and other instances of white terrorism helped to keep black demands and concerns high among national political priorities. And because the black drive for civil rights occupied so much domestic attention, it was to be expected that foreign onlookers would also be concerned about how the United States dealt with its largest racial minority. Thus, international interest served to reinforce the strength of black political demonstrations.

Until the eruption of political violence in urban America during the middle sixties, black protest had centered on acquiring *political* rights to complement the *legal* rights which were being pursued by the NAACP. Blacks were attempting to secure what appeared to be the two fundamental parts of citizenship.[32] A third part identified by Marshall as *social* rights is difficult to separate from the broad conception held by many blacks of political rights. In other words, the black American believed that social welfare concerns would be met as a result of achieving legal and political rights. The type of difficulty facing black Americans could be remedied only in part through legal and political means.

Table 4-1 indicates how white Americans felt about blacks' rights in 1963 when the civil rights drive was at its height. There is a clear pattern of white approval. But when these areas are made subject to legislative protection one finds a sharp drop in white approval. (See Table 4-2.) Specific governmental acts to enforce the existing laws (1963) protecting black civil rights did not meet with similar levels of support. Nor was there strong southern support for other legislative measures in civil rights areas. (See Table 4-3.) These lower levels of support for legislative action to protect black rights may have resulted from the mistaken belief

TABLE 4-1
The White View of Negro Rights

	NATIONWIDE %	SOUTH %
Approve:		
Voting in elections	93	88
Unrestricted use of buses and trains	88	75
Job opportunities	88	80
Decent housing	82	76

SOURCE: William Brink and Louis Harris, *The Negro Revolution in America.* Copyright © 1963, by Newsweek, Inc. Reprinted by permission of Simon & Schuster.

---

[32] For an extended discussion of the concept of citizenship the reader should consult T. H. Marshall, *Class Citizenship, and Social Development* (Garden City, N.Y.: Doubleday Anchor Books, 1965); also worth reviewing is the essay by Talcott Parsons, "Full Citizenship for the Negro American," in *Daedalus* 94,4 (Fall, 1965): 1009-1054. Our discussion draws on these two works.

TABLE 4-2
Whites Assess Federal Action

	NATIONWIDE %	SOUTH %
Approve:		
Eisenhower use of troops in Little Rock, Ark.	71	44
Kennedy use of troops at Oxford, Miss.	65	37
The original Supreme Court decision	64	35
Overall role of federal government in civil rights	64	35
Overall role of federal courts in civil rights	60	33

SOURCE: Brink and Harris, p. 143

TABLE 4-3
White Support for Civil Rights Legislation

	NATIONWIDE %	SOUTH %
Approve:		
Federal vote-enforcement law	57	31
Federal Fair Employment Practices law	62	40
Kennedy civil rights bill	63	31
Public accommodations bill	66	29

SOURCE: Brink and Harris, p. 142.

TABLE 4-4
White Stereotypes About Negroes

	NATIONWIDE %	SOUTH %
Agreement with statement:		
Negroes laugh a lot	68	81
Negroes tend to have less ambition	66	81
Negroes smell different	60	78
Negroes have looser morals	55	80
Negroes keep untidy homes	46	57
Negroes want to live off the handout	41	61
Negroes have less native intelligence	39	60
Negroes breed crime	35	46
Negroes are inferior to whites	31	51
Negroes care less for the family	31	49

SOURCE: Brink and Harris, pp. 140-41.

that no such laws were necessary. After all, one might reason, "white citizens don't need that kind of special interest legislation." For many blacks, however, without specific guarantees the nation might have once again, as it had in 1876, left the problems of blacks to the South. The basis for black insistence on legislative protection can be seen by examining stereotypes about blacks. (See Table 4-4.) It is the nationwide existence of such attitudes, their strength among white southerners, which has inhibited corrective action on black concerns. And because these attitudes were held by larger numbers of white southerners, it is understandable that resistance to changes in black status would be strongest in the South.

Through 1963 the coalition of black organizations working for civil rights remained more or less intact. Out of this period emerged the most effective black spokesman of the century, Rev. Martin Luther King, Jr. of Birmingham, Alabama. Until the March on Washington in August of 1963 King was the black leader. Part of his effectiveness was undoubtedly the result of his religious role. As for earlier influential blacks, the church provided an organizational base for mass leadership. But King's leadership did not go unchallenged. There were critics, especially among the young workers for SNCC. Almost as soon as the March on Washington was concluded younger and more aggressive blacks began to move to the forefront. This change occurred because some blacks, especially the young, saw the solution of black problems as requiring more than formal civil rights. For the new activists the political program for black Americans, at a minimum, would require fundamental changes in the distribution of power in society. Their ideology was "black power." With it, they believed, black Americans would be able to change American institutions. They could effectively counteract the pervasive racism in American life (as seen in Table 4-4). To be sure some blacks were dissatisfied with the outcomes of the civil rights struggle. But for the majority of black Americans in the South, a long sought-after political resource had been secured — that was the right to vote as recognized by the passage of the Voting Rights Act of 1965. Almost immediately black Americans began to test the use of the franchise as a political resource.

Resource Use and Political Outcomes

Local political offices do represent a first step toward acquiring political strength. This is one of the reasons why the decline of the political machine discussed earlier is important in understanding blacks' limited political strength. At this point it is difficult to know how many blacks holding local offices have higher ambitions. However, if

Wide World Photos

The black vote: How valuable a resource? As a result of demonstrations, and the subsequent passage of the 1965 Voting Rights Act, blacks in the South can now vote. The above scene shows blacks lining up to vote in a 1969 special election in Green County, Alabama.

they do it will be interesting to watch their political careers. For in view of the large number of black mayors we may find that the office will continue to be a dead-end as far as higher office is concerned.

Table 4-5 shows the extent of black elective political gains as of 1972.* Note that of the total (2,264), more than half the officeholders are to be found at the local level. Councilmen and school board members alone comprise almost 52 percent of the total. State legislatures, however, were the scene of significant increases in the 1972 elections. And despite the Republican campaign to field black candidates, they managed to capture only 2 percent of the contests. Moreover, these Republican challengers were unable to unseat any of the Democratic incumbents.

---

* By 1975, the number of black elected officials had increased to more than 3,500. Even so, blacks still occupy only a very small proportion (less than 3 percent) of the large number of elective offices in the United States.

TABLE 4-5
Black Elected Officials in the United States*

		CONGRESS		STATE				COUNTY			CITY			LAW ENFORCEMENT				EDUCATION		
	Total	Senator	Representatives	Senators	Representatives	State-wide Elected Offices	Others	Commissioners, Supervisors	Election Supervisors	Others	Mayors Vice Mayors	Councilmen, Aldermen	Others	Judges, Magistrates	Constables, Marshals	Justices of the Peace	Others	College Trustees	School Board Members	Others
Alabama	83				2			7			4	38	9	1	11				11	
Alaska	3				2														1	
Arizona	10			1	3										1				5	
Arkansas	97										8	27	9			5			48	
California	134		2	1	5	1		1			7	34	2	15					66	
Colorado	7			1	2							3		1						
Connecticut	51			1	5						3	25			5				12	
Delaware	11			1	2			1				6							1	
Washington, D.C.	8		1																7	
Florida	51				2			1			4	38	3		1				2	
Georgia	65			2	13			6		1		31	1	1					10	
Hawaii	1											1								
Illinois	123		2	5	14			3			7	35	5	13	2	2		1	38	
Indiana	52				2			3			1	22	5	3	2	2			11	

TABLE 4-5 (continued)

	TOTAL	CONGRESS		STATE				COUNTY			CITY			LAW ENFORCEMENT				EDUCATION		
		SENATOR	REPRESENTATIVES	SENATORS	REPRESENTATIVES	STATE-WIDE ELECTED OFFICES	OTHERS	COMMISSIONERS, SUPERVISORS	ELECTION SUPERVISORS	OTHERS	MAYORS VICE MAYORS	COUNCILMEN, ALDERMEN	OTHERS	JUDGES, MAGISTRATES	CONSTABLES, MARSHALS	JUSTICES OF THE PEACE	OTHERS	COLLEGE TRUSTEES	SCHOOL BOARD MEMBERS	OTHERS
Iowa	10				1							2	1	1					5	
Kansas	18			1	3			3			2	3		5	4				7	
Kentucky	57				2			1			3	32			15	14			9	
Louisiana	119		1	4	8			31			3	24		5			1		23	
Maryland	54				14						3	20					2		5	
Massachusetts	16	1			3							5					2		5	
Michigan	179		2	3	13	1		35		1	8	41	2	11	2		6	6	48	
Minnesota	8											2		1			1		4	
Mississippi	129				1			7	15		3	31	5		23	18	6		20	
Missouri	77		1	2	13						2	24	1	8	1		4	2	18	1
Nebraska	3			1								1							1	
Nevada	4				1							1		1		1				
New Hampshire	1																			1
New Jersey	121		1	1	4			4			8	34					2		68	

State																				
New Mexico	4	1																		3
New York	163		2	3	9		4	2				13	3	24					103	
North Carolina	103		2					3			4	64		1	1				29	
Ohio	110		1	2	10	1					7	50	3	13	1				22	
Oklahoma	62			1	5			5				24	6	1					19	
Oregon	5											1	1						3	
Pennsylvania	63		1	2	9			1				14	1	15	4				16	
Rhode Island	7				1							2							4	
South Carolina	66			3				7			3	38		9					6	
Tennessee	48		2		6			4			3	16	1	7		6			6	
Texas	61			1	2						2	35							21	
Vermont	1												1							
Virginia	54		1		2			13		2	2	30	2	15		4				
Washington	9		1	2								1		4					1	
West Virginia	5				1						2		2							
Wisconsin	9			1	2							5							1	
Wyoming	2													1					1	
Total	2264	1	13	37	169	2	2	132	15	29	86	780	66	141	70	50	2	9	657	3

NOTE: Six states have no black elected officials: Idaho, Maine, Montana, North Dakota, South Dakota and Utah.

*Official Count as of March 1972 by Joint Center for Political Studies.

SOURCE: Reprinted with permission from Joint Center for Political Studies, JCPS *Guide To Black Politics*: Part II The Republican National Convention (Wash. D.C., 1972), p. 60.

Black disenchantment with the Democratic party was not serious enough to cause a shift in party allegiance.

If state offices continue to be a launching pad for national political careers, then blacks may have an opportunity to add to the size of the Congressional Black Caucus in the future. One observation should be made to temper the optimism of the black electorate: of the 58 congressional districts in which blacks are 25 percent or more of the population, 37 are in the South. In addition, there were (in 1972) 13 districts in which blacks were a majority; 12 of these districts have black members of Congress. However, black members of Congress serve only two districts in which blacks constitute 40 to 49 percent of the population. These two are Andrew Young of Georgia and Barbara Jordan of Texas. The black political strength in the national legislature may continue to grow if the gains of the past several years continue.

But in view of the distribution of the black vote — that is, its urban concentration — there may also develop an *intra-racial* competition for some of the present seats. If, however, black voter turnout can be increased, especially in the South, conceivably the Congressional Black Caucus will come to speak with more of a southern accent. Nevertheless, national black turnout figures present a difficult problem, as can be seen from Table 4-6. The habit of nonparticipation among southern blacks is strong. Until 1972, it was consistently higher than among white southerners. And, while the table shows more "never voted" among northern blacks as well, the differences between non-South blacks and whites is not nearly so great as in the South. In addition, the trend suggests that blacks are beginning to equal the white turnout rates.

Although the Caucus members share a racial bond, they are not a monolith. Like their white colleagues, the members of the Caucus come from the middle class. Several had prior political experience in their local communities as councilmen or ward committeemen. But only a few of the seventeen had prior legislative experience in their respective states. Some have been involved in activities connected with the War on Poverty to various degrees. And at least two achieved national prominence in that connection. Interestingly, both (Walter Fauntroy and Andrew Young) are ministers who were associated with Rev. Martin Luther King, Jr. during the height of the civil rights demonstrations of the sixties. Perhaps the most significant committee assignments have gone to Louis Stokes (D., Ohio) and Ronald Dellums (D., Calif.).* In terms of functional importance the Stokes seat on the House Committee on Appropriations offers the greatest potential for the development of political power in Congress itself. Members of this committee tend to

---

* However, as the 94th Congress convened in 1975, other black members were appointed to important committees. For a more detailed discussion of these appointments and of the Black Caucus as an organized group, see Chapter 8.

TABLE 4-6
The Distribution of Adults Who Have Never Voted, According to Race and Sex for the South and Non-South in 1952, 1956, 1960, 1964, 1968, and 1972

	1952		1956		1960		1964		1968		1972	
	WHITE	BLACK	WHITE	BLACK	WHITE	BLACK	WHITE	BLACK	WHITE	BLACK	WHITE	BLACK
SOUTH[a]												
Men	12%	65%	14%	60%	8%	33%	5%	26%	9%	25%	13%	12%
Women	33%	87%	27%	70%	17%	63%	14%	39%	26%	31%	20%	25%
NON-SOUTH[b]												
Men	6%	17%	6%	17%	6%	11%	7%	10%	9%	0%[c]	8%	7%
Women	7%	11%	10%	32%	7%	28%	7%	18%	7%	17%	9%	10%

[a] The states included in the South are Alabama, Arkansas, Florida, Georgia, Kentucky, Louisiana, Maryland, Mississippi, North Carolina, Oklahoma, South Carolina, Tennessee, Texas, Virginia, and West Virginia.
[b] The states included in the Non-South are the remainder.
[c] This "unrealistic" finding may reflect sampling problems in central cities of the North.

SOURCE: Survey Research Center, University of Michigan. Reprinted with permission from William H. Flanigan, Nancy H. Zingale, *Political Behavior of the American Electorate*, 3rd ed. (Boston: Allyn and Bacon, 1975), p. 28.

119

come from relatively **safe districts;** thus, seniority, one of the bases of influence in Congress, is likely to be attained. Moreover, the House Appropriations Committee exerts a powerful influence on the shape of the executive budget.[33]

Because of his strong opposition to the Vietnam War Congressman Dellums surprised longtime analysts of Congress when he sought a seat on the House Armed Services Committee. If they had looked a bit more carefully at Dellums' constituency, they might have been less surprised. Dellums' district includes the University of California-Berkeley, which is known for its liberalism (some would say radicalism). In addition, however, his district contains part of the Oakland community which had become concerned with the racial aspects of American military involvement in Asia. Dellums is now in his second term. He just may gain some seniority on the Armed Services Committee despite the recent inclusion of a more conservative and predominantly white region of the East Bay region in his district. His seat is difficult to classify as "safe," however, for blacks constitute only 25.5 percent of the population. The Dellums seat is interesting from another point of view as well. It is difficult to find a white opponent to run against him. In this regard Congressman Dellums' race is a political advantage which is difficult to overcome. There is fear that a white opponent would be charged with racism. But the Republican party did try to offset this advantage by running a black candidate. The Republican was soundly defeated by the substantial Democratic majorities in the district. This pattern may be repeated in other parts of this country.

Rewards From Political Activism

Although blacks made some political inroads at the state and local levels prior to the sixties, the most dramatic gains have come since 1965. A number of blacks were able to gain elective offices on school boards, city councils, state legislatures, and the like, some years before the black revolution in the middle sixties. Thus, in the late 1950's Cleveland had two black councilmen. And in 1958, an unknown black lawyer named Carl Stokes entered the Democratic primary for a vacancy

---

[33] A general study which can be consulted is William L. Morrow, *Congressional Committees* (New York: Scribners, 1969); Nelson W. Polsby, ed., *Congressional Behavior* (New York: Random House, 1971); Nelson W. Polsby, *Congress and the Presidency*, 2nd ed. (Englewood Cliffs, N.J.: Prentice-Hall, 1971). Two more specialized works on the House Appropriations Committee are Richard F. Fenno, Jr., *The Power of the Purse* (Boston: Little, Brown, 1966); and Aaron W. Wildavsky, *The Politics of the Budgetary Process*, 2nd ed. (Boston: Little, Brown, 1974). The latter work is not exclusively devoted to the House Committee, but it does deal in some detail with its activities; see especially pp. 47-62, and chapter 3.

in the state senate in Columbus, Ohio. At this early date Stokes had no illusions about his chances for election.

> I had no serious thought that I would win the nomination, and didn't campaign beyond the routine appearances before the endorsing bodies — the newspapers, the Citizens' League, the League of Women Voters, the Cleveland Federation of Labor, AFL-CIO.[34]

For Stokes, this initial try was simply a way of testing the political climate. He was also aware that he was unlikely to get the backing of the Democratic party. Stokes viewed the party as allowing blacks to run for offices, but only at the council level. Stokes did not want to be a councilman. Nonetheless, the desire to gain a statewide political office is one thing; getting it is another. Moreover, the lack of party organization help and the disadvantages of being black added to his difficulties. Stokes ran a vigorous campaign in 1960 but lost.

In 1962 Stokes again ran for the Democratic nomination and won handily. Stokes interpreted his success as meaning that the system had worked. Specifically, Stokes described his victory as one of "ethnic-coalition politics." This point is worth some elaboration. It bears on the potential for further black political gains. Blacks may be a large part of the population in many of the largest cities, but they are not yet a majority. As a result, the black vote is not enough for sending black candidates to offices where the electoral base is at-large, countywide or larger. If the contested office requires approval from a relatively small base — for example, a city ward — it is possible for a black candidate to get a majority among blacks, doing away with any need for coalition-building. Since blacks do not constitute majorities in the big cities they have to find allies. A number of blacks have criticized the coalition strategy adopted by Stokes and other black political actors as being effective only in the short-term and on minor issues.[35]

Carl Stokes was not the only black man to take a more active interest in running for political office in the urban North. Given hope, perhaps, by the strength of the direct action campaigns throughout much of the South, blacks began to set their sights on something more than local elective offices. Local office-holding had, of course, lost one of its major attractions through the loss of patronage as cities came more and more under the influence of the latter day reformers. In addition, the kinds of jobs which are available through the patronage system in most cities (custodial and service jobs, laborers and the like) are no longer as

---

[34] Carl B. Stokes, *Promises of Power: A Political Autobiography* (New York: Simon and Schuster, 1973), p. 48.

[35] Stokely Carmichael and Charles V. Hamilton, *Black Power* (New York: Vintage Books, 1967), pp. 60–62.

attractive as they once were.[36] These jobs were similar to those which many blacks were rejecting in the open labor market. And, they were also the kinds of employment which the War on Poverty had criticized as being dead-ended.

But electing blacks to national office had to await other changes in the nation's political climate. One of these changes came about through Supreme Court actions; they have come to be known as the **Reapportionment** Cases beginning with *Baker* v. *Carr* (1962). The other change was the use of political violence as an instrument of black political action beginning in 1964. (Violence as a political resource is discussed in Chapter 10 and elsewhere in this volume.)

One Man — One Vote

As we have seen, there had been some major changes in the distribution of the American population. Although these changes had been apparent for some time prior to 1962 many states had done little to redraw their congressional district boundaries. Tennessee, the state in which Baker filed his suit, had not redistricted since 1901 Although *Baker* v. *Carr* and the subsequent cases led to the creation of electoral bases from which blacks might start a political campaign, the legal questions have not been completely resolved. Nor, because of the scarcity of black representation in the state legislatures which would determine the character of the new districts, were the interests of the minority communities always given first consideration. Party strength was a principal concern of these legislators. Whichever party was in control of the state house would naturally try to preserve what it had as its first redistricting objective.

A second objective would be attempting to create new districts; this led to an expansion of the party's base of support. In the context of expanding the base, therefore, blacks stood to gain in those states where the Democratic party controlled the legislatures; if the states contained any large cities it was reasonable to assume that blacks would make up a sizable portion of their populations. To meet the demands for black districts, however, required in some cases that white incumbents run from a new district or share their original base with the black newcomer. This was the case with Charles Vanik in Cleveland. Before Stokes left the state legislature to become mayor of Cleveland, a congressional district was created in the predominantly East Side black community from which Stokes' brother, Louis, would run for Congress. Vanik, who

---

[36] Cf. Fred I. Greenstein, "The Changing Pattern of Urban Party Politics," *The Annals of the American Academy of Political and Social Science* 353 (May, 1964): 1-13.

previously had part of this east Cleveland population among his constituents, ran for reelection in a new district. This district included substantially more Republicans for it now contained some of the supporters of former Rep. Frances Bolling, a conservative Republican.

The influence of Carl Stokes was one result of political experience and bargaining. But it should also be recognized that the price of political influence is high. It led Stokes to give up a public political career, although there are other black mayors in cities such as Atlanta, Los Angeles and Detroit. It is too early to assess these men. But it might be pointed out that Maynard Jackson of Atlanta has encountered problems similar to those about which Stokes complained.[37] In addition, many of the electoral victories of blacks since 1967 have come in small, poor cities of the South. One cannot expect that they will be able to develop the kinds of resources which allow their big-city colleagues to rise to national prominence. And, finally, it remains to be seen if this relatively small base of resources can be "pyramided."

Bureaucracy As A Representative Institution

Blacks have done less well in another area of political resources. Appointive positions within the government have not come as quickly as have elective offices. Nor have bureaucratic positions gone to blacks in the national administrative system in significant numbers. By significant, we mean only that the office is one which plays an identifiable and important role in making public policy decisions. Thus, some of the positions in the Executive Office of the President and the White House Staff would constitute a significant post. Similarly, the "super-grades" among Civil Service ranks would also be considered as significant from the point of view of policy formulation.

Figure 4-1 indicates this problem. The figure shows the classification and distribution of black federal employees as of 1969. But the past several years have not substantially altered this picture. It is immediately apparent that blacks are mostly found among the lowest grades of federal employment. In part, this results from the surge of black recruitment which took place under the past three administrations (especially under President Johnson during the War on Poverty). The abrupt downward trend in the figure clearly reflects concentration in the lower grades. Notice also the inverse relationship of black-to-white employment between grades 1-5 and 6-11. In spite of the claims which have

---

[37] Cf. the article by Drummond Ayres, Jr. in the *New York Times* (Feb. 26, 1975), 18C; and also see William E. Nelson, Jr. and Winston Van Horne, "Black Elected Administrators: The Trials of Office," *Public Administration Review* (Nov./Dec. 1974): 526-33.

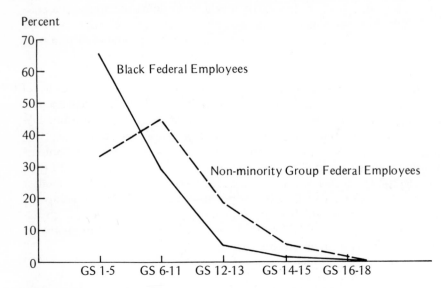

FIGURE 4-1
Distribution of Negro Employees by Selected Grade Groupings, as of November 30, 1969

SOURCE: *Study of Minority Group Employment in the Federal Government.* U.S. Civil Service Commission, Washington, D.C. Government Printing Office, November 30, 1969.

been made for increases in black employment, the total figures are far from spectacular. (See Table 4-7.) The summary figures for all black employment are found in the right-hand column; the other columns show the percentage of black employees in the particular grades.

These data show that the proportion of blacks in the bureaucracy is about equal to their numbers in the general population. However, the problem of black underemployment by the government or the distribution within the bureaucracy has been largely ignored. Not until the Kennedy administration did the government seriously examine itself with regard to minority employment. Ironically, the study which was ordered by Kennedy was published just four days after his assassination. The following extract, entitled Government Employment Census, reveals the extent of the problem at the time.[38]

> Prior to the issuance of Executive Order 10925, the belief was widely held that minority group employees of the Federal Government, particularly

---

[38] The President's Committee on Equal Employment Opportunity, *Report to the President* (Washington, D.C.: U.S. Government Printing Office, Nov. 26, 1963); the discussion in the text is based upon information contained in the Report at pp. 34-35.

Wide World Photos

A "second" being sworn in by a "first." William T. Coleman, center, being sworn in as Secretary of Transportation by Justice Thurgood Marshall (right), the first black ever to serve on the U.S. Supreme Court. Coleman is only the second black appointed to a cabinet position. Robert Weaver, appointed by President Lyndon Johnson as Secretary of Housing and Urban Development, was the first black appointed to the cabinet.

Negro employees, were denied equal opportunity in employment. No accurate measure existed, however, of the extent of such alleged discrimination.

Accordingly, the late President Kennedy included in his Order instructions to conduct a government-wide survey of employees to provide statistics on current employment patterns. By direction of the Committee, that survey was made as of June, 1961. It was repeated in June, 1962 and June, 1963.

The results of the 1961 survey bore out in large measure the contention that Negroes were being denied equal access to employment opportunity. And it provided the Committee and the agencies with the necessary information for undertaking programs to insure equal opportunity.

TABLE 4-7
Blacks in the Bureaucracy

Date	General Schedule Classification				
	1-4	5-8	9-11	12-18	Total*
June, 1962	18.1	7.7	2.6	.8	13.0
June, 1963	18.6	8.4	2.9	1.0	13.1
June, 1964	19.0	9.1	3.1	1.1	13.2
June, 1965	19.3	9.6	3.4	1.3	13.5
June, 1966	18.6	10.1	3.8	1.6	13.9
Nov. 1967	20.5	11.6	4.3	1.8	14.9
Nov. 1968			Unavailable		
Nov. 1969	21.6	13.0	5.1	2.3	15.0
Nov. 1970	22.3	14.0	5.3	2.6	15.2
Nov. 1971	21.8	14.8	5.7	2.5	15.0
Nov. 1972	21.7	15.0	5.9	3.0	15.1

* All pay systems.
Source: President's Committee on Equal Employment Opportunity, *Report to the President* (Washington, D.C.: Government Printing Office, Nov. 26, 1963).
U.S. Civil Service Commission. *Study of Minority Group Employment in the Federal Government* (Washington, D.C.: Government Printing Office, 1966, 1967, 1969, 1970, 1971, 1972.

The report provided the administration with the following details:

— While Negroes held 8.9 percent of the 1,012,447 Classification Act or similar positions, 72 percent of their jobs were concentrated in the lower level of GS-1 through GS-4 where the starting salary range was from $3,185 to $4,985. Only 35 percent of all employees were in this job bracket.
— Only 27 percent of the Negroes in Classification Act or similar systems held jobs in the middle range of positions, GS-5 through GS-11 (salary range, $4,345 to $9,640), while 50 percent of all employees held jobs in this bracket.
— Only 1 percent of the positions from GS-12 through GS-18 ($8,995 to $18,500) were held by Negroes.
    In the Postal Field Service, the situation was similar — the great bulk of the Negroes concentrated in the lower grades, disproportionately small numbers in middle and upper grades.[39]

Even before the survey figures were available, however, the committee and the various agencies had undertaken programs to ensure equal opportunity in government employment.

By the time of the second annual survey of government in June, 1962, the committee was able to report substantial progress toward equal opportunity for Negroes in federal employment.

---

[39] Until after the Korean War many upwardly mobile blacks believed that the Postal Service had the most highly educated black work force of all government agencies. They also recognized the irony in the levels of educational attainment and the predominantly low-status jobs which blacks filled in this branch of government.

Some highlights:

— The percentage of Negro Federal employees in Classification Act jobs in Grades 1-4 dropped from 72 percent to 68 percent while the number in the middle level GS-5 through GS-11 positions climbed from 27 percent to 30 percent.

— Of the net increase of 62,633 jobs from June, 1961, to June, 1962 Negroes accounted for 10,737 or more than 17 percent.

— In Classification Act jobs, Negro employment in the middle grades, GS-5 through GS-11, increased 19.2 percent compared with an overall increase of 2.4 percent, while in the upper grades, GS-12 through GS-18, the increase of Negroes was 35.6 percent compared with an overall increase of 9.5 percent.

The second and third surveys also provided information (not obtained in the 1961 census) on employment of the Spanish-speaking nationwide; of people of Mexican origin in five southwestern states; of people of Puerto Rican origin in four northeastern states; of people of Oriental origin in three western states, and of American Indians in seven states.

Since this survey was the first to cover the additional minority groups, there was no basis for comparison as to progress being made, but the picture presented was similar, although to varying degrees, to the picture of Negro employment. This material is still being tabulated for the 1963 census.

At the time this report was being prepared, only preliminary information was available from the third census. What was available, however, showed that sound and steady progress was still being made.

Some highlights:

— Twenty-two percent of the net increase in Federal employment during the period represented increased Negro employment. This compares to 17 percent for the previous census period.

— This net increase brings total reported Negro employment to a new high of 301,899 — up 3 percent from 293,353 in June, 1962. The cumulative percentage increase from June, 1961, to June, 1963, amounted to 6.8 percent.

— There were 545 more Negroes in the grades GS-12 through GS-18 (paying $9,475 to $20,000) than there were a year earlier, an increase of 38.7 percent. The total number of jobs in these grades increased 12.4 percent during the same period.

— Negroes in the middle grades (GS-5 to GS-11) increased by 4,278 or 14.7 percent, while total employment in these grades increased 5.1 percent.

— The number of Negroes in Wage Board positions paying more than $8,000 increased by 183, or 122 percent, while the total number of these positions increased 41.5 percent.

— In the Postal Field Service, the number of Negroes in higher paying positions increased 56.3 percent, despite a 2 percent decline in the total number of such jobs. . . .

By 1970, blacks made up just over 15 percent of the total federal work force. Given the low point from which the government started, it is not surprising, although it is depressing, to find that blacks, along with other nonwhite groups, predominate in the lower pay grades.

Clearly, one does not expect that some sort of *quid pro quo* will exist between the legislative élite and increased black representation in the nation's bureaucratic system. Nevertheless, it is reasonable to suggest that the presence of blacks in the administrative hierarchy of government could influence the shape of policy-making. It could lead to a decrease in the number of task forces and other ad hoc groups that tend to treat many unrelated policy questions. And even then it is only after some severe dislocation of the social order has taken place. Most important, perhaps, would be the educational purposes that might be achieved if blacks were to acquire more influence in government bureaucracies. This was, in fact, a point which received close attention when the War on Poverty was being developed.[40] If the problem of attitudes is the key to getting desired changes in policy areas of concern to blacks, then it makes sense to have blacks inside the system working with others who have a responsibility in those areas. Reshaping bureaucratic procedures is not a simple task. And, even with increased black representation the task will require much time. Much of the opposition to bureaucratic change comes from outside the organization. In part, this opposition is based on the belief that bureaucracy is simply unable to do the job because of "red tape." In addition, there is the problem of *clientele groups*, that is to say, organized recipients of the agencies' services, whose interests might be jeopardized, or seen as being so, with the kind of personnel changes and task reformulation we are suggesting here.

At the close of a decade of their most intense and diverse political activity, black Americans could look back on some successes. With qualifications they could speak of a growing black middle class. As in the past, this part of the black minority showed some anxieties about its status. In a feature story in *Time Magazine*, one black told the reporter: "We constantly live with the paranoia that we'll get sick or fired. I'm constantly aware of the fact that if I were out of work for six months, I'd be on the skids."[41] At the same time that blacks are moving up the income ladder, there is a dilemma which must be faced: what happens to those who are left behind? The black underclass is still large. There is still a belief among blacks that they have some degree of responsibility for helping the black lower class to better their lot. In some respects this

---

[40] See discussions in John C. Donovan, *The Politics of Poverty*, 2nd ed. (Indianapolis: Pegasus, 1973); Daniel P. Moynihan, *Maximum Feasible Misunderstanding* (New York: Free Press, 1970); and Richard Blumenthal, "The Bureaucracy: Antipoverty and the Community Action Program," in Allan P. Sindler, ed., *American Political Institutions and Public Policy* (Boston: Little, Brown, 1969).

[41] "America's Rising Black Middle Class," *Time Magazine*, June 17, 1974, p. 20.

is a responsibility that the white majority has suggested. It provokes some bitterness among the successful blacks. As one of the respondents in the *Time* essay phrased it: "I'm tired of white liberals always reminding you that if you take two steps forward, you always have to remember your unfortunate brethren. Look at white people who live in the rich suburbs. . . . They don't go down . . . and mingle with the blue-collar workers."[42]

These comments do suggest that the highly praised black unity may be little more than wishful thinking. Except on matters of real racial importance, black Americans divide themselves along traditional lines of class separation.

In electoral politics, however, racial solidarity has shown itself. This unity contributed significantly to the black mayoral victories in large

Wide World Photos

The big city black mayor: How influential a resource? John B. Swainson, of the State Supreme Court (left) and Damon J. Keith of the U.S. District Court for the Eastern District of Michigan (right) during swearing in of Coleman A. Young as Detroit's first black mayor (January 2, 1973). Keith is one of the few black federal judges.

---

[42] Ibid.

TABLE 4-8

Reported Voter Registration for Persons of Voting Age, by Region: 1966, 1968 and 1970 (Numbers in thousands)

SUBJECT	NEGRO			WHITE		
	1966	1968	1970	1966	1968	1970
All persons of voting age	10,533	10,935	11,473	101,205	104,521	107,997
North and West	4,849	4,944	5,277	72,593	75,687	77,158
South	5,684	5,991	6,196	28,612	28,834	30,839
Number who reported they had registered:						
United States	6,345	7,238	6,971	72,517	78,835	74,672
North and West	3,337	3,548	3,406	54,125	58,419	54,591
South	3,008	3,690	3,565	18,392	20,416	20,081
Percent of voting-age population:						
United States	60	66	61	72	75	69
North and West	69	72	65	75	77	71
South	53	62	58	64	71	65

SOURCE: U.S. Department of Commerce, Social and Economic Statistics Administration, Bureau of the Census.

TABLE 4-9

Reported Voter Participation for Persons of Voting Age, by Region: 1966, 1968, and 1970 (in millions)

SUBJECT	NEGRO			WHITE		
	1966	1968	1970	1966	1968	1970
All persons of voting age:	10.5	10.9	11.5	101.2	104.5	108.0
North and West	4.8	4.9	5.3	72.6	75.7	77.2
South	5.7	6.0	6.2	28.6	28.8	30.8
Number who reported that they voted:						
United States	6.4	6.3	5.0	57.8	72.2	60.4
North and West	2.5	3.2	2.7	44.8	54.4	46.1
South	1.9	3.1	2.3	12.9	17.9	14.3
Percent who reported that they voted:						
United States	42	58	44	57	69	56
North and West	52	65	51	62	72	60
South	33	52	37	45	62	46

SOURCE: U.S. Department of Commerce, Social and Economic Statistics Administration, Bureau of the Census. (Figures rounded by authors.)

urban areas. And, of course, electoral strength was a major factor in the emergence of the Congressional Black Caucus. But bringing together these few gains will require a substantial change in black political participation rates. As yet, their middle class is still too small to ensure that the interests of the black American will be expressed in the political process.

Although the number of voting age blacks who are registered has increased, it should be recalled that the years 1964 to 1970 covered some of the most wrenching domestic events of this century. In addition, during this same period black political activity moved away from non-violent protest demonstrations to the politics of confrontation in the War on Poverty and political violence in the rebellions of 1964 through 1968.

Despite the increases, voter turnout among blacks continues to be a problem. Also, the potential of black political strength is difficult to realize due to the lags in registration as well. Tables 4-8 and 4-9 reveal the relevant figures for the most volatile period of black political activity. The surges in black registration and turnout which are evident in the tables are associated with unique events. Political violence during the mid-sixties, and strenuous efforts to give effect to the various voting rights acts of the previous decade, combined to stimulate formal political activity. If these rates of participation cannot be maintained, or increased, the gains made thus far may be lost. And if, as many blacks believe, there has been relatively small improvement in the socioeconomic standing of the black masses, the right to vote may turn out to be of little but symbolic value. There is no indication that the relationship between income and voting is lessening. Moreover, the unique combination of circumstances that gave rise to aggressive black political activism does not occur often. Let us then, in the remainder of this volume, attempt to assess the extent to which these gains — legal, economic and political — have contributed to the achievement of black objectives. We begin with an examination of one of the most pervasive institutions in American political life; our system of legal institutions, the law and the courts.

Topics for Discussion

1. What qualities make an effective political leader? How have the leadership characteristics of blacks changed over time?

2. How did the black church serve as a "protector and political depressant" to black political aspirations? Has the role changed over time? In what ways?

3. How important is voting in the United States? Why is voting sometimes called a symbolic action? How much influence do elections have on government officials' behavior?

Suggested Readings

Aiken, Charles. *The Negro Voter*. San Francisco, 1962.

A study of the voting behavior of black Americans and the distribution of the black vote.

Bachrach, Peter and Morton S. Baratz. *Power and Poverty: Theory and Practice*. New York: Oxford University Press, 1970.

An analysis of political power, authority, influence and force in the policy-making process.

Edelman, Murray. *The Symbolic Uses of Politics*. Chicago: University of Illinois Press, 1964.

An examination of the impact of symbolic action on both spectators and players in the political game.

Lewinson, Paul. *Race, Class and Party*. New York: Russell, 1965.

A study of black suffrage and white political strategies in the South.

Lipset, Seymour Martin. *Political Man*. Chapters 6 and 7. Garden City, N.Y.: Doubleday, 1960.

In these chapters Lipset examines who votes and why in Western democracies.

Mitchell, William. *Why Vote?* Chicago: Rand McNally, 1971.

A counter to the argument that voting is merely a symbolic event.

Rose, Peter I. et al., eds. *Through Different Eyes: Black and White Perspectives on American Race Relations*. New York: Oxford University Press, 1973.

A reader on differing perspectives of black and white Americans on race relations.

Verba, Sidney and Norman Nie. *Participation in America*. New York: Harper & Row, 1972.

An analysis of the relationship between education and voting behavior.

Woodward, C. Vann. *The Strange Career of Jim Crow*. New York: Oxford University Press, 1966.

A study both of Southern segregation under the "Jim Crow" system and of the extension of these ideas into contemporary society.

5

CHANGE THROUGH LAW: COURTS, POLITICS AND THE LEGAL PROCESS

. . . A majority of black law students are repelled early in their law school careers by the degree to which the views expressed by their teachers reflect a far from analytical allegiance to a **legal system** that since its inception has systematically suppressed black people. Blacks do not expect the law schools to advocate revolution. They do, however, expect a view of the world, the law, and society more encompassing than that held by Louis XIV. And in this expectation, they are often disappointed. By defini- tion, a law professor is one upon whom law and society have looked with favor. Evidently, as an expression of appreciation for their good fortune, many law professors hold unthinkingly to political and legal views so conserva- tive that black students quickly, and I fear correctly, con- clude that there is nothing they wish to learn from such men.

Derrick A. Bell, Jr.*

For white lawyers and legal thinkers, the concept of law is one imbued with such fundamentally liberal values as "due process," "equal justice under law," and "a gov- ernment of laws and not of men." For blacks, on the other hand, law has traditionally meant violence, repression,

---

* Reprinted with permission from *The University of Toledo Law Review,* Volume 1970, at 548.

but above all, the police. . . . [F]or the ordinary ghetto resident, what the police officer says or does *is* the law.

Michael Katz, "Black Law Students in White Law Schools: Law in a Changing Society"†

Blacks will be the engine of Black progress in America; or, to a lesser extent, Blacks will be the engine of societal destruction if there is not sufficient recognition by the establishment that there must be an input of the Black vision in the societal process. To the extent that the norms generated in the societal process are the product of, or are influenced by, the legal profession, and to the extent that major law firms and corporations in partnership with important government officials and members of the judiciary occupy the lion's role in that process, there is an undeniable need for more Black lawyers to exert a full measure of Black power within those councils of the lions.

Harry T. Edwards, "A New Role for Black Law Graduates, a Reality or an Illusion?"‡

The truth is that our court system, state and federal, and our whole machinery of law enforcement remains even to this day the most racially segregated and class oriented institution in our public life. The special irony of this is that all law enforcement machinery and personnel are ultimately responsible to the judge; and we judges have assumed the vanguard role in breaking down the barriers of racism and classism in all the other aspects and institutions of our public life. One is tempted to say, "Physician heal thyself!"

Judge George W. Crockett, Jr., "Black Judges and the Judicial Experience"§

────────────

† Reprinted with permission from *The University of Toledo Law Review,* Volume 1970, at 599.

‡ Reprinted with permission from Harry T. Edwards and *Michigan Law Review.*

§ Reprinted with permission from 19 *Wayne Law Review* (1972), p. 61.

Courts, Politics, and the Legal Process

De Tocqueville observed that sooner or later major political issues are translated into legal issues. This observation is certainly supported by the involvement of courts in racial problems. And this involvement has been anything but neutral, above politics. Indeed, given the American tendency for legalism, courts and other participants in the legal process have played a central role in determining who gets what, when, and how.[1]

This importance of courts and judges in the political process was illuminated very early in the nation's history in the classic case of *Marbury* v. *Madison*. The decision of Chief Justice John Marshall in this case, made in 1803, went far toward establishing **judicial review:** the authority of courts to declare legislative acts (e.g., Congress) unconstitutional. To be sure, there was fairly strong support for judicial review with respect to state actions. However, there was no such support as to whether the Court's authority extended to actions of a coordinate branch of government, such as the Congress. But *Marbury* v. *Madison* presented the Court a chance to find out. Chief Justice Marshall seized the opportunity.

The case arose from circumstances involving the election of 1800. In this election President John Adams and his Federalists were defeated by Thomas Jefferson and his followers. But before leaving office, the Federalist-controlled lameduck Congress hastily created a number of new federal judicial posts that would conceivably allow Federalists to maintain some control over the Jeffersonians whom they did not trust. How much authority and what role such federal judges would have was unclear. But Adams and his followers were apparently ready to find out. In short, even though defeated at the polls, the Federalists made a strategic retreat to the judiciary where new Federalist appointees of the lameduck President Adams could now hold office for life, pending good behavior. The plan seemed quite plausible and altogether suited to the Federalist cause. For certain, the Constitution does give the president, with the consent of the Senate, the authority to fill such judicial positions. Given the circumstances President Adams and the Federalist Senate exercised their authority willingly and quickly. In any event, by March 3, 1801, the date he was to leave office, Adams had signed the commissions that authorized the new judicial appointments. He had also turned them over to his secretary of state, John Marshall, to be sealed and delivered. Marshall himself had just been appointed. He received

---

[1] Harold Lasswell, *Politics: Who Gets What, When, How* (Cleveland, Ohio: Meridian Books, 1958).

his commission as chief justice of the United States but continued in office as secretary of state until Adams left office. By the March 3 deadline Marshall had delivered most of the commissions and left the few that remained for his successor to deliver. Quite naturally, however, President Jefferson instructed his new secretary of state (Madison) not to deliver the commissions. Jefferson was incensed over this "packing" of the judiciary by those who had been defeated in the election. Among the few commissions not delivered was one for William Marbury who had been appointed as a justice of the peace for the District of Columbia. Marbury took his case directly to the Supreme Court. He asked the Court to order Madison to deliver the commission. Marbury based his case on a provision (section 13) of the Judiciary Act of 1789 that extended the original jurisdiction of the Supreme Court to issue **writs of mandamus** in such situations. (A writ of mandamus is a court order that instructs an official to perform a ministerial act.)

At first, Marbury seemed to have been in a good position. After all, John Marshall, who should have delivered the commission in the first place, was now chief justice. And in any event, the very purpose of the many last-minute judicial appointments was to allow the outgoing Federalists to restrain the newly elected opposition. But the situation was not this easy. At least John Marshall and his colleagues did not so construe it. At the time the Supreme Court was literally the *third* branch of government, and a distant third. The authority and prestige of the Court were quite low. Consequently, the Court was in no position to clash with a hostile president and Marshall knew it. This would have presented Jefferson an excellent opportunity to ignore the court order. He also could have done it in a way that could do great harm to the Court. But neither could the Court simply play dead to difficult issues that came to it. For to do so would also impair its authority and prestige.

Given such considerations, Marshall and his colleagues came upon a brilliant no-lose strategy. As expected, Marshall ruled that Marbury was entitled to his commission and that Madison should have delivered it to him. But now came the unexpected. Marshall held that the section of the Judiciary Act which gave the Supreme Court **original jurisdiction** to issue writs of mandamus was unconstitutional. The original jurisdiction of the Court, said Marshall, is outlined in Article III of the Constitution. It is restricted to cases involving ambassadors, foreign ministers, or in which a state is a party. Obviously, observed Marshall, Marbury is not covered by any of these categories. Consequently the only way the Court could assume jurisdiction in Marbury's case was by section 13 of the Judiciary Act of 1789. But to do so, reasoned Marshall, would mean that the Court was following an act of Congress that was contrary to the Constitution. Clearly, said Marshall, the Court was bound to follow the

Constitution, not a congressional act. The Constitution, he stated, is the supreme law of the land. Courts cannot uphold actions that conflict with the supreme law. But perhaps most important, Marshall made it very clear that whether or not an act of Congress conflicts with the Constitution is in the final analysis a matter for the Court to decide.

> It is emphatically the province and duty of the judicial department to say what the law is. Those who apply the rule to particular cases, must of necessity expound and interpret that rule. If two laws conflict with each other, the courts must decide on the operation of each.
>
> So if a law be in opposition to the Constitution; if both the law and the Constitution apply to a particular case, so that the Court must either decide that case conformably to the law, disregarding the Constitution; or conformably to the Constitution, disregarding the law; the Court must determine which of these conflicting rules governs the case. This is the very essence of judicial duty.
>
> If, then, the courts are to regard the Constitution, and the Constitution is superior to any ordinary act of the legislature, the Constitution, and not such ordinary act, must govern the case to which they both apply.

IMPORTANCE OF *MARBURY* v. *MADISON*

It is indeed difficult to overstate the importance of Marshall's reasoning in *Marbury* v. *Madison*. Its impact on the role of courts and judges in American politics was great. To be sure, Marshall denied Marbury his commission. But this was undoubtedly a wise course to take. Certainly one would not have expected Jefferson to have obeyed the order even had it been issued. Understandably, then, Marshall did not give Jefferson an order that he could disobey. He did, however, give Jefferson a "lecture" that he could hear. And though Jefferson did not like it, there was very little he could do. In essence, what Marshall told Jefferson, and the entire country, was that it is within the special competence of courts and judges, not presidents and congressmen, to determine whether actions of the executive and Congress conform with the Constitution, the supreme law of the land.

While there is no specific basis or authority in the Constitution for the Court's power to declare acts of Congress unconstitutional, the force of Marshall's argument in *Marbury* v. *Madison* is now fully imbedded in our constitutional system. More than this, that power not only refers to actions of the national government, but to actions of state and local governments as well. In short, it is the special province of courts and judges authoritatively to decide conflicts over constitutional interpretation. And such decisions are anything but neutral. When, for example, the Supreme Court decided in *Plessy* v. *Ferguson* (1896) that "separate but equal" facilities were constitutional, it strongly supported the segregation policies of southern whites. It was a major setback to civil rights for black Americans. But when the Court decided in *Brown* v. *Board of Education* (1954) that "separate but equal" was unconstitutional, it strengthened the rising civil rights movement and dealt a severe blow to segregationists. The *Plessy* and *Brown* examples also show how the interpretation of law might change over time. We shall return to this topic in the next chapter.

STATUTORY INTERPRETATION

Thus far we have focused on the highly visible role of the court in judicial review. This emphasis, however, is quite understandable since the "interpretation of the Constitution . . . is the highest and most difficult responsibility that American judges are called on to perform."* Nonetheless, we should mention here that a major part of the workload of courts in America consists of cases dealing with **statutory interpretation** as opposed to constitutional interpretation. Statutory interpretation refers to the work of courts in applying and enforcing laws (statutes) that are enacted by Congress, state legislatures and city councils. Constitutional interpretation refers to the role of courts in applying and enforcing various provisions of the Constitution.

In deciding conflicts concerning statutory law, the role of courts can become crucial in determining who wins or who loses as a result of specific legislative enactments. For example, in 1969 the Supreme Court interpreted the public accommodations section of the Civil Rights Act of 1964 to apply to a privately owned recreational facility (the Lake Nixon Club). Black patrons won the right to use such facilities while the white club owner lost in his attempts to keep racial segregation. Consider the language of the 1964 act. Generally, the act forbids racial discrimination in "places of public accommodation." But whether a particular establishment is a "place of public accommodation" within the meaning of the statute (the Civil Rights Act) depends on whether its business operations involve interstate commerce. In applying the statute to the Lake Nixon Club, the Court found that the club's operations were so affected by interstate commerce that the facility was a "place of public accommodation" within the coverage of the statute. Often, then, what a statute means is what the courts say it means. And the vague language inevitably found in statutes, which more or less reflects compromises needed to enact such legislation, obviously means that "the oppor-

---

* See footnote #2, at p. 442.

tunities for the exercise of judicial discretion in statutory interpretation are both frequent and wide."[2]

When we combine this traditional function of courts in statutory interpretations with that of judicial review, we begin to see more clearly the enormous importance of courts and judges in the political process. We begin to see more clearly the influence of courts in determining who gets what, when, and how. This influence is undoubtedly enhanced by the strong attachment Americans have to doing things "legally" and "according to law." Under our system of government, courts exercise a very crucial role in determining what is "legal" and "according to law." Accordingly, courts are the focal point of the legal process. However, we should not overlook the very fundamental role of other participants in that process. A discussion of these other participants, especially lawyers, allows us better to understand the nature of courts and the legal process and their importance to the overall political system. To this discussion we now turn.

Participants in the Legal Process: An Overview

Lawyers make up the legal profession from which judges come. They are the principal gatekeepers to the courts and to the legal process in general. Their special training gives them the knowledge needed to negotiate the details of the process on behalf of their clients. The legal process is indeed controlled by lawyers. Such control is, stabilized, as we shall discuss later, by the strong influence and representation of lawyers in government and in the private sector. This presence further indicates the influence of legalism in the political system.

The dominant role of lawyers in the legal process, however, should not obscure the importance of other participants. Indeed the most visible symbols of the law are the police, from the rural deputy sheriff to the city patrolman to the state police. How these *initial* enforcers (and interpreters) of the law carry out their responsibilities does much to shape the functioning of the legal process. It also helps shape the perceptions that groups hold of law and the legal process. Indeed "law in action" (police) can impair if not overcome in short order "law as doctrine" (Supreme Court decisions). Less visible but no less important roles are performed by investigative agencies attached to local police departments or the FBI, among others. Correctional institutions, prisons and prison officials, are

---

[2] Walter Murphy and C. Herman Pritchett, *Courts, Judges and Politics,* 2nd ed. (New York: Random House, 1974), p. 408.

likewise parts of the legal process. They are becoming increasingly visible as parts of "the system."

Overall, the functions (roles) of these various participants (judges, lawyers, prosecutors, police, prison officials) in the legal process are usually quite definite and narrowly specialized. However, it is the inter-dependence of these participants as they carry out their various functions that provide the dynamics of the legal process. And it is this interaction — this working together — that permits us to refer to these participants collectively as the legal system. They are all in one way or another concerned with the interpretation and/or enforcement of law. But since Americans generally try to resolve conflicts *according to law* let us take a closer look at those who have a primary responsibility for shaping the law.

Lawyers and the Legal Profession

The legal process is controlled by lawyers. These are the persons who by specialized training become certified as "learned in the law." And in a nation which seems to prefer legal solutions to social and political problems, lawyers naturally dominate the legal process. It is nevertheless interesting to learn, as we shall discuss later, that this same profession exercises a disproportionate influence (in terms of sheer numbers) throughout the various structures of American government. Long ago Count de Tocqueville observed that if he had to describe where the aristocracy lies in America it would be in the lofty role and deference accorded lawyers. De Tocqueville's observation is even more valid today. Lawyers and the public alike acknowledge the importance of lawyers and the legal profession. This, too, is remarkably consistent with de Tocqueville.[3]

In 1972 the legal aristocracy was composed of some 300,000 lawyers of whom about 4,000 were black. This aristocracy is sustained by the controls imposed on who enters the profession as well as by the be-havior expected once in the legal fraternity. The controls that determine who enters the profession tell us much about the nature of the profession. Generally, entrance into the profession depends upon successful completion of law school and admission to the bar, usually by state bar examination.

---

[3] Cf. Alexis de Tocqueville, *Democracy in America,* ed. J. P. Mayer and Max Lerner, trans. George Lawrence (New York: Harper & Row, 1966), pp. 242–48.

A CLOSER LOOK AT LAW SCHOOLS

Most law schools today are associated with or are a part of the nation's universities and colleges. This affiliation, however, does not shield law schools from requirements imposed by the profession (mainly the organized bar) through the American Bar Association and the Association of American Law Schools. To remain in good standing (and accredited) a law school must meet a number of requirements. For example, the number of credits students need to receive a law degree, the number of weeks in a law school semester, faculty salary rates, teaching loads, and autonomy are all requirements.

The biggest headaches for law schools in recent years, however, have revolved around admissions and curricula. The admission problem is becoming more, not less, acute. To be sure, one must be *admitted* to law school before receiving the training necessary to gain entrance to the profession. In addition, given the scarcity of jobs, legal training offers a variety of career opportunities, including the choice to become self-employed. A third reason why the admissions problem remains acute is that those who are politically disadvantaged, and who have previously been excluded from the legal profession, now perceive the law (and courts) as ways to rectify or overcome many of the nation's social ills.

When these and other factors are combined with the overall standing and prestige of the legal profession in the political system, it becomes quite understandable why blacks and other minorities want to become a part of the legal aristocracy. But many white Americans also want to become lawyers to enhance job opportunities and security. However, unlike blacks they do not necessarily view the law and courts as a way to effect basic social and political change. Rather, they see law and courts as conserving and maintaining the "good life" as it is, with such marginal changes as may be necessary to accomplish this end. Hence, the problem of law school admissions can become sharply joined. Consider, for example, the celebrated *DeFunis* case,[4] which the Supreme Court sidestepped in 1974. DeFunis was a white applicant to the University of Washington Law School. He was denied admission to law school even though his academic transcript and Law School Admission Test scores were higher than a number of blacks and other minority students who were admitted. As a result, DeFunis charged "reverse discrimination." He argued that his rejection was contrary to the equal protection provisions of both the state and federal constitutions. The university acknowledged that DeFunis' grades and LSAT scores were higher than

---

[4] *DeFunis* v. *Odegaard* (416 U.S. 312, 1974).

certain minority students who were admitted. However, university officials argued that in addition to raw grades and LSAT scores, they could
consider a broad range of factors in the admissions process. For instance, they could consider providing opportunities for legal education
to groups whose access to the legal profession in the past had been quite
restricted.

A state trial court agreed with DeFunis and ordered his admission in
1971. The state supreme court, however, reversed this ruling. But De-
Funis was allowed to remain in school pending appeal to the U.S.
Supreme Court. However, by the time the case was ready for decision in
the Supreme Court in 1974, DeFunis was ready to graduate from law
school only a few weeks later. Hence, since DeFunis was nearing the
end of his legal education, and since the case was not instituted as a class
action, the Supreme Court majority saw no need to decide the issue
involved. But the majority did concede that the widespread use of such
admissions policies would undoubtedly cause the issue to reach once
again the Court for decision. In any event, for our purposes here, the
DeFunis case vividly illustrates the problems in law school admissions.

However, the immediate admissions problem only scratches the
surface of what is undoubtedly the more fundamental concern: the
future role and nature of law, the courts, and the legal profession in the
American political system. Some indication of this more fundamental
concern can be seen in the curriculum problems of law schools. The
admission of more blacks and others who wish to use "the law" to
overcome certain inequities has made problems for those who wish to
stay with the traditional law school curricula. These problems relate to
more than instituting new courses. In fact, this may be considered the
easier way to satisfy the new breed (mainly black) law student, especially if such courses (for example, Urban Law, Legal Problems of the
Poor, Civil Rights) are taught by newly recruited black professors. Even
so, these courses can prove useful. They have natural appeal to many
students from minority backgrounds. They also can give upper class
white students a view of the "Other America" which they otherwise
might never get.

The more difficult problems, however, might relate to the pressures
which the newly admitted black and other minority students place on
their professors and others to rethink their way of offering traditional
courses. In addition, these pressures may also lead the various law
faculties to examine the whole concept of the role of law and lawyers in
the American political system, and how legal education might be
adapted accordingly. Obviously this poses a dilemma for the law professor and the profession generally. For the very presence of increasing
numbers of students from previously unrepresented groups challenges
the professor to see how the law and its associated institutions in the

"real world" are often disadvantageous to minorities. Moreover, they may recognize that perhaps it is time to reexamine the traditional role that law and the legal aristocracy have played and might play in making the real world a better place for all. Meeting this challenge is a big order. It could mean, as black law professor Derrick Bell puts it, that "if white law professors are to teach effectively black law students . . . they must make the effort to see the world and the legal issues as black students see them."[5] White students would also profit from insights that could be gained from such teaching and curriculum reforms.

To meet this challenge successfully does imply that *institutional racism* in law schools must be eliminated. Let us look at the example of place-ment activities. Certainly, providing legal services to those who are disadvantaged by poverty and racism is an acute problem in a political system that highly values and so strongly depends on lawyers and the legal process. Because of the poor's need for legal assistance — and because many of the poor are black — it is plausible for placement officers and others to expect some blacks to pursue careers in predomi-nantly black communities. But law schools and placement officers should not automatically assume that all black law students will do so. Comments from two black law professors put this career problem well and in broader context.

Comment #1:

> There seems to be a developing presumption that the recruitment efforts undertaken by many law schools to increase the number of minority students exists in the main, if not exclusively, for the purpose of directing minority students toward the legal profession so that such students may re-enter "their communities" in some kind of legalistic social work em-ployment or service status. This is a troublesome development.[6]

Comment #2:

> . . . the need for Black lawyers in the offices of major law firms, corpora-tions, brokerage houses, and banks — the real power pockets in American society — is plainly apparent.
> . . . institutions of legal learning are busy at the task of increasing Black admissions, developing "relevant" curriculums, and in general focusing institutional resources upon the preparation of a corps of young Black lawyers who can "return to their community." . . . The law schools,

---

[5] Derrick Bell, "Black Students in White Law Schools: The Ordeal and the Opportu-nity," 2 *Toledo Law Review*, 539 at 547–48 (1970).

[6] Walter Leonard, "Placement and the Minority Student: New Pressures and Old Hang-Ups," 2 *Toledo Law Review*, 583 at 586 (1970).

the professional associations, and the major law firms are rendering an egregious disservice to society in general and the profession in particular when, by acts of omission or commission, Blacks are "nudged" or "forced" to limit their professional career choice to "neighborhood practice" or practice with "legal services programs," both of which emphasize such matters as criminal defense, divorce and family law, personal injury and landlord-tenant. Black lawyers must have the opportunity to move into all areas of concentration and specialty within the profession. In addition to dealing with problems of poverty, discrimination, and criminality, the upcoming generation of young black lawyers must face no barriers to specializing in such areas as taxation, anti-trust, securities, admiralty, corporate, labor, and administrative law.[7]

It would indeed be a "troublesome development" for law schools and others to automatically "place" blacks in those careers that seem more "natural" or of "immediate concern" to the problems of minority groups. To do so is an example of the institutional racism to which we referred above. Of equal importance, however, is that such placements will tend to deny black lawyers the opportunity to learn and exercise wider influence in large basic industries and prestigious law firms. As the American political system presently operates, fundamental changes in the black (and minority) communities cannot come about without the support of those who possess power. Law schools and their placement officers surely understand this. But whether they act accordingly is another matter. In any event, there are indications that more blacks are being sought and placed in these previously off-limits areas.[8] But it remains to be seen whether this is "merely a manifestation of contemporary tokenism."[9]

ADMISSION TO THE BAR

Graduation from law school does not automatically or necessarily mean that one can enter the legal profession and practice law. Each state sets its own requirement for admission to the bar. Almost two-thirds of the states require candidates for admission to the bar to be graduates of law schools approved by the ABA. In addition, most states require applicants to pass the state bar examination. The exam is administered by a Board of Bar Examiners or state supreme court. Applicants must also receive certification, usually from practicing attorneys in the particular state, that they are of good moral character

---

[7] Harry Edwards, "A New Role for Black Law Graduates," 2 *Black Law Journal,* 21 at 24-25.
[8] Bell, "Black Students in White Law Schools, " pp. 541-42.
[9] Ibid.

and reputation. These requirements ensure state control, usually through the organized bar, over who is admitted to practice.

Such control has its spillover effects. The bar examination, which may be weighted in certain subject matter areas, may affect the basic curricula of the law schools. In most instances this means that traditional subjects must be taught in traditional ways. No law school can continue to flourish if a number of its graduates fail the state bar. Moreover, just as traditional curricula in law schools can pose problems for blacks and other newly admitted groups, traditional and standardized bar examinations can prove likewise. The same could be true where "certification" as to good moral character is a requirement for admission to the bar. The lack of black attorneys in a particular state suggests that such certification must come from local white practicing attorneys. In any event, such built-in institutional biases in bar examinations and in "certification" procedures can, of course, influence whether previously excluded groups gain entrance to the legal aristocracy.

NATURE AND STRUCTURE

Once admitted to the bar, lawyers engage in a variety of practices. By far, the largest number of lawyers are in private practice, either alone or in partnership with others as in law firms. The larger of these firms, some of which number 100 or more attorneys, generally (but not always) allow for departmentalization and specialization within the firm — for example, specialists in labor law, insurance law, business law, and so forth. The majority of black lawyers are in private practice as solo practitioners in what may be called "the neighborhood practice." "They serve individual clients regarding such matters as personal injury, workmen's compensation, divorce and custody, and criminal defense. . . ."[10] One study, for example, found that of the graduates of Howard University Law School (the largest predominantly black law school) who are in private practice, five-sixths are solo practitioners.[11] Such practice is not geared to yield great financial returns. Nor is it likely to bring black lawyers into power centers that would more likely come through association and partnership in major law firms. And here there are few black lawyers. In other words, most black lawyers are in private practice. Their numbers are few in the kind of practice that ranks high in financial reward and in influence, in either the legal profession or in American society generally.

A large number of lawyers are in government service at the federal,

---

[10] Jerome Schuman, "A Black Lawyers' Survey," 16 *Howard Law Journal*, 225 at 239 (1971).

[11] Martin Mayer, *The Lawyers*, 3rd ed. (New York: Harper & Row, 1973), pp. 97-98.

state and local levels. Federal employment is extremely varied. It ranges from securities and corporation specialists for the Securities and Exchange Commission to tax lawyers for the Internal Revenue Service to labor lawyers for the National Labor Relations Board. And, of course, the Justice Department is the largest government employer of lawyers. Virtually every federal department and agency has some legal staff. A similar pattern exists in state government with the office of the state attorney general and office of local prosecuting attorney being the most visible symbols. Cities also have legal departments and other positions which require legal counsel.

The corporate community also depends heavily upon the expertise of lawyers. Many corporations, rather than employing a law firm on a retainer basis, have established corporate legal departments. These are usually referred to as "in house" counsel. The attorney working for a corporation is much like the private practitioner, except that he has but one client — the corporation. Still another aspect of practice is in the public interest law area. This area includes not only the "Nader's Raider" type lawyers, but also legal aid attorneys and public defenders. The latter two, of course, are supported by government.

The basic structure of the legal profession is provided by its "unions" — the organized bar associations — national, state, and local. Membership in about half of the state bar associations come automatically upon passing the state bar examination. In the other states, membership in the state bar is optional, but many attorneys do belong to their state organizations. Membership in the national organization — the American Bar Association (ABA) — is maintained by about half of the nation's lawyers. In 1971, for example, the ABA membership was approximately 150,000. [12]

The ABA has an enormous influence in the legal profession and in the American system generally. Most of the nation's outstanding lawyers in the corporate, government, and academic sectors are members of the ABA. What these leaders say carries weight. They are especially influential with regard to the ABA Committee on the Federal Judiciary. This in turn affects the quality of the nation's courts. This committee, consisting of twelve members, stands ready to review the qualifications of individuals nominated to the federal judiciary, from the district court judgeships up to the justices of the Supreme Court. The use of this extragovernmental screening may, of course, vary with incumbent presidents. However, nominations to judgeships in the lower federal courts are usually sent to the ABA Committee for evaluation. A president may, however, as did Nixon in the Carswell and Haynesworth cases, bypass

---

[12] Edward L. Wright, "An Overview of the Association in its 93rd Year," 57 *ABA Journal* 760 (August, 1971).

the ABA in choosing his nominees to the Supreme Court. Even so, as in these instances, such attempts usually prove unsuccessful since the Senate can also ask for the ABA advice. The plain fact is that the prestige of the ABA and its Committee on the Federal Judiciary is such that judicial nominees who do not receive the committee's stamp of approval are unlikely to weather the appointment process.[13] This strong influence of the ABA in the selection of federal court judges is not without consequence. As Nimmo and Ungs have shown:

. . . The ABA has consistently urged the President to appoint judges who demonstrate qualities of intelligence, legal scholarship, and honesty rather than make "political" appointments. Nevertheless, the ABA stands on socioeconomic policies over the years have indicated a strong conservative bias. In this respect, the organization is no different from other groups that seek to influence judicial policy-making by urging appointment of justices with views similar to their own. That the ABA represents the legal profession, however, lends an aura of prestige to its views that is not usually accorded to other pressuring interests.[14]

The ABA has other key committees and commissions; among them are those set up to review and restate various areas of substantive law with recommendations for change, such as the Commission of the Restatement of Tort Law or on the Law of Property.[15] These recommendations, just as the ABA's views on judicial nominees, carry great weight with those who hold authoritative positions — for example, judges, state legislators — which could bring about changes in their areas of responsibility. State and local bar associations are similar in character and function to the ABA. They usually command a standing and prestige in state and local politics far beyond that of other interest groups, especially as related to legal matters.

In general, the membership of the several bar associations reflects the ideology and racial composition of the prevailing power structures. As stated previously, leaders in the bar associations are usually those successful (in terms of wealth) and distinguished men of the bar (in terms of their standing in the legal profession and their being a part of or interacting with other élites, that is, business, corporate, political, academic). By and large then, the organized bar reflects the views of the establishment with corresponding attachments and allegiances to the existing patterns

---

[13] For a detailed account of the role of the ABA in judicial selection see Joel Grossman, *Lawyers and Judges: The ABA and the Politics of Judicial Selection* (New York: John Wiley, 1965).

[14] Dan Nimmo and Thomas Ungs, *American Political Patterns* (Boston: Little, Brown and Co., 1967), p. 431.

[15] Wright, p. 760.

of power distribution. Groups which are not presently represented in the establishment and seek to change the distribution of power will find little sympathy or support from the organized bar or the legal profession generally. Small wonder then that for many years the ABA, as well as state and local bar associations, did not permit black lawyers to join their ranks. In short, the profession generally and the organized bar in particular mirrored the racism in other areas of American life. Consequently, just as in other areas, black lawyers formed their own organizations. The organization of black lawyers at the national level is the National Bar Association, formed in 1925.

Although the ABA (and state and local bar associations) now admits blacks, the NBA (and other black bar groups) still functions — and flourishes. This is shown by the recent formation under NBA auspices of a judicial council, composed of black judges. In explaining "Why We Organize," one black judge and a member of the judicial council put it this way:

> We organize as blacks and around our blackness because the melting pot ideology has been ineffective in producing meaningful progress in our heterogeneous society. . . .
> We assemble with the realization that in unity there is strength and that our society interprets formal organization as an index of a group's sense of urgency and concern. This union will provide protection and support. Together we hope to articulate a consensus of opinion, command more respect, exert more influence, champion more causes, challenge accepted practices, and promulgate our positions better than before. . . .[16]

Regardless of the nature of practice, or membership in the organized bar, lawyers are expected to live up to "almost idealistic" standards of professional conduct.[17] As put elsewhere: "Like the boy scout, the attorney is supposed to be loyal, truthful, trustworthy, courteous, kind, clean, and prompt."[18] There are codes of ethics of various state bar associations and the ABA. Each state provides some way to discipline attorneys who engage in unethical or illegal conduct. This function may be lodged in bar associations, the state courts (usually the state supreme court), or a structure provided for participation of both judges and the organized bar. Among other things, Watergate has shown dramatically the importance of policing the legal aristocracy.

---

[16] Judge Joseph C. Howard, "Why We Organize," 20 *Journal of Public Law*, 381 at 382 (1971).

[17] Murphy and Pritchett, p. 128.

[18] Ibid.

Courts and Judges

Judges, like legislators, are also engaged in the business of allocating resources, making rewards and imposing deprivations. The fact that a judge is so involved, as Peltason puts it, is "not a matter of choice but of function."[19] "Judicial participation," continues Peltason, "does not grow out of the judge's personality or philosophy but out of his position."[20] Thus, it is his *position* with authority to *render decisions*, to support certain interests and not support others that leads us to describe judges no less than legislators as participants in the political process. Consequently, courts, the institutional structures in which judges operate, become important forums in managing and resolving conflict in the governing system.

To be sure, certain factors that tend to remove or insulate courts and judges from politics can sometimes obscure their crucial role in American politics. Consider our attachment to the belief in a "government of laws and not of men." Consider, moreover, that courts stand as constant reminders of these attachments and are to rule according to *law*. While general public opinion and special interests may influence other decision-makers, the judge's influence is believed to come from the law and what the law requires. Consider also the methods of selecting judges; these methods, which increasingly emphasize their expertise in the law and their judicial temperament, are based upon the judges' accountability to no one save the law and their own consciences. In addition, consider the formal and informal expectations (norms) concerning how judges are to act, behave, and carry on their high duties. Moreover, these jurists must show impartiality and neutrality. And, above all, judges are to be *above* politics. Admittedly these and other factors do shape judicial behavior and how courts function. They also shape our perceptions of courts and judges and how we think they should carry out their responsibilities. All this, however, does not change the crucial and often determining roles that courts perform in the business of governing. Indeed, rather than lessening their functions, these perceptions and expectations strengthen the judicial hand.

We are not attempting here to equate the functions of courts with legislatures, or judges with elected politicians. Rather, we suggest that courts, through proper judicial procedures, also make decisions that determine who gets what, when, and how. However, decision-making

---

[19] Jack Peltason, *Federal Courts in the Political Process* (New York: Random House, 1955), p. 3.

[20] Ibid.

in the judicial forum — unlike the legislature, for example — does not supposedly turn on numbers, wealth, or social standing. Rather it turns on *the law*. And though much of *the law* is itself influenced by these very factors (for example, social standing),[21] once enacted it may be subject to judicial interpretations which might or might not support interests that led to its original enactment. In any event, the structure of courts is such that they do not necessarily respond to the same interests as do other political institutions, such as legislatures. This element of discretion, and the authority of his decisions, places the judge in a position of power and influence in the American government system. How one gains such a position and what manner of person becomes a judge are of obvious importance to those interested in the allocation of values. To these questions we now turn.

COURTS AND JUDICIAL SELECTION

In keeping with basic federal structure, we have a federal (national) court system and a state court system. Selection of state court judges, as would be expected, can be through partisan and **nonpartisan elections** and by executive and legislative appointment, or variations of these basic methods. Our purpose in this section, however, can perhaps best be met by focusing on courts that are familiar to most of us, the federal courts. Yet we should all remember that state (and local) courts and judges make determinations that can affect our everyday living in ways that may be more immediate than actions of federal courts. It is sufficient to say here that those interested in building "power bases" at the grassroots should not neglect the role of state and local courts.[22]

The federal courts that we hear most about are the Supreme Court, the courts of appeals and the federal district courts. These are **constitutional courts** of general jurisdiction. That is, they are based on Article III of the Constitution. They have authority to hear cases covering a variety of matters. Judges in these courts are appointed by the president and must be confirmed by the Senate. They have life tenure, assuming they conform to expected norms of good behavior.

---

[21] See, for example, John P. Heinz, Robert W. Gettleman, and Morris A. Seeskin, "Legislative Politics and The Criminal Law," LXIV *Nw. Law Review:* 277–358 (1969). See also discussion on the politics of the development of criminal legislation in Herbert Jacob, *Urban Justice* (Englewood Cliffs, N.J.: Prentice-Hall, 1973), pp. 17–20.

[22] Increasing attention is being given to the role of state and local courts in the political process. See, for example, James Klonoski and Robert Mendelsohn, "The Allocation of Justice: A Political Approach," XIV *Journal of Public Law,* 326–42 (1966); Kenneth Dolbeare, *Trial Courts in Urban Politics* (New York: John Wiley, 1967); and Jacob, *Urban Justice.*

The federal district courts are at the base of the federal court system. Each state has at least one district court. Large states have up to four such courts. The number of judges in these courts range from one to twenty-four, though each judge normally sits separately to hear cases.

The district courts are courts of *original jurisdiction;* that is, most cases involving federal law (and the U.S. Constitution) begin in these courts. They have no **appellate jurisdiction.** The district courts are the trial courts of the federal system. They are the only federal courts where one can get the classic picture of a trial with counsel, witnesses, judge, and jury. These courts also regularly use the grand jury to bring indictments which may result in trials. In addition to judges, the personnel of the district court includes stenographers, law clerks, court reporters, probation officers, and magistrates. These positions are all filled with persons appointed by the district judge. United States marshals, assigned to each district court, are appointed by the president. The president also appoints the United States Attorney, who serves as federal prosecutor and who represents the government in most civil actions in the district court.

But the ultimate authority of the district court is vested in the some 350 judges who preside over these courts. These are the judicial decision-makers in the district courts. And since a majority of their decisions are not appealed, the type of justice one gets in federal courts is given out by the district court judges.

Three main criteria stand out in the selection of federal judges. These "**selection variables**" are competence, party affiliation, and ideological considerations.[23] The latter two factors are primarily political. Thus, they will be determined largely by *political* officials, such as the president, U.S. senators, state and local party officials. The potential nominee must be a member of the president's party; also, the kinds of support he has given to the party, as well as the "right" ideological positions on important policy issues define more accurately the *best* nominee for a federal judgeship. However, the *competence* part, having to do with the legal ability, experience, and judicial nature of the nominee, are primarily "legal" matters to be determined through institutionalized legal channels such as the ABA Committee on Federal Judiciary. The role and influence of these key participants in the selection process, as we shall see, varies widely depending upon a number of factors — for example, the particular judgeship to be filled (Supreme Court, court of appeals, district court) and the political context in which the appointment is being made.

---

[23] Sheldon Goldman and Thomas Jahnige, *Federal Courts as a Political System* (New York: Harper & Row, 1971).

Appointments to federal district courts have long been seen as patronage positions by the officials and leaders of the president's party in
the state where the appointment is to be made. Of these officials the
U.S. senator from the particular state has traditionally been accorded
the most influential role in the selection. There is some evidence, however, that senators do not play the crucial role that many believe.[24]
Indeed, the senator's role in selection must be shared by others within
and outside the state. These include the U.S. deputy attorney general
and his staff, members of the bar and bench (sitting judges in the district
may be asked for opinions), the FBI in terms of its background investigation, and of course, the Senate Judiciary Committee. While the roles of
these participants vary, they can nevertheless prove to be crucial. The
influence of the organized bar in the selection process is especially
noteworthy. Through its Committee on the Federal Judiciary, the ABA is
asked routinely to evaluate all nominees. The Committee in turn rates
the nominees as "exceptionally well-qualified," "well-qualified," or
"not qualified." To be sure, as mentioned previously, how much weight
the Committee's recommendations carry may vary given particular situations. But so does and has the influence of individual senators. Nevertheless, a nominee who does not have the support of the ABA Committee (and of course the U.S. senator) will have trouble winning confirmation.

Appointments to the courts of appeals follow a similar procedure,
except that the president (and his administration) exercises far greater
control and influence in the selection.[25] Many factors differentiate the
selection of judges to the courts of appeals from those in the district
courts. For instance, at the court of appeals level there are fewer judges
and fewer courts with enlarged jurisdiction to hear cases from a number
of districts covering several states, not just one. For example, the nation
is divided into ten large circuits, each of which has a court of appeals. In
addition there is one court of appeals in the District of Columbia. The
number of judges in these courts range from three to nine and the court
usually sits in panels of three, except that in decisions of utmost importance and visibility the court will sit **en banc** — all members sitting to
hear the particular case. Altogether there are some 97 judges who
occupy the circuit court bench.

But, as suggested earlier, the relative influence of participants in the
selection process varies at the circuit court level. For example, the influence of individual United States senators is not as great here as at the

---

[24] Harold W. Chase, *Federal Judges* (Minneapolis: University of Minnesota Press, 1972),
p. 47.

[25] Sheldon Goldman, "Judicial Appointments to the U.S. Courts of Appeals," 1967
Wisconsin Law Review: 186.

district court level. Nevertheless, by practice and tradition, individual states within a given circuit attempt, often successfully, to claim at least one seat on their court of appeals. If, for example, a judge in a given circuit should resign or retire, the state from which he was originally appointed would attempt to claim the seat. In this context (in the instance of such occurrences) the senator and other officials from the particular state, provided they are of the president's party, will have a voice in the selection process. Apparently, though, they have less influence than in the case of district courts. Because the decisions of the courts of appeals have much broader policy impact than those of district courts, the president and his advisers give more attention and exercise more control over who occupies the circuit court bench.

Appointments to the U.S. Supreme Court are undoubtedly the most visible to the public. There is only one Supreme Court with *final* authority to interpret and apply the law. This means that the stakes are very high in terms of who serves on that Court. There are, of course, nine positions on the Supreme Court. But the size of this Court, just as with other federal courts, is not set by the Constitution but is rather determined by the Congress. Given the authority and prestige of the Supreme Court, plus that vacancies occur only occasionally, it becomes obvious that the president will use the influence of his "nominating" authority in such appointments with more care than in lower federal courts. While certain other considerations such as race, ethnic affiliation, and geographic balance may enter, a president will perhaps be *most* concerned about the ideological and policy dispositions of potential nominees. Indeed, decisions of the Supreme Court have nationwide implications. They can do much to promote, frustrate, or negate presidential policies and programs. But by the same token, other participants in the selection process — both official and unofficial — attach added importance to Supreme Court nominations for the same reasons. Consequently, senators and other public officials, the ABA and leaders of the bar, organized interest groups and concerned citizens will all use the full range of their influence to make certain the "right" person is selected. And, of course, all it takes is a "controversial" appointment to bring the dynamics of selecting a Supreme Court Justice into full focus. The story of one such appointment, that of Judge Harold Carswell, is brilliantly told by Richard Harris in his description of the unsuccessful attempt of President Nixon to appoint Carswell to the Court.[26] The Carswell episode, it will be recalled, followed the earlier unsuccessful Nixon effort to place Judge Clement Haynesworth on the Court.

What kinds of judges have come out of this selection process? There is evidence suggesting linkages between life experiences of decision-

---

[26] Richard Harris, *Decision* (New York: E. P. Dutton, 1971).

makers and the kind of decisions they make. Thus, more and more attention is being given to seeing the nature, extent, and impact of such linkages in the judicial arena. Studies of this nature have initially focused on the social, economic, and political background of decision-makers. Such research, as applied to judges, turns up interesting and revealing information. For one thing, men of wealth and high social status have historically been overrepresented in the federal courts. Schmidhauser's study of the background of Supreme Court Justices, for example, reveals that about 90 percent of the Justices have come from economically comfortable families. Only about 10 percent come from what may be described as "humble backgrounds."[27] With only two exceptions (James Wilson, a Federalist, and Earl Warren, a Republican) all Supreme Court Justices of humble backgrounds were Democrats. By and large then the overwhelming majority of Supreme Court Justices have come from the upper strata of society.[28]

Lower federal court judges have tended to be drawn as well from high socioeconomic backgrounds. But only in relatively recent times has attention been focused on the lower federal courts. Undoubtedly, this is in part due to the upper court myth that captured the fancy of so many for so long. Consequently, lower federal courts (and state courts) have generally escaped the exacting scrutiny that scholars, journalists and others have given to the U.S. Supreme Court. A striking example is again seen in the case of Judge Carswell. When Carswell was nominated and won approval to a district judgeship, and was later elevated to the court of appeals, very little attention was focused on his record and qualifications. But we all know what happened once he was nominated for the Supreme Court. Now, however, the situation is changing. The growing awareness of the importance of lower federal (and state) courts is reflected by the increasing attention being given to them. As a result, we can now say something more about such judges.[29] For example, a study of Eisenhower and Kennedy appointments to the courts of appeals shows that about three-fourths of Eisenhower's appointees and about one-half of Kennedy's appointees came from middle and upper classes.

The overwhelming majority of federal judges are white, Anglo-Saxon and Protestant. The few who come from other racial (black), ethnic and religious backgrounds (Jewish, Catholic) were mainly appointed by Democratic presidents. This, of course, may be explained in part by the

---

[27] John Schmidhauser, *The Supreme Court: Its Politics, Personalities, and Procedures* (New York: Holt, Rinehart, and Winston, 1960).

[28] Jerry Lansauer, "Shaping the Bench," *Wall Street Journal*, December 10, 1970, p. 1.

[29] Sheldon Goldman, "Characteristics of Eisenhower and Kennedy Appointees to the Lower Federal Courts," 18 *Western Political Quarterly:* 758 (1965); and "Johnson and Nixon Appointees to Lower Federal Courts," 34 *Journal of Politics:* 936 (1972).

attachment that economically disadvantaged and ethnic groups have for the Democratic party.

In addition to being WASPs, federal judges generally have been "politically active"; that is, they have been actively involved in politics prior to their appointments. A good number of judges have held political or legal offices associated with government, such as service in the Justice Department or in the office of the U.S. Attorney General. Many judges have indeed had prior experience on the bench. Those appointed to the courts of appeals have had more prior judicial experience than those appointed to the federal district courts and Supreme Court. For example, about half of Eisenhower, Kennedy, Johnson, and Nixon appointees to the courts of appeals had had prior judicial experience, mostly at the federal district court level.[30] But while service on a district court may lead to appointment to a court of appeals, there is little evidence to support a similar pattern for appointment to the Supreme Court. However, appointments to the Supreme Court have gone in large measure to those who have held important political or legal office (for example, U.S. Senator or Attorney General) or those who had achieved prominence in the legal profession (for example, in the ABA or in prestigious law schools).

This discussion about courts and judicial selection leads to a major conclusion: those who are selected as federal judges mostly represent the dominant political interests at any given time. Hence those who are disadvantaged in "political" arenas will find, as far as representation is concerned, that they are similarly disadvantaged in the judicial forum. It should come as no surprise then that the black representation in the third branch *at all levels* (national, state, and local) is very small. For example, a 1970 report of the National Bar Association indicated that there were only 325 black judges in courts of every description in the entire United States, state and federal. This, in large measure, is a consequence of built-in selection biases that have determined and continue to determine who becomes a judge. While tradition, structures, and insulation of the judicial office serve to hide these selection biases, their visibility becomes all too clear when one takes a closer look at the facts. Of the 350 federal district court judges, eleven are black; of the 97 judges in the courts of appeals, only three are black; and the only black to serve on the U.S. Supreme Court (Thurgood Marshall) was appointed in 1968 by President Johnson. The number of black judges at the state level is also small, even in states with sizable black populations. (See Table 5-1.) As we might expect, the largest number of black judges are found in cities with large black populations. Even so, however, the number of such judges and their influence in judicial politics is relatively

---

[30] Pritchett and Murphy, *Courts, Judges, and Politics,* p. 161.

TABLE 5-1
Number and Distribution of Black Judges, September, 1972

STATE	STATE COURTS					FEDERAL COURTS		
	APPELLATE COURT	GENERAL JURISDICTION	LIMITED JURISDICTION	SPECIAL COURTS	TOTAL STATE JUDGES	APPELLATE COURT	TRIAL COURT	TOTAL BLACK JUDGES
Alabama			2	1	3			3
Arizona			1		1			1
California	1	6	12		19		1	20
Colorado			2		2			2
Connecticut		1	1	1	3			3
Delaware			1		1			1
Dist. of Col.	2	12			14	3	4	21
Florida			2	1	3			3
Georgia			1	2	3			3
Illinois	1	27			28		1	29
Indiana		2	2		4			4
Iowa			2		2			2
Kansas			2		2			2
Kentucky			4	1	5			5
Louisiana		1		1	2			2
Maryland		4	5		9			9
Massachusetts		1	2	1	4			4

Michigan*		9	3		12		1	13
Minnesota		1			1			1
Missouri		4	5		9			9
Nebraska			1		1			1
Nevada			1		1			1
New Hampshire			1		1			1
New Jersey		3	6	1	10			10
New York	4	10	30	7	51		5	56
North Carolina		1	2		3			3
Ohio	2	3	7	1	13	1		14
Oklahoma			2		2			2
Oregon			2		2			2
Pennsylvania	2	17	3		22	1	2	25
South Carolina			4		4			4
Tennessee		2	5		7			7
Texas			4	1	5			5
Virginia			3		3			3
Washington	1	1	2		4			4
West Virginia		1			1			1
Virgin Is.		1			1		1	2
Totals	13	107	120	18	258	5	15	278

* This chart does not reflect the results of the November 1972 election. In Michigan, for example, five new black judges were elected.
SOURCE: Adapted with permission from George W. Crockett, Jr., "Black Judges and the Judicial Experience," 19 *Wayne Law R.* 61 at 70–71 (1972).

small when compared to the proportion of blacks in those areas. Overall then, very few blacks occupy the powerful position of judge in the American governing system.

But the small number of black judges has not been overlooked by black judges themselves and by other black leaders. They recognize the important role that American courts perform in the distribution of benefits (rewards) and costs (deprivations). Moreover, they are sensitive to the relationship of this role to the need for more black judges. The following comment from a black judge illustrates that sensitivity:

> We who are products of the American common law are always extolling the virtues of a common law system and its ability to adapt to the growing needs of the people. In the past, white judges have really made the common law adaptable to what they conceive to be the desires of the American people. We black judges have to take a page from that book. If the common law is so adaptable, let's get down to books and find the remedies, and apply them to the old evils that have plagued the poor and the underprivileged in our society for so long. The answers are there. The special role of the black judge is to see what justice requires and then go to the books and get the remedies to apply to it. Most people assume that the law is something that is clear cut, it's written out, it's black and white; it's not so. Most of the law is a matter of discretion. What is discretion? Discretion is whatever the judge thinks it is as long as he can give a sound reason for it. A judge is a product of his own experiences, of his own history, of the people from whom he came. So a black judge's exercise of discretion is not going to necessarily be the same as that of a white judge. But as long as it is reason, and the law is made by precedents established by white people, that discretion stands. That's the one record that is available.[31]

However, the need for more black judges goes beyond the "position of power" argument. There is also a value to be gained by having judges who understand black experiences. Bruce Wright, a black judge from New York, comments:

> Black judges who have themselves escaped the gravitational pull of the ghetto, but who still bear the marks of their narrow escape, know the rough tensions of a two-culture existence. There is, therefore, a special insight of compassion which only a Black judge can bring to the law.[32]

Professor Beverly Blair Cook, in her pioneering study on black judges, provides yet another reason why more black judges are needed and the role they can perform.

---

[31] George W. Crockett, Jr., "The Role of The Black Judge," 20, *Journal of Public Law:* 398–99 (1971).

[32] *Black Law Journal*, 241 at 243.

The presence of a black judge on an important trial bench might attract cases which lawyers would not invest resources to bring before another judge. It has been suggested that the most vital exercise of power is not in winning old conflicts but in raising new issues. At a minimum, the black judge by his visibility on the trial bench opens the judicial door for the articulation of different complaints. . . .[33]

These comments — especially the latter two — explicitly acknowledge the relation of *social background* to judicial decision-making and judicial outcomes.

Some Concluding Remarks

As the American political system has evolved, courts have come to play an important role in determining who gets what, when and how. The intimate nature of this involvement was set out early by John Marshall in *Marbury* v. *Madison* (1803). Here Marshall reasoned (assumed) that the Constitution empowered the Court with judicial review, the authority to review acts of the Congress, president and others as to their constitutionality. In short, according to Marshall, it belonged to the judiciary, and no one else, to have the final say as to what the Constitution means. While this assertion of judicial authority has been challenged from time to time, it has nonetheless become firmly engrained as part of our constitutional–legal structure. It comes as no surprise then, as de Tocqueville observed long ago, that sooner or later courts become involved in the major political issues of the day.

But *how* and *for what ends* judges exercise judicial review has been a subject of continuous debate among judges themselves and others. Among the many schools of thought that have resulted from this debate two stand out: **judicial self-restraint** and **judicial activism.** Murphy and Pritchett describe vividly those who embrace these two views.

Advocates of self-restraint stress the dangers to judicial prestige and the damage to the judicial image if judges become entangled in debate over proper public policies. The continued acceptance of judicial authority, it is argued, depends on the maintenance of a mystique of judicial aloofness and noninvolvement in political matters. Problems of policy are for politicians, not judges, to decide. "Courts are not representative bodies," wrote Justice Frankfurter, the leading spokesman for judicial restraint, in *Dennis* v. *United States* (1951). "They are not designed to be a good reflex of a democratic society." The restrained judge sees his major task as the skillful manipulation of judicial techniques. He submerges himself in the judicial

---

[33] Ibid., 260 at 270.

tradition and thinks of himself as dominated by roles with tightly prescribed limitations and expectations.

The activist judge, on the other hand, may be described as goal-
oriented. His interest in achieving the "right" result in the controversies
that come before him is stronger than his interest in the process by which
the court arrives at the result. His tests for the rightness of a decision are
whether it is politically and morally acceptable and whether its effects will
be beneficial to society. Since he views law as one form of social control, he
will be more creative in developing new legal doctrines to support his
conclusions about public policy and more willing to overrule precedents
that stand in the way of desired results. He is less hesitant to challenge the
political branches and less fearful of becoming involved in controversy.[34]

Thus, the debate over judicial review is not so much over whether
courts *should have* such authority, but over *how and when* it should be
used.

We should again emphasize that as far as the involvement of the
judiciary in politics is concerned, it does not matter whether a judge
takes an "activist" or a "self-restraint" position. For, as Peltason has
stated: "[Courts] are in the political process . . . not as a matter of choice
but as a matter of function."[35] Those judges who *do not* wish to become
involved are supporting certain interests as much as those judges who
do become involved. And this involvement, of course, concerns not only
judicial review, but also the role of courts in applying and enforcing
statutes. Indeed, as discussed earlier, what a particular statute means is,
in many instances, what courts say it means.

Overall, the participation of courts in both constitutional and statutory interpretation has increased the visibility of the judiciary in politics.
As a consequence, the role of courts generally has grown in political
importance for blacks and other minorities. And blacks who have gained
judicial positions do not seem reluctant to use this "awesome state
power," as one black judge put it,[36] to overcome injustices in the
political system. Thus black judges will more often than not be found
supporting and practicing "judicial activism."

The judicial process is the focal point of bringing about change
through *law*. But we cannot overlook the broad influence of lawyers in
that process. Lawyers, as we have indicated, are the "gatekeepers" to
the judicial forum. They determine, in large measure, what issues are
brought to courts and how those issues will be shaped for final determination. More than this, what the lawyers say in their **briefs, oral argu-**

---

[34] Murphy and Pritchett, *Courts, Judges, and Politics*, pp. 30-31.
[35] Peltason, *Federal Courts in the Political Process*, p. 3.
[36] George W. Crockett, Jr., "Racism in the Courts," 20 *Journal of Public Law* 385 at 388
(1971).

ments (and law reviews) can go far in determining judicial outcomes on particular questions. In short, lawyers are an indispensable part of the judge's "company." And, as we have seen, those who become judges are themselves selected from among, and in large measure by, lawyers and the legal profession. However, because there are few black lawyers, there are also few black judges. In view of their importance in American political life, the small number of blacks in the legal profession is another example of the unequal distribution of political resources. For lawyers and the law play important and sometimes crucial roles in determining what changes can (or will) come through the political process.

In the next chapter we offer a closer examination of the interaction between courts, judges, lawyers and others in attempting to bring about change through the judicial process.

Topics for Discussion

1. The authors have outlined the important powers that courts have in the American political process. *Should* courts have such powers? Why or why not?

2. Lawyers and the legal profession exercise a very crucial and dominant influence in American politics. What is the basis of this influence? *Should* lawyers (as opposed to other groups and professions) exercise such influence?

3. The number of blacks in the legal profession is very small. Blacks comprise less than 3 percent of the legal profession in America. *How* and *in what ways* does this shortage of black lawyers disadvantage blacks in American politics? Discuss.

4. Discuss the advantages and disadvantages of black lawyers being primarily engaged in private (neighborhood) practice as opposed to corporate practice or practice in a large firm. What are the costs/benefits to the black community and to black politics generally as a result of this predominance of black lawyers in private (neighborhood) practice in contrast to the very few black lawyers in the other types of practice?

5. The "selection variables" referred to by the authors in choosing federal judges inevitably mean that few black and minority judges will be chosen. Do you agree or disagree with this statement? Are there different selection criteria you would suggest? What are they and will they result in an increase of black representation in the "third" branch?

Suggested Readings

Abraham, Henry J. *Justices and Presidents: A Political History of Appointments to the Supreme Court.* New York: Oxford University Press, 1974.

An historical analysis of the president's role in the selection of Supreme Court Justices.

Bickel, Alexander. *The Least Dangerous Branch: The Supreme Court at Bar of American Politics.* Indianapolis: Bobbs-Merrill, 1962.

Attempt to chart an appropriate role for the Court.

Black, Charles L., Jr. *The People and the Court.* Englewood Cliffs, N.J.: Prentice-Hall, 1960.

A vigorous defense of the importance of judicial review in the American political system.

Cardozo, Benjamin. *The Nature of the Judicial Process.* New Haven: Yale University Press, 1921.

A former judge and associate justice of the U.S. Supreme Court gives an unusually vivid description of his view of the role of judges and the nature of judicial decision-making.

Casper, Jonathan D. *Lawyers Before the Warren Court: Civil Liberties and Civil Rights.* Urbana, Ill.: University of Illinois Press, 1972.

A study of lawyers who argued civil liberties and civil rights cases before the Warren Court.

Chase, Harold. *Federal Judges.* Minneapolis: University of Minnesota Press, 1972.

An examination of the appointment process of federal judges during the Eisenhower, Kennedy, and Johnson administrations.

Cook, Beverly. "Black Representation in the Third Branch," *Black Law Journal,* Vol. I, No. 1 (Spring, 1971).

Crockett, George W., Jr. "Racism in the Court," 20 *Journal of Public Law* (1971).

A dynamic exposition of how racism is interwoven in the American judicial process.

Crockett, George W., Jr. "The Role of the Black Judge, 20 *Journal of Public Law* (1971).

A black judge attempts to define the role of black judges in a predominately white judicial process.

Edwards, Harry T. "The New Role for the Black Law Graduate — A Reality or an Illusion?" 2 *Black Law Journal* 21 (1972).

A study of the present and potential job and status possibilities of blacks in the legal profession.

Eisenstein, James. *Politics and the Legal Process.* New York: Harper & Row, 1973.

An evaluation of the role, function, and interaction of various participants in the legal process.

Goldman, Sheldon and Thomas P. Jahnige. *The Federal Courts as a Political System.* New York: Harper & Row, 1971.

Viewing the federal courts as a political system within the American scheme of government.

Grossman, Joel. *Lawyers and Judges: The ABA and the Politics of Judicial Selection.* New York: John Wiley & Sons, 1965.

A detailed study of the role of the American Bar Association in the selection of federal judges.

Jacob, Herbert. *Justice in America.* 2nd ed. Boston: Little, Brown, 1972.

A systematic overview of the nature, structure, and role of American courts in the political system.

Jacob, Herbert. *Urban Justice: Law and Order in American Cities.* Englewood Cliffs, N.J.: Prentice-Hall, 1973.

Focuses on the administration of justice in urban areas.

Krislov, Samuel. *The Supreme Court in the Political Process.* New York: Macmillan Company, 1965.

A concise and very readable analysis of the role of the Supreme Court in American politics.

Murphy, Walter and C. Herman Pritchett. *Courts, Judges and Politics.* 2nd ed. New York: Random House, 1974.

A valuable collection of essays and readings that describe the role and functioning of courts in the American political system.

Peltason, Jack W. *Federal Courts in the Political Process*. New York: Random House, 1962.

Pioneer work on role and interaction of courts in the political system.

Schuman, Jerome. "A Black Lawyers' Survey." 16 *Howard Law Journal* 225 (1971).

Data and discussion on the status of black lawyers in the legal profession.

6

CHANGE THROUGH LAW:
COURTS AND POLICY-MAKING

. . . Litigation is not a technique of resolving private differences; it is a means for achieving the lawful objectives
of equality of treatment by all government, federal, state
and local, for the members of the Negro community in this
country. It is thus a form of political expression. Groups
which find themselves unable to achieve their objectives
through the ballot frequently turn to the courts. Just as it
was true of the opponents of New Deal legislation during
the 1930's, no less is it true of the Negro minority today.
And under the conditions of modern government, litigation may well be the sole practicable avenue open to a
minority to petition for redress of grievances. . . .

Justice William J. Brennan, Jr.
(N.A.A.C.P. v. Button, 371 U.S. 415 at 429–430, 1963)

It might be that there are some issues on which the
judiciary must act as a safety valve for the elected political
branches, providing leadership when it is reasonably ascertained that the elected institutions are either unwilling
or unable to act. This does not mean that in every instance
where elected institutions fail to act, the Court must step
in. Such a notion simplifies too much, both the delicate
operation of our governing system as well as the role of
the Court in that system. On the contrary, by deciding
and fashioning policy on such issues, the Court gives to
the governing system that necessary viability and capacity
needed to survive.
. . . There remains the inescapable and hard responsibility for judges no less than for other policy makers to try

as best they can to assume and fulfill their proper roles while carrying on the practical operation of a government under law. Law and tradition help chart particular roles, especially for judges, but law and tradition cannot chart automatic roles for the complex business of governing, not even for judges. Judgment (discretion) inevitably remains.

Lucius J. Barker, "Third Parties in Litigation: A Systemic View of the Judicial Function"*

Introduction

In the previous chapter we discussed the role of law and courts in the political system. The uniqueness of that role is highlighted by the authority of American courts to exercise judicial review. How courts exercise this authority and for what ends inevitably brings them into the business of policy-making. It also brings them into the thick of political controversy. The history of the Supreme Court in dealing with civil rights questions, especially since 1954, clearly shows these various factors. Particularly does it shed light on the role of the court in the political system, and the nature and limitations of the judiciary in forming public policy. In the present chapter we consider these matters. We will give special attention to how the transition from the Warren Court to the Burger Court has affected civil rights policy and the aspirations of black Americans generally.

Courts, Policy-Making, and Civil Rights

Prior to the Civil Rights Act of 1964 the political branches had done almost nothing to deal with the problem facing blacks in America. The Civil Rights Act of 1957 — the first such legislation passed by Congress since Reconstruction — and the later Civil Rights Act of 1960 were little more than sympathetic gestures toward civil rights interests. It was not until the passage of the 1964 Act that the political branches at

---

* *The Journal of Politics*, Vol. 29 (February, 1967) No. 1, pp. 63-65. Reprinted with permission.

last began to come to grips with the problem. But, as we shall see, the 1964 Act did not just come about. Dire circumstances and enormous resources created the environment conducive to its passage. A crucial element in this environment was the strong support given blacks by the Warren Court, beginning with the famous *Brown* decision of 1954. Indeed, the Warren Court did not shy away from the problem of race. It met and directly addressed issues that had long been brushed aside and stymied in the political process. In so doing, the Supreme Court engaged in policy-making not unlike other political institutions.

Courts in many ways are the forums of last resort, especially for those who are politically disadvantaged. The resources needed to achieve desired objectives through the judicial process are much more attainable and available to minorities than those needed to prevail in the political process. It stands to reason then that blacks who were (and are) certainly disadvantaged in the political system have for some time resorted to the judiciary rather than to the political branches to protect their interests. These efforts were primarily the work of the NAACP and later the NAACP Legal Defense staff. Here was a small group of lawyers whose only armor included the good will and help of a large lay organization (NAACP); a modest amount of money coming mainly from voluntary contributions; courageous litigants with good causes; and most important the keen intellect and endless devotion of the legal staff itself which made good cases out of good causes. The successes achieved by the NAACP, although limited, give support to those who argue for a legal strategy to resolve *the problem*.

Yet, the emergence of the Burger Court suggests that judicial victories, like political victories, are not etched in concrete. The fact that the Burger Court seems bent on reading the Constitution differently from the Warren Court illustrates vividly that the meaning of the Constitution (and law) is not fixed and unchanging. Indeed, that law and the courts stand as barriers to the tyranny of the majority is not at all certain. In fact, time and again we are reminded of the reverse — that law and courts are indeed instruments of majority rule. If judges interpret the law contrary to persistent majorities, sooner or later the judges (and the law) will change. Whether this *should* be the case in a democratic government — as the government of the United States is described — is not of concern here. What does matter is that blacks and others who place their hopes and trust in courts should be aware that the nature of law and the judiciary is anything but static. Though blacks were greatly encouraged by actions of the Warren Court, the Supreme Court of earlier years had much to do with legitimating and perpetuating the very racial inequities with which the Warren Court and the national government had to deal. Let us take a brief look at history.

Constitutionalizing Racism: Its Birth and Decline

Decisions of the Supreme Court did much to *constitutionalize* racism. They helped create a climate conducive to fostering rather than eliminating racial segregation. (For a more detailed review of some earlier decisions see Chapter 1, pp. 12–22.) In the *Civil Rights Cases* (1883), for example, the Court rebuffed attempts of the Reconstruction Congress effectively to get rid of some of the badges and incidents of slavery. In 1875 Congress had passed the first public accommodations statute in history. It forbid racial segregation in various places of accommodation open to the public — for example, hotels, inns, theaters. But the Supreme Court ruled that neither the Thirteenth nor the Fourteenth Amendment provided constitutional support for the congressional action. A significant holding of the Court in that case was that the Fourteenth Amendment applied to **"state" action** and not to **"private" action** (that is, to action by individuals). Privately owned accommodations could discriminate among their customers without fear of constitutional restrictions. This *state-private* action distinction of the *Civil Rights Cases* has not been wholly abandoned. But its effect has been largely overcome by the 1964 Civil Rights Act and by subsequent decisions of the Warren Court. Nonetheless, the decision in the *Civil Rights Cases* in 1883 reflected the waning of Reconstruction policies in the South and the return of white control/black subordination in that region.

An even more ominous decision, as we discussed in Chapter 1, was made by the Court in *Plessy* v. *Ferguson* (1896). In this case, the Court upheld a Louisiana statute that required racial segregation of passengers on trains as a valid exercise of state police power. Specifically, the Court held that segregation of the races was not the discrimination proscribed by the equal protection clause of the Fourteenth Amendment. In short, classification by race was not arbitrary and without reason and was within the state's authority. States, under this formula, could provide separate facilities for the races if they were equal. Here then, the Court sanctioned "separate but equal." In so doing it effectively constitutionalized racism. To be sure, state laws and practices certainly treated blacks *separately*, but not at all *equally*. The *Plessy* decision, in effect, legitimated racial segregation not only in transportation, but in every aspect of life including education, voting, public accommodations, employment, and so on.

Take education, for example. Just three years after *Plessy*, the Court upheld the actions of a Georgia county school board in maintaining a high school for whites but discontinuing a high school for blacks because of financial difficulties (*Cumming* v. *Board of Education*, 1899). The Court reasoned that the black high school was discontinued temporarily for economic reasons and did not indicate that the school board was discriminating because of race. In this way, the Court got around the constitutional issue of segregation. But once again blacks (and minorities) suffered because of the state authorities' (and now the Supreme Court) decision. Likewise, the Court avoided the racial segregation issue in two other school cases. In *Berea College* v. *Kentucky*, 1908 (Berea is a private college), the Court sustained a Kentucky law that required segregation of blacks and whites in both public and private institutions as a valid regulation by the state of corporate charters. In the second case, *Gong Lum* v. *Rice*, 1927, the Court upheld Mississippi in its exclusion of Orientals from white public schools. This Court action upheld Mississippi segregation laws generally and gave them constitutional legitimacy.

Some change in the Supreme Court stance toward racial segregation in public education began to surface in 1938 in a Missouri law school case (*Missouri* ex rel *Gaines* v. *Canada*). Missouri maintained a law school for whites but refused to accept blacks. Missouri did, however, offer blacks scholarships to attend law schools outside the state. This "out-of-state scholarship" arrangement became one of the many avenues used by southern states to foster racial segregation. However, the Court ruled that where the state did maintain certain educational opportunities for whites, it must furnish such opportunities to all of its residents "upon the basis of an equality of right." More importantly, the Court gave notice that it would begin to scrutinize more closely the "equal" part of the "separate but equal" doctrine (*Pearson* v. *Murray*, 1936). But Missouri and five southern states (Texas, Louisiana, Florida, North Carolina and South Carolina) responded to the Court decision in *Gaines* by establishing separate law schools for blacks. This action quite naturally led to legal challenges as to the standard of equality required by the "equal protection clause" of the Fourteenth Amendment.

The Texas law school case (*Sweatt* v. *Painter*, 1950) provided the opportunity for the Supreme Court to explain the meaning of the "equal protection" provided by the "separate but equal" formula. While not overturning "separate but equal," the Court ruled that the legal education Texas had offered to blacks was not equal to that provided by the state to whites. And most importantly, the Court defined equality in such a way as to signal the end of "separate but equal." In terms of faculty, curriculum, size of student body, and scope of the library, the University of Texas law school was superior to the law school for blacks. Chief Justice Vinson, who spoke for the Court, reasoned that:

What is more important, the University of Texas Law School possesses to a far greater degree those qualities which are incapable of objective measurement but which make for greatness in a law school. Such qualities, to name but a few, include reputation of the faculty, experience of the administration, position and influence of the alumni, standing in the community, traditions and prestige. It is difficult to believe that one who had a free choice between the law schools would consider the question close.

That the "separate but equal" doctrine was being subjected to a more rigid test was also evidenced by another 1950 Supreme Court decision, *McLaurin* v. *Oklahoma*. McLaurin, a black graduate student, was admitted to the University of Oklahoma but was segregated from white students through special seating arrangements in classrooms, and in the use of the library and cafeteria. The Court ruled that the Fourteenth Amendment (equal protection) required that black students (in this instance McLaurin) be accorded the same treatment as other students. In general *Sweatt* and *McLaurin*, though at the professional and graduate school level, signalled the declining support of the Supreme Court for racial segregation. And, as we shall see later, while the Court finally declared "separate but equal" unconstitutional, it can never be forgotten that the Court (and the judiciary generally) supported and furthered racial segregation in education.

Political participation by blacks in voting provides another example of how decisions of the Supreme Court legitimated racism in America. It was not until 1944, for example, that the Court finally declared the **white primary** unconstitutional as a deprivation of the Fifteenth Amendment (*Smith* v. *Allwright*). Though the focus of the litigation was in Texas, the white primary was one of the chief methods used by southern states to prevent blacks from voting and from participating in politics generally. (Of course, many other devices were used to disfranchise blacks including the "grandfather clause," the poll tax, and literacy tests. The **grandfather clause** was declared unconstitutional in 1915, but the **poll tax** and literacy tests were not overcome until the 1960's through combined efforts of the Court and the Congress.) The "white primary" was as simple as it was effective. Since the Democratic party was the dominant party in the South, and since the winner of that primary was inevitably the winner of the general election, the way to prevent blacks from having any real effect on the election of southern officeholders was to prevent them from joining the Democratic party and hence voting in that party's primary election. But in 1944, the Supreme Court overruled one of its earlier decisions and held that the primary was not the "private" affair of the Democratic party. The Court ruled that the party (and its primary) was so enmeshed in and supported by state law and state election machinery that it had become an agent of the state. Consequently, if the party engaged in racial discrimination, its actions amounted to "state action" forbidden by the Fifteenth Amendment.

Blacks suffered inequities and deprivations as a result of discrimination in other areas as well. In addition to education and politics, the plight of blacks and other minorities in their efforts to obtain jobs and housing, to gain service in places of public accommodations, were similarly stymied by laws and legal action. As we shall see later, it was only after the 1954 *Brown* decision and well into the 1960's before the national government began to act to improve the quality of life for blacks and other minorities in these areas. But even these actions, as we shall also see, have still not secured equality of treatment and opportunity for blacks in this country. Nonetheless, just as in the past, the Supreme Court (and the judiciary generally) continue to play an important role.

The importance of the Court's role to policy outcome is demonstrated by the generally favorable position of the Warren Court toward racial problems. But, the early position of the Burger Court shows that the role of the Court is subject to change. The remainder of this chapter examines how the law of the Warren Court has been and is being changed by the law of the Burger Court. Hopefully, this discussion will explain the role and limitations of courts as instruments of policy-making and social change. The study of the Warren and Burger Courts is followed by a brief examination of factors that affect the impact of and compliance with Court decisions.

The Supreme Court from Warren to Burger: Implications for Black Americans and the Political System*

In recent years there has been considerable commentary on the posture of the Burger Court toward black Americans and civil rights interests. During the Warren era, the Supreme Court was generally pictured as supporting these interests. However, under Chief Justice Warren Burger, this image of the Supreme Court seems to be fading. Former President Nixon's 1968 campaign pledge to reverse the trends of the Warren Court by appointing "strict constructionists" to the Court appears to be meeting with some success. After less than three years in office, Mr. Nixon had the rare opportunity to fill four vacancies on the nine-man court, including the office of Chief Justice.[1] The long

---

* Adapted and revised with permission from Lucius J. Barker, "Black Americans and the Burger Court: Implications for the Political System," *Washington University Law Quarterly* (Fall, 1973), pp. 747-77. A few footnotes have been omitted and others revised to coincide with revisions.

[1] Over the history of the Court, Robert Dahl has found that a president can expect to appoint one new justice about every 21 months, or about two new justices during one term of office. See generally Robert Dahl, "Decision-Making in a Democracy: The Supreme Court as a National Policy-Maker," 6 *Journal of Public Law* (1957).

confirmation battles that attended several of these nominations, plus the behavior of the Nixon appointees once on the Court, show clearly that some changes in the Court's decision-making were expected and are indeed coming about.

The central purpose here is to view these changes in the broader context of the role and importance of the Supreme Court in helping blacks (and others) to achieve their objectives within the political system as it presently operates. This framework allows us to see clearly several factors concerning the Court's role in policy-making and conflict resolution. For example, how might changes in the decisions made by the Warren and Burger Courts affect those groups and interests that have resorted to the judiciary (and with some success) in pursuit of their objectives? How might this changed posture and, indeed, role of the Court affect the political system's capability to deal with these problems? What implications does this changed posture and role of the Court have with respect to the role and function of other political institutions, primarily Congress and the presidency? What implications does this change in function and role of the Court have for the future function and role of the Court itself? What implications might this phenomenon have for the governing system generally?

This case study covers several policy issue areas. A major portion of the study discusses the position of the Warren and Burger Courts regarding racial segregation. In addition, we will examine the general stance of the two Courts on the developing area of poverty law (rights of the poor), and rights of persons accused of crime. That policies in these two areas are nonracial on the surface should not obscure their practical and often critical influence in the everyday life of black Americans. The last part of the study focuses on the implications that the change from the Warren Court to the Burger Court might hold for blacks and the political system.

The Warren Court and Racial Discrimination

The School Segregation Cases (*Brown* v. *Board of Education*, 1954) set the tone that the Warren Court was to follow in matters relating to racial segregation. The tone was one of "great policy pronouncement" followed by less grandiose and certainly less definite decisions to implement such policies. Concerning school segregation, for example, the Court boldly declared that black schools where racial segregation was based upon law were inherently unequal. In short, racial segregation in public school education was unconstitutional. But the Court hedged in 1955 when it made its decision to implement the 1954 policy. The force of the Court's decision was blunted both by its **remanding** (sending back) cases to federal district courts and by the flexibility given those courts to implement school desegregation "with all deliberate speed." In later decisions, the Warren Court had to deal bit by bit with a variety of schemes and strategies designed to circumvent the decision. But the Court did so, finding most of these schemes unconstitutional. Moreover, the Court applied the principle of its 1954 *Brown* decision to other areas that involved public facilities such as parks and recreational facilities.

Then in the 1960's when the elective political institutions joined the battle, the Court found ways to legitimate their legislative response to civil rights demands. The Civil Rights Act of 1964, for example, was by far the most pervasive such legislation since Reconstruction. It forbade discrimination against persons in places of public accommodation and in employment. The Act also provided substantial new weapons to fight against discrimination, including a mandate to cut off federal funds to agencies that practice discrimination. Nonetheless, despite strong constitutional challenges and precedents (especially the *Civil Rights Cases* of 1883), the Warren Court supported this congressional exercise of legislative authority.

The Court also handed down important decisions concerning racial segregation in housing. For example, the Court declared unconstitutional California's attempt to incorporate a policy in its state constitution that would permit racial segregation in the sale or rental of housing (*Reitman* v. *Mulkey*, 1967). This was an especially important decision since Proposition 14, by which the California constitutional amendment was popularly known, was put into the state constitution by popular referendum through a majority vote in the 1964 election. This constitutional amendment in effect repealed existing state fair housing laws. The importance of the Court decision is that it signalled that a popular vote even to amend a state's constitution cannot be used as a way to overcome or to impair constitutionally guaranteed rights. The debate within the Court highlighted the division of opinion that existed not only on this question, but on the role of the Court generally. The majority saw Proposition 14 as intending to authorize, and authorizing, racial discrimination in housing. As such the Court believed that it would significantly encourage and involve the state in private discrimination. Such state involvement would, of course, be unconstitutional.

But the dissenters, speaking through Mr. Justice Harlan, thought the decision was not only "constitutionally *un*sound, but in its practical potentialities short-sighted." Harlan said that opponents of state antidiscrimination statutes now had additional reason for opposing enactment of such legislation, namely, because once enacted they may be unrepealable. He thought this most unfortunate since "the lines that have been and must be drawn" with respect to the "delicate and troublesome problems" in the area of race relations, "fraught as it is with human sensibilities and frailties of whatever race or creed, are difficult ones," and should be left to political processes. Said Harlan:

> Here the electorate itself overwhelmingly wished to overrule and check its own legislature on a matter left open by the Federal Constitution. By refusing to accept the decision of the people of California, and by contriving a new and ill-defined constitutional concept to allow federal judicial interference, I think the Court has taken to itself powers and responsibilities left elsewhere by the Constitution.

But despite this sharp dissent — one that focused on the role of the Court in the political system — the Warren Court majority had once again provided legal support for those interested in fighting racial segregation.

Another important housing decision was that of *Jones* v. *Mayer* (1968). The Court held that a provision of the Civil Rights Act of 1866 that guarantees blacks the same right "enjoyed by whites . . . to inherit, purchase, lease, sell, hold, and convey real and personal property" prohibits racial discrimination in the sale of housing by a private developer. Justice Stewart, who spoke for the majority, concluded that the statute's language was "plain and unambiguous" in its declaration of property rights available to all citizens. "[O]n its face [it] . . . appears to prohibit all discrimination against Negroes in sale or rental of property." The importance of this decision cannot be overestimated: it came just two months after the passage of the 1968 Fair Housing Law. This statute prohibits racial discrimination in 80 percent of the nation's housing. But the effect of the *Jones* decision is to extend such policy to cover the remaining 20 percent of the housing market. The dissenters, Harlan and White, attacked the majority opinion. They said that the action was "most ill-considered and ill-advised" since the political branches had enacted a fair housing law geared to the current dynamics of society. But the heart of Harlan's dissent is that neither the 1866 Act nor its legislative history support the majority conclusion that the Act was to extend to private action.

In another decision, the Warren Court interpreted the Civil Rights Act of 1964 to cover a privately owned recreational facility that catered to interstate travelers. The Court brushed aside attempts of the recreational facility to evade the act by becoming a "private club." In so doing it gave particular scrutiny to the operations and services of the "club." The decision had significant implications for one of the remaining symbols of white racism in America, the so-called private club.

There are of course many other decisions rendered by the Warren Court dealing with the problems of racial injustice. (See the Suggested

Readings at the end of this chapter for further literature on the Warren Court.) Our central point here is that by and large civil rights causes found strong representation in the Warren Court.

Crime and Poverty: Old Problems, New Law

The Warren Court also fashioned new law in certain areas that could properly be termed nonracial; in practice, however, they have great relevance to the everyday life of blacks. For example, in strengthening the rights of those accused of crime, the Warren Court must have been aware of the importance of these rights to the civil rights revolution. As one commentator aptly put it:

> The Court's concern with criminal procedure can be understood only in the context of the struggle for civil rights. . . . Concern with civil rights almost inevitably required attention to the rights of defendants in criminal cases. It is hard to conceive of a Court that would accept the challenge of guaranteeing the rights of Negroes and other disadvantaged groups to equality before the law and at the same time do nothing to ameliorate the invidious discrimination between rich and poor which existed in the original process. It would have been equally anomalous for such a Court to ignore the clear evidence that members of disadvantaged groups generally bore the brunt of most unlawful police activity.[2]

In any event, beginning in 1961 the Warren Court brought about major changes in our criminal law.

Essentially what the Court did was to make certain provisions of the Bill of Rights, which govern criminal procedures in federal courts, applicable to states also. The Court held and insisted that states, just as federal authorities, must provide certain guarantees to those accused of crime. Such guarantees included the right to assistance of counsel (*Gideon* v. *Wainwright*, 1963, and *U.S.* v. *Wade*, 1967); the right to be free from self-incrimination (*Griffen* v. *California*, 1965, *Miranda* v. *Arizona*, 1966); and the right to be free from unreasonable searches and seizures by excluding evidence secured through such means (*Mapp* v. *Ohio*, 1961).

Similarly, in the emerging area of poverty law,[3] the Warren Court also tended to protect the rights of the poor. As mentioned earlier, the

---

[2] A. Kenneth Pye, "The Warren Court and Criminal Procedure," in Richard H. Sayler, Barry B. Boyer, and Robert E. Gooding, Jr., eds., *The Warren Court* (New York: Chelsea House, 1969), p. 65.

[3] For a summary overview of this developing area of the law, see "A Note on The Supreme Court and The Legal Needs of The Poor," in Joel Grossman and Richard Wells, *Constitutional Law and Judicial Policy Making* (New York: John Wiley & Sons, Inc., 1972), pp. 767–74.

Court strengthened such rights in the enforcement and administration of criminal justice. It also struck down the poll tax in voting as an unconstitutional burden on poor persons. Further, in *Shapiro* v. *Thompson* (1968), the Court held the one-year residency requirement for public welfare assistance unconstitutional as violating the Equal Protection Clause of the Fourteenth Amendment. Moreover, in one of its last decisions, the Warren Court found as violating "due process" a Wisconsin prejudgment garnishment of wages procedure that allowed the wages of garnishees to be frozen without notice or prior hearing. And Justice Douglas' opinion for the Court in this case, over the bitter dissent of Justice Black, demonstrates vividly how the Warren Court interpreted the Constitution to take account of the plight of poor people.

The Warren Court and Civil Rights: An Overview

We have attempted to indicate thus far the general thrust of the Warren Court on racial segregation and related problems. In general, the Court seems to have protected and expanded the constitutional rights of black Americans, as well as individuals generally, against governmental authority. True, there were Court decisions out of line with this general posture. And in large measure the Warren Court could be viewed as merely attempting to right many of the wrongs that had previously been judicially approved. In the area of racial segregation, for example, Lewis Steele makes some plausible arguments that the decisions of the Supreme Court, including those of the Warren Court, were rendered by "Nine Men in Black Who Think White." [4]

Overall, however, it seems that the importance of the Warren Court is that by acting on certain problems of racial segregation, the Court helped to place racial problems generally on both the formal and informal agendas of other political institutions. The very symbolic effects of a Supreme Court decision, such as that in *Brown*, forced many Americans — including Congress, the president, state officials and others — to begin to consider *seriously*, not just ceremonially, the general plight of a very large segment of its people. Even so, however, serious attention that resulted in some concrete actions by the president and Congress did not take place until more dramatic actions — demonstrations, riots, and violence — forced these institutions to give such problems a high priority on a national agenda that is always filled.

---

[4] See Lewis Steele in the *New York Times Magazine*, October 13, 1968, pp. 56–57ff.

Wide World Photos.

New judges, new trends: the Burger Court. Members of the Supreme Court from left: front row — Associate Justices Potter Stewart, William O. Douglas, Chief Justice Warren E. Burger, Associate Justices William J. Brennan, Jr., and Byron R. White; back row — Associate Justices Lewis F. Powell, Jr., Thurgood Marshall, Harry A. Blackmun, and William H. Rehnquist.

New Judges, New Trends: The Burger Court

Generally, the Burger Court has tempered the trend and tone of the Warren Court in combatting racial segregation and discrimination. To be certain, the Court has continued to pursue the command of *Brown* v. *Board of Education* to eliminate racial segregation in public schools. In 1969, for example, the Court unanimously held against the attempts of the Justice Department to delay beginning integration plans in certain Mississippi school districts. In so doing the Court stated again the formula established late in the Warren Court era that integration of public schools must begin "at once." They tried to eliminate any fears of a return to the "all deliberate speed" guideline of *Brown*. Further, in

Swann v. *Charlotte-Mecklenburg Board of Education* (1971) the Court approved busing as a judicial tool in integrating public school districts in which officials had deliberately created or enforced a "dual" system on racial lines. *Swann* granted federal judges wide discretion to establish remedial measures in combatting state-enforced segregation. At the same time, however, *Swann* may be seen by lower courts as lessening judicial presence in this area, especially if in their view a unitary school system has been achieved.

In *Keyes* v. *School District No. 1, Denver, Colorado* (1973) the Court declined to build on the "activism" of the Warren Court's desegregation decisions. It continued to recognize the distinction between de facto and **de jure segregation**. *Keyes* did put northern school districts on notice that where intentional segregation occurred in particular units within a school district, those units must be desegregated. It also held that the burden of proving that a policy of intentional segregation in that unit did not demonstrate a segregative intent with respect to the entire district rested on the defendant school board. *Keyes* shows important legal support for improving the quality of education for minority school children in northern areas. But one cannot help but note the apparent gradual steps of the Court in judging constitutional rights of black and other minority children. Specifically, the Court's reluctance to abandon the de jure/de facto distinction in determining the constitutional rights of minority school children and the obligations of school districts seriously slows down meaningful changes of racial balances in the North. The Court continues to be unwilling to deal squarely with the inequities faced by minorities in de facto segregated school systems. Yet, their effects on minorities are identical to those of de jure segregation. As a consequence, the Court places on blacks and other minorities the "initial tortuous effort" of showing segregative intent before constitutional guarantees come into play.

Two other decisions of the Burger Court may be viewed as supporting the interests of black Americans. In *Griggs* v. *Duke Power Co.* (1971) a unanimous Court declared invalid under Title VII of the Civil Rights Act of 1964 a standardized intelligence test. The effect of this test had been to bar a disproportionate number of blacks from employment. Although the test was "neutral," or not intended to discriminate against blacks, it was not "directed or intended to measure the ability to learn to perform a particular job or category of jobs." Without a "demonstrable relationship" to job performance, concluded the Court, any "artificial, arbitrary, and unnecessary barriers to employment [which] operate invidiously to discriminate" cannot stand. And in *Griffin* v. *Breckenridge* (1971) a unanimous Court construed an earlier civil rights statute to permit suits for damages for racially motivated private conspiracies to commit violence in deprivation of civil rights, despite an earlier decision restricting the statute to conspiracies under color of state law.

When considered in context, however, the promise of these decisions has been clouded by other actions of the Burger Court. Indeed, despite these decisions judicial policies toward racial justice generally appear to have taken on a negative, or at least a more restraining, tone. For example, Chief Justice Burger himself, in denying a stay of a lower court desegregation order, somewhat blurred the effect of the Court's busing decision.[5] In an unusual ten-page memorandum, he interpreted the Court's decision in *Swann*. He thought *Swann* was being misinterpreted by lower courts which read the decision as requiring a fixed racial balance or quota. But whatever his intention, it seems clear that Chief Justice Burger's memorandum softened the impact of the Court's decision that busing may be used to effect public school integration. In addition, the Court's first attempt to decide the "city-suburbs" (inter-district) busing issue was left essentially unresolved by a 4-4 deadlock.[6]

Still other actions of the Burger Court indicate its apparent trend away from the strong support given blacks by the Warren Court. For example, in *Whitcomb* v. *Chavis* (1971) the Burger Court rebuffed the efforts of blacks to gain political representation in the Indiana legislature. Blacks had alleged that the Indiana statutes that established Marion County (Indianapolis) as a **multi-member district** for the election of state senators and representatives deprived them of a realistic opportunity to win elections. Specifically, they charged that the laws diluted their votes in the predominantly black inner-city areas of Indianapolis. A three-judge federal district court agreed with this position. But the Supreme Court overturned the lower court decision, 6-3. Chief Justice Burger and Justice Blackmun voted with the majority. Justice White, who wrote for the Court, said there was no suggestion that the multi-member district in Marion County or similar districts in the state were "conceived or operated as purposeful devices to further racial or economic discrimination." Justice White maintained that "the failure of the ghetto to have legislative seats in proportion to its population emerges more as a function of losing elections than of built-in bias against poor Negroes." He specifically disagreed with the trial court's view that inner-city voters could not be adequately or equally represented unless some of Marion County's general assembly seats were reserved for such residents serving the interests of the inner-city majority. "The mere fact," said Justice White, "that one interest group or another concerned with the outcome of Marion County elections has found itself outvoted and without legislative seats of its own provides no basis for invoking constitutional remedies where, as here, there is no indication that this segment of the population is being denied access to the political sys-

---

[5] See *The New York Times*, September 1, 1971, p. 1.

[6] *School Board* v. *State Board of Education* (1973). (Referred to hereafter as *Richmond, Va.* case.) The case is discussed in greater detail later in this chapter.

tem." Furthermore, reasoned Justice White, to uphold the position of one racial group would make it difficult to reject claims of any other groups — for example, Republicans, Democrats, or organized labor — who find themselves similarly disadvantaged.

But Justice Douglas, joined by Justices Brennan and Marshall, filed a strong dissenting opinion in *Whitcomb*. Justice Douglas supported the position of the district court that "a showing of racial motivation is not necessary when dealing with multi-member districts." Justice Douglas maintained that the test of constitutionality for multi-member districts is whether there are "invidious effects," and that in this case the test was met by a showing of (1) an identifiable voting group; (2) discrepancies of representation between middle and lower class townships; (3) the "pervasive influence of the county organizations of the political parties"; and (4) the "undifferentiated positions" of legislators on political issues. Justice Douglas compared multi-member districting to **gerrymandering** in that both "dilute" or "surround" the minority vote, causing the requisite segregative effect. He concluded, "Our cases since *Baker* v. *Carr* have never intimated that 'one man, one vote' meant 'one white man, one vote.' "

Further evidence of eroding judicial support for civil rights interests was reflected by the Burger Court in *Palmer* v. *Thompson* (1971). By a 5–4 vote, the Court refused to force the city of Jackson, Mississippi, to reopen its municipal swimming pools. The city had closed them following a district court's ruling that operating them on a racially segregated basis was unconstitutional. The Court based its decision on evidence that the city had closed the pools because they could not be economically or safely operated on an integrated basis. The dissenting opinion of Justice White deserves particular mention. Justice White made specific reference to the fact that though he had spoken for the majority only a week earlier in *Whitcomb* he now found himself at odds with four of the Justices — Chief Justice Burger and Justices Black, Stewart, and Blackmun — who supported his opinion in that case. To Justice White, the closing of swimming pools in Jackson, unlike the multi-member district scheme in Indiana, was an obvious attempt to continue racial segregation.[7] However, it was left to Justice Thurgood Marshall, the only black ever to serve on the Court, to put the matter in sharp perspective: "By effectively removing publicly owned swimming pools from the protection of the Fourteenth Amendment . . . the majority and concurring opinions turn the clock back 17 years [to the situation prior to *Brown*]."

---

[7] White's dissenting opinion said in part: "[T]he city is adhering to an unconstitutional policy and is implementing it by abandoning the facilities. It will not do in such circumstances to say that whites and Negroes are being treated alike because both are denied use

Some of the strongest clues of the increasingly negative judicial posture toward civil rights are provided in two 1972 decisions in which all four Nixon appointees participated. In *Wright* v. *Council of City of Emporia* a bare 5-4 majority followed the strong pro-civil rights stance of the Warren Court. But perhaps most significant is that the entire five-man majority consisted of holdovers from the Warren Court while the four dissenters — Chief Justice Burger, and Justices Blackmun, Powell, and Rehnquist — were Nixon appointees. This marked the first dissent from a majority ruling on school desegregation since the 1954 *Brown* decision.[8] In *Wright* the "holdover" majority enjoined a city from setting up a separate school system where the separation might adversely affect an existing desegregation order from a federal court to dismantle a dual school system on a countywide basis. "Only when it became clear," said Justice Stewart for the majority, "that segregation in the county system was finally to be abolished did Emporia attempt to take its children out of the county system." The majority focused again on the practical effect of the city's withdrawal on the overall desegregation plan, rather than on the specific intent of the city.

Chief Justice Burger wrote for the four dissenters. His focus concerned the limits of judicial power and the discretion that must be left to local authorities. "A local school board plan," wrote the Chief Justice, "that will eliminate dual schools, stop discrimination and improve the quality of education ought not to be cast aside because a judge can evolve some other plan that accomplishes the same result or what he considers a preferable result. . . . Such an approach gives controlling weight to sociological theories [but] not constitutional doctrine."

The other 1972 ruling that suggests the emerging posture of the Burger Court toward civil rights is *Moose Lodge No. 107* v. *Irvis*. In this case the Court majority, including all four Nixon appointees, construed the "state action" doctrine as upholding a private club's refusal to serve blacks despite state issuance of a liquor license to the club. The decision broke the trend of the Warren years by limiting the application of the "state action" doctrine. Under this doctrine the equal protection clause of the Fourteenth Amendment may not be invoked without a sufficient level of state activity in the alleged denial of equal protection of the laws. It could have found the requisite state involvement in the state's discretionary control over liquor licenses.[9] Yet the majority chose to em-

---

of public services. The fact is that closing the pools is an expression of official policy that Negroes are unfit to associate with whites. Closing pools to prevent interracial swimming is little different from laws or customs forbidding Negroes and whites from eating together or from cohabiting or intermarrying."

[8] See Fred Graham, "Four Nixon Appointees End Court's School Unanimity," *New York Times,* June 23, 1972, p. 1.

[9] This was the holding of the district court. The question is one of degrees. As Justice

phasize that the state did not influence the club's policies on serving guests and therefore did not encourage the club's discrimination.

Justices Douglas, Brennan, and Marshall thought otherwise. To Justice Brennan, for example, the liquor licensing laws involve the state in such detail with the licensee's business that "when Moose Lodge obtains its liquor license, the State of Pennsylvania becomes an active participant in the operation of the Lodge Bar." This involvement was especially disturbing to Justice Brennan since to him "something is uniquely amiss in a society where the government, the authoritative oracle of community values, involves itself in racial discrimination."

A Setback to Busing: The Detroit Case

Additional insight into the Burger Court position toward civil rights is provided by the "city-suburbs" busing issue. Earlier, it will be recalled, the Court had approved busing as a permissible tool to effect public school integration. However, it had left the extent to which this "tool" could be used somewhat unclear. In dealing with the city-suburbs busing issue, the position of the Burger Court toward busing has become clearer. The Court called a halt to the Detroit metropolitan-wide (interdistrict) busing plan.

The thorny issue is whether students may be bused across district lines to remedy the segregative effects of central city school districts which are predominantly black. As is well known, the overwhelming black majorities in central cities, which exist because of the flight of whites to suburban areas, make it virtually impossible to effect an integration remedy of a central city school district even though that central city district were found to have purposefully engaged in de jure segregation practices (for example, drawing of attendance zones, location of new school buildings). The black central city school district, hemmed in with a suburban ring of white school districts, is a familiar pattern in America today. To break this pattern some have suggested a metropolitan-wide solution (interdistrict busing) for what they consider a metropolitan-wide problem (rigid segregation patterns in city and suburban schools).

Rehnquist, writing for the six-man majority, pointed out, "The Court has never held, of course, that discrimination by an otherwise private entity would be violative of the Equal Protection Clause if the private entity receives any sort of benefit or service at all from the state, or if it is subject to state regulation in any degree whatever. Since state-furnished services include such necessities of life as electricity, water, and police and fire protection, such a holding would utterly emasculate the distinction between private as distinguished from state conduct. . . ." The Court distinguished earlier "state action" cases as reflecting state involvement in the ostensibly private discriminatory practice under attack. It found insufficient or "neutral" state activity in *Moose Lodge*.

As would be expected, this multifaceted issue eventually came to the Supreme Court. The first time around, however, in the 1973 Richmond, Virginia, case, the Burger Court left the issue essentially unresolved when the Court divided in a 4–4 deadlock. Justice Powell did not participate in the case, apparently because of his involvement in the Virginia school situation prior to his appointment to the Supreme Court. But it was not long before the issue was again before the Supreme Court. And this time, in the 1974 Detroit case (*Milliken* v. *Bradley*), the Burger Court, with Justice Powell joining a five-man majority, made its position clear. A multi-district remedy, said Chief Justice Burger who spoke for the 5–4 majority, could not be used to solve single-district de jure segregation unless other affected districts had engaged in constitutional violations. Since earlier rulings of the Court had been confined to violations and remedies within a single school district, Burger said that for the first time the Court was asked to decide "the validity of a remedy mandating cross-district or interdistrict consolidation to remedy a condition of segregation found to exist in only one district." In holding against such a remedy, the Chief Justice stated that:

> Before the boundaries of separate and autonomous school districts may be set aside by consolidating the separate units for remedial purposes or by imposing a cross-district remedy, it must first be shown that there has been a constitutional violation within one district that produces a significant segregative effect in another district. Specifically it must be shown that racially discriminatory acts of the state or local school district or of a single school district have been a substantial cause of inter-district segregation.

Burger concluded that since the record contains evidence of de jure segregated conditions only in Detroit city schools, the remedy (of the lower courts) was inappropriate. "It is clear, . . ." said Burger, "that the district court, with the approval of the court of appeals, has provided an interdistrict remedy in the face of a record which shows no constitutional violations that would call for equitable relief except within the city of Detroit." However, since "the constitutional right of the Negro respondents in Detroit is to attend a unitary school system in that district," and since that district had engaged in unconstitutional segregation policies, Burger remanded the case for "prompt formulation of a decree directed to eliminating the segregation found to exist in Detroit city schools. . . ."

Justices Douglas, White, and Marshall filed dissenting opinions, the latter two being joined by Justice Brennan. Douglas felt that to rule against the metropolitan area remedy was a step "that will likely put the problems of the blacks and our society back to the period that antedated the 'separate but equal' regime of *Plessy* v. *Ferguson.*" Indeed Douglas saw the reason as "simple." Since Detroit is rather largely black, and since blacks are mostly poor and since the Court has ruled that poor districts must pay their own way (see *Rodriguez*, discussed on pp. 186–87), it is simple enough to see that black schools will not only be "separate" but will be "inferior" as well. "So far as equal protection is concerned," said Douglas, "we are now in a dramatic retreat from the 8–1 decision in 1896 that blacks could be segregated in public facilities provided they received equal treatment."

In his dissenting opinion Justice White chided the majority on several grounds. First, said White, the majority does not challenge the district court's findings, supported by the court of appeals, that "including the suburbs in a desegregation plan would be impractical and infeasible because of educational considerations." "Indeed," said White, "the Court leaves unchallenged the district court's conclusions that a plan including the suburbs would be physically easier and more practical and feasible than a Detroit-only plan. . . . Whereas the most promising Detroit-only plan, for example, would have entailed the purchase of 900 buses, the metro plan would involve the acquisition of no more than 350 new vehicles." White also expressed surprise "that the Court, sitting at this distance from the State of Michigan, claims better insight than the court of appeals and district court as to whether an interdistrict remedy for equal protection violations practiced by the State of Michigan would involve undue difficulties for the state in the management of its public schools." White called the Court's attention to its own practice during the past 16 years in relying "on the informed judgment" of the district courts and courts of appeals in determining what constitutes an "acceptable desegregation plan."

White was "even more mystified" that the majority could "ignore the reality that the constitutional violations, even if occurring locally, were committed by governmental entities for which the State is responsible and that it is the State that must respond to the command of the Fourteenth Amendment." Under Michigan law, said White, such remedies were and are especially appropriate in this case where the state had both directly and indirectly contributed to the current segregation in Detroit city schools.

Justice Thurgood Marshall, who at one time led the NAACP's attack against segregation, bitterly attacked the Court's decision and called it a "giant step backwards." "The rights at issue in this case," he said, "are too fundamental to be abridged on grounds as superficial as those relied on by the majority today." Marshall continued:

> We deal here with the right of all of our children, whatever their race, to an equal start in life and to an equal opportunity to reach their full potential as citizens. Those children who have been denied that right in the past deserve better than to see fences thrown up to deny them that right in the

future. Our Nation, I fear, will be ill-served by the Court's refusal to remedy separate and unequal education, for unless our children begin to learn together, there is little hope that our people will ever learn to live together.

Marshall found that the "great irony" and the "most serious analytical flaw" in the majority opinion lay in its concluding sentence in which the Court remanded the case for "prompt formulation of a decree directed to eliminating the segregation found to exist in Detroit city schools, a remedy which has been delayed since 1970." What the majority seems to have forgotten, said Marshall, is "the district court's explicit finding that a Detroit-only decree, the only remedy permitted under today's decision, 'would not accomplish desegregation.'" And most important, he said, the majority neither confronts nor responds to the district court's conclusion "that a remedy limited to the city of Detroit would not effectively desegregate the Detroit city schools."

In addition, Marshall, just as the other dissenters, cited specific instances whereby the state itself, as opposed to the local school district, actively contributed to the present segregation in Detroit. And in Marshall's view the state had both the responsibility and the authority to take appropriate remedial actions. Marshall concluded his opinion on a very pessimistic note. Said he:

> Desegregation is not and was never expected to be an easy task. Racial attitudes ingrained in our Nation's childhood and adolescence are not quickly thrown aside in its middle years. But just as the inconvenience of some cannot be allowed to stand in the way of the rights of others, so public opposition, no matter how strident, cannot be permitted to divert this Court from the enforcement of the constitutional principles at issue in this case. Today's holding, I fear, is more a reflection of a perceived public mood that we have gone far enough in enforcing the Constitution's guarantee of equal justice than it is the product of neutral principles of law. In the short run, it may seem to be the easier course to allow our great metropolitan areas to be divided up each into two cities — one white, the other black — but it is a course, I predict, our people will ultimately regret.

The Burger Court and Rights of the Poor

The Burger Court has also rendered decisions in another area that is of importance to black Americans: poverty law. In general, these decisions indicate that the Court is not disposed to break new ground in expanding rights of the poor. The issue in *James* v. *Valtierra* (1971), for example, was whether an amendment to the California constitution which provided for mandatory popular referenda on low-rent housing proposals violated the equal protection clause of the federal Constitution. A three-judge district court had enjoined enforcement of the amendment, relying chiefly on *Hunter* v. *Erickson* (1969). Here the Court held that a referendum law violated equal protection by requiring that any ordinance that regulated real property on the basis of race, color, religion, or national origin must be approved by a majority of qualified voters. The Burger Court distinguished *Hunter* on the ground that California's referendum provision did not rest on "distinctions based on race." Instead, the amendment "requires referendum approval for any low rent housing project, not only for projects which will be occupied by a racial minority." Further, wrote Justice Black for the majority, the record "would not support any claim that a law seemingly neutral on its face is in fact aimed at a racial minority."

Justice Marshall dissented, joined by Justice Brennan and, interestingly, by one of the then-two Nixon appointees, Justice Blackmun. To Justice Marshall, the California amendment created a distinction between rich and poor which, particularly since it should be subject to "closer scrutiny" as a **suspect classification**, violated equal protection. The distinction that troubled Justice Marshall was that only projects for persons "of low income" must obtain prior approval. And, while none of the Justices discussed the possibility, California's scheme of involving local judgment in the location of federally assisted housing may permit racial majorities to maintain patterns of racial housing — patterns which make meaningful "equal protection" extremely unlikely.

The poor did not fare any better in *San Antonio Independent School District* v. *Rodriguez*, a 1973 decision. In *Rodriguez* the Court rejected challenges to the local property tax system that provides a significant part of public school finances in 49 of the 50 states. The contention was that the Texas system of supplementing state aid to school districts by means of property tax levied within the jurisdiction of the individual school district violated the equal protection clause. Rodriguez' children attended schools in a district with lower per pupil expenditures but higher property tax rates than in other area districts. He argued that substantial differences in per pupil expenditures among the districts resulted from differences in the value of property taxed within each district. Speaking for a 5-4 majority, Justice Powell said that the financing system, although not perfect, "abundantly satisfies" the constitutional standard for equal protection since the system "rationally furthers a legitimate state purpose or interest," namely, the maintenance of local control of public education. Justice Powell applied the traditional equal protection standard since "the Texas system does not operate to the peculiar disadvantage of any suspect class," and since education, although an important state service, is not a "fundamental" right because it is not "explicitly or implicitly guaranteed by the Constitution."[10]

Justices Brennan, White, Douglas, and Marshall dissented. Justice Marshall's dissent was especially strong. He called the Court's decision "a retreat from our historic commitment to equality of educational opportunity" and an "unsupportable acquiescence in a system which deprived children in their earliest years of the chance to reach their full potential as citizens." He emphasized the disparities in per pupil expenditures and tax rates among the districts involved. In addition, he sharply attacked the majority's attempt "to force this case into the same category for purposes of equal protection analysis as decisions involving discrimination affecting commercial interests." "By so doing," said Justice Marshall, "the majority singles this case out for treatment at odds with what seems to me to be the clear trend of recent decisions . . . and thereby ignores the constitutional importance of the interest at stake and the invidiousness of the particular classification, factors that call for far more than lenient scrutiny of the Texas financing scheme which the majority pursues." Justice Marshall insisted that if the discrimination inherent in the Texas scheme is scrutinized with the care demanded by the interest and classification involved, the unconstitutionality of the scheme is "unmistakable."

Rodriguez, while not posed in racial terms, has a direct impact on equality of opportunity for racial minorities. Since minorities tend to be concentrated in areas where property values are lower and where consequently, regardless of the willingness in some of these areas to pay a substantial *rate* of tax for education, less money can be made available for educational services.

The Burger Court has also considered the protections afforded welfare recipients. At issue before the Court in *Wyman* v. *James* (1971), for example, was whether a welfare recipient must permit a social worker to visit her home as a condition of eligibility for benefits under the program of Aid to Families of Dependent Children. On the basis of past decisions, chances appeared good that the Court would knock down home visit requirements. But Justice Blackmun, who spoke for the Court majority, viewed home visits by social workers as a "reasonable administrative tool" that served a valid purpose and did not unconstitutionally infringe on the right of privacy or any other rights guaranteed by the Fourth Amendment. "The caseworker," said Justice Blackmun, "is not a sleuth but rather, we trust, is a friend to one in need."

---

[10] While education is not explicitly guaranteed in the federal Constitution, it is so guaranteed by many state constitutions. These provisions have provided the basis for relief against unfair property tax assessments and expenditures in several states.

The dissenters — Justices Marshall, Brennan, and Douglas — reacted sharply. Justice Marshall, joined by Justice Brennan, charged the majority with ignoring an "unbroken line of cases." He said he could not understand "why a commercial warehouse deserves more protection than does this poor woman's home." "This Court," observed Marshall, "has occasionally pushed beyond established constitutional contours to protect the vulnerable and to further basic human values." He concluded, "I find no little irony in the fact that the burden of today's departure from principled adjudication is placed upon the lowly poor." Justice Douglas' dissent was equally sharp:

> Is the search of [the welfare recipient's] home without a warrant made "reasonable" merely because she is dependent on government largesse? . . . [C]onstitutional rights — here the privacy of the *home* — are obviously not dependent on the poverty or the affluence of the beneficiary. It is the precincts of the *home* that the Fourth Amendment protects, and their privacy is as important to the lowly as to the mighty.

The majority and dissenting Justices thus revealed a basic difference in attitude about the role of constitutional protections in the lives of the poor.

The Burger Court rendered several other decisions concerning welfare recipients. For example, on the one hand, the Court held that welfare benefits are a matter of statutory entitlement that may not be ended without procedural due process. On the other hand, in *Dandridge v. Williams* (1970) the Court upheld a Maryland statute that limited welfare payments to a single family unit to a maximum of $250 per month regardless of the size of the family. In general, however, the thrust of the activity of the Burger Court appears to counter what looms as the key issue in this developing area of the law: whether poor people are, or should be, entitled to some minimal level of protection as a matter of right against economic deprivation.

Still other decisions of the Burger Court relate to the access of poor people to courts in **civil litigation**. In *Boddie* v. *Connecticut* (1971), for example, the Court held that states cannot deny access to their courts by persons seeking divorce solely because of inability to pay court costs. But in *United States* v. *Kras* (1973) the Court held that *Boddie* could not apply as precedent when the issue involved the inability of an unemployed indigent to pay a $50 filing fee in a federal bankruptcy petition. Writing for the majority, Justice Blackmun interpreted *Boddie* as requiring both that the interest sought to be protected must be "fundamental" and that there be no effective alternative available to the prospective litigant. Since one seeking bankruptcy seeks no "fundamental" right, and may have the debts discharged without judicial assistance, due process is not violated by charging a filing fee as a condition to an adjudication of bankruptcy.[11] The *Kras* majority's reading of *Boddie* will likely have the effect of preventing expansion of the *Boddie* rationale to any but a few classes of litigation. As a practical matter, it will also prevent a significant number of poor black Americans from initiating judicial proceedings to vindicate their rights.[12]

"Law and Order": The Nixon Pledge and the Court Performance

The Burger Court has also blunted the thrust of Warren Court decisions regarding the rights of persons accused of crime. In *Harris* v. *New York* (1971) the Court, with Chief Justice Burger writing for a 5–4 majority, held that statements of an accused obtained by police in violation of *Miranda* rules,[13] provided the statements were made voluntarily, could be used to attack the credibility of a defendant if he took the stand. They were not admissible as evidence of the defendant's guilt, however. Indeed, wrote Chief Juctice Burger, once he has taken the witness stand, the defendant has an obligation to tell the truth, and "the prosecution . . . did no more than utilize the traditional trust-testing devices of the adversary process. . . . The shield provided by *Miranda*," concluded Burger, "cannot be perverted into a license to use perjury by

---

[11] Justice Marshall, dissenting, indicated that *Boddie* established access to the courts itself as a fundamental right which cannot be denied on the basis of poverty. Justice Stewart's dissent argued that while *Boddie* did not open the courts to indigents under all circumstances, neither did it require that the interest be "fundamental" for the indigent to gain free access to the judicial process. Justice Douglas argued that all filing fees create a classification based on wealth which violates equal protection.

[12] To illustrate, in another 1973 case, *Ortwein* v. *Schwab*, the Court upheld the imposition of a $25 filing fee as a condition of obtaining a review of administrative action affecting welfare recipients in Oregon. The Court cited *Kras* rather than *Boddie* as authority. The Court, as it had in *Kras*, weighed the constitutional significance of the interest of the prospective litigant, and found that it was not "fundamental." On the second issue of available alternatives, the Court cited the welfare recipients' opportunities for administrative hearings.

The *Kras* dissenters again dissented in *Ortwein*. As Justice Douglas put it, the majority's decision simply "broadens and fortifies the 'private preserve' for the affluent [by upholding] a scheme of judicial review whereby justice remains a luxury for the wealthy."

The uncertainty of the effect of *Kras* and *Ortwein* on the *Boddie* rationale is augmented by two other Burger Court decisions, in which prejudgment garnishment procedures and the seizure of property of defaulting debtors without notice and hearing were declared unconstitutional as denials of due process.

[13] In *Miranda* v. *Arizona* the Warren Court held that statements elicited from an accused who has not been advised of his rights to remain silent and to an attorney are inadmissible against him at trial to establish guilt.

way of a defense, free from risk of confrontation with prior inconsistent utterances." But Justice Brennan, joined by Justices Douglas and Marshall, thought the Court had "seriously undermined" *Miranda*. Wrote Justice Brennan:

> The Court today tells the police that they may freely interrogate an accused incommunicado and without counsel and know that although any statement they obtain in violation of *Miranda* can't be used on the state's direct case, it may be introduced if the defendant has the temerity to testify in his own defense. This goes far toward undoing much of the progress made in conforming police methods to the Constitution.

Other criminal cases illustrate the Court's support of President Nixon's pledge to strengthen society's "peace forces" against the "criminal forces." For example, even though the Court found capital punishment unconstitutional,[14] it should be noted that all four Nixon appointees dissented. Moreover, though a unanimous Court expanded the right to counsel to apply to misdemeanor cases, it also strengthened the discretion of authorities before indictment or formal charges are brought. And it is at this stage — after arrest but prior to formal charges — that blacks and others can experience their greatest difficulties with law enforcement officers. For example, the Court held that a suspect in a police lineup is not entitled to counsel if he has not been formally indicted. Also, the Court approved the right of a policeman to stop and frisk a suspect even if the officer's suspicion is based on information supplied by an unnamed informant. Still further, the Court allowed an unconstitutional pretrial confession to be admitted against a criminal defendant as evidence, brushing aside the unconstitutional taint as "harmless error" on the ground that the jury had independent and sufficient evidence to convict. In each of these cases all four Nixon appointees were included in the majority.

In addition, *Johnson* v. *Louisiana*, one of the 1972 non-unanimous jury verdict cases, illustrates vividly the implications of the Burger Court's "law and order" decisions for blacks and other minorities. In *Johnson* the Court, with all Nixon appointees in agreement, upheld nonunanimous jury verdicts in criminal cases. The Court held that a verdict of guilty or not guilty returned by nine of twelve jurors did not deprive the defendant of due process or equal protection.[15] The basis of the majority's holding was that permitting non-unanimous convictions serves the

---

[14] *Furman* v. *Georgia* (1972). The failure of any two of the concurring justices to agree on a rationale in *Furman* leaves the future of capital punishment in doubt, for example, where unlike *Furman* its imposition is not discretionary.

[15] In another case decided the same day, the Court upheld a ten-to-two jury conviction as not violating the Sixth Amendment. *Apodaca* v. *Oregon* (1972).

valid state objective of "facilitat[ing], expedit[ing], and reduc[ing] expense in the administration of criminal justice. . . ." However, four of the remaining five Warren Court Justices — Brennan, Douglas, Stewart, and Marshall — dissented. Questioning whether the decision amounted to a "watered down" version of the Bill of Rights, Justice Douglas observed that "these civil rights — whether they concern speech, searches and seizures, self-incrimination, criminal prosecution, bail, or cruel and unusual punishment — extend of course to everyone, but in cold reality touch mostly the lower castes in our society. I refer of course," said Justice Douglas, "to the blacks, the Chicanos, the one-mule farmers, the agricultural workers, the off-beat students, the victims of the ghetto." In a similar vein, Justice Brennan observed:

> When verdicts must be unanimous, no member of the jury may be ignored by the others. When less than unanimity is sufficient, consideration of minority views may become nothing more than a matter of majority grace. In my opinion, the right of all groups in this Nation to participate in the criminal process means the right to have their voices heard. A unanimous verdict vindicates that right. Majority verdicts could destroy it.

On the other side of the ledger, certain Burger Court decisions have served to bolster rights of indigents in the criminal justice system. Mostly, however, these decisions support the rights of indigents *after* conviction. For example, the Court ruled that a state could not sentence an indigent to jail for failure to pay a fine or court costs in a lump sum if the consequent time in jail would exceed the maximum jail term set by statute for the particular crime. Indigents must be offered some alternative to lump sum payment of fines, such as installment payments. Still further, the Court held that in view of the equal protection clause of the Fourteenth Amendment an indigent cannot be compelled to "work out" traffic fines by spending time in jail.

Continuity and Change: From Warren to Burger

Generally, the decisions of the Burger Court have been mixed. While there is some continuity between Warren Court policies and those of the Burger Court — for example, on school desegregation — there are also increasing signs of toning down and departing from these and other policies. This, of course, is exactly what Nixon had hoped the Court would do. For example, concerning criminal procedures, the Burger Court is apparently disposed to minimize or reduce the rights of those interacting with administrative bureaucracies (police) until litigation is initiated. At this time the Court will apparently uphold traditional constitutional values such as the right to counsel. The practical consequences of this trend, if it continues, are obvious. It is this daily interaction with bureaucracies that determines the quality of life (repressive or less so) for many persons, especially blacks. Of course, at this early stage of comparison, there are certain organizational and functional characteristics of the Court, such as continuing input by holdover Justices from the Warren Court and allegiance to precedent, that tend to blunt any abrupt policy changes. Nonetheless, even at this stage, some change is evident.

This review of judicial policies indicates a change in substance and tone between the decisions of the Warren Court and those of the Burger Court. Indeed, Professor Kurland's intended pun that "the [Court's] shift has not been . . . a simple change from black to white" seems to have already lost its punch. Changes in Court personnel are certainly bringing about a change in the judicial stance toward blacks' constitutional rights. This is not to say that the Warren Court was the great "white savior" of black Americans.[16] That would overstate what the Warren Court did or what any Court actually could do. Nor can we say that the Burger Court has not supported certain rights of blacks. In some instances the Court has done so. But we can say that the legal fate of problems confronting black Americans is much more uncertain under the Burger Court than it was during the Warren Court. What we have observed here indicates that we may expect three trends: (1) less inclination by the Court to apply or to expand judicial policies supporting racial justice; (2) less support for blacks and others who wish to use litigation to achieve objectives that they cannot attain in political forums; and (3) less judicial support for individual or group claims as against governmental authority.

Implications For Black Americans

The present trends of the Burger Court, if continued, could hold important implications for blacks and for the political system. First, continuing certain decisional outputs of the Burger Court could weaken one of the most vital points of access that blacks have to the political system. Indeed, one of the chief functions assumed by the Warren Court was to express and to respond to certain key demands of those who were unpopular, unrepresented, or underrepresented in the political system. The characteristics of the American judiciary, as opposed to Congress and the presidency, seem unique to this function. Particularly,

---

[16] See Steele, "Nine Men in Black Who Think White."

isolating the federal judiciary from the pressures of conforming to majority will make judges more likely to protect minority rights. It seems much too late to argue whether the judiciary *should* respond to minority demands. The fact is that judges are a part of the political process "not by choice, but by function."[17]

In any event, the problems that affect blacks and press the governmental system for solution are not trivial. They are the great issues of our time, which, as de Tocqueville observed long ago, sooner or later are resolved into judicial issues. The American political system, as it has developed, tends to translate economic and social conflicts into legal conflicts. This, it seems, accounts for the unique significance of the Supreme Court. Consider the kinds of major issues that occupied the Warren Court:

1. how to overcome problems of racial injustice.
2. how to strengthen and extend political democracy — for example, fair and effective systems of representation.
3. how to ensure fairness to all persons in administering criminal justice.
4. how to safeguard the rights of the poor in distributing legal, political, and economic benefits.
5. how to give maximum protection to individual freedoms.

As to all these problems, it seems quite obvious that the current dominant interests are unlikely to be in the vanguard of change. Those who are the victims of these problems — the politically disadvantaged — would quite naturally turn to the judicial system. Here numbers, social status, wealth, and influence presumably have less bearing on the decisions. In short, one of the important contributions of the Warren Court is that it was in a position to place items important to such groups on its institutional agenda. It also could deal with them. Among the results of these actions was placing the symbol of constitutionalism and law on the side of such interests.

As a result, blacks were able initially to overcome many of the defects of coalition-building and isolationism that so often characterize minority group politics. Coalition politics, for example, would appear to be necessary for a minority group to achieve favorable policies in the majority-rule-oriented electoral system. But to gain coalition support a minority more often than not must soften its original objectives, since failure to do so lessens the possibilities of success in coalition-building. Or, a minority may hold to its original objectives but find itself isolated without the

---

[17] J. W. Peltason, *Federal Courts in the Political Process* (New York: Random House, 1962).

support necessary to achieve success. Then again the minority group may subscribe to general, vague, though favorable policies. These policies either postpone the specific goals or shift their realization to another arena. This is the more plausible course for a minority group to follow in elective-political arenas. Indeed, such policies are more likely to involve matters that affect the very self-esteem and dignity of individuals and the group itself. Hence, it would be most difficult for the group to soften its original objectives. It would be equally difficult for the group to hold to its original objectives in isolation without any viable chance of even limited success.

The judicial process can offer a minority group a way to overcome certain limitations that are part of the elective-political process. In the judicial process a minority group may push its original objectives to obtain fully specific constitutional–legal guarantees. Moreover, the entire judicial drama, though not separate from politics, is carried on in a strictly "nonpolitical" manner; the language used addresses outcomes in terms of what the Constitution — and justice and fairness — "command." "Reasoned argument" and "legal principles" replace advice and majority rule as the "critical" determinants. The "myth" and structure of the judicial forum, unlike the practice and structure of elective-political forums such as Congress, strengthen minority group chances of success. In addition, since courts also serve important functions for political élites and the political system generally — for example, resolution of conflict in terms of "law and order" — a victory for a minority group in the judicial system takes on added significance. Specifically, favorable court action may increase and constitutionalize (legitimize) pressures on and in elective-political institutions to deal with the issues involved. Indeed, the minority group may now, as a result of victory in the courts, seek to put into effect constitutional–legal rights, not mere interest group objectives. This, in large measure, is what happened during the Warren Court.

Today, however, the situation is different. The Supreme Court's leadership and strong support for civil rights and civil liberties no longer exist. Decisions of the Warren Court included a creative use and application of law to stimulate basic policy changes. However, the Burger Court shows no such inclination. An off-the-bench comment by Chief Justice Burger suggests this shift in the direction of the Court. "Those [young people] who decide to go into law primarily on the theory that they can change the world by litigation in the courts," cautioned the Chief Justice, "may be in for some disappointments." Litigation, he said, is not "the route by which basic changes in a country like ours should be made. That is a legislative and policy process, part of the political process," he continued, "and there is a very limited role for courts in this respect." [18] If this posture of the Burger Court continues, the problem for blacks will not be how to forge new changes through litigation. It will be rather how to prevent the "chipping away" of legal supports already gained.

Importance of Judicial Support

A second implication of present trends of the Burger Court is that without strong judicial support, blacks and other minorities might find it increasingly difficult to achieve their objectives — quality education, decent jobs, and adequate housing. Indeed, given the nature of the political system, it seems unlikely that leadership on civil rights and related problems can be expected from elective-political institutions. [19] This observation finds strong support in Professor Dawson's study of 1968 and 1970 Survey Research Center public opinion data concerning government action in certain policy areas. [20] Dawson argues that:

> increased intensity and polarization of opinions regarding government race relation policies, the relatively small proportion of blacks in the population, and the increasing divisions within the Democratic Party over race related issues make it increasingly difficult to deal with the issues of racial equality and integration through the normal electoral system and policy making processes.

In other words, elective-political institutions, in large measure, respond to constituencies that have the resources necessary to win elections. These resources include votes, financial wealth, support from influential groups, and so on. The only resource that blacks have in potentially adequate supply is votes. However, even if blacks should achieve maximum voting strength, this would not be enough to balance the scale, much less assure favorable action from elective-political institutions.

More active political participation such as voting and holding public office might appear desirable. Yet it is not wise to build expectations

---

[18] *The New York Times*, July 4, 1971, p. 24.

[19] For commentary on the inability of the political system to deal with these problems, see James M. Burns, *Uncommon Sense* (New York: Harper & Row, Inc., 1972); Theodore J. Lowi, *The End of Liberalism* (New York: W. W. Norton, 1969). See also Walter D. Burnham, *Critical Elections and the Mainspring of American Politics* (New York: W. W. Norton, 1970), pp. 91–193.

[20] Richard Dawson, *Public Opinion and Contemporary Disarray* (New York: Harper & Row, Inc., 1973), pp. 116–24, 154–202.

about such activity beyond what we might reasonably expect. Reliance on political participation as the main way to correct basic sociopolitical and legal problems must be tempered by the limitations in American electoral politics. This latter point, as well as the overall efficiency of elective–political institutions in dealing with racial problems, is illustrated in a study by Professor Mack Jones on black officeholders in the South.[21] "While voting and holding office are necessary conditions," writes Jones, "they are not sufficient ones for realization of the democratic creed." This suggests, for example, that more than emergent black political majorities and elected officials in the nation's central cities may be needed for blacks to receive the full benefits of American society.[22] The authority and resources which cities need to deal with the problems involved make them greatly dependent, as the system presently operates, upon institutions beyond their control, such as state and federal legislatures. This situation has led one scholar to conclude that future control of central cities appears to offer blacks "very limited" opportunities for gains and may well prove a "hollow prize."[23] But this need not be the case. The unique role and powers of the judiciary, symbolized by the Supreme Court during the Warren era, could be a determining factor in these circumstances.

It could very well be that given the nature and operation of the American political system, strong judicial support — similar to and even more than that given by the Warren Court — is one of the *necessary* conditions for the full realization of the "democratic creed" by minority groups. The Court has had a long history of blocking and slowing down the constitutional rights of blacks, even when faced with strong congressional opposition. (An example is the Civil Rights Cases of 1883.) Even in relatively recent times, decisions of the Court offered only slight support for black interests. As long as the Court impeded black interests or supported them only slightly, nothing much was done to improve blacks' status. But once the Court began making decisions that strongly supported and expanded the constitutional rights of blacks, the situation began to change. Impetus was given to the civil rights movement. Support for its objectives was broadened. Congress and the president began to take action to deal with the problems of racial injustice. Initia-

---

[21] M. Jones, "Black Officeholders in Local Governments of the South: An Overview" (paper prepared for delivery at the Annual Meeting of the American Political Science Association, 1970).

[22] For searing commentary on the problems which face a black mayor (and in many ways, problems common to elected executives generally), see Carl Stokes, *Promises of Power: A Political Autobiography* (New York: Simon and Schuster, Inc., 1972), pp. 118–20.

[23] H. Paul Friesena, "Black Control of Central Cities: The Hollow Prize," *Journal of the American Institute of Planners* (March 1969): 75–79.

tives taken by the Warren Court stand out as crucial in stimulating and developing policies designed to overcome these problems.

Viewed from an overall perspective, the decisions of the Warren Court suggest that safeguarding constitutional rights of a minority group requires the Court to do more than just police the *process* by which public policies are made (for example, *Baker* v. *Carr*). It must also judge the *output* of that process (for example, the *Brown* decision). But so far at least, the Burger Court, unlike the Warren Court, does not seem inclined to face these issues so as to overcome weaknesses of the elective-political process. Even so, however, recent data indicate that blacks still apparently place more trust and hope in the Supreme Court than in any other of our national political institutions.[24]

Impact on Lower Courts

If the Burger Court continues to make uncertain, to narrow, or to negate the policies and posture of the Warren Court, we might expect such actions to have an important impact on lower federal and state courts. These courts, after all, perform very crucial functions. They exercise a "gatekeeping" function to determine what issues enter the judicial arena. They determine, in large measure, how the few major issues that do finally reach the Supreme Court are phrased for decision by that body. Lower courts also implement Supreme Court mandates.[25] Moreover, decisions of lower courts are final in most cases. How lower courts exercise these functions may be determined largely by what they

---

[24] Responding to the question as to "which part of government . . . do you most often place more confidence and trust to do what's right," over 52 percent of blacks responding placed more "confidence and trust" in the Supreme Court. This represented a small increase of about 2 percent over the same question when asked in 1972. There was, however, a significant increase in white "confidence and trust" in the Court, from 23 percent in 1972 to about 38 percent in 1973. This differential rate of increase between blacks and whites might reflect that whites more than blacks approve of how the Burger Court is toning down (or eroding) policies of the Warren Court. These specific data are taken from Table 3 of Illustrative Materials distributed by Arthur H. Miller, Center for Political Studies, University of Michigan, in a lecture to the Department of Political Science of Washington University, St. Louis, March 8, 1974. Table 3 is reprinted in Lucius Barker, "Black Americans and the Burger Court," *Washington University Law Quarterly*, Vol. 1973, p. 772.

[25] For a detailed and interesting account of lower court implementation of the school desegregation cases, see J. Peltason, *Fifty-eight Lonely Men: Southern Federal Judges and School Desegregation* (Chicago: University of Illinois Press, 1961). A more recent study of lower court implementation of federal law is found in Charles Hamilton, *The Bench and the Ballot: Southern Federal Judges and Black Voters* (New York: Oxford University Press, 1973).

perceive to be, and what is, the actual posture of the Supreme Court. The same holds true for the potential influence of the Supreme Court on other government institutions and officials, including, for example, state legislators, school superintendents, and policemen.

The Role of the Supreme Court: A Summary View

The importance and relationship of policy shifts from the Warren to the Burger Courts can be more fully understood when viewed in a broader political context. Some years ago Robert Dahl presented a formulation about the role of the Supreme Court in the political system.[26] Dahl argued essentially that the Court both defines and legitimates the basic political decisions which are made by dominant majority coalitions rooted in the political branches and, ultimately, in the electorate. The Warren Court, as Dahl himself recognized, does not fit this formulation. The Warren Court did more than "define and legitimate" basic decisions made elsewhere. It fashioned decisions of its own. True, as Dahl explains, there was division among political élites on the issues involved. The resulting decisions did put the Court's authority and prestige on the line. However, in these decisions the Warren Court indicated a role for the Court that was somewhat different from the past. The Court used an opportunity to lead rather than delay the nation on matters that seemingly went to the heart of the "democratic creed." It forged a really unique, and perhaps necessary, role for the Court in the political system.

However, on the basis of our discussion here the Burger Court does not seem likely to assume this role by safeguarding, and perhaps expanding, policies that came from the Warren Court. Ironically the Burger Court appears to be "following the election returns" more than it is following the decisions of the Warren Court. Indeed, recent presidential elections have not yet brought about a critical realignment or a new dominant majority coalition. But they have nevertheless mirrored a current of opinion on the problems of race, crime, and poverty. The policies of the Burger Court increasingly agree with this current of opinion. Consequently, whether viewed as "legitimating" or "capitulating" to current political majorities,[27] the thrust of Dahl's formulation about the constituent role of the Court is valid in light of present trends in judicial policy. However, it is this role that now contributes to the

---

[26] See Note 1, above.

[27] See David Adamany, "Legitimacy, Realigning Elections, and the Supreme Court," 1973 *Wisconsin Law Review*, p. 790 at 842.

worsening of current problems and to the capability of the political system to deal with them.

This suggests that the somewhat negative and uncertain posture of the Burger Court toward civil rights, including "new" civil rights areas such as rights of the poor, could hurt advances already made. A strong judicial posture over a long period of time on civil rights goes far toward *institutionalizing* these civil rights concepts as part of the basic sociolegal structure of the political system. This is the prime example of the **educative function** that the Court can serve in a democratic government. On the other hand, the actual or apparent uncertainty coming from the nation's highest court could easily provide the excuse for many to return to pre-1954 racial practices in schools, in politics, in the administration of justice, and in daily life generally.

Moreover, other political institutions have crucial roles to play. Yet judicial weakness on issues of racial justice could seriously weaken the capability of the political system successfully to overcome these problems.

> It might be that there are some issues on which the judiciary must act as a safety valve for the elected political branches, providing leadership when it is reasonably ascertained that elected institutions are either unwilling or unable to act. This does not mean that in every instance where elected institutions fail to act, the Court must step in. Such a notion simplifies too much, both the delicate operation of our governing system as well as the role of the Court in that system. On the contrary, by deciding and fashioning policy on such issues, the Court gives to the governing system that necessary viability and capacity needed to survive.[28]

These issues are so important that the Court in resolving them is faced with perhaps its highest duty under the Constitution: to lead the way in the protection of minority rights against majority abuses. This duty is especially appropriate for the Supreme Court since it commands some "additional reverence because of the American devotion to 'law' and to the Constitution."[29]

But Not by Judges Alone: Impact and Compliance

The central point in examining the Supreme Court from Warren to Burger is that strong and persistent support from the Court can prove crucial (even determinative) in gaining policy objectives. But

---

[28] Lucius Barker, "Third Parties in Litigation: A Systemic View of the Judicial Function," *Journal of Politics* 41 (1967): 64–65.

[29] Adamany, see note 27, at 844.

Court action in itself may not be enough to achieve the very goals and objectives expressed in Court decisions. Action from other quarters may be needed to achieve the benefits. Court pronouncements may be viewed as authoritative (and final) as to the law and the Constitution. Yet they are not necessarily authoritative and final as to ultimate policy and practice. Consequently, we will conclude this chapter with a brief commentary on the impact of and **compliance** with Court decisions.

Impact and compliance studies of Court decisions have multiplied greatly in the past decade or so.[30] Undoubtedly these efforts were spurred by the increasing role of the judiciary, especially the Supreme Court, in dealing with the tough issues of our time — race, reapportionment, crime. Specifically, the active support given by the Warren Court to those interests that were unable to accomplish their objectives in other arenas stimulated attention as to the role and influence of judicial policies in the governing system.

Impact of Court decisions is much more difficult to grasp. It involves a range of factors that so far at least have not been dealt with systematically. For example, to discern the impact of a Court decision it would seem that we need to be concerned with both the *anticipated* and the *unanticipated* consequences of particular decisions. But such concerns, if considered at all, are invariably a part of judicial decision-making itself. We all know the limitations of our knowledge in this area. Nonetheless, we do get some clues as to the anticipated consequences — for example, the problems or hardships a particular decision might cause. The anticipated consequences seem to have weighed particularly heavy on the Court in the school segregation cases. The Court chose compliance with "all deliberate speed" rather than immediately. This shows the Court's concern with both the anticipated and the unanticipated consequences of its decision.

Still further, in measuring the impact of a particular judicial policy it might be necessary to consider other decisions from which the policy has come. For example, in the school desegregation cases, as well as in the reapportionment cases, it seems clear that the eventual Court decrees benefited from the initial reactions and responses to the basic decisions in those two areas. In *Brown*, reactions were sharp and divided. Impact of the decision was seen as uncertain. Here the Court fashioned its decree accordingly. In *Baker*, the response to judicial intervention in the reapportionment was quite popular. In subsequent deci-

---

[30] Increasing attention is being given to studies of impact and compliance. Studies of more general and theoretical interest include: Stephen Wasby, *The Impact of the United States Supreme Court: Some Perspectives* (Homewood, Ill.: Dorsey Press, 1970); Samuel Krislov, *The Supreme Court in the Political Process* (New York: Macmillan, 1965), ch. 6; and Harrell Rodgers, "Law as an Instrument of Public Policy," 17 *American Journal of Political Science* 638 (1973).

sions the Court defined its position quite clearly — that is, the "one man, one vote" formula.

Also, in dealing with the effect of Court decisions on such complex issues we can never be certain that the impact was due to one or a number of Court decisions, to other factors such as the passage of new legislation, or to a combination of these and other factors. In other words, measuring the impact of Court decisions still poses research problems. We are yet working *toward* a theory of impact.

Compliance, on the other hand, is much more narrow in focus than impact. In fact, compliance may be considered a "subset of impact."[31] Here our primary concern is finding out to what extent a given Court decision has been followed, or obeyed, complied with, evaded, ignored or modified. Most of our studies of the aftermath of judicial decisions focus on these points (that is, on compliance). Several factors have been suggested in assessing compliance.[32]

1. The context of the decision. Here one needs to consider the circumstances out of which litigation arose. For example, had other remedies been exhausted, was the issue highly explosive, controversial, and so on.

2. The nature and clarity of the decision so that people to whom it is addressed will understand. This has to do with both what the Court is asking to be done as well as to the clarity of what it wants to be done. Also involved here is a communications process. Do lawyers, lower courts, public officials and the public understand the decision?

3. The extent to which the decision coincides with established values. This also involves the nature of the opinion written to support the decision, its clarity, and its agreement with established values. The role of public opinion, and how it perceives the decision, also enters here.

4. The authority of the Court to render the decision. Is there great controversy over whether the particular problem involved in the decision is within the province of the Court?

Why people comply raises the question of the Court's authority, the basis on which people accept its decisions as ones which the Court has a *right* to give, and which they, for that reason, ought to obey. Bases for that authority might include a formal allocation of power to the Court to decide constitutionality; the Court's expertise, the formal setting in which the Court operates, which evokes respect; charismatic leadership of some judges; and people's need for some body or institution which can confine conflict and fulfill security needs. The Court's authority is related to the *legitimacy* people grant it.[33]

---

[31] Wasby, p. 28.
[32] See especially material in Note 30, above.
[33] Wasby, p. 29.

5. The relative costs/benefits of compliance/noncompliance. Here the relevant questions are, what do I stand to gain or to lose? or, what can be done if I do not comply? Since compliance with most cases involving civil rights and liberties takes place in the context of a local community, the matter of compliance/noncompliance might depend on the characteristics of the community.

6. Specific and generalized support for the Court from other institutions, public officials and various publics. This relates to specific support for a particular Court decision that might come from key officials such as president, governors, mayors, and so on. It also relates to the general esteem with which other institutions and various publics hold for the Court. In short, *prestige* of the Court among the various "others" is a crucial factor in compliance. This is especially true since the Court has neither the sword nor the purse.

We cannot (at least not yet) measure all these factors. Yet together they emphasize the interrelation of laws and politics. They also show that court decisions, even the Supreme Court, are not necessarily the last word in the American political system.

Topics for Discussion

1. The text states that "emergence of the Burger Court suggests that judicial victories, like political victories, are not etched in concrete." Do you agree or disagree? How and in what ways do "judicial" victories differ from "political" victories? Are they interrelated? What are implications of your discussion for the prevailing view that in America we are a "government of laws, not of men?"

2. Lewis Steele has described the Supreme Court, including the Warren Court, as "Nine Men in Black Who Think White." Do you agree or disagree? Justify your position citing concrete decisions by the Court.

3. Do you agree with the authors' view that "judicial abstinence or ambivalence on issues of racial justice could seriously weaken the capability of the political system" to deal with such problems? Justify your position.

4. The authors believe that "if judges interpret the law contrary to persistent majorities, sooner or later the judges (and the law) will change." Assuming this is true, are favorable judicial policies, such as those rendered by the Warren Court, of any *real* value to securing the rights of blacks and other minorities? Discuss.

Suggested Readings

Barker, Lucius J. "The Supreme Court From Warren to Burger: Implications for Black Americans and the Political System." *Washington University Law Quarterly*, Vol. 1973 (Fall, 1973), No. 4.

A study of decisional trends of the Warren and Burger Court with respect to their impact on black Americans and the political system.

Becker, Theodore and Malcolm Feeley. *The Impact of Supreme Court Decisions*. 2nd ed. New York: Oxford University Press, 1973.

A collection of readings that focus on an impact analysis of Supreme Court decisions.

Bell, Derrick, Jr. *Race, Racism and Law*. Boston: Little, Brown, 1973.

A collection of cases and materials that portray racism in American law.

Blaustein, Albert and Clarence Ferguson. *Desegregation and the Law*. 2nd ed. New York: Random House, 1962.

The story of the importance of the 1954 school desegregation cases and the immediate aftermath.

Cox, Archibald. *The Warren Court: Constitutional Decision as an Instrument of Reform*. Cambridge: Harvard University Press, 1973.

A sympathetic appraisal of the revolutionary changes brought about by the Warren Court in constitutional law.

Mitau, G. Theodore. *Decade of Decision: The Supreme Court and the Constitutional Revolution, 1954-1964*. New York: Scribner's, 1967.

An analysis of the Warren Court and the constitutional implications of its decisions.

Peltason, J. W. *Fifty-eight Lonely Men: Southern Federal Judges and School Desegregation*. Chicago: University of Illinois Press, 1971.

An examination of the political behavior of southern federal judges and the integration of schools in the South.

Sayler, Richard H., Barry B. Boyer, and Robert E. Gooding, Jr. *The Warren Court: A Critical Analysis*. New York: Chelsea House, 1969.

A collection of articles that evaluate the work of the Warren Court in various issue areas.

Tollett, Kenneth. "The Viability and Reliability of the Supreme Court as an Institution for Social Change and Progress Beneficial to Blacks." 2 *Black Law Journal* 197 (Winter, 1972).

An examination of the status of blacks in relation to the transition from the Warren to Burger Courts.

Vose, Clement E. *Caucasians Only: The Supreme Court, the NAACP, and the Restrictive Covenant Cases.* Berkeley and Los Angeles: University of California Press, 1967.

Traces the role of the NAACP and the Supreme Court in the conflict over restrictive covenants.

Wasby, Stephen. *The Impact of the United States Supreme Court: Some Perspectives.* Homewood, Ill.: Dorsey Press, 1970.

An overview and evaluation of impact and compliance with decisions on the U.S. Supreme Court.

7

CHANGE THROUGH POLITICS: INTEREST GROUPS AND POLITICAL PARTIES

The new black politics demands a reevaluation of the old concept that "what is good for the Nation is good for minorities." Those who embrace the new black politics must couch their thinking in the fundamental concept that "what is good for minorities is good for the Nation." This position out of necessity requires the development of a new philosophy that must be practical and selfish — the same as all others that presently exist in this country. Black politics must start on the premise that we have no permanent friends; no permanent enemies, just permanent interests. In matters strictly of a political nature, we must be determined to "take what we can, give up what we must." Those in politics who disagree with this approach should first analyze the composition of their own philosophy and if it does not parallel ours — they are qualified to disagree.

. . . The second qualification for the new black politics is a relative degree of political independence. Those black politicians who are subservient to white controlled political machines cannot possibly stand the kinds of pressures which will come when the new black politics launches the campaign for total black equality in all areas of American life. This is not to say that blacks in politics cannot have a reasonable, legitimate coalition with white politics. To think otherwise would be absolute folly. But the kinds of techniques necessary to employ at this stage in black politics must be abrasive, retaliatory, obstructionist — all of which may be offensive to whites, even white liberals. Without political independence or a deep sense of commitment the pressures will be too great and some "colored" politicians may not be able to stay in the kitchen.

The new black politics will cast the traditional white liberal in a new and perhaps uncomfortable role. For many years now the white liberal has planned, strategized, organized the fight for racial justice in this country. He has determined the priorities, the issues, the battle plan; and the time of execution. He has skillfully involved many forces into the fight and has provided dedicated leadership in helping to create the national climate for racial change. But now he is confronted with the possibility that blacks will be planning, directing, and leading the onslaught. The question is — can the white liberal follow the lead of blacks who have followed them for so many years?

Congressman William Clay (D., Mo.)*

Introduction

By now it is quite clear that in the American political system change through law is also dependent on change through "politics." Even so, one can understand why blacks and other disadvantaged groups have resorted to "judicial" politics as opposed to "political" politics. Indeed, success in the judicial arena, as shown by the civil rights movement, has had enormous impact on the political arenas. Judicial decisions have broadened the protection of those who have to resort to both traditional and non-traditional means to communicate and act on their views. The scope of the First Amendment guarantees has been interpreted so as to protect protest demonstrations and other forms of political expression. These latter include limitations on the law of libel as applied to public officials and public figures; permitting those with common objectives to join in association with others without fear of recrimination; permitting **interest groups** to use litigation and to promote and advocate objectives which they perhaps could not otherwise achieve in other arenas. Court actions have also eliminated the white primary and other similarly restrictive devices. In addition, the Court has upheld the Voting Rights Act of 1965. Moreover, in the reappor-

---

* *Congressional Record*, Feb. 19, 1971, p. E936.

tionment cases electoral districts were drawn so that representation would be based on people rather than acres or trees.

Such decisions have had variable effects on black participation and influence in the political arena. Mainly, however, their overall impact has had a healthy effect by stimulating blacks and others to use "politics" as a way to gain their objectives. Of course, it could very well be that both the judiciary and black groups recognized, and not without glaring evidence, that except for strong support in and from political institutions, judicial policies would not go very far. In any event, favorable judicial decisions have broadened participation and stimulated the use of political forums by blacks and others to deal with their concerns. And without doubt, these groups have attempted to take advantage of the "new" openings in the political process. In the present chapter we present: (1) a general overview of the nature and operation of interest groups and political parties in the political system; (2) a discussion of black civil rights groups and the experience of blacks in the activities of the two major political parties; and (3) some general comments and observations about interest groups and political parties as they affect the problems of blacks and other minorities.

Interest Groups: Nature and Operation

Interest groups are a dominant feature of the American political landscape. More than this, they are constitutionally based; that is, their formation is guaranteed by the First Amendment guarantees of the freedom of assembly, petition, and association. The number and variety of such groups indicate their importance in the American political system. These groups seek various goals and objectives; they reflect a wide range of society. There are, for example, business groups, farmers groups, labor groups, professional groups, and racial, ethnic and nationality groups. Organizations such as the AFL-CIO, American Bankers Association (ABA), American Medical Association (AMA), American Association of University Professors (AAUP), American Farm Bureau Federation (AFBF), and NAACP readily come to mind. That sooner or later these groups resort to the political process to promote the interests of their varied memberships shows their intimate relation and involvement in public policy-making.[1] Policies advantageous to some groups

---

[1] Arthur Bentley's *The Process of Government* (Chicago: University of Chicago Press, 1908) germinated much of the scholarship in this area. David Truman, for example, in *The Governmental Process* (New York: Alfred A. Knopf, 1951) acknowledges the strong influence of Bentley on his work. Truman's book, however, stands as perhaps the most definitive study of the political role of interest groups. For a penetrating and critical

are harmful to others. At this point we can see politics more clearly as reconciling conflict and competition among interests. However, some groups are more capable and influential in such conflict and competition than others. What accounts for differences in group influence in political conflict?

THE NATURE OF GROUP MEMBERSHIP

Perhaps the most important factor in group effectiveness is the nature of the membership of the particular group. These elements include the basis of group membership — that is, why people join certain groups — the commitment and attitude of group members toward group goals, and the position and standing of the group and its members.

Robert Salisbury indicates that most groups organize, and that people join such groups, for three main reasons.[2] The first, and most important, reason is that members expect to receive, and leaders hope to deliver, **material benefits.** These could include better wages, improved working conditions, special tax advantages, and so on. Individual members may differ as to how much and what benefits are most important. They nevertheless agree that some material benefits must be forthcoming. Consequently, organization cohesion could be affected by the group leaders' ability to deliver such benefits. A second reason why people join groups — and why groups exist — is for **social solidarity.** This expresses the need for people who hold similar views to enjoy the support, fellowship, and solidarity of one another. A third reason is to provide a more effective avenue for *expression of opinion* in the political marketplace. **Expressive interest groups,** as Salisbury indicates, are easy to organize: "about all you need is some stationery and an appealing point of view."[3] But such groups are fragile since other groups could spring up that more nearly represent particular opinions. Of course, some persons undoubtedly join groups expecting both material and non-material — that is, social solidarity — benefits. When viewed in overall perspective, membership satisfaction may well depend on whether individual members feel that their reasons for joining are being sufficiently met to warrant their continued participation. Thus, membership satis-

---

analysis of Truman and other interest group theorists see Mancur Olson, *The Logic of Collective Action*, rev. ed. (New York: Schocken Books, 1971). For a carefully selected and well-organized collection of materials on interest groups see Robert Salisbury, *Interest Group Politics in America* (New York: Harper & Row, 1970).

[2] Robert Salisbury, *Governing America* (New York: Appleton-Century-Crofts, 1973), p. 87. Also see Salisbury, *Interest Group Politics*, esp. pp. 32–67.

[3] Salisbury, *Governing America*, p. 87.

faction relates directly to the commitment of group members toward group goals.

Another factor influencing commitment and attitudes of group members is **overlapping memberships.** When persons belong to more than one group, their loyalties are frequently divided. This results in less than total commitment to any particular group. Individuals who identify strongly with a particular group or cause tend to join groups which *reinforce* rather than strain their allegiance to that group or cause. While the concept of overlapping membership could theoretically affect group cohesion, it does appear that the hard core, activist members — those who attend meetings and vigorously support policy positions — are unlikely to join organizations that have conflicting values. It is certainly unlikely that those whites who are strong identifiers or members of the NAACP would be found joining the Ku Klux Klan.

The *prestige* and *social standing* of the group and its members also influence membership for these features say something about a group's influence in politics. The influence of groups in politics depends in part on how much the group and its members possess those characteristics that society values. Since occupation, income, and social status are held in high esteem in most industrial societies, individuals and groups that possess these characteristics are able to have much greater political influence and power. But, group standing and influence are also dependent on how much the group's purposes, goals, and activities are seen as agreeing with traditional American values. Groups that advocate "socialism," for example, will find the going more difficult than groups that advocate "free enterprise."

GROUP RESOURCES AND GROUP INFLUENCE

The resources that groups can bring to bear in achieving their goals is another major factor to consider in assessing their influence in the political process. These resources relate to such elements as leadership, money, and size of group membership. For example, groups with leaders who can minimize internal friction and express group objectives while preserving and promoting these objectives can have considerable influence. That is, leaders who can maintain the viability of their organizations are likely to make those organizations politically effective. Similarly, the influence of a group in politics also depends upon the money at its disposal and its use of this valuable resource. Money can pay for those things that a group needs in the political process. For example, money can help to create a favorable public opinion through propaganda; it can elect friendly, sympathetic public officials by supporting campaigns, and it can influence public officials through lobbying. Those groups with members of high socioeconomic status — for example, doctors, lawyers, businessmen — naturally have more influence.

But the size of membership as a group resource may in some ways make up for a group's lack of other resources. Nominal dues from large membership groups such as labor organizations may overcome or at least minimize the influence of large contributions of more affluent members of smaller organizations (for example, the AMA). In addition, the one-man, one vote principle means that votes remain an important resource of large membership groups. Whether this resource can be used, however, is another matter. Group members do not automatically follow group leaders. But leaders may still use the size of their membership (and vote) as a weapon in political conflict.

There are, of course, other resources that may determine the effectiveness of groups in politics. The time and skills that individual members can give to an organization can free its money resources to be used in other ways. Here is where the higher socio-status groups with small memberships overcome or minimize the advantages of mass membership organizations. Also, groups that are disadvantaged in politics may possess special skills that protect and promote group goals. For example, the use by the NAACP of its legal talent as a political resource is well known. (It is discussed later in this chapter.)

The organization of a group may also affect how the group operates in politics. Some groups have no formal organization, and yet respond as united. Black Americans as blacks, for example, have no formal organization, but when faced with common problems — such as race discrimination — they have reacted as a group. Of course, organized groups that promote black causes (for example, NAACP) have done much to mold this kind of "organizational" behavior on the part of blacks.

When groups are formally organized, organization structure can influence the operation and policies of the group. For example, some groups are centrally organized; that is, the central organization is dominant and has final say over local units. Other groups are *federally* organized; they have a division of authority which corresponds in many ways with our federal system of government. But, of course, the organizational structure of these groups has been influenced by the governmental structure. In any case, in federated groups local units operate with a certain measure of authority and independence from the authority of the national unit. Federated structures are more likely to experience problems of cohesion than do unitary or centrally controlled organized groups. Thus, national leaders might find it more difficult to represent the unified view of their organization.

As suggested previously, the influence of groups also depends upon the nature of the political system, in terms of both its values and its structures. The First Amendment, for example, fosters group participation. Similarly, the separation of powers doctrine allows groups to focus on various policy-making arenas. Both of these governmental features, it can be said, have strengthened the NAACP's ability to use the federal judiciary to achieve its objectives. The division of powers between nation and states (the federal system) also affects the influence of groups. Groups whose memberships may be large but concentrated in a few states may have great influence in those states and their cities. But they may not have too much influence nationally. And, groups who claim fairly wide distribution of members and who can harness other resources may have more impact on national policy.

EXERCISING INFLUENCE — GROUPS IN ACTION

We will now examine how groups use their resources. How and in what ways do they try to achieve their objectives in the political process? In large measure, of course, this depends upon the resources available to the group and how well it uses those resources. Within this framework, let us look at some of the techniques that groups use as they try to attain their policy objectives.

Public Opinion. First of all, groups try to stimulate a *favorable public opinion* toward their objectives.[4] Some call this propaganda; others refer to it as "educational" campaigns. In either case, communications media — newspapers, radio, television, billboards, and newsletters — play a major role. Eye-catching advertisements and easy-to-remember commercials (announcements) show the efforts of a good public relations department. However, groups sometimes use more subtle ways to create a favorable public image and opinion. They provide free educational materials, offer free expert lecturers, and give special grants to universities to endow professorships and establish special centers. The good will created by these soft-sell or "public interest" ventures could prove valuable when and if the group finds it necessary to make more direct efforts to influence particular public policies.

Electioneering. Groups also use this technique to achieve their policy objectives. In **electioneering** groups seek to influence election outcomes by supporting candidates who are favorable (or at least not opposed) to their goals. Group participation in elections may take several forms. It may range from outright endorsement and support of particular candidates to outright opposition in other situations. This, of course, leaves other options in between. In any event, the concern of groups in elections is quite understandable; election outcomes can determine the access that particular groups may have to those who win public office.

---

[4] Truman, *The Governmental Process,* esp. ch. 8.

Lobbying. Groups also **lobby** to influence public policy. Much of this activity focuses on Congress where groups spend large amounts of money each year to protect and promote their interests. In 1973, for example, registered lobbies reported spending $9,700,000.[5] But loopholes in the Federal Regulation of Lobbying Act of 1946 offer easy ways for organizations to avoid its registration and reporting requirements. For example, as interpreted by the U.S. Supreme Court,[6] the act applies only to those groups (and individuals) who collect and receive money "for the principal purpose of influencing legislation through direct contact with members of Congress." So, those groups who can *rely on their own funds* and do not "collect or receive" funds, or who argue that they do not use such funds for the *principal purpose* of influencing Congress, can and do escape the terms of the law. Many well-known organizations do not feel bound to report lobbying activities. For example, the National Association of Manufacturers spent more than $2,500,000 on "staff research, printing, mailing, and telegraphing that related to lobbying," but did not report such expenses since "grassroots" lobbying is not covered by the 1946 legislation.[7] Apparently, situations such as this led a lobbyist for the American Nurses Association to remark: "I just have to laugh every time that I see these [annual] lobby spending totals."[8] In this respect, it is interesting to note that Common Cause, the "citizens' lobby" that reports all its lobby expenditures, was "easily" the top spender in 1973. (See Table 7-1.) Small wonder then that Common Cause Chairman John Gardner called the Act "almost totally useless."[9]

A variety of groups engage in lobbying though some operate on a larger and more sophisticated scale than others. Lobbying has indeed become an art and profession. Making the right approach at the right time is the key to the successful lobbyist. This could involve supplying legislators with useful information. A lobbyist could provide professional analysis of the many bills that are introduced (or that a member of Congress might wish to introduce). Or he could summarize the views of the various publics with which particular legislators might be concerned. Or he could give testimony before congressional committees. This "information" function suggests that effective lobbyists, not unlike legis-

---

[5] For a summary review of lobby spending and proposed reforms see *Congressional Quarterly Weekly Report* (July 27, 1974, pp. 1947-1955). This discussion is based largely on materials found in this review.

[6] *United States* v. *Harriss* (347 U.S. 612, 1954).

[7] *Congressional Quarterly Weekly Report* (July 27, 1974, p. 1949). Comments on testimony of Common Cause Chairman John Gardner before Senate Government Operations Subcommittee.

[8] Ibid.

[9] Ibid.

TABLE 7-1
Twenty-five Top Spenders

Organization	1973	1972
Common Cause	$934,835	$558,839
International Union, United Automobile, Aerospace and Agricultural Implement Workers.	460,992	no spending record
American Postal Workers Union	393,399	208,767
American Federation of Labor–Congress of Industrial Organizations	240,800	216,294
American Trucking Associations Inc.	226,157	137,804
American Nurses Association Inc.	218,354	109,642
United States Savings and Loan League	204,221	191,726
Gas Supply Committee	195,537	11,263
Disabled American Veterans	193,168	159,431
The Committee of Publicly Owned Companies	180,493	no spending record
American Farm Bureau Federation	170,472	180,678
National Education Association	162,755	no spending record
National Association of Letter Carriers	160,597	154,187
National Association of Home Builders of the United States	152,177	99,031
Recording Industry Association of America Inc.	141,111	88,396
National Council of Farmer Cooperatives	140,560	184,346
American Insurance Association	139,395	82,395
The Farmers Educational and Co-operative Union of America	138,403	113,156
Committee of Copyright Owners	135,095	no spending record
National Housing Conference Inc.	125,726	77,906
American Petroleum Institute	121,276	38,856
American Medical Association	114,859	96,145
Citizens for Control of Federal Spending	113,659	no spending record
American Civil Liberties Union	102,595	73,131
National Association of Insurance Agents Inc.	87,422	50,924

SOURCE: Reprinted with permission from *Congressional Quarterly* (July 27, 1974), p. 1948.

lators, must and do have good supportive staffs. In any event, the major concern of the lobbyist is to protect and promote the group's interest by maintaining access to the legislator. This access, of course, may be attained through "information," or in other ways such as through electioneering. Or it could come from giving favors such as expense-paid vacations, rides on corporate jets, campaign contributions, and meals and entertainment.[10] All of these things, of course, cost money. But much of this access comes from lobbyists "knowing their way around Washington" — from years of long experience and contact with legislators, administrators, newspapermen and other Washingtonians. Indeed it is often just this kind of knowledge (information) that both the legislator and lobbyist need to do their jobs. Even more, however, such information and lobbying activities in general also allow the group to protect and promote its interests in the executive and administrative offices. After all, this is where legislative policies are defined and their benefits (and costs) distributed.

Litigation. Groups also use the judicial process to influence public policy. The two principal ways by which groups do this are by sponsoring (initiating, financing, and conducting) *litigation*, and by filing **amicus curiae** (that is, friend of the court) **briefs.** For example, the NAACP has been quite vigorous in using litigation to achieve its goals. And the U.S. Supreme Court has held that such vigorous advocacy is constitutionally grounded in the First Amendment. As Justice Brennan put it:

> In the context of NAACP objectives, litigation is not a technique of resolving private differences; it is a means for achieving the lawful objectives of equality of treatment by all government, federal, state and local for the members of the Negro community in this country. It is thus a form of political expression. Groups which find themselves unable to achieve their objectives through the ballot frequently turn to the courts. Just as it was true of the opponents of New Deal legislation during the 1930's, no less is it true of the Negro minority today. And under the conditions of modern government, litigation may well be the sole practicable avenue open to a minority to petition for redress of grievances.[11]

In general the success of the NAACP and other such groups in this respect has been well documented elsewhere.[12] We will not repeat it here except to reemphasize that litigation remains a chief avenue by which groups seek to accomplish their objectives.

---

[10] Ibid.

[11] *NAACP* v. *Button* (371 U.S. 415, 1963), pp. 429-430.

[12] See Lucius Barker, "Third Parties in Litigation," 29 *Journal of Politics* (1967): 41-69, and sources cited therein.

Direct Action and Violence. Marches, demonstrations, sit-ins, and violence have long been used by groups to promote their causes. This is particularly true of groups that lack the traditional resources (money, skills, votes) needed to influence public policy. The more recent and widespread use of direct action and violence occurred during the civil rights movement of the 1950's and 1960's. But even though these methods have long been part of the American political scene, they have never really been *accepted* as consistent with American beliefs and traditions of resolving conflict through peaceful (even nonobstructive) means. But accepted or not, the potential use of such methods may yet be determined by whether politically disadvantaged groups gain a greater share of the *traditional* and *accepted* resources (for instance, money, political offices) they need to protect and promote effectively their interests in the American political system.

Black Interest Groups: Problems Old and New

The major black interest groups have been and are now concerned with those problems that affect black people and other minorities. These problems have been called civil rights problems; groups that focus on these problems have been labeled civil rights groups. Obviously, the nature and scope of civil rights problems and civil rights groups have changed over time. Until late in the 1960's these groups were mostly concerned with the formal recognition and definition of constitutional and legal rights. Today their chief concern is with the practical implementation of these legal rights so as to improve the quality of everyday living for black Americans. While these were and are the chief concerns of civil rights groups, it is no secret that black groups have differed and continue to differ in how best to achieve these objectives. What objectives should be sought has been and is a source of disagreement as well.

The difference between and among groups and their objectives, as we discussed in the first part of this chapter, may be explained by such factors as the nature of group membership and the nature of group resources — that is, how groups attempt to achieve their objectives. To illustrate many of these factors as they relate to black interest groups we have chosen to reprint an article that describes the problems and successes of major black groups in forming a coalition that would give unity and direction to the civil rights movement in the 1960's. The article is followed by a brief account of what has happened to civil rights groups and the civil rights movement since that time.

COALITIONS
IN THE CIVIL RIGHTS
MOVEMENT*

Lucius J. Barker
Donald Jansiewicz

On July 2, 1964, President Lyndon Johnson signed into law the Civil Rights Act of 1964. This enactment is important in two respects. First, it is one of the most significant pieces of civil rights legislation to get through Congress. Secondly, and most important for our purposes, the 1964 legislation displayed the strength and unity of the civil rights coalition. The 1964 legislation (along with the 1965 Voting Rights Act) marks the high point of the civil rights movement. More than forty major interest groups united their efforts in order to pass it.[1] Anthony Lewis states that the passage of the 1964 legislation "emphasized the breadth of national commitment"[2] to civil rights.

The events of the more recent past, however, stand in sharp contrast to the unity and success of 1964. The coalition which rallied around the 1964 legislation is all but dead. Even the hard center of that coalition (NAACP, Urban League, SCLC, CORE, and SNCC) has splintered. The once-effective civil rights coalition is today rent by truculent diatribe. There is not only a debate over means, but over ends as well. The coalition is divided into suspicious, tense, and warring factions. The sympathetic white liberal, a basic component of the 1964 coalition, now watches with anxiety.[3] The Reverend Martin Luther King, Jr., once a rallying point, was at the time of his assassination struggling to maintain

---

* From "Coalitions in the Civil Rights Movement" by Lucius J. Barker and Donald Jansiewicz, in *The Study of Coalition Behavior: Theoretical Perspectives and Cases from Four Continents*, edited by Sven Groennings, E. W. Kelley, and Michael Leiserson. Copyright © 1970, by Holt, Rinehart, and Winston, Publishers. Reprinted with permission of Holt, Rinehart, and Winston, Publishers. (Footnotes in the original.)

[1] For a complete list of participating groups, see "Intensive Lobbying Marked House Civil Rights Debate," *Congressional Quarterly Report*, 22 (week ending February 21, 1964), pp. 364–366.

[2] Anthony Lewis, *Portrait of a Decade: The Second American Revolution* (New York: Bantam Books, 1965), p. 106.

[3] See Murray Friedman, "The White Liberal's Retreat" in Alan F. Westin, ed., *Freedom Now: The Civil Rights Struggle in America* (New York: Basic Books, 1964), pp. 320–328.

a viable leadership position. The NAACP, the major force behind the *Brown* Supreme Court decision, now struggles to maintain some vestige of its moderate civil rights leadership.[4] The whole concept of racial integration has been rejected by some black leaders.[5] Nonviolence is now being challenged by Black Power[6] advocates; in short, disunity has struck the entire civil rights movement.

Among other things, this state of affairs focuses attention on the admittedly narrow political problem of maintaining a coalition among civil rights groups, that is, among groups championing civil rights as their central purpose. This study is limited to six civil rights groups. Five of these groups are of major importance: the Urban League, the NAACP, SCLC, SNCC, and CORE. The sixth group, the Muslims, is important to the extent that it acts as a viable alternative to civil rights for Negroes (in the form of separatism) and commands considerable support.

This [article] is divided into three parts: a general profile of group characteristics and attitudes, a brief history of the rise of a coalition of civil rights groups, and an account of the factors leading to disunity among the groups.

The Major Civil Rights Groups

Civil rights groups are hardly cut out of the same cloth. They exhibit a variety of characteristics which tend to associate with, and perhaps produce, differing political outlooks. First of all, these groups can be visualized in terms of a continuum of high-low integration into the existing political system, as in Figure 1.[7] Clearly, some civil rights

---

[4] See Louis Lomax, "The Crisis of Negro Leadership," in *The Negro Revolt* (New York: New American Library, 1963), pp. 160-176.

[5] Louis Lomax, "The Crisis of Negro Leadership," pp. 178-193. For more complete references see Louis Lomax, *When the Word is Given* (Cleveland: World Publishing, 1963) and Elijah Muhammad, *Message to the Blackman in America* (Chicago: Muhammad Mosque of Islam No. 2, 1965).

[6] See Stokely Carmichael and Charles V. Hamilton, *Black Power: The Politics of Liberation in America* (New York: Vintage Books, 1967).

[7] This continuum is a reflection of group efforts to work within the institutional framework of American politics. It represents the percentage of actions or statements of a group that conform to normal American institutional expectations.

The data for the figure were drawn from nineteen and one-half months (January 1, 1966, through September 15, 1967) of the *New York Times Index*. Every time a group's representative went to formal government for redress of grievance, spoke positively about the viability of American institutions or established and participated in complementary nongovernmental institutions, this group was given credit for one "integrated action." Every march, boycott, threat of picketing, or anti-institutional statement (or antisystem

FIGURE 1
Percentage of Institutionally Directed Incidents as Indicative of Relative System Integration, 1966–1967

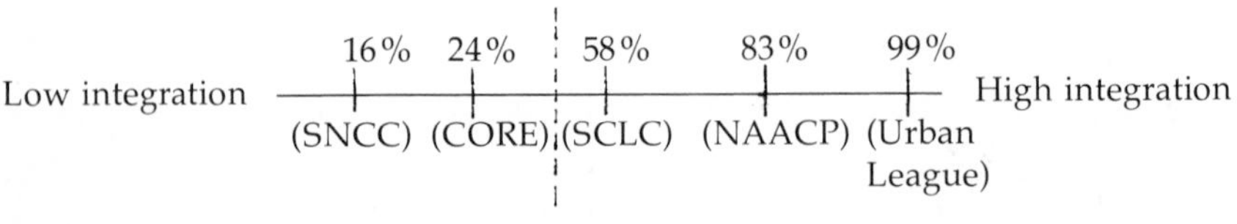

```
                  16%   24%  ┊ 58%      83%      99%
Low integration  ──┼─────┼──┊┼─────────┼─────────┼──  High integration
                 (SNCC) (CORE)┊(SCLC)  (NAACP) (Urban
                              ┊                 League)
```

groups seek to achieve their goals by using normal institutional approaches and channels, such as lobbying and electioneering. On the other hand, other groups consider these techniques ineffective in terms of institutional response and accordingly resort to "direct action" and "militant" methods to achieve their goals. Though generally within the legal limits of the political system, these direct-action approaches nevertheless defy traditional norms and political styles, and in the process evoke strong negative reactions from many people including those in the policy-making positions. Initially, then, we are discussing group behavior patterns in terms of their relative integration into the "normal," conventional political system.

At one end of the continuum we find two groups. Both of these, the Urban League and the National Association for the Advancement of Colored People, are deeply integrated into the political and social structure of American life.

---

statement) are coded as an "alienated action." The assumption here is that picketing, boycotting, and threats of violence do not constitute institutionally oriented behavior patterns. Final calculations were then made in terms of a group's percentage of institutional incidents. The complete table follows:

Organization	Total Reported Actions	Alienated Actions	Integrated Actions	Percent Integrated
Urban League	47	1	46	98
NAACP	133	23	110	83
SCLC	140	38	82	59
CORE	98	72	26	27
SNCC	101	85	16	16

Three major methodological qualifications should be noted. The continuum does not weigh the intensity and forms of political behavior. Rather, it weighs the direction. In this respect it does not distinguish between peaceful march and the threat of violence. These forms of political behavior are merely classified as being institution-alienated.

Secondly, the Muslims were left out of the analysis. Despite their consideration later in this chapter, the paucity of data prohibited useful analysis. In light of the organization's goals, the Muslims might be given a score of absolute zero, but in the absence of the necessary data they have been excluded from Figure 1. . . .

The National Urban League[8] was founded in 1910 for the purpose of aiding Southern Negroes in their adjustment to the urban North. Over time, it has evolved into a large-scale social agency operating on a national level. Today, the Urban League is a highly structured, biracial organization, run from the top, with a professional staff of about 8000. The league attempts to achieve its objectives through research, consultation, and persuasion. Since its beginnings, it has sought to integrate Negroes into American society through the establishment of equal opportunities. The Urban League hastens to add that with new opportunities come responsibilities for Negroes. In this light, then, the Urban League divides its time between the white and Negro communities. Under the leadership of Whitney M. Young, Jr.,* the league has proposed in recent times a "Marshall Plan for American Negroes." This program would make available billions of dollars to improve Negroes' health, education, and welfare. The league's plan is to integrate the Negro within the general structure of American life.

In attempting to push its social welfare approach to race relations, the Urban League has gone to the white community for most of its financial support. The main sources of funds are foundation grants and monies donated through United Fund drives and so forth. Consequently, even though the league devotes its major efforts to the unemployed and the poor, it tends to do so in the framework of "established" America. It could be said that the league uses middle-class methods to achieve middle-class goals for lower-class people. The league normally avoids participation in direct-action campaigns. It emphasizes welfare lobbying within the limits of existing institutions and practices, and, of the organizations discussed in this article, it is probably the most integrated into the American political system.

The National Association for the Advancement of Colored People (NAACP)[9] and the Urban League have much in common. Founded in

---

[8] See Louis Lomax, *The Negro Revolt*, pp. 112–132; Kenneth B. Clark, "The Civil Rights Movement: Momentum and Organization," in Talcott Parsons and Kenneth B. Clark, *The Negro American* (Boston: Houghton Mifflin, 1966), pp. 601–602; R. Joseph Monsen, Jr., and Mark W. Cannon, "Negroes," in *The Makers of Public Policy: American Power Groups and Their Ideologies* (New York: McGraw-Hill, 1965), pp. 143–144; Whitney Young, "The Urban League and Its Strategy," in Arnold M. Rose, ed., *Annals of the American Academy*, 357 (January 1965), pp. 102–107; Norman Jackman and Jack Dodson, "Negro Youth and Direct Action," in *Phylon*, 28 (Spring 1967), p. 13; James H. Lane, "The Changing Nature of Negro Protest," in Arnold M. Rose, *Annals of the American Academy*, 1965, pp. 120–125.

* The reader should be aware that this article was written in 1968–1969, prior to the death of Whitney M. Young, Jr. A number of changes have occurred since that time. One was the appointment of a new head of the League, Vernon Jordan.

[9] Lomax, *The Negro Revolt*, pp. 224–236; Clark, *Negro American*, pp. 598–601; Monsen and Cannon, "Negroes," pp. 141–142; Morsell, "The NAACP and Its Strategy," in Arnold M. Rose, *Annals of the American Academy*, 1965, pp. 97–101; Jackman and Dodson, "Negro Youth and Direct Action"; Lane, "The Changing Nature of Negro Protest," pp. 120–122.

1909, the NAACP has attempted to work for change within the established political structure. While the Urban League has emphasized integration through massive social welfare programs, the NAACP has dedicated much of its effort to conventional political arenas in an effort to make and change laws that would improve the legal status of American Negroes. This legalistic approach can be observed in the NAACP's active role in legislative, administrative, and judicial decision-making.

The organization has attempted to avoid direct-action approaches. The Executive Board, under the leadership of Roy Wilkins, uses political and legal channels rather than direct action. Yet, the NAACP does support the right of protest and has increasingly participated in direct-action programs and the more action-oriented tenor of the civil rights movement. Nevertheless, power in the NAACP is concentrated in the hands of the National Executive Board. Although there are more than 400,000 dues-paying members and 1600 local chapters throughout the country, NAACP policy is largely determined at the top.

Membership is fundamentally middle class and middle age. There are two outside bases of support, namely, the white liberals and the religious community. Like the Urban League, the NAACP is well-financed, "elitist," and highly integrated into the present structure of American politics.

Toward the low-integration end of the continuum, we find a cluster of three organizations: the Black Muslims, SNCC, and CORE. These organizations, unlike the NAACP and the Urban League, are not highly integrated into the structure of American Politics. These groups, especially SNCC and CORE, tend to emphasize direct action techniques.

The Muslims[10] are one of the most alienated groups in American society; they are dedicated to the complete cultural and spatial separation of races. The Muslims are a religious group, strongly anti-Christian and antiwhite, and their organization is theocratic. Their membership exceeds 100,000 and is concentrated in the Negro urban areas of the Northern and Western United States. Most of the members are black students, workers, and the dispossessed. The Muslims gained national attention during the early 1960's, under the leadership of Elijah Muhammad and Malcolm X, as an alternative to racial integration. The organization maintains no ties with the white community. Indeed, the Muslims regard the white man as the Devil incarnate. Although it is not a political action group in the usual sense (members are forbidden to vote), it does give direction to some elements of the black community.

The Student Non-violent Coordinating Committee (SNCC)[11] is the

---

[10] Lomax, *The Negro Revolt*, pp. 178–192; Monsen and Cannon, "Negroes," pp. 145–146; Lomax, *When the Word is Given.*

[11] Lomax, *The Negro Revolt*, pp. 133–159; Clark, *Negro American*, pp. 615–619; Monsen and Cannon, "Negroes," pp. 144–145; Lane, "The Changing Nature of Negro Protest,"

youngest of civil rights organizations, having begun in 1960. Whereas students originally constituted the bulk of SNCC's membership, today the organization is primarily composed of a young nonstudent Negro working class membership. Financed by contributions, SNCC has few, if any, ties with the white middle class, or with whites in general. Accordingly, the organization is less influenced by the interests and pressures of the political establishment than are the more integrated groups. SNCC is unlike the NAACP and the Urban League in another way: it is more of a grassroots organization. Its national body, the Coordinating Committee, represents a variety of protest groups. As a result of this system of representation, there is a close relationship between the national organization and its local units.

SNCC has not used normal political channels to achieve its goals. It champions the use of Black Power to achieve equality for black Americans. However, Black Power, even as defined by SNCC leaders, is a changing concept subject to varying interpretations. Stokely Carmichael, former SNCC chairman and still a leading spokesman for the organization, once viewed Black Power as the political, economic, and social mobilization of an oppressed people, an effort to gain power through direct action (pickets, marches, and boycotts) and electioneering. In more recent times, however, Carmichael and other SNCC leaders have defined Black Power and the goals of SNCC in more militant terms. Recently, for example, Carmichael defined Black Power as "the unification of the Negro population to fight for their liberation . . . to take up arms."[12] This new, militant stance contrasts sharply with the "nonviolent direct action" emphasis which characterized the founding of SNCC. Perhaps partly as a result of its new image, SNCC today faces a dwindling of both finances and membership.

Much like SNCC, the Congress of Racial Equality (CORE)[13] has grown up with a history of protest. Founded in 1942, CORE has generally tried to abolish racial discrimination through the application of Gandhian philosophy and techniques of nonviolent direct action. Under the leadership of Floyd McKissick, however, CORE also adopted the rhetoric of Black Power. As in the case of SNCC, this more militant Black Power stance has affected the organization in a number of ways. Its

---

pp. 125–126; Jackman and Dodson, "Negro Youth and Direct Action," pp. 12–15; Howard Zinn, *SNCC: The New Abolitionists* (Boston: Beacon Press, 1964), pp. 1–40.

[12] See, generally, Don McKee, "SNCC Turns to Black Violence as Members' Support Dwindle," *Milwaukee Journal* (November 26, 1967), p. 24.

[13] Lomax, *The Negro Revolt*, pp. 133–159; Clark, *Negro American*, pp. 608–610; Monsen and Cannon, "Negroes," pp. 144–145; Lane, "The Changing Nature of Negro Protest," pp. 125–126; Marvin Rich, "The Congress of Racial Equality and Its Strategy," in Arnold M. Rose, ed., *Annals of the American Academy*, 357 (January 1965), pp. 113–118; Jackman and Dodson, "Negro Youth and Direct Action," pp. 12–15.

biracial character is giving way to uniracial emphasis. While a number of liberal whites are leaving the group, many [urban blacks] have been attracted to it. Losing the financial support of liberal whites has hampered certain CORE programs, such as its "target city" program. The "target city" program combines a mild welfare approach with a strong dose of protest. However, reductions in programs of this kind have been somewhat offset by an increased black membership and a program which more directly appeals to lower-class Negroes.

As in the case of SNCC, CORE has few connections with the political establishment. Because of its philosophy and its orientation to the lower-class Negro, CORE rarely enters conventional political arenas. It relies primarily on direct-action methods. Consequently, CORE, just like SNCC, is becoming increasingly alienated from the political system and from the more established moderate civil rights organizations such as the NAACP and the Urban League.

The Southern Christian Leadership Conference (SCLC)[14] falls in the middle of the continuum shown in Figure 1. It holds this position probably because of its mixed characteristics. On the one hand, SCLC's organization, support, and connections with liberal whites have tended to integrate it into the political system. On the other hand, however, its techniques resemble those of low-integration groups. This mixture of characteristics probably accounts for SCLC's central position in the 1964 coalition.

SCLC was organized in 1957 and has been one of the most effective groups in civil rights. It is based on a philosophy of racial reform through creative nonviolence. Martin Luther King, Jr., was until his assassination in the spring of 1968 the president of SCLC. In fact, the organization was considered the personal embodiment of King. SCLC under King's leadership was very highly centralized: despite elections, the organization was a synonym for the name Martin Luther King. It depended not only on his leadership and philosophical guidance, but also upon his ability to raise money. King's speaking tours helped SCLC to become one of the best financed civil rights groups. Given King's charisma, the organization has been able to enlist the support of more than one hundred church-affiliated groups. This religious support, in combination with the support of white liberals, provided King with many points of access.

During the past two years, however, SCLC's power position has been highly unstable. Some white liberals shied away from King because of his increased use of direct-action techniques. (Yet King gained other

---

[14] Clark, *Negro American*, pp. 610–615; Monsen and Cannon, "Negroes," pp. 142–143; Jackman and Dodson, "Negro Youth and Direct Action," pp. 12–15; Lane, "The Changing Nature of Negro Protest," pp. 123–124.

white liberal support for his stand on Vietnam.) In contrast, however, some Negroes were disappointed by his refusal to become more militant in his direct-action activities. At the time of his death, Martin Luther King seemed caught in the center. The year 1968 found SCLC in a central position, but the center may no longer be the rallying point in civil rights. Wherever that "rallying point" was, it appeared likely that Dr. King would try to find it. Whether Ralph Abernathy and his associates will be able to pilot SCLC and the civil rights movement as skillfully is not clear.

The Politics of Coalition Building

Between 1963 and 1965, the civil rights coalition proved to be a potent force in the American political scene. The question of how this coalition came about leads us to the politics of coalition building.

World War II brought the country into a new phase of civil rights.[15] This new era was an outgrowth of several factors. First, we had just fought a war in the name of human freedom. This attuned the population, both black and white, to the importance of equality. Secondly, the war marked the end of the Great Depression. The depression reoriented the thinking of many Americans. The market had failed the United States in 1929. At last, the American people were willing to place other values above the rights of private property. As a result of this rethinking, Americans now placed a greater emphasis on political, economic, and social equality. Finally, the war directly affected Negroes' lives by making them mobile. Able to compare two styles of life (thanks to military service or a wartime job in some Northern factory), Negroes could see that the Southern caste system was not inevitable. Taken together, these factors set the stage for a new revolution in America.

The 1940s produced a flurry of civil rights activities. It was in this era that groups like CORE gained attention.[16] Frustrated by the gradualism of established civil rights groups, the younger groups dedicated themselves to more militant approaches. But during the tensions of the 1940s, groups tended to be concerned with their own immediate problems. For the most part, civil rights was still considered in terms of local interests. A civil rights movement per se did not yet exist.

Only in the 1950s can we observe the development of a coalition. Through a series of Supreme Court cases, one could note a gradual

---

[15] Samuel Eliot Morison and Henry Steele Commager, *The Growth of the American Republic*, pp. 916–928.

[16] Lomax, *The Negro Revolt*, p. 145.

convergence of interested parties. There was now evidence that a civil rights coalition could be effective. This new realization sparked the desire finally to destroy the "separate but equal doctrine." In *Brown* v. *Board of Education* (1954), several groups, under the leadership of the NAACP, pooled their resources[17] and won a monumental victory when on May 17, 1954, the Supreme Court declared racial segregation in public schools unconstitutional.

The 1954 decision fostered new hope in the civil rights movement. It also aroused in Negroes a sense of impatience with racial conditions generally. In 1955, for example, nearly all Negroes in Montgomery, Alabama, boycotted segregated transportation facilities. Indeed, "the once dormant and quiescent Negro community," as Martin Luther King expressed it, "was now fully awake."[18] The success of the 1955 bus boycott paved the way for subsequent nonviolent techniques including sit-ins and freedom rides of the early 1960s. (It also skyrocketed Martin Luther King into national prominence.) These direct-action efforts were engineered primarily by the more recently established, more action-oriented groups, that is, CORE, SCLC, and SNCC. In the early 1960s, however, these newer civil rights groups and the older groups were not united, and there were many who felt that unity was needed. The 1963 March on Washington represented, among other things, an attempt to promote and demonstrate unity among the various groups.

A. Philip Randolph, veteran civil rights leader and President of the Brotherhood of Sleeping Car Porters, AFL–CIO, issued the call for the march at a time when there was considerable division and personal rancor between civil rights groups and their leaders.[19] Randolph originally conceived the march as a demonstration for jobs, but Martin Luther King thought the goals should be broadened to include all Negro rights, not just economic ones. Randolph accepted King's "broadening proposal" and the march began to take shape. To actually plan the march, Randolph secured the services of Bayard Rustin. Rustin had had a rich and varied background of experiences in civil rights activities and other human rights causes, and at one time had served as secretary to Dr. King. In any case, planning could now begin for the march, which was intended to demonstrate as much as anything else the unity and dimensions of the civil rights movement, and to bring its various fac-

---

[17] For an account of the *Brown* litigation, see Barker and Barker, *Freedoms, Courts, Politics: Studies of Civil Liberties* (Englewood Cliffs, N.J.: Prentice-Hall, 1965), pp. 137–185. Also see Barker, "Third Parties in Litigation: A Systematic View of the Judicial Function," *The Journal of Politics* (February 1967), pp. 41 ff.

[18] Martin Luther King, Jr., *Stride Toward Freedom* (New York: Harper & Row, 1958), p. 40.

[19] M. Kempton, "March on Washington," *New Republic*, 149 (September 14, 1963), pp. 19–20.

tions together. Attention had to be given not only to unity among basically Negro groups — the focus of this essay — but also to promoting a coalition between Negro organizations and white groups such as labor.

Achieving unity and cooperation among black civil rights groups was not easy. Ordinarily, for example, one would have expected the June 13, 1963, murder of Medgar Evers, Field Director of the Mississippi NAACP, to serve as a rallying point among the various groups. But such was not the case. Groups suspected each other of trying to "use" an emotional situation to demonstrate and promote particular causes. Frictions inevitably developed. Perhaps because of this and other "irritating incidents" largely caused by "local eager beavers," Roy Wilkins, Executive Secretary of the NAACP, openly criticized CORE, SNCC, and SCLC for taking "the publicity while the NAACP provides the manpower and pays the bill."[20] "The only organization that can handle a long sustained fight," said Wilkins, "is the NAACP. We are not here today, gone tomorrow." However, a few days later Wilkins called for cooperation among the various groups, noting that such collaboration was especially important at the "present time" because of civil rights legislation pending in Congress. "Intelligent work in the Capitol lobbies," said Wilkins, "could be more important than mass marches on Washington or sit-downs or sit-ins in the halls of Congress." SNCC and CORE leaders disclaimed any divisions and did not, at the time at least, join the argument, but Martin Luther King did. King said:

> We all acknowledge that the NAACP is the oldest, the best established, it has done a marvelous job for many years and has worked rigorously. But we feel we also have a role to play in supplementing what the NAACP has done. Unity is necessary. Uniformity is not. The highway that leads to the city of freedom is not a one-lane highway. New organizations such as SCLC are not substitutes for the NAACP, but they can be wonderful supplements.[21]

King's remarks seemingly sounded a note upon which there could be unity and cooperation among the various groups. The commonality of their goal overcame, for the time being at least, group differences in strategy and tactics and led to cooperative ventures. For example, in July 1963 SNCC, CORE, SCLC, and NAACP, the Urban League, and two other groups formed an Ad Hoc Council on Civil Rights Leadership to coordinate planning and activities for "racial integration and equal opportunity."[22] A major goal of the Ad Hoc Council was to raise

---

[20] *New York Times*, June 17, 1963, p. 12.
[21] *New York Times*, June 23, 1963, p. 56.
[22] *New York Times*, July 3, 1963, p. 10, and July 17, 1963, p. 15.

emergency funds for aiding organizations to meet rising and unexpected costs resulting from the "tremendous increase in civil rights activities . . . since their 1963 budgets were adopted."[23] Evidence that this cooperative fund-raising effort met with some success can be found in the more than one-half million dollars distributed among the various participating groups in July 1963.[24]

The cooperative mood of the times was further enhanced by pronouncements and resolutions emanating from the 1963 national conventions of the various organizations. CORE national delegates, for example, were warned against "rivalry" between organizations and were told of the necessity of cooperation.[25] But perhaps the most dramatic example of the growing cooperation and understanding among civil rights groups was pointed up by a resolution passed by the 1963 National Convention of the Urban League. While continuing to pursue its goals through negotiations and professional social work, the league nevertheless resolved to support legal picketing and sit-ins by other groups. The league even acknowledged that certain "stubborn problem situations have not responded to Urban League methods."[26]

The August 1963 March on Washington was the highpoint of coalition activity among civil rights groups and their allies up to that time. (The "Big Six" civil rights organizations, SNCC, CORE, the NAACP, SCLC, the Urban League, and Randolph's Negro American Labor Council, even agreed to accept as equal partners Walter Reuther, Vice President of AFL–CIO and one white officer from Protestant, Catholic, and Jewish organizations.) For the moment, group priorities were set aside, each group yielding something for the coalition. The Urban League and the NAACP agreed to participate actively in the form of direct action. On the other hand, the militants such as CORE and SNCC agreed to seek and be content (for a while at least) with action through relatively conventional channels. Moreover, the militants were dissuaded from other actions that tended to offend white liberal sympathizers. Archbishop O'Boyle of the Washington, D.C., Archdiocese threatened not to give the invocation at the March program unless John Lewis, then President of SNCC, changed his prepared speech. Lewis' original speech read:

> The non-violent revolution is saying we will not wait for the others to act for we have been waiting for hundreds of years. We will not wait for the President, the Justice Department nor Congress, but we will take matters into our own hands and create a source of power outside of any national structure that could and would assure us victory.[27]

---

[23] *New York Times,* August 16, 1963, p. 9.
[24] *New York Times,* July 18, 1963, p. 10.
[25] *New York Times,* July 18, 1963, p. 10.
[26] *New York Times,* June 29, 1963, p. 10.
[27] *New York Times,* August 2, 1963, p. 11.

Wide World Photos

1963 March on Washington: Highpoint of Coalition. Leaders of the March hold up their hands to greet crowd as they walk along parade route followed by placard-carrying marchers. Third from left is Rev. Martin Luther King, Jr. At right is Walter Reuther of the United Auto Workers and third from right is Roy Wilkins of the NAACP.

O'Boyle discussed this part of Lewis' speech with Randolph and Reuther, who both agreed that the speech was not consistent with the tenor "of the rest of the program." Upon the urgings of Randolph and Reuther, Lewis revised this part of his speech. The revision read:

> To those who are saying, "Be patient and wait," we will say that we cannot be patient. We do not want our freedom gradually, but we want to be free now.[28]

Great care was taken to nurture March unity. For example, representatives of each of the ten sponsoring groups were given a place on the program. In this way no group could feel slighted. Again however, as on other occasions, it was the charisma and powerful oratory of Martin

---

[28] *New York Times,* August 26, 1963, p. 20. Also see Paul Good, "Odyssey of Man and a Movement," *New York Times Magazine,* June 25, 1967, p. 45.

Wide World Photos

LBJ talks with Civil Rights Leaders. Soon after the tragic assassination of President John F. Kennedy, the new President Johnson stated his determination to push vigorously civil rights goals. Here Johnson talks with civil rights leaders in January 1964, a few months prior to passage of the most far-reaching civil rights legislation since Reconstruction, the Civil Rights Act of 1964. From left: Roy Wilkins, executive secretary of the NAACP, James Farmer, national director of the Congress of Racial Equality; Dr. Martin Luther King, Jr., head of the Southern Christian Leadership Conference; and Whitney Young, executive secretary of the Urban League.

Luther King that highlighted the program and cemented a coalition unity that paved the way for future coordination and cooperation among civil rights groups and their allies.

The fruits of the cooperation and spirit of unity exemplified in the 1963 March on Washington were reaped in 1964 and 1965, when Congress passed the most far-reaching civil rights legislation since the Reconstruction era. These acts contained provisions legally guaranteeing Negroes the right to vote, access to most public accommodations, desegregated schools, and equal employment opportunities. Not only was the scope of these acts far broader than the earlier Civil Rights Acts of 1957 and 1960, but the provisions for enforcement by the federal government gave hope that the provisions would be obeyed. Of course, passage of these two acts was not due solely to intensive lobbying; the Northern Democratic-Republican coalition and vigorous assistance from the White House were crucial elements of the victory. Nevertheless, behind the near-consensus among the pro-civil rights coalition of politicians (in Senate Republican Leader Dirksen's words "the time has come"[29]) was a national mood; in the creation of that national mood the coalition of civil rights groups was perhaps the primary moving force.

But there were signs, even in 1964–1965, that the coalition was in jeopardy. First, the less integrationist members of the coalition such, as SNCC, CORE, and SCLC, had always made their support contingent upon success in the society at large, and not merely in Congress. As it gradually became clear that even the historic Acts of 1964–1965 would not change the life situations of Negroes rapidly, these groups began to search for means other than legislation for promoting that change. Secondly, even with the provisions for enforcement, considerable discrimination remained even in the areas covered by these two acts. For example, in 1967 the Civil Rights Commission reported that, in the area of public education, the field in which federal government action had been tried *longest* (since 1954), "racial isolation in the public schools was intense and growing worse."[30] And thirdly, there was the failure of the coalition to obtain legislative enactment of desegregation in certain crucial areas, such as housing. "Open housing" was not included in the 1964–1965 acts, and when it was included in the 1966 Civil Rights Bill the Senate killed the bill. Such legislation was finally passed in 1968.

The Politics of Disintegration

In July 1964, the leaders of the NAACP, SCLC, the Urban League, and NALC signed a statement urging major civil rights groups to curtail or postpone mass demonstrations until after the 1964 presidential elections.[31] SNCC (Lewis) and CORE (Farmer) did not sign the statement. "Our own estimate of the present situation," said the four leaders, "is that it presents a serious threat to the implementation of the

---

[29] Congressional Quarterly Service, *Revolution in Civil Rights,* 3d ed. (Washington, D.C., 1967), p. 68.

[30] *Revolution in Civil Rights,* p. 22.

[31] See generally George D. Blackwood, "Civil Rights and Direct Action in the North," *Public Policy* (1965), p. 311.

Civil Rights Act of 1964."[32] The "present situation" was described as including the passage of the Civil Rights Act, the nomination of Barry Goldwater, and recent big-city riots. "Therefore," the four leaders continued, "we propose a temporary change of emphasis and tactics because we sincerely believe that the major energy of the civil rights forces should be used to encourage Negro people, North and South, to register and to vote. The greatest need in this period is for political action."[33] Although Roy Wilkins said that SNCC and CORE leaders agreed with the statement "personally" and were withholding their signatures pending meeting of their steering committees, there is no evidence that they ever agreed to the statement. In a second statement issued by the group, all but SNCC joined. This statement condemned rioting and looting and drew a sharp distinction between such activity and legitimate protest.

The year 1965 was the turning point for coalition activity within the civil rights movement. The year began on a cooperative note. A. Philip Randolph (NALC), who led the 1963 March on Washington, was once again in the forefront. He convened a two-day closed meeting of civil rights leaders to outline aims for 1965. Some twenty-nine organizations attended, including representatives from all major civil rights groups, including SNCC, SCLC, CORE, the NAACP, and the Urban League.[34] In a carefully and broadly worded statement, the organizations agreed that "the thrust of the civil rights movement this year . . . would be toward guaranteeing the right to vote through increased registration, legislation, and peaceful demonstrations."[35] Randolph called the conference evidence of the "continued dialogue and shared experience" among civil rights groups.[36]

But support for the Voting Rights Act of 1965 was perhaps the final manifestation of a viable coalition among civil rights groups and their allies. Indeed, the "continued dialogue" was already almost finished. Disaffection, frustration, and friction began to develop and, ironically, the passage of the Civil Rights Act of 1964 and the Voting Rights Act of 1965 gave further impetus to these developments. Some reasoned that since legal barriers were now removed, they could turn their attention to other issues, such as the peace movement. The Negro masses were frustrated because, though sweeping legislation had been passed, their social and economic situation remained the same; to them, nothing had changed. It was this latter factor as much or more than anything else which led to friction among civil rights groups. Some groups, such as SNCC and CORE, wanted results *now,* while the NAACP was willing to

---

[32] *New York Times,* July 30, 1964, pp. 1,12.
[33] *New York Times,* July 30, 1964, pp. 1,12.
[34] *New York Times,* February 1, 1965, p. 12.
[35] *New York Times,* February 1, 1965, p. 12.
[36] *New York Times,* February 1, 1965, p. 12.

pursue enforcement through regular legal processes. Actually, this "division of labor,"[37] that is, the testing of laws through demonstrations by the more militant groups, and legal support from the NAACP, seemed tailor-made for the situation. But, although their goals may have been the same, the difference in temperament and approach between the militants and the more established organizations posed too great an obstacle to overcome for a sustained period. The disposition of the more militant groups to link the "peace movement" (Vietnam) with civil rights also proved a friction point among the groups. For example, in August 1965 SNCC and CORE members openly joined the Assembly of Unrepresented People and staged a march on Washington, D.C. On the other hand, the NAACP's Roy Wilkins warned his members not to participate since the focus of the march was on Vietnam, not civil rights.[38]

The smoldering frictions of the coalition exploded into the open in 1966. This was the year that saw Stokely Carmichael and Floyd McKissick take over the reins of SNCC and CORE. Undoubtedly, these changes in leadership in SNCC and CORE did much to bring the battle into the open. In May 1966, for example, Carmichael attacked integration as a goal of the civil rights movement and called it "irrelevant."[39] "Political and economic power is what black people have to have."[40] This kindling of black nationalism flew in the face of everything civil rights leaders had previously sought to accomplish. Even so, however, the man in the "middle" of the civil rights movement, Martin Luther King, remained in the middle in his criticism of Carmichael. "While I can't agree with the move toward a kind of black nationalism developing in SNCC," said King, "it is an indication of deep discontent, frustration, disappointment, and even despair in many segments of the Negro community."[41]

The June 1966 White House Conference on Civil Rights also pointed up the developing split among civil rights groups. SNCC refused to participate since it did not believe the Johnson administration was sincere in helping the Negro and because of United States involvement in Vietnam. And though CORE participated, it did so, as its new national chairman, Floyd McKissick, put it, so that militants could "bring forth ideas that otherwise would not be brought forth."[42] This "militant" view included a CORE-sponsored resolution calling for American with-

---

[37] Actually, this "division of labor" is suggested by Anthony Lewis in his *Portrait of a Decade;* that is, SNCC and CORE would protest while the NAACP would provide counsel and bail (pp. 118–120).

[38] *New York Times,* August 15, 1965, p. 73.

[39] *New York Times,* May 28, 1966, p. 1.

[40] *New York Times,* May 28, 1966, p. 1.

[41] *New York Times,* May 28, 1966, p. 1.

[42] *New York Times,* June 1, 1966, p. 33.

drawal from Vietnam. Though soundly defeated, the resolution nevertheless evidenced the growing schism between militants such as CORE
and SNCC and the more established groups such as the NAACP. Martin
Luther King attended the White House Conference but apparently, and
perhaps discreetly, remained "behind the scenes."

Other incidents also demonstrated the growing rift among the various groups. In June 1966, for example, James Meredith was wounded
while walking through Mississippi on his "pilgrimage against fear."
Major civil rights organizations came to his rescue and agreed to continue the march. For the moment, at least, it seemed as if the groups had
patched up their differences. But this appearance was short-lived. The
groups did not agree on what they hoped to accomplish by continuing
the "pilgrimage." Three leaders — King, Carmichael, and McKissick —
issued a joint statement declaring the march to be a "massive public
indictment and protest of the failure of American society, the government of the United States, and the State of Mississippi to 'fulfill these
rights.'" [43] "Most important of all," the statement continued, "the President of the United States must enforce those laws justly and impartially
for all men." [44] However, Roy Wilkins of the NAACP and Whitney
Young of the Urban League refused to sign the statement. Sub-
sequently, Wilkins openly denounced CORE and SNCC and shed light
on the apparent disagreement among the groups at the time of the
Meredith march. Wilkins said:

> The refusal of the . . . organizations . . . to join in a strong nation-wide
> effort to pass the Civil Rights Bill (1966) was a civil rights tragedy. The
> Meredith shooting should have been and could have been a rallying cry for
> scores of organizations and groups in a concerted push for the Bill . . . The
> whole business showed the NAACP again how difficult it is to have
> genuine cooperation on an equal responsibility basis with groups that do
> not have the same commitments and which may well be pursuing certain
> goals that have nothing to do with civil rights at all. [45]

Wilkins decried the fact that his organization had to bear the major
burdens in order to get cooperation with other groups. He recalled
instances in which his group had helped SNCC, CORE, and SCLC. He
talked of the $5000 the NAACP sent to King during the Selma-to-
Montgomery march in 1965 and said it was some six months later before
his organization even got an acknowledgment, and then for only $3000

---

[43] *New York Times,* June 9, 1966, p. 1. For a general discussion of the Mississippi march
and its consequences see Martin Luther King, *Where Do We Go from Here: Chaos or
Community* (New York: Harper & Row, 1967, pp. 1–66.
[44] *New York Times,* June 9, 1966, p. 1.
[45] *New York Times,* July 8, 1966, p. 1.

(this was apparently the first hint of strained relations between Wilkins and King). Wilkins also denounced the Black Power aspirations of SNCC and CORE. This latter denunciation brought a sharp rebuttal from CORE's Floyd McKissick: "I think it is regrettable that Mr. Wilkins, a man whom I respect . . . has reached the point where he does not understand the community, possibly because of lack of contact."[46] Undoubtedly, the Mississippi "pilgrimage against fear" widened the split among civil rights groups and "Black Power" became the symbol of that split. It was on this march that Carmichael popularized "Black Power,"[47] and angry crowds repeated it time and again.

Black Power now became the divisive force among civil rights groups. Carmichael (SNCC) and McKissick (CORE) championed the new concept and expounded its meaning, including black mobilization, black leadership for black organizations, the promotion of self-pride, and the right of self-defense.[48] But the better-established civil rights groups and leaders denounced the new concept. They viewed Black Power as damaging to the civil rights movement and alien to its principles. Accordingly, seven civil rights leaders, including Wilkins (the NAACP), Young (the Urban League), and Randolph and Rustin (leaders of the 1963 March on Washington), issued a joint statement reaffirming these principles lest Black Power advocates "be interpreted as representing the civil rights movement."[49] In this restatement of principles, the leaders reaffirmed their commitment to achieving racial justice through democratic institutions such as courts and legislatures, their commitment to integration and to "the common responsibility of all Americans, white and black, for bringing integration to pass." The leaders strongly denounced the violent "implications" of Black Power.

Once again, Martin Luther King took a "middle" position.[50] He endorsed the principles set forth by the moderate civil rights leaders but refused to sign the statement.[51] He called Black Power "confusing" but did not denounce those who espoused it. He said it was a false assumption that the slogan had brought about the so-called white backlash when actually, it had been "exploited by the decision-makers to justify resistance to change."[52] In an oblique criticism of those who signed the statement, King said:

---

[46] *New York Times,* July 8, 1966, p. 1.

[47] See King, *Where Do We Go From Here.*

[48] *New York Times,* July 8, 1966, p. 16; See also *New York Times,* July 3, 1966, p. 28; Carmichael and Hamilton, *Black Power.*

[49] *New York Times,* October 10, 1966, p. 35.

[50] See, generally, Gene Roberts, "Dr. King on Middle Ground," *New York Times,* July 17, 1966, Part IV, p. 5.

[51] *New York Times,* October 15, 1966, p. 14.

[52] *New York Times,* October 15, 1966, p. 14.

Some consider certain civil rights groups inclusively and irrevocably committed to error and wish them barred from the movement. I cannot agree with this approach because it involves an acceptance of the interpretation of enemies of civil rights and bases policy on their distortion. Actually, much thinking, particularly by young Negroes is in a state of flux . . . the intensified resistance to civil rights goals has outraged and dismayed very sincere Negroes and . . . in frustration and despair, they are groping for new approaches. Negro unity and Negro-white unity, both of which are decisive, can only be harmed by a

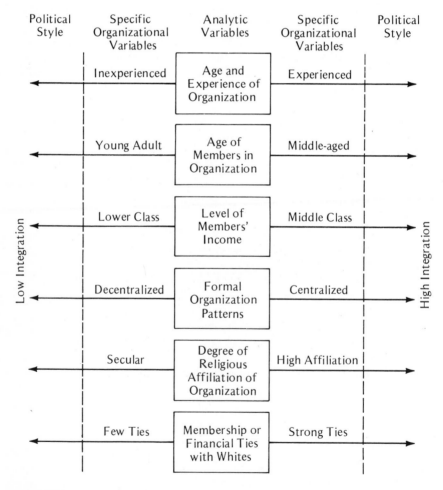

FIGURE 2
Factors Contributing to the "Integration" of Civil Rights Groups in the Existing Political System

precipitated effort to excommunicate any group, even if silencing or isolating some groups is unintended.[53]

Basically, this general division among civil rights groups and leaders — with SNCC and CORE on the one side, the NAACP and the Urban League on the other, and Martin Luther King and his organization somewhere in between — was the pattern that emerged in early 1968.

Conclusion

Basically, the civil rights groups' policies differ because of substantial differences in the nature and structure of the groups. Moreover, these organizational differences tend to be cumulative in civil rights organizations. As these factors reinforce one another, coalition disintegration accelerates. In sum, it appears that the breakdown of the civil rights coalition stems from the organizational characteristics of its member groups. Thus, we might conceptualize civil rights coalition behavior in terms of Figure 2.

In the view presented here, the highly effective civil rights coalition of 1963–1964 was able to function in spite of a large number of factors tending toward disunity because of the central position of the SCLC and Dr. Martin Luther King, Jr. However, events after 1964–1965 exacerbated the frictions between the various civil rights groups and, of course, in the spring of 1968, assassination removed Dr. King from his position of leadership. The implication of this analysis is that there is no basis for the expectation that the civil rights coalition will re-form. Of course, it is possible that factors and events outside the scope of the present study will intervene and bring some coherence and unity to the civil rights movement.

The Civil Rights Movement: New Groups, New Directions, New Problems

The 1960's were the high point of the civil rights movement. Certainly the unity and direction of that movement no longer exist. The focus of civil rights activity has changed. In the 1960's the push for *formal recognition* of legal rights provided a broad base around which civil rights groups and their white allies could rally. But in the 1970's the push for the *actual implementation* of those rights commands

---

[53] *New York Times*, October 17, 1966, p. 42.

far less appeal and support. In fact, civil rights and racial problems no longer enjoy priority status in national politics.[13] In October 1965, for example, more people (27 percent) considered civil rights the *most* important problem facing the country.[14] While the saliency of the issue fluctuated throughout the 1960's, by September 1972 only 5 percent considered civil rights the most important issue.

It is interesting to observe how Vietnam, crime, and the economy compare with race as "most important problems" of the sixties and early seventies. (See Figures 7–1, 7–2, and 7–3.) Notice, for example, in Figure 7–2 how "crime and lawlessness" entered the "most important problem" category in 1968. This probably reflected public concern over widespread riots in the nation's urban areas. And this concern was undoubtedly sparked by Nixon's campaign pledge to return the country to "law and order" — a euphemism for "being tough on blacks." In any event, corresponding with the decrease in the importance of civil rights issues was the development of a more favorable attitude by whites toward racial questions. This, of course, underscores the view that the unsympathetic posture of the Nixon administration toward civil rights, which considerably slowed progress in the area,[15] met with popular approval among whites. As a consequence, civil rights groups have come in for hard times.[16]

Of the five major organizations that sparked the civil rights movement of the 1960's — the NAACP, Urban League, CORE, SNCC, and SCLC — only the NAACP and the Urban League continue to thrive. And these are the two organizations that show the highest degree of "system integration." Some groups, such as CORE and SNCC (and especially the latter) have all but faded from the scene. And the SCLC, since the assassination of Martin Luther King, has been struggling to maintain its organizational and financial vitality.

To be sure, several forces and factors have brought about these changes. For one thing, as mentioned earlier, the legalization of rights has now been replaced by the implementation of rights. And it seems quite clear that such implementation as might occur must come in a social and political climate that has increasingly become more hostile to black goals. This climate was fostered and perpetuated by the presi-

---

[13] For a discussion of race and civil rights as salient political issues, see Richard E. Dawson, *Public Opinion and Contemporary Disarray* (New York: Harper & Row, 1973), pp. 52–77.

[14] The question asked was, "What do you think the *most* important problem facing this country today?" Multiple answers were possible.

[15] See Report of U.S. Commission on Civil Rights, Civil Rights Enforcement Effort, 1973.

[16] See Paul Delaney, "Civil Rights Unity Gone in Redirected Movement," *New York Times* (August 29, 1973), p. 1, c. 2.

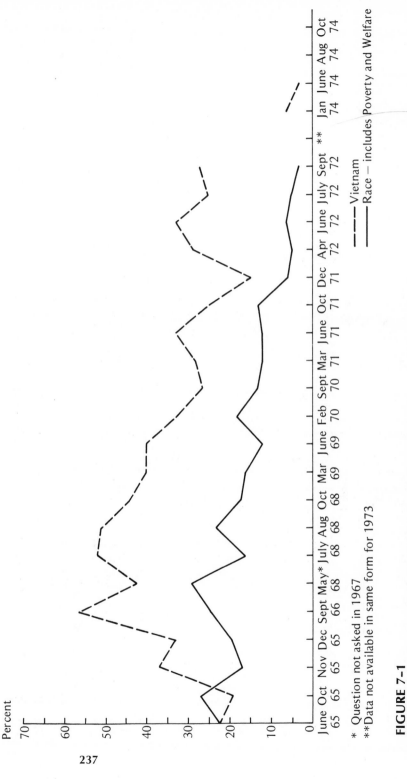

237

Percent

June Oct Nov Dec Sept May* July Aug Oct Mar June Feb Sept Mar June Oct Dec Apr June July Sept ** Jan June Aug Oct
65 65 65 65 65 66 68 68 68 68 69 69 70 71 71 71 71 72 72 72 72   74 74 74 74

* Question not asked in 1967
**Data not available in same form for 1973

– – – Vietnam
——— Race – includes Poverty and Welfare

FIGURE 7-1
Trends in Most Important Problems: Race and Vietnam

Source: Gallup Poll Index.

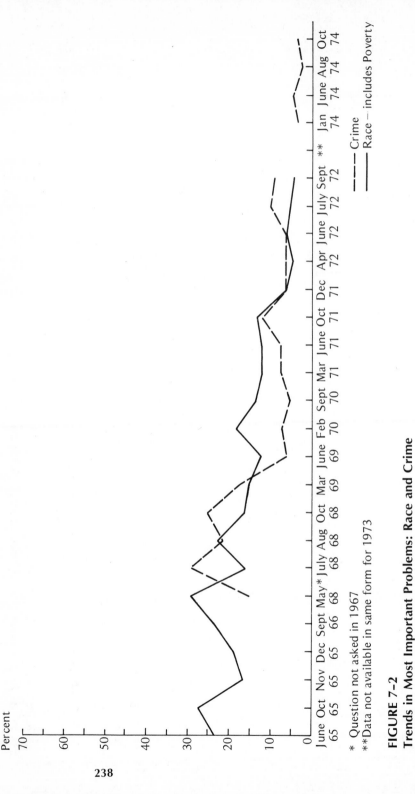

FIGURE 7-2
Trends in Most Important Problems: Race and Crime

SOURCE: Gallup Poll Index.

* Question not asked in 1967
**Data not available in same form for 1973

— — — Crime
———— Race — includes Poverty

238

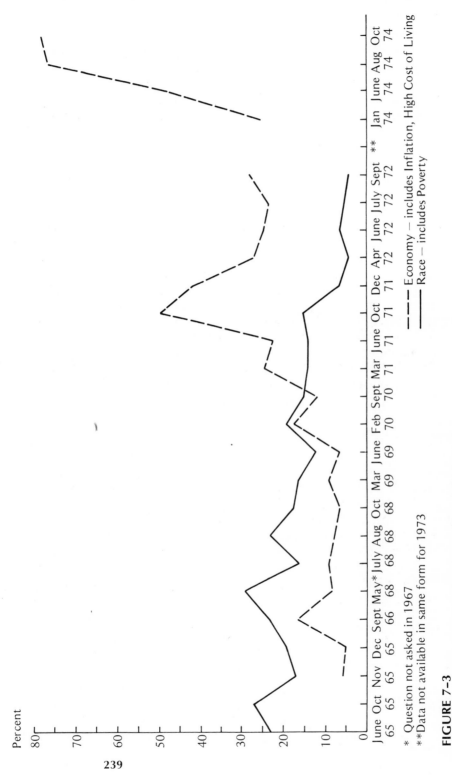

FIGURE 7-3
Trends in Most Important Problems: Race and Economy

SOURCE: Gallup Poll Index.

* Question not asked in 1967
**Data not available in same form for 1973

– – – Economy – includes Inflation, High Cost of Living
——— Race – includes Poverty

Percent

239

dency of Richard Nixon and shows few signs of abating. Some organizations, such as the NAACP, have been able to cope with this changed environment and have adjusted accordingly; other organizations have not been as successful. They have fallen by the wayside. On the other hand, several new more issue-oriented groups, such as Operation PUSH (People United to Save Humanity) and the National Welfare Rights Organization, have emerged. Operation PUSH, for example, was founded by the Rev. Jesse Jackson, a former close associate of Martin Luther King and former national director of SCLC's Operation Breadbasket. But apparent differences between Jackson and the Rev. Ralph Abernathy, King's successor as president of SCLC, led Jackson to launch a new organization devoted mainly to the economic development of blacks and minority groups.

In addition, the activation of the black vote and black interest in the political process has led to an increasing number of black elected officials. These officials, in turn, have formed organizations of their own. The most widely known is the Congressional Black Caucus. The nature and activity of the CBC is discussed in the next chapter. However, it is sufficient to say here that black elected officials, both individually and organizationally, are now trying to solidify the lofty goals and achievements of the civil rights movement through the political process. Obviously, the extent of their success is important for the future course of civil rights groups and black Americans generally.

Political Parties

To bring about change through politics in the American political system necessarily involves change in and through political parties. And undoubtedly the most striking feature of political parties in America is the **two-party system.** This refers to the dominant and overwhelming role of the Democratic and Republican parties in performing the major function of parties — the recruitment and election of public officials at all levels of government. The lifeblood of parties is to control government by electing its members to office. This is the central concern of parties, of their every move; every other function is geared toward this central concern.

THE TWO-PARTY SYSTEM

That two parties and only two parties dominate the American political scene has been explained by several factors.[17"] At the

---

[17] See explanatory factors discussed in Frank J. Sorauf, *The American Party System* (Boston: Little Brown, 1972), pp. 37–40.

root of the explanation," as Sorauf puts it, "lies the basic, long-run American consensus on fundamental beliefs. No deep rifts over the kind of economy, society or government we want have marked our politics."[18] But the more practical explanation by which this "consensus" is fostered lies perhaps in the symbiotic relationship that has developed between parties and the constitutional–legal system. In attempts to win control, parties have actually given life to our constitutional–legal structures, and have in turn been influenced by these very structures.

Consider such features as federalism, the **electoral college,** separation of powers, regular and frequent elections, and the **single-member district.** Federalism, for example, means that a party must be organized to contest national and state elections. Federalism has also come to mean, of course, that frictions which inevitably erupt between national and state interests also erupt along these lines within the party organization. Overcoming such frictions could hold enormous consequences for party success. Consider the election of the president, by far the single most important government official. To win the presidency, the party must win a majority of the electoral votes. And electoral votes of each state are awarded on a winner-take-all basis. This calls for viable party organizations in all states — organizations that can work together under a central umbrella. And given the varied politics of the states, that central umbrella must be large indeed to cover and hold many divergent interests. Obviously the resources needed by the party to win the presidency (such as nature of organization, type of candidate, the platform, money) can differ from the resources needed by the party to capture other government offices (for example, state governors, U.S. senators and representatives). Yet somehow the major problem for the central party organization is that these very resources must be made to work together if the party is to succeed and win the presidency and other offices. In any event, the party must be able to adjust to the many structures such as federalism that exist in the political system.

One way in which a party tries to adjust to and overcome these structures in presidential elections is through the national party convention. Meeting every four years to coincide with presidential elections, the main business of the convention is to nominate candidates for president and vice president. But it must conduct that business so as to maximize party chances in the subsequent election. What this means essentially is that at every turn party leaders must be alert to the tenuous foundations upon which party organizations are built and upon which they depend. Indeed, party organization generally corresponds with governmental organizations; that is, there is a national party organization, a state party organization, and local (county, city, ward, precinct) party organizations. And some of the same problems that plague opera-

---

[18] Ibid., p. 39.

tions at the various government levels also plague the party organization. Essentially then, one may well describe the two major parties as
"grand **coalitions**." More often than not one can find this coalition flavor
reflected both in the party platform (statement of policies) as well as in
the presidential ticket. By and large, however, both the platform and
party nominees represent the same interests. That is, the dominant
interests that coalesce to mold the party platform also prevail in fashioning the presidential ticket and vice versa. What this all means is that it is
highly unlikely (although not unknown) that any one group or interest
in a given party will have its way. Put another way, party conventions as
forums of decision-making, similar to other national forums, are not
likely to come up with sharp, clear, concise actions that might jeopardize
their mass/broad support base. Consequently, *compromise* and *moderation*
rather than *conflict* and *clarity* usually characterize the operation of parties at the national level. As such the character of the national party
tends to support those interests who favor the status quo, or those who
believe in gradual change.

It becomes obvious then why black participation in national party
politics has for the most part been frustrating. Let us take a brief look at
black experience with the two major parties.

BLACKS AND THE REPUBLICANS: FROM FRIENDSHIP TO ALIENATION

Lincoln's Emancipation Proclamation and the policies of
the Republican Reconstruction Congress stand out as historic bench-
marks in black Americans' struggle for freedom. The circumstances
surrounding these actions have led some to ascribe various motivations
for them. But the fact remains that these actions were taken by Republicans. To be sure, Lincoln's Proclamation did free the slaves. Moreover,
the support of the Republican Congress for black interests was symbolized not only through legislation, such as the Civil Rights Act of 1866,
but also through the eventual enactment of the Civil War Amendments,
the Thirteenth, Fourteenth, and Fifteenth Amendments. Quite naturally
these historic policies benefited the Republican party by attracting black
voters.

But this strong support given blacks by Republicans during Reconstruction was short-lived. As we have seen earlier, in the disputed
election of 1876 Republican candidate Rutherford B. Hayes, in exchange
for southern electoral votes, agreed to withdraw federal troops from the
South and in effect adopted a "hands-off" policy toward the newly freed
blacks. This agreement, called the Compromise of 1877, led to a widespread feeling among blacks that they had been abandoned by the
Republican party and once again offered up to the whims of their former

slaveholders. Consequently, black Republicans who had prospered during Reconstruction were brushed aside both by the reemergence of the Democratic party as well as by southern white Republican leaders who wanted to rid the party of its black image. This led to warfare between two factions of the party: the white faction known as the Lily White Republicans and the black faction, the Black and Tan Republicans. And although national Republican leaders sought to overcome this factionalism and effect a viable party organization in the South, they were unable to do so.

Southern whites took full advantage of the situation. They solidified their control of state governments through the Democratic party. They also instituted various devices that disfranchised black voters and relegated blacks in general to a subordinate status. In 1928 President Hoover squashed any hope that the Republican party would once again come to the rescue of blacks. Indeed Hoover, sensing an increasing wave of race prejudice throughout the country, sided with the Lily White Republicans and dealt a severe blow to the Black and Tan faction in the South. This move by Hoover, coupled with the attractive economic policies of President Roosevelt's New Deal, had by 1936 brought most blacks to the Democratic party. But though Democrats controlled national politics until 1952, they did little to unravel the web of subordination that enveloped the life of blacks in the South.

However, the National Republicans did even less to alleviate the plight of blacks and poor people. The GOP was pictured as the party of the rich and well-born WASP. It is, of course, true that the Republicans with General Eisenhower recaptured the White House from 1952 through 1960. And these were crucial years in the civil rights movement. These were the years of the Supreme Court's decision on public school desegregation, the Montgomery bus boycott, and the Little Rock school integration crisis. These were all situations that provided opportunities for the Republicans to regain some credence with black Americans. But, as is well known, President Eisenhower refused to endorse the Court decision. He remained aloof and uninvolved in the expanding civil rights controversy. For certain, the president did use federal troops to enforce federal court orders during the Little Rock crisis, but only as a last resort.

The Republicans did not regain the White House until 1968 when Richard Nixon was elected president. Between 1960 and 1968, however, the Democrats through Kennedy and Johnson strengthened their hold on black voters. This black support for the Democrats was, of course, enhanced by the strong anti–civil rights posture and conservatism of the 1964 Goldwater campaign. In 1968, however, the Republicans won the presidency with a campaign that appealed to white America. The "law and order," "anti-busing," and "southern strategy" themes that characterized the 1968 and 1972 Nixon campaigns — as well as his administrations — were definitely not calculated to appeal to black voters. It was as if Nixon had written off the black vote and he apparently had. But President Nixon and leading figures of his administration, including his chief law enforcement officer, Attorney General John Mitchell, became trapped in their own "law and order" rhetoric, in word and in (mis)-deed. This, of course, included Vice President Spiro Agnew, who along with Mitchell, symbolized the antipathy of the Republican administration toward blacks, minorities and the poor. The ensuing Watergate scandal led not only to the conviction of leading officials of Mr. Nixon's administration, but also to the resignation of the president himself.

Predictably, the elevation of Gerald Ford to the presidency has done little to improve the civil rights image of the Republican party. And it is too early to tell whether President Ford's call for a "broadly" based Republican party, a call which has been echoed by Vice President Nelson Rockefeller, will be made *broad* enough to encompass significant numbers of black and minority voters. Black delegate representation at the 1968 and 1972 Republican conventions has been anything but encouraging. (See Table 7–2.) It should be noted, however, that the party has formulated a plan that calls on state party organizations to "take positive action and endeavor to assure greater and more equitable participation of women, young people, minority and heritage groups, and senior citizens and to increase their representation at the 1976 national convention."[19] But even if such "positive action" programs are implemented, it is unlikely that they will end, as some had hoped, the "country club" image of the Republican party. More than "positive action" is needed to change this image.

BLACKS AND DEMOCRATIC PARTY POLITICS

Black ties to the Democratic party stem in large part from the economic benefits which accrued during Franklin Roosevelt's New Deal era. These ties were strengthened during President Truman's Fair Deal administration. Truman not only continued Roosevelt's policies, but he also exhibited some concern for the civil rights of black Americans. This concern was symbolized by the report of a 1947 presidential commission on civil rights, "To Secure These Rights." In addition, black attachment to the Democratic party was undoubtedly strengthened by the sympathetic support given the Civil Rights Movement from Democratic leaders (the Kennedys, Johnson, Humphrey) and Democratic-oriented groups (Labor, Catholics and Jews).

Moreover, the issue orientation of the Democratic party, in contrast to

---

[19] *Congressional Quarterly Weekly Report*, 32:50 (7/14/74), 3332.

TABLE 7-2
**Black Delegate Representation at Republican National Conventions 1968
and 1972**

STATE	NUMBER BLACK DELS 1972	TOTAL NUMBER DELS 1972	PER CENT BLACK DELS 1972	PER CENT BLACK DELS 1968	PER CENT BLACK POP
Alabama	1	18	5.5	0.0	26.2
Alaska	0	12	0.0	0.0	3.0
Arizona	1	18	5.5	0.0	3.0
Arkansas	3	18	16.6	11.0	18.3
California	4	96	4.1	1.0	7.0
Colorado	0	20	0.0	0.0	3.0
Connecticut	0	22	0.0	0.0	6.0
Delaware	2	12	16.7	1.0	14.3
District of Columbia	3	9	33.3	33.0	71.1
Florida	1	40	2.5	0.0	15.3
Georgia	1	24	4.1	4.0	25.9
Hawaii	0	14	0.0	0.0	1.0
Idaho	0	14	0.0	0.0	0.3
Illinois	2	58	3.4	3.0	12.8
Indiana	1	32	3.1	3.0	6.9
Iowa	1	22	4.5	0.0	1.2
Kansas	1	20	5.0	11.0	4.8
Kentucky	1	24	4.1	0.0	7.2
Louisiana	2	20	10.0	0.0	29.8
Maine	0	8	0.0	0.0	0.3
Maryland	3	26	11.5	11.0	17.8
Massachusetts	0	34	0.0	6.0	3.1
Michigan	5	48	10.4	2.0	7.2
Minnesota	1	26	3.8	0.0	0.9
Mississippi	1	14	7.1	0.0	36.8
Missouri	1	30	3.3	0.0	10.3
Montana	0	14	0.0	0.0	0.3
Nebraska	0	16	0.0	0.0	2.7
Nevada	1	12	8.3	0.0	5.7
New Hampshire	0	14	0.0	0.0	0.3
New Jersey	2	40	5.0	0.0	10.7
New Mexico	0	14	0.0	0.0	1.9
New York	8	88	9.0	4.5	11.9
North Carolina	2	32	6.2	0.0	22.2
North Dakota	0	12	0.0	0.0	0.4
Ohio	1	56	1.8	1.5	9.1
Oklahoma	0	22	0.0	0.0	6.7
Oregon	0	18	0.0	0.0	1.3
Pennsylvania	1	60	1.7	1.5	8.6
Rhode Island	0	8	0.0	0.0	2.7
South Carolina	1	22	4.5	0.0	30.5

TABLE 7-2 (continued)
Black Delegate Representation at Republican National Conventions 1968 and 1972

State	Number Black Dels 1972	Total Number Dels 1972	Per Cent Black Dels 1972	Per Cent Black Dels 1968	Per Cent Black Pop
South Dakota	0	14	0.0	0.0	0.2
Tennessee	1	26	3.8	0.0	15.8
Texas	0	52	0.0	0.0	12.5
Utah	0	14	0.0	0.0	0.6
Vermont	0	12	0.0	0.0	0.2
Virginia	3	30	10.0	0.0	18.5
Washington	0	24	0.0	0.0	2.1
West Virginia	0	18	0.0	0.0	3.9
Wisconsin	0	28	0.0	0.0	2.9
Wyoming	0	12	0.0	0.0	0.8
Guam	0	3	0.0	0.0	—
Puerto Rico	0	5	0.0	0.0	—
Virgin Islands	1	3	33.0	0.0	80.0
	56	1348	4.2	1.9	11.2

1. According to the best information available to the JCPS, the number of black delegates is accurate as of August 1, 1972.
2. Total number of votes equal to actual number of delegates.
3. Republican National Committee.
4. *1970 Census of Population* U.S. Department of Commerce, Bureau of the Census.
Source: Reprinted with permission from Joint Center for Political Studies, *Guide to Black Politics '72*, Part II: The Republican National Convention (August, 1972), p. 21.

the Republicans, has been more supportive of black concerns. Consider the positions taken by the two parties in their 1972 platforms.[20] Indeed the tone and substance of the Democrats in such key issue areas as civil rights, employment, housing, welfare, health insurance, education, law enforcement, and tax reform were undoubtedly more clearly attuned to black interests than was the Republican position. Let us look at a few examples. With respect to *busing*, the Democrats viewed it as "another tool to accomplish desegregation," while the Republicans flatly said they were "irrevocably opposed to busing for racial balance." The GOP said that busing "fails in its stated objective — improved learning opportunities — while it achieves results no one wants — division within communities and hostilities between classes and races."

[20] This comparison is taken from *Congressional Quarterly Weekly Report*, 30:35 (8/26/72), 2146–50. Text of the Democratic platform is in 30:29 (7/15/72), 1726ff; and the Republican platform is in 30:35 (8/26/72), 2151ff.

Take welfare. Both parties agreed that the present welfare system needs replacing. But agreement stopped there. The Democrats would replace welfare with "an income security program" that includes a guaranteed annual income "substantially more than the poverty level" to ensure standards of decency and health. In contrast, the Republicans flatly opposed "programs or policies which embrace the principle of a government-guaranteed income" and rejected as "unconscionable the idea that all citizens have the right to be supported by the government, regardless of their ability or desires to support themselves or their families." As to health insurance, the Democrats supported a federally financed and federally administered National Health Insurance. The Republicans opposed "nationalized compulsory health insurance" and called for a plan "financed by employers, employees and the federal government." On law enforcement, the GOP platform praised President Nixon's anti-crime program and his strongly articulated "law and order" stance. The platform called for increased support for law enforcement. The Democrats were likewise against crime, but stated that

we can protect all people without undermining fundamental liberties by ceasing to use "law and order" as justification for repression and political persecution, and by ceasing to use stop-gap measures as preventive detention, "no-knock" entry, surveillance, promiscuous and unauthorized use of wire taps, harassment, and secret dossiers. . . ."

The Democratic platform concluded that "the problems of crime and drug abuse cannot be isolated from the social and economic conditions that give rise to them."

This sample of issue positions of the two parties clearly supports the disposition of blacks to favor the Democratic party. This should not be construed to suggest that blacks are satisfied with the position taken by Democrats on particular issues. It simply means that as between the two major parties blacks tend to favor the Democrats. This is a matter to which we shall return later in this chapter. It is sufficient to state here, however, that it has been "good politics" for Democrats to be considerate of black interests. Indeed, blacks, more than any other emergent minority group such as women and youth, have given strong and consistent support to the Democrats.[21] That support continued to be apparent in the 1972 presidential election. (See Table 7-3.)

In terms of party identification, blacks have shown an overwhelming preference for the Democratic party, although in recent years that preference seems on the decline. Nonetheless, such support would certainly

---

[21] Robert Axelrod, "Where the Votes Come From: An Analysis of Electoral Coalitions, 1952-1968," *American Political Science Review*, 66:1 (March, 1972), 11-20.

TABLE 7-3
Black and White Voting Patterns — 1952-1972

Year	Race	Democratic	Republican	Other
1952	Black	80%	20%	—
	White	40	60	—
1956	Black	64	36	—
	White	39	61	—
1960	Black	71	29	—
	White	48	52	—
1964	Black	100*	0	—
	White	65	35	—
1968	Black	97	3	—
	White	36	52	12%
1972	Black	87	13	—
	White	30	70	—

* The 100 percent voting of blacks for the Democratic party probably results from the small size of sample. Certainly a few blacks voted for Goldwater as probably a very few voted for Wallace in 1968. Furthermore, the reported 100 percent Democratic support is consistent with a bias to report having supported the winner — a well-known artifact in re-call data.
Source: Survey Research Center, University of Michigan (Presidential Elections from 1952-1972).

suggest that blacks would expect and demand (which they did) more voice and representation in Democratic party councils. One obvious target was the national convention. Indeed, as has been suggested elsewhere, black claims for more representation in the 1972 convention went beyond the "issue of societal justice."[22] Based on past history, blacks "had a concrete claim to increased representation." Let us take a closer look at how the Democratic party handled this matter of increased representation for blacks and other minority groups in the 1972 convention.

Formulas for selection of delegates to national conventions are determined by the national party committees which act under the authority of their previous conventions. Accordingly, the Democratic National Committee, acting on the recommendations of the McGovern-Fraser Commission, announced two major reforms for selection of delegates to the 1972 convention. First, each state delegation was to include representation of blacks, women, and youths in "reasonable relationship to their presence" in the population of each state. This thus became known as the "group quota" formula. A second important reform was designed to

---

[22] Except as otherwise indicated, this account is based on Denis Sullivan et al., *The Politics of Representation* (New York: St. Martins, 1974), esp. chapters 1 and 2.

open up state selection procedures to non-party regulars, especially at the local-caucus and state convention levels. The result of these reforms was to increase representation of these heretofore excluded groups as delegates in the Democratic National convention. Even so, however, as Table 7-4 shows, only blacks achieved a percentage equal to their percentage of the total population.

However, after the 1972 elections, party regulars charged that it was this very quota system (and the intrusion of "outsiders" in party councils) that led to the disastrous defeat of the McGovern-led Democratic ticket. They could recall vividly and with rancor how "upstart insurgents" such as Alderman William Singer of Chicago and the Rev. Jesse

Wide World Photos

Prelude to McGovern Nomination. Willie Brown, Jr., a leader of Senator George S. McGovern's California delegation, and Frank Mankiewicz, his campaign coordinator, rejoice on floor of the 1972 Democratic National Convention when the Convention voted to overturn the credentials committee which had taken 151 California delegates from McGovern. The victory virtually assured McGovern of the party's presidential nomination.

TABLE 7-4
Representation of Blacks, Youth, and Women

	1968 CONVENTION	1972 CONVENTION	POPULATION PERCENTAGE
Blacks	6%	14%	11%
Under thirty	2	23	30
Women	14	36	51
Total	2,528	3,100	

SOURCE: Denis Sullivan et al, *The Politics of Representation* (New York: St. Martins Press, 1974), p. 23. Reprinted with permission.

Jackson had successfully ousted the "veteran-loyal-party regular" — Mayor Richard Daley — not only from his perennial king-making role in Democratic party conventions but from the floor of the convention as well. And, of course, other party regulars were also left watching from the sidelines.

Consequently, in its first mid-term conference to consider recommendations for a new party charter, the Democrats shied away from the quota provisions of the 1972 convention. Rather, the 1974 Kansas City mini-convention, as it was known, called for the adoption and implementation of "affirmative action programs" in delegate selection and party organizations "at all levels."[23] Reaching compromise on this issue represented a major problem for the Democrats. In the end, however, under the orchestration of National Chairman Robert Strauss and other leaders, the new "affirmative action" compromise for delegate representation in the 1976 national convention was approved by the 1974 Kansas City conference.

Whether the compromise will hold remains to be seen. Much depends on how the affirmative action formula works out in practice; that is, in how many delegates are selected from minority groups. Given the history of black support of the Democratic party, it stands to reason, for example, that if the percentage of black delegates is not reasonably proportionate to the black population, the "unity under a cloud"[24] of the Kansas City convention could easily fade away. Indeed, as one study has carefully shown, "a valid assessment of group quotas must separate out the insurgent effect (of candidates such as McCarthy in 1968 and McGovern in 1972) and it must state the specific groups included in a

---

[23] For commentary and text of charter, see *Congressional Quarterly Weekly Report*, 32:50 (12/14/74/), 3330–36. Affirmative action provisions are found in Art. 10 of the charter, "Full Participation," at 3336. See also 32:48 (11/30/74), 3209ff.
[24] Ibid., p. 3330, "Democratic Conference: Unity Under a Cloud."

Wide World Photos

The Victor and the Vanquished. Jesse Jackson, a leader of the Illinois delegation which succeeded in ousting Mayor Richard Daley's delegation from the 1972 Democratic National Convention, uses the shoulder of Daley aide Clyde Choate to hoist himself up in celebration as the results of the roll call were announced. Lower left is another defeated Daley aide, John Toughy.

quota system. By almost any measure . . . ," the study continues, "the costs in representing blacks in some reasonable relation to their numbers in the population do not involve much sacrifice in terms of political experience or, . . . in representativeness of opinion."[25] The study concludes with this succinct observation:

> It is clear . . . that in terms of representation of issue opinions of a constituency, and in terms of political experience, the increase in representation of blacks in 1972 was least costly and, in fact, represented an adjustment to the political reality of the party's dependence on black support.
>
> To comprehend fully why some party leaders have advanced the proposition that the so-called quota system was responsible for the radicalization of the convention, one must understand that such an assertion has political functions; that believing it to be true may affect the distribution of power within the party. Its political functions seem to have been (1) to discredit spokesmen for the new constituencies as being radical and as a consequence, without broad support, and (2) to signal the old constituencies in the party-labor, blue-collar factions, . . . that they are returning to positions of leadership within the party. Thus, for some, it becomes convenient to attribute a variety of the party's current ailments to the quota system.[26]

Even if blacks have legitimate bases for preferential treatment (as opposed to being lumped under a "minority" umbrella) they might nevertheless find that their lot must be fused (and not necessarily to their specific benefit) with other minorities. An invariable result of such fusion appears to be that black claims to what is rightfully theirs are considerably muted.

PARTY POLITICS IN PERSPECTIVE

Black participation in national party politics has for the most part been frustrating. To be sure, blacks have gravitated to the Democratic party and have generally tended to support its candidates. Attitudes and benefits that carry over from Roosevelt's New Deal, and the Truman, Kennedy, and Johnson administrations still claim a dominant allegiance from blacks. Moreover, when one views the membership characteristics of the two major parties (such as education, race, income, occupation) blacks and other minorities still continue to have more in common with Democrats than with Republicans.

But something is happening. For example, data from the Survey

---

[25] Sullivan et al., *The Politics of Representation*, p. 30.
[26] Ibid., pp. 35–36.

Research Center of the University of Michigan in 1968 indicate that about 85 percent of black adults identify with the Democratic party and only about 2 percent with the Republican party. (See Table 7-5.) However, in 1972, black identification with the Democratic party had dropped to 69 percent, with a slight rise in the percentage of blacks favoring the Republican party. The most striking shift among blacks, however, occurs in the number who identify themselves as Independents. In 1968 this figure was about 10 percent; in 1972 the percentage of blacks who called themselves Independents had risen to more than 23 percent! Even if one considers that the 1972 figures include for the first time the 18–21 year old group, it still represents a strong trend away from the Democratic party and from the two parties in general. This is consistent with a general trend toward "independence." Yet, it remains a striking development, especially when we compare the black increase from 1968 to 1972 to that of whites.

It is true, of course, that recent studies have pointed to an increasing dissatisfaction with both Republicans and Democrats in general.[27] Blacks undoubtedly perceive a growing insensitivity and inaction coming from both major parties with respect to the very serious problems, such as poverty, that they still face. One manifestation of this dissatisfaction is afforded by the national black political conventions held in Gary (1972) and Little Rock (1973).[28]

These conventions and their follow-up activities reflect divisions and factionalism among blacks. But more important they also reflect the perception of many blacks that "something else," in addition to working through traditional forums such as the two major political parties, needs to be done. That "something else" might be voting for friendly candidates regardless of party label, or holding black national conventions, or by the use of these or other strategies. If that "something else" can dramatize black protests to the two major parties, then it must be pursued in order to foster black participation and influence in the political process. For despite differences in the two parties — and there are differences — they nonetheless have much in common, particularly regarding racial issues. This is because in appealing for voting majorities, especially in presidential elections and in national elections generally, both parties apparently perceive that they must remain in the mainstream of American life. And no matter how socioeconomic data are manipulated, the majority of blacks are not yet in that mainstream.[29]

---

[27] See, for example, Arthur H. Miller, "Political Issues and Trust in Government, 1964–1970," *American Political Science Review* 68 (September, 1974), 951–972 at 971. Also see Comment by Jack Citrin and Rejoinder by Miller, ibid., pp. 973–1001.

[28] For more commentary on black political conventions see Hanes Walton, Jr., *Black Political Parties: An Historical and Political Analysis* (New York: Free Press, 1972).

[29] See Chapter 2.

TABLE 7-5
Social Characteristics of Party Identifiers: 1968* and 1972**

	Strong Democrat	Weak Democrat	Independent	Weak Republican	Strong Republican	Other	Totals
Race							
White	12.6 (16.1%)	25.0 (24.8%)	36.6 (31.0%)	14.5 (16.1%)	11.3 (10.5%)	1.4 (1.4%)	100.0 (99.9%)
Negro	37.2 (55.7)	31.8 (28.9)	23.4 (10.1)	3.8 (0.7)	3.8 (1.3)	3.4 (3.4)	100.0 (100.1)
Others	10.5 (21.7)	50.0 (39.1)	28.9 (34.8)	5.8 (0)	5.3 (4.3)	0 (0)	100.0 (99.9)
Occupation							
Professional	10.3 (11.6)	24.2 (18.1)	37.4 (37.1)	16.6 (20.3)	11.6 (12.9)	0 (0)	100.1 (100.0)
Manager, official	10.4 (17.1)	20.7 (22.0)	33.3 (33.6)	18.5 (16.6)	17.1 (9.3)	1.5 (1.5)	100.0 (100.1)
Clerical, sales	13.6 (15.3)	26.9 (23.5)	36.9 (32.3)	13.6 (17.6)	9.0 (11.2)	0 (0)	100.1 (99.9)
Skilled, semiskilled	18.6 (18.3)	25.9 (29.7)	38.4 (30.3)	9.9 (12.7)	7.3 (7.3)	0 (0)	100.1 (99.9)
Unskilled, service	17.6 (33.3)	29.2 (26.2)	35.1 (24.3)	8.2 (6.0)	10.0 (7.1)	3.0 (3.0)	100.1 (99.9)
Farmer	20.8 (25.7)	24.5 (27.0)	17.0 (10.9)	15.1 (23.0)	22.6 (12.2)	1.4 (1.4)	100.1 (100.2)
Other (retired, etc.)	14.6 (28.0)	26.8 (27.0)	33.0 (19.0)	15.0 (10.6)	10.6 (11.6)	3.7 (3.7)	100.0 (99.9)
Income							
0–$1,999	21.5 (29.4)	28.5 (28.4)	30.8 (17.7)	12.8 (10.3)	6.4 (10.3)	3.7 (3.7)	100.0 (100.1)
$2,000–3,999	19.2 (28.2)	28.2 (25.8)	27.6 (24.0)	12.8 (10.8)	12.2 (8.9)	2.3 (2.3)	100.0 (100.0)
$4,000–5,999	17.4 (19.8)	26.9 (25.7)	34.8 (29.7)	9.8 (11.9)	11.1 (9.9)	3.0 (3.0)	100.0 (100.0)
$6,000–9,999	13.8 (18.6)	28.5 (25.3)	38.5 (30.8)	10.8 (13.9)	8.4 (10.1)	1.3 (1.3)	100.0 (100.0)
$10,000–14,999	14.3 (17.7)	26.7 (28.0)	33.7 (30.5)	14.6 (15.8)	14.6 (7.7)	0.3 (0.3)	100.1 (100.0)
$15,000 and over	10.8 (9.4)	21.0 (16.5)	37.6 (39.5)	17.2 (24.1)	13.4 (10.0)	0.6 (0.6)	100.0 (100.1)
Education							
None–8 grades	24.4 (31.0)	27.3 (31.8)	23.6 (15.9)	13.8 (10.6)	10.9 (7.5)	3.1 (3.1)	100.0 (100.1)
9–12 grades	14.4 (19.2)	28.2 (27.3)	37.0 (28.9)	11.5 (14.6)	8.9 (8.3)	1.7 (1.7)	100.0 (100.0)
Some college	11.3 (10.8)	26.6 (18.8)	37.9 (42.5)	12.0 (15.7)	12.2 (11.7)	0.4 (0.4)	100.0 (99.9)
Baccalaureate degree	5.7 (10.0)	21.0 (15.7)	39.3 (37.1)	20.2 (20.7)	13.7 (16.4)	0 (0)	99.9 (99.9)
Advanced degree	17.9 (21.0)	14.0 (12.9)	38.3 (40.3)	8.3 (12.9)	10.9 (12.9)	0 (0)	99.1 (100.0)
Religion							
Protestants	13.5 (19.1)	24.8 (24.1)	33.5 (26.9)	15.5 (16.3)	12.6 (11.5)	1.9 (1.9)	99.1 (99.8)
Catholics	18.9 (23.1)	31.7 (29.4)	35.3 (31.2)	8.1 (9.5)	6.1 (5.6)	1.2 (1.2)	100.1 (100.0)
Jews	27.7 (33.3)	25.0 (19.0)	38.3 (42.9)	8.3 (4.8)	1.7 (0)	0 (0)	100.7 (100.0)

NOTE: The figures in parentheses represent 1968 Party identifiers.
SOURCE: * Survey Research Center of the University of Michigan, data made available through the Inter-University Consortium for Political Research. Reproduced from Frank Sorauf, *Party Politics in America*, 2nd ed. (Boston: Little, Brown & Company, 1972), p. 149. Reprinted by permission.

** Data for 1972 made available through the Survey Research Center of the University of Michigan.

Interest Groups and Political Parties: Some Concluding Observations

This discussion of interest groups and political parties permits us to make several conclusions and observations about these forums, especially as they relate to black politics.

1. "Social solidarity" and "expression of opinion" might best characterize black interest groups. Yet the stability and viability of these groups are related directly to *material benefits* they can secure for the causes they represent. Hence the successes of the NAACP in the courtroom and the successes of the Urban League in employment have kept these organizations more viable than those where tangible successes are less continuously evident (for example, SCLC, CORE). Nonetheless, both the NAACP and Urban League have had to modify or broaden the posture of their "non-material" benefits (such as participation in direct action) to retain support and increase interaction with various segments of the black community.

2. *Staff* and *money*, as we have seen, are important resources that groups need to promote their objectives in the political process. However, with the possible exception of the NAACP, black interest groups have such resources only in small measure, if at all. The lack of black resources is vividly portrayed by Harold Wolman and Norman Thomas in their study of black influence in the federal policy process as related to two policy areas that are of crucial importance to blacks, housing and education.[30] Wolman and Thomas found that "the civil rights movement did not result in extensive involvement by black groups in the federal policy process" in these two areas. Indeed, black groups suffer from problems such as small staffs, lack of technical expertise and the resulting inability to influence policy at crucial stages of its formulation. When such groups do attempt to influence policy, say Wolman and Thomas, they do so in largely "formal and visible" ways such as testifying before congressional committees. More than this, these attempts occur "fairly late in the policy process, particularly at the stages of legislative consideration and implementation." "At those stages," the authors conclude, "certain actions can be prevented and marginal changes in policy outputs affected, but the major thrust of policies cannot substantially be altered, for they have been shaped in the earlier innovative and formulative stages when the basic agenda is set." In general, however, the lack of staff and money have forced black groups

---

[30] Unless otherwise indicated, the materials in quotes are taken from Harold L. Wolman and Norman C. Thomas, "Black Interests, Black Groups, and Black Influence in the Federal Policy Process: The Cases of Housing and Education," *Journal of Politics*, 32, 875–897.

to concentrate what meager resources they have in ways and areas which they believe to be most useful. This might call for activities that are open and visible rather than those of the behind-the-scene-low-profile variety, which ordinarily might indeed be most effective. However, that black interest groups do not possess adequate resources or the kind of temperament necessary for good lobbying ("compromise, accommodation, patience"[31]) is not at all surprising given the long history of factors that have retarded for so long the social, economic, and political development of black Americans.

3. Blacks can count on neither mass membership organizations (labor) nor high socioeconomic status groups (ABA, AMA) to support their goals. And, these are the groups that wield significant influence in American politics. The political arsenal of the AFL-CIO, for example, includes a large potential vote, a good amount of money, and lots of manpower to supplement and expand those things money can buy — for instance, time. To be sure, there are elements among labor that apparently still offer strong support to black interests. Witness, for example, the role of certain liberal unions such as the United Auto Workers and American Federation of County, State, and Municipal Employees, in adopting the new Democratic Charter in the 1974 Kansas City conference.[32] But support from organized labor generally, except for general policy declarations such as the Civil Rights Act of 1964, may turn out to be only marginal, if favorable at all, to black aspirations. Racial friction and apprehension between labor's rank-and-file and blacks, for example, over such issues as school integration and job competition and job security, has tended to lessen labor's traditional support for blacks and other minorities. This phenomenon has many implications, including the problems it could cause for black candidates who now enjoy labor support in elections. No longer can it be assumed that the policy positions of blacks and organized labor are compatible or closely related. That they *should* be compatible or related is another matter.

The high socioeconomic status groups — for example ABA, AMA — have money and standing as their major resources. While there is an increasing number of black lawyers and doctors, their numbers and success in terms of material wealth do not yet have a significant impact on these organizations and the policies they support.

4. Black interest groups, in many ways, are somewhat caught in a bind. This is so because a group's influence in politics may be related to how much its purposes and activities are congruent with American values and traditions. To be sure, to advocate freedom and equality for all is certainly in keeping with American values. But many perceive that

---

[31] Ibid., p. 893.

[32] See *Congressional Quarterly Weekly Report*, 32:50 (12/14/74), 3330.

it is not consistent with American values when groups seek to achieve such ends through means such as marches, demonstrations, and violence. This view persists even though such means have long been used by whites (for example, farmers, organized labor) to achieve their goals. That this situation has not caused more explosions (violence) in the 1960's and now is due in large measure to the moderating influence of black organized groups, especially the NAACP, and black leaders such as Martin Luther King. By the same token, such moderating influence helped to create the environment wherein some progress toward black goals has been made. Moreover, that progress has come *incrementally*. It is therefore consistent with how change occurs in American politics.

5. The central concern of the two major parties is to win elections — all else must be conducive or subordinate to this end. At the national level this means that above all the party wants to win the presidential election. Consequently, drafting the party platform, nominating its candidates, and even conducting convention business are geared toward fashioning a winning majority. This calls for the presentation of policy positions (platforms) and candidates (president and vice president) that have broad appeal. Special efforts are made to minimize controversy and to promote harmony. Given this situation, party policies or candidates are rarely strongly committed to the interest of black Americans. For in the context of American politics, those interests (goals) involve the type of controversy that party leaders more often than not wish to avoid.

6. Winning presidential elections, however, might require support from black and minority voters. As we discuss in the next chapter, the structure of the electoral college and the concentration of black voters in key states offer certain advantages to blacks in a presidential election situation. Strong black support for one of the two major parties, for example, could prove decisive in closely contested elections. Thus, party leaders may consider ways to attract these votes while simultaneously attempting to keep a "mainstream" or "middle of the road" stance. In practice this could mean recognition of black and minority concerns in the party platform but not in the candidates or vice versa. But in either case, party leaders (presidential candidates) strive to maintain a broad appeal in elections that not only attracts votes but precludes definite commitments (policy or otherwise; for instance, future appointments) to particular groups such as blacks. That party leaders and presidential candidates have been largely successful in doing this is reflected in the relatively few number of blacks who have won appointments to important government positions.

But they may not be so successful in the future. As blacks gain in political influence, in voting and office-holding, they will undoubtedly expect and demand a greater role in the activities of the major parties, especially in the selection of nominees for president and vice president.

Given the present pattern of party participation, however, the matter is not as crucial for the Republicans as it is for the Democrats. There are already clear indications that blacks expect to wield their increasing political influence in shaping the policies and selecting the nominees of the Democratic party. And while the Republicans are less pressured in this regard, the sheer size and distribution of the potential black vote makes it almost necessary for the Republican party to make some effort to attract black votes. In any event, whether and how the expectation and demands of blacks can be met by the major parties will tell us much about the nature of our two-party system, as well as about the future course of black politics.

Topics for Discussion

1. From time to time we hear of internal warfare erupting in both major parties between "liberal" and "conservative" factions. We have also heard the suggestion that new parties should be formed with the Liberal Republicans uniting with the Liberal Democrats to form one major party; and the Conservative Democrats uniting with Conservative Republicans to form the other major party. Roughly, then, we would still have two major parties that we might call "The Liberal Party" and "The Conservative Party." First, what problems do you think such a party reorganization would encounter? Why? Do you think these problems can be overcome? Assuming they can be overcome, what difference (if any) might this new party organization make for black politics and minority politics generally? Discuss.

2. It has become obvious in some instances that both the Democratic and Republican parties have abandoned (or refused to give high priority to) the political aspirations of black Americans. Would you suggest that blacks organize a political party to represent their interests? Do you think that blacks could overcome such differences and problems as might exist among themselves to form a viable party organization? What would be the costs and benefits to blacks (and to the political system generally) if such a political party were organized?

3. Consider the following passage from the text: " 'Social solidarity' and 'expression of opinion' might best characterize black interest groups. Yet the stability and viability of these groups is related directly to *material benefits* they can secure for the causes they represent. Hence the successes of the NAACP in the courtroom and the successes of the Urban League in employment have kept these organizations more viable than those where tangible successes are less continuously evident (for example, SCLC, CORE)." Do you agree with this view? Justify your position.

4. The authors state that "black interest groups, in many ways, are somewhat caught in a bind. This is so because a group's influence in politics may be related to how much its purposes and activities are congruent with American values and traditions." Assuming this to be true, comment on the *relative effectiveness* that various black interest groups (for example, NAACP, CORE, SCLC, SNCC) have had or do now have in achieving their objectives.

Suggested Readings

Bentley, Arthur. *The Process of Government.* Chicago: University of Chicago Press, 1908.

A classic work on the whole body of literature on group analysis and interest group theory.

Burnham, Walter D. *Critical Elections and the Mainsprings of American Politics.* New York: W. W. Norton & Co., 1970.

An excellent analysis of aggregate electoral behavior in historical perspective.

Carmichael, Stokely and Charles V. Hamilton. *Black Power: The Politics of Liberation in America.* New York: Vintage Books, 1967.

Pioneering work on the explanation and formulation of the meaning of the concept of black power.

Dawson, Richard. *Public Opinion and Contemporary Disarray.* New York: Harper & Row, 1973.

Describes and analyzes the distribution of opinions on current social and political issues.

Key, V. O. *Public Opinion and American Democracy.* New York: Alfred A. Knopf, 1961.

The formation of public opinion and its political implications.

Key, V. O. *Parties, Politics and Interest Groups.* New York: Crowell, 1958.

An examination of American politics in light of the activities of parties and interest groups.

Olson, Mancur, Jr. *The Logic of Collective Action: Public Goods and the Theory of Groups.* New York: Schocken Books, 1970.

Explores the nature of interest groups, the behavior of members, the importance of size and how these and other factors interact in realizing group objectives.

Salisbury, Robert. "Interest Groups." In Fred I. Greenstein and Nelson Polsby, *Handbook of Political Science,* Vol. 4. Reading Mass.: Addison-Wesley Publishing Co., 1975.

Analysis of interest groups over a broad spectrum.

Schattschneider, E. E. *The Semi-Sovereign People.* New York: Holt, Rinehart and Winston, 1960.

A forceful commentary on the role of the people in the American political system.

Sorauf, Frank J. *Party Politics in America.* Boston: Little, Brown, 1972.

Considers the nature, role, and functions of political parties in the American political system.

Sullivan, Denis G., Jeffrey L. Pressman, Benjamin I. Page, John J. Lyons, *The Politics of Representation.* New York: St. Martin's Press, 1974.

A case study of representation and decision-making at the 1972 Democratic National Convention.

Walton, Hanes. *Black Political Parties: An Historical and Political Analysis.* New York: Free Press, 1972.

Traces the historical development of black political parties.

8

CHANGE THROUGH POLITICS: THE PRESIDENT AND CONGRESS

The essence of a President's persuasive task with Congressmen and everybody else, *is to induce them to believe that what their own appraisal of their own responsibilities requires them to do is in their interest, not his.* Because men may differ in their views on public policy, because differences in outlook stem from differences in duty — duty to one's office, one's constituents, oneself — that task is bound to be more like collective bargaining than like a reasoned argument among philosopher kings. This is the reason why: persuasion deals in the coin of self-interest with men who have some freedom to reject what they find counterfeit.

Richard E. Neustadt, *Presidential Power**

Although congressional institutions and procedures do not have an inevitable negative or conservative impact on social policy, they do limit the contributions of many extremely talented younger members, particularly in the House. Far more serious than deficiencies within Congress, however, are some glaring defects in the process of getting into Congress. Since this book argues that the rules and procedures are less important than had been thought, and that real change depends upon a change in the membership, this is an extremely serious problem.

Perhaps the gravest distortions in congressional representation come from the extraordinary difficulty of defeat-
ing incumbents, and the great dependence of congressional campaigns on large contributions from interests
with very specific legislative objectives. The slow turnover
of members causes Congress to be always dominated by
members with a vested interest in the organizational
status quo. Sometimes it also isolates the legislative
branch from changes in public attitudes. The members'
dependency on business, unions, and the more affluent
professions greatly increases the difficulty of enacting
legislation to reform these institutions.

Gary Orfield, *Congressional Power: Congress and Social
Change**

Introduction

The president and Congress are the chief elective forums in
which interest groups, political parties, and others attempt to achieve
their policy objectives. These are the two "political" branches of the
national government, the judiciary being the third branch. This chapter
examines the president and Congress: their recruitment and selection;
their organization and structure; their functions and interdependence.
An examination of the processes and interactions of these institutions
shows some of the problems and prospects of blacks and other
minorities in dealing with their grievances through the "political"
branches. The chapter concludes with a case study and discussion of the
Congressional Black Caucus.

The President

Truman, Eisenhower, Kennedy, Johnson, Nixon, Ford:
these men connote many things to many people. But they all have one
thing in common: they all sat in the Oval Office as president of the
United States. Those who become president do indeed sit at the pinna-
cle of power in the American political system, and in many ways in the
entire world. The responsibilities and expectations of the office are

---

* Reprinted with permission of the publishers, Harcourt Brace Jovanovich, Inc.

enormous. There are many **presidential roles.** The president is indeed the chief executive and must take care that the laws be faithfully executed. This, in a sense, casts the president in the role of chief administrator. But the president is also chief legislator. He not only supervises the administration of the laws, but he is expected to suggest laws that are needed. In addition, as the office has developed in terms of both the formal requirements of Article II of the Constitution (see Appendix) and the practices and uses of power by particular occupants, the president performs many other roles. He is commander-in-chief of the armed forces, chief foreign policy-maker, chief of party, and chief of state. When combined these roles make the president, as many others have suggested, both king and prime minister.[1] Because these roles tend to overlap and reinforce one another, of course, they add to the powerful position of the president in the political system.

BECOMING PRESIDENT

But as powerful as the president is, he is not all powerful. Both the process by which he is selected and the way in which he is able to carry out his various roles limit his power. Take the process of selection. "To win the presidency," as one writer put it, "the aspirant must travel a long, hard, treacherous road abounding in bumps and quicksand and divisible into three distinct segments: the pre-convention build-up, **the national nominating convention,** and the post-convention electoral campaign."[2]

But before one can start this long journey with any viable chances of success one must possess more than the formal requirements for the presidential office. It is not enough to be a native born citizen, at least 35 years of age, and to have lived in the country for at least 14 years. Indeed, one must also meet (or have a reasonable chance of meeting) the informal requirements. One must have secured or be able to secure great financial backing. One must be well known, perhaps by having held high office or having rendered distinguished service to the country in some other way. Nor can one be too controversial; a candidate needs the support of a broad, often diverse, spectrum of people and interests.

---

[1] James W. Davis, Jr., *An Introduction to Public Administration* (New York: The Free Press, 1974), p. 21. Of course, literature on the presidency is voluminous. Among the most useful are: Richard Neustadt, *Presidential Power* (New York: John Wiley and Sons, 1964); Clinton Rossiter, *The American Presidency* (New York: Harcourt Brace Jovanovich, 1960); Louis Koenig, *The Chief Executive* (New York: Harcourt Brace Jovanovich, 1964); Nelson Polsby and Aaron Wildavsky, *Presidential Elections,* 2nd ed. (New York: Scribners, 1968); and Nelson Polsby, *Congress and the Presidency,* 2nd ed., (Englewood Cliffs, N.J.: Prentice-Hall, 1971).

[2] Koenig, *The Chief Executive,* p. 35.

What is "controversial" could include those things over which a person has control: for example, his stand on major issues. Or it could involve matters over which he has little or no control — religion, race, color, sex. A potential candidate can and may alter his stand on issues as the campaign develops. But in terms of ethnic consideration, a candidate has to convince many others that such factors should not stand as barriers to his efforts to become president. For example, it was not until 1960 that John F. Kennedy, who had everything going for him (money, organization, charm) was able to overcome the traditional anti-Catholic barrier, and even then just barely. Consequently, one shudders to guess, despite an increasing number of blacks and women in public office, how long race, sex, and other factors will continue to make particular candidates too "controversial."

Generally, the "pre-convention" phase provides a testing ground in which a presidential aspirant can assess his chances. Through **presidential primaries,** state party conventions, and other campaign forums one might indeed overcome or gain the necessary informal prerequisites to become a viable candidate for his party's nomination. He can gain publicity and become better known. He might also attract more financial backing, assuming he has enough money *initially* to gain additional funds.* One might also overcome or temper apprehension or controversy with respect to his position on issues, or regarding his religion, race, or sex. Finally, and very important, one might gather the kind of popular support and delegate commitment needed to do battle at the "convention" stage.

To win the party's nomination at the convention, the candidate must be able to fashion a majority of the delegates. That is, he must be willing to form coalitions through negotiating and practicing the art of compromise. He might have to compromise in such areas as the party platform, a credentials fight, the vice presidential nominee, the national party chairman, and his likely position with respect to key issues and appointments if he should become president. Managing and overcoming conflict over any of these areas may determine not only who wins the nomination, but also how well the nominee can carry on in the third stage — the "post-convention election campaign."

In the post-convention phase the nominee must try to hold to the coalition that fashioned his nomination in the convention; he must also try to add to it. He needs more campaign workers. He needs to appeal to a broader spectrum of voters. He invariably needs more money. But gaining new support involves risks of losing old support. A candidate and his staff must constantly assess costs and benefits, advantages and disadvantages. In the end, the candidate who receives a majority of

---

* Candidates, of course, might qualify for funds under the Federal Elections Campaign Act of 1974.

the electoral vote (and almost always a plurality of the popular vote) becomes president. But in his becoming (or winning) the president he needed the kind of broad support that he will continue to need to exercise effectively the various roles and responsibilities of his office.

ONCE IN OFFICE

In addition to this broad popular support, the president also needs the support of those specifically charged with helping him fulfill his various roles. The president appoints many people in offices and agencies of the executive branch. The heads of the major departments — for example, State, Defense, Housing and Urban Development (HUD), Health, Education and Welfare (HEW) — are all appointed by the president. These officials (or secretaries) and several others form the cabinet. In making these and other appointments, the president has to remain alert to factors that affect the policies and programs of his administration. For example, will a particular appointment dampen support from an important party leader, an important member of Congress, or endanger the support for an important segment of those who supported him in the presidential election. By and large, however, the overwhelming majority of the thousands of employees in these departments are under civil service and are not subject to presidential appointment.

The president also relies heavily on the **Executive Office of the President.** This office, just as the larger departments, consists of presidential appointees and career civil servants. It is divided into various units such as the White House Office, National Security Council, Office of Management and Budget, and Council of Economic Advisers. While these various units are all directly responsible to the president in helping to carry out his many functions, the White House Office is composed of the president's "own men." This allows the president to overcome certain political considerations (such as, satisfying different factions of his party) that may dictate whom he can appoint to administer the more formal governmental structures, such as the various cabinet departments. But in the White House Office the president can appoint aides and assistants of his *own* choosing. And their influence with the president in a given area might be greater than the cabinet member charged with that responsibility. However, the Watergate scandal, and subsequent revelations that some of President Nixon's closest "personal" assistants were involved, will undoubtedly cause presidents in the future to be more careful in making such appointments and in assigning responsibilities. In any event, to carry out his many roles the president needs the help of these administrators, both in the Executive Office and in the farflung bureaucracies of the large departments, such as

HEW. And the kind of help he gets determines how well the president does his job.

In conclusion, the person who occupies the office of the president has enormous influence in American politics. Through his various messages to Congress and to the nation (for example, in his **State of the Union Address**), he sets the nation's agenda. He can thus *propose* legislation; and through his **veto** power he can *dispose* of legislation passed by the Congress. Further, the president sets the nation's priorities, and his budget, legislative, and administrative powers give him great leverage to make those priorities stick. Also, his many ceremonial functions serve to strengthen him in exercising his formal powers.

The Congressional Arena

"All legislative power herein granted," says the Constitution, "is vested in a Congress of the United States. . . ." But the Constitution says much more. It makes similar statements about the executive power being vested in the president and the judicial power being vested in the federal courts. However, as discussed in Chapter 3, the Constitution follows the separation of powers doctrine only so far. After seeming to delegate total power to each of the three branches, the Constitution goes on to clothe each branch with just enough of the other's powers to make them *interdependent* rather than *independent* of each other. Accordingly, it is not accurate, either in theory or in practice, that the whole of any of these powers resides in any one branch exclusively. But exclusiveness aside, however, the fact is that Congress is the chief repository of legislative power under our system of government. As such Congress has been and remains a major forum in the formation of public policy.

For one thing, the composition of Congress enhances its role in the policy-making process. Congress, as we know, is a **bicameral** institution consisting of the House of Representatives and the Senate. All of its 535 members are elected directly by the people and are called the people's representatives in Washington. The members of the House are closest to the people because they are from smaller districts. House members are elected for two-year terms from 435 single-member districts into which the various states are apportioned. This apportionment is figured on the basis of population[3] and is done by the respective state legislatures. Whereas there are 435 members of the House, there are only 100 senators elected for six-year terms with equal representation (two) from

---

[3] Wesberry v. Sanders (376 U.S. 1, 1964).

Wide World Photos

Conferring with Counsel at Impeachment Hearings. Representatives Barbara Jordan (D., Tex.), center, and Charles Rangel (D., N.Y.), right, confer with John Doar, chief counsel for the House Judiciary Committee's impeachment inquiry during a committee recess in July, 1974.

each state. The Senate elections are staggered, so that one-third of the senate members are elected every two years.

The core organization and working unit in both houses is the **standing committee.** These committees are generally organized along subject matter lines such as labor, finance, agriculture, and foreign policy.[4] There are 17 such committees in the Senate with from 7 to 27 members. Important committees in the Senate are Foreign Relations, Finance, and Appropriations. In the House, there are 22 standing committees with an

---

[4] The most recent addition to the standing committees of Congress include budget committees for both the House and Senate. These committees, established in 1974, are designed to allow Congress with the aid of its own budgetary analysts to focus attention on the overall budgetary totals—both taxing and spending—and how individual authorization and appropriation measures square with budget projects. See generally *CQ Guide to Current American Government* (Spring, 1975), pp. 75-78.

average membership of about 30. Important committees in the House include Appropriations, Rules, and Ways and Means. (Of course, as the role of the House Judiciary Committee in the Nixon **impeachment hearings** clearly demonstrates, any given committee can prove important under the particular circumstances.) These committees in turn have many subcommittees; there are also joint committees with membership from both houses.

Membership on the major working committees of the Congress — the standing committees — is bipartisan. Each party is represented roughly in proportion to its strength in the particular house. Both parties provide structures for making committee assignments; these structures are usually dominated by veteran leaders of the respective house. And while several factors (for example, desires of individual members) are considered in assigning members to committees, in the end it is these veteran party leaders who have the final say.

The main work of the Congress takes place in these committees. How they function determines in large measure what Congress actually does. Bills introduced in a particular house are referred to the appropriate committee of that house. Most such bills stay in committee — they die there. Bills that do finally reach the floor have been the focus of much work by the committee. The committee reviews, redrafts, or drafts anew such legislation as it deems appropriate. In the process the committee might conduct public hearings. While these hearings might focus on particular bills, they might also be used by Congress (and particular committees) to oversee the work of the president and the far-flung executive bureaucracy. Such hearings, of course, might reveal the need for additional (or remedial) legislation.

COMMITTEE CHAIRMAN

But what comes out of the committee as well as how the committee conducts its work depends in large part on the committee chairman. The power of an individual chairman, of course, depends on many factors — his personal prestige and standing among colleagues, the traditions and norms of the particular committee, and so on. Nonetheless, the committee chairman occupies a central position in the work of the committee. He controls the committee staff, schedules or postpones committee meetings, determines the agenda, and generally sets the pace of the committee.

How does one gain such an important status? Generally, the chairman receives his position based on **seniority.** He is the member of the majority party with the longest continuous service on the particular committee. His counterpart on the committee from the minority party is designated as the *ranking* minority member; he usually becomes chairman if his party should gain the majority in a given house. Thus, those who stay around longest, who can be reelected time and again, will sooner or later gain a position of power and prestige in the Congress. Committee chairmen are therefore likely to be in the hands of those who come from fairly *stable* constituencies; that is, constituencies that do not find or see sufficient reason to change their representative in Washington.

Only three blacks have ever served as chairmen of congressional committees. These were all in the House of Representatives. Representative Charles Diggs (D., Mich.), elected to Congress in 1954, became chairman of the Committee on the District of Columbia in 1972; he is presently the only black in Congress holding a chairmanship. But the two men who became committee chairmen prior to Diggs are names familiar to many of us: Representative William L. Dawson (D., Ill.) and Representative Adam Clayton Powell (D., N.Y.). Dawson was elected to Congress in 1942 and served as chairman of the House Committee on Government Operations from 1955 until his retirement in 1970. Powell was elected to Congress in 1944 and became chairman of the very important House Committee on Education and Labor in 1961. Powell remained as chairman of the committee until 1967 when he was ousted from that position and eventually from Congress. Let us take a more detailed look at the politics and chairmanships of Dawson and Powell.

Since the Depression there has always been at least one black member of the House. (See Table 8–1.) But until Dawson and Powell came on the scene, blacks did not hold positions of significant influence in congressional policy-making. Dawson's situation is especially important, we believe, since he seemed so enmeshed in the Chicago **political machine** that it was difficult, if not impossible, for him to attend to black interests. However, it should be stated that Dawson's committee did not at the time handle matters of salient interest to blacks. The jurisdiction of the committee has been described as

> [b]udget and accounting measures other than appropriations, reorganization in executive and legislative branches of government, studying intergovernmental relations between U.S. and the states and municipalities, general legislative oversight of executive branch.[5]

Possessing institutional power in this instance did not lead to generalized political gains for blacks. In this regard Hanes Walton has stated:

> . . .Dawson used his institutional and personal power to enhance his political position and influence in Congress and did not serve blacks in general. . . .[6]

---

[5] Polsby, *Congress and the Presidency*, Table 3, p. 79.

[6] Hanes Walton, Jr., *Black Politics: A Theoretical and Structural Analysis* (Philadelphia: Lippincott, 1972), p. 171.

TABLE 8-1
Blacks in U.S. Congress 1869–1976

Year	Name	Party	State
U.S. Senate			
1868–1870	Hiram Revel	R	Mississippi
1874–1880	Blanche K. Bruce	R	Mississippi
1966–1972	Edward W. Brooke	R	Massachusetts
1972–	Edward W. Brooke	R	Massachusetts
U.S. House of Representatives			
1868–1870	Jefferson F. Long	R	Georgia
	Joseph H. Rainey	R	South Carolina
1870–1872	Benjamin S. Turner	R	Alabama
	Josiah T. Walls	R	Florida
	Joseph H. Rainey	R	South Carolina
	Robert B. Elliott	R	South Carolina
	Robert C. De Large	R	South Carolina
1872–1874	James T. Rapier	R	Alabama
	Josiah T. Walls	R	Florida
	John R. Lynch	R	Mississippi
	Robert B. Elliott	R	South Carolina
	Richard H. Cain	R	South Carolina
	Alonzo Ransier	R	South Carolina
	Joseph H. Rainey	R	South Carolina
1874–1876	Jeremiah Haralson	R	Alabama
	Josiah T. Walls	R	Florida
	Charles E. Nash	R	Louisiana
	John R. Lynch	R	Mississippi
	John A. Hyman	R	North Carolina
	Joseph H. Rainey	R	South Carolina
	Robert Smalls	R	South Carolina
1876–1878	Robert Smalls	R	South Carolina
	Joseph H. Rainey	R	South Carolina
	Richard H. Cain	R	South Carolina
1880–1882	John R. Lynch	R	Mississippi
	Robert Smalls	R	South Carolina
1882–1884	J. E. O'Hara	R	North Carolina
	Robert Smalls	R	South Carolina
1884–1886	J. E. O'Hara	R	North Carolina
	Robert Smalls	R	South Carolina
1886–1888	None		
1888–1890	Henry P. Cheatham	R	North Carolina
	Thomas E. Miller	R	South Carolina
	John M. Langston	R	Virginia
1890–1892	Henry P. Cheatham	R	North Carolina
1892–1894	George W. Murray	R	South Carolina
1894–1896	George W. Murray	R	South Carolina

Year	Name	Party	State
1896–1898	George H. White	R	North Carolina
1898–1900	George H. White[1]	R	North Carolina
1928–1930	Oscar DePriest	R	Illinois
1930–1932	Oscar DePriest	R	Illinois
1932–1934	Oscar DePriest	R	Illinois
1934–1936	Arthur W. Mitchell	D	Illinois
1936–1938	Arthur W. Mitchell	D	Illinois
1938–1940	Arthur W. Mitchell	D	Illinois
1940–1942	Arthur W. Mitchell	D	Illinois
1942–1944	William L. Dawson	D	Illinois
1944–1946	William L. Dawson	D	Illinois
	Adam Clayton Powell, Jr.	D	New York
1946–1948	William L. Dawson	D	Illinois
	Adam Clayton Powell, Jr.	D	New York
1948–1950	William L. Dawson	D	Illinois
	Adam Clayton Powell, Jr.	D	New York
1950–1952	William L. Dawson	D	Illinois
	Adam Clayton Powell, Jr.	D	New York
1952–1954	William L. Dawson	D	Illinois
	Adam Clayton Powell, Jr.	D	New York
1954–1956	William L. Dawson	D	Illinois
	Charles C. Diggs, Jr.	D	Michigan
	Adam Clayton Powell, Jr.	D	New York
1956–1958	William L. Dawson	D	Illinois
	Charles C. Diggs, Jr.	D	Michigan
	Adam Clayton Powell, Jr.	D	New York
	Robert N. C. Nix[2]	D	Pennsylvania
1958–1960	William L. Dawson	D	Illinois
	Charles C. Diggs, Jr.	D	Michigan
	Adam Clayton Powell, Jr.	D	New York
	Robert N. C. Nix	D	Pennsylvania
1960–1962	William L. Dawson	D	Illinois
	Charles C. Diggs, Jr.	D	Michigan
	Adam Clayton Powell, Jr.	D	New York
	Robert N. C. Nix	D	Pennsylvania
1962–1964	Augustus F. Hawkins	D	California
	William L. Dawson	D	Illinois
	Charles C. Diggs, Jr.	D	Michigan
	Adam Clayton Powell, Jr.	D	New York
	Robert N. C. Nix	D	Pennsylvania

[1] White was the last black Congressman from the South and the last black Congressman for 28 years. (Barbara Jordan of Texas and Andrew Young of Georgia were elected in 1972. Harold Ford of Tennessee won election in 1974.)

[2] Nix was elected in a special election held in May 1958.

TABLE 8-1 (continued)

Year	Name	Party	State
1964–1966	Augustus F. Hawkins	D	California
	William L. Dawson	D	Illinois
	John Conyers, Jr.	D	Michigan
	Charles C. Diggs, Jr.	D	Michigan
	Adam Clayton Powell, Jr.	D	New York
	Robert N. C. Nix	D	Pennsylvania
1966–1968	Augustus F. Hawkins	D	California
	William L. Dawson	D	Illinois
	John Conyers, Jr.	D	Michigan
	Charles C. Diggs, Jr.	D	Michigan
	Adam Clayton Powell, Jr.	D	New York
	Robert N. C. Nix	D	Pennsylvania
1968–1970	Augustus F. Hawkins	D	California
	William L. Dawson	D	Illinois
	John Conyers, Jr.	D	Michigan
	Charles C. Diggs, Jr.	D	Michigan
	William L. Clay	D	Missouri
	Shirley Chisholm	D	New York
	Adam Clayton Powell, Jr.	D	New York
	Louis Stokes	D	Ohio
	Robert N. C. Nix	D	Pennsylvania
1970–1972	Ronald V. Dellums	D	California
	Augustus F. Hawkins	D	California
	Walter E. Fauntroy	D	District of Columbia
	George W. Collins	D	Illinois
	Ralph H. Metcalfe	D	Illinois
	Parren J. Mitchell	D	Maryland
	John Conyers, Jr.	D	Michigan
	Charles C. Diggs, Jr.	D	Michigan
	William L. Clay	D	Missouri
	Shirley Chisholm	D	New York
	Charles B. Rangel	D	New York
	Louis Stokes	D	Ohio
	Robert N. C. Nix	D	Pennsylvania
1972–1974	Yvonne Burke	D	California
	Shirley Chisholm	D	New York
	William L. Clay	D	Missouri
	Cardiss Collins[3]	D	Illinois
	John Conyers, Jr.	D	Michigan
	Ronald V. Dellums	D	California
	Charles C. Diggs, Jr.	D	Michigan

[3] Cardiss Collins won special election in 1973 to fill seat of her late husband, George Collins.

YEAR	NAME	PARTY	STATE
	Walter E. Fauntroy	D	District of Columbia
	Augustus F. Hawkins	D	California
	Barbara Jordan	D	Texas
	Ralph H. Metcalfe	D	Illinois
	Parren J. Mitchell	D	Maryland
	Robert N. C. Nix	D	Pennsylvania
	Charles B. Rangel	D	New York
	Louis Stokes	D	Ohio
	Andrew Young	D	Georgia
1974–1976	Yvonne Burke	D	California
	Shirley Chisholm	D	New York
	William L. Clay	D	Missouri
	Cardiss Collins	D	Illinois
	John Conyers, Jr.	D	Michigan
	Ronald V. Dellums	D	California
	Charles C. Diggs, Jr.	D	Michigan
	Walter E. Fauntroy	D	District of Columbia
	Harold Ford	D	Tennessee
	Augustus F. Hawkins	D	California
	Barbara Jordan	D	Texas
	Ralph H. Metcalfe	D	Illinois
	Parren J. Mitchell	D	Maryland
	Robert N. C. Nix	D	Pennsylvania
	Charles B. Rangel	D	New York
	Louis Stokes	D	Ohio
	Andrew Young	D	Georgia

SOURCE: List through 1973 compiled and reprinted with permission from Joint Center for Political Studies. *Black Politics '72* (Part II. The Republican National Convention, pp. 61–64). Updated by authors from 1973–1976. Notes reprinted in original and updated where necessary.

By the time Dawson became chairman he had reached an advanced age and his health was deteriorating. Effective use of power requires a degree of vigor and energy which he also did not possess. And, finally, the amount of bargaining with colleagues for the interest of a black constituency was limited since Dawson's position furnished few sources with which to negotiate.

Unlike his colleague from Chicago, Adam Clayton Powell, Jr. was a maverick. The minister of the largest black Protestant congregation in New York City, Congressman Powell exploited this resource in fighting the Tammany machine of New York. Powell emerged at an opportune time. The influence of political machines was declining, but of equal importance was a growing political consciousness among northern urban blacks. This consciousness partly resulted from long-standing frustration over unresponsive government institutions. Black Americans were becoming increasingly resentful of the continued discrimination and other forms of social injustice to which they were subjected.

Because of his flamboyant style and the explicit emphasis which Powell placed on race, he has generally been criticized by political commentators and scholarly analysts. James Q. Wilson, for example, characterized Powell as a political leader who substituted "personal charisma and bellicose militancy" for organization.[7] We agree that Powell had charismatic appeal and that he was (for his time) militant. But personalizing leadership is a characteristic of black ministerial style, especially in the Baptist denominations. And in the absence of more tangible rewards, charisma is a functional substitute for holding a constituency together. It should also be kept in mind that a religious congregation is similar to a political machine; it provides welfare services to members. This function is, of course, more limited in scope in a church because of its private nature.

As a political base, Powell's congregation was both durable and large enough to return him to office repeatedly. In consequence, he became chairman of the House Committee on Education and Labor when Graham Barden resigned from Congress in protest against packing the committee with new members who favored more liberal legislation. Chairman Powell's tenure as chairman included the years of the poverty program. His committee was a focal point for many of the crucial legislative debates on this effort. Powell's committee leadership has not been favorably evaluated. Unlike some of the other chairmen, Powell was not considered an "expert" in his assigned responsibilities. Much of the work of Education and Labor, as with other House committees, was done by subcommittee chairmen. The flamboyant style that characterized Powell's leadership also militated against his effectiveness as chairman. In addition, he could not be attentive to the business of the committee because of a high rate of absenteeism from Congress.

Perhaps his fall from power was an inevitable consequence of Powell's behavior. He was never a popular figure in Congress. His troubles grew in New York and Washington as well. Powell had gone against congressional norms, including what a special House Committee found to be a misuse of federal funds. As a result, the House fined Powell, stripped him of seniority, and of his chairmanship. The racial themes which he espoused offended the white majority at the same time that they gained him widespread admiration among blacks. But in the end it

---

[7] Cf. James Q. Wilson, "The Negro in Politics," in *Daedalus* 94:4 (Fall, 1965), 961. For a more extended analysis of Powell, see Wilson's "Two Negro Politicians: An Interpretation," *MJPS*, 4 (November 1960), 360–69.

was Powell's Harlem constituents who did what his House colleagues wanted to do but could not: deprive him of a seat in Congress.[8] Powell was defeated in the 1970 primary and died soon thereafter.

OTHER CONGRESSIONAL LEADERS

In addition to committee chairmen, there are other key positions in the Congress where seniority is also an important and perhaps a decisive consideration. In the House there is the Speaker of the House, the majority **floor leader,** and the minority floor leader. Though each of these officials is selected by his party **caucus,** only the Speaker (the presiding officer) is officially elected by the entire House. The speaker is by far the single most important official in the House. He wields great influence in his party, the House, and the Congress generally. Together the Speaker and the majority and minority floor leaders significantly influence the outcome of business in the House. Similarly, the majority and minority leaders in the Senate set the pace of business in that house.

THE LEGISLATIVE PROCESS

Now to the main business of Congress, the business of legislation. As mentioned earlier, the initiative in lawmaking comes primarily from the president, not the Congress. Nonetheless, before any proposals (bills) can become law they must survive the legislative gamut in the Congress. That gamut includes: (1) introduction and referral to committee; (2) committee consideration including the full range of options open to the committee; for example whether or not to hold public hearings, whether the bill should be amended, redrafted or substituted altogether, whether or not the bill should be reported out; and (3) consideration, or debate, and vote by the entire house. If passed by one house, the bill is sent to the other house where basically the same procedures are followed. If both houses pass the bill in identical form, then the bill has run the legislative gamut in the Congress. However, if a similar but different version of the bill is passed by one house, a conference committee composed of members of both houses convenes to resolve differences. If such differences are resolved, the identical measure worked out by the conference committee is presented to both houses. If passed in this identical form the bill is then sent to the president for his approval or disapproval (veto). If he approves and signs, the bill becomes law; if he disapproves (vetoes), the bill might still become law if two-thirds of both houses of Congress vote to override the president's veto. The overriding of a presidential veto, however, is seldom accomplished.

---

[8] Actually the House denied Powell his seat in 1967 but the Supreme Court later ruled that he had been unlawfully excluded. (*Powell* v. *McCormack*, 395 U.S. 486, 1969).

The President, Congress, and Black Americans: Some General Observations

This brief overview of Congress and the president permits us to make several observations about the Congress and the president as decision-making forums, especially as they relate to problems of blacks and other minorities.

1. Given the structure of presidential election politics, it would be most difficult for a black person to garner the necessary resources and overcome the other informal requirements to mount a viable presidential race. Realists (and optimists), of course, can always point to the incremental character of American politics and the slow but steady progress of blacks that could conceivably allow a black to become president. From our vantage point, however, that will require a remarkable degree of optimism and an accelerated pace of incrementalism. Should the racial barrier be overcome sooner than implied here, it could very well be that the coalitions and alliances necessary at this time for a black to become president would make him little more than a prisoner of established norms, policies and practices. As such, he could hardly articulate, much less push, policies favorable to blacks and other minorities. Of course, these are the very kinds of problems that face other black elected officials although in different settings, such as black mayors.

2. As the system presently operates, a president has to remain alert to political considerations and realities in filling his chief appointive positions. These considerations and realities invariably involve such questions as the past experiences and competencies as related to position concerned; the standing of the potential appointee with other influentials; and the reception of the appointment by those upon whom the president relies for support. While each of these factors is on its face "neutral" insofar as race or color is concerned, a closer look reveals that they are anything but neutral. Any one of these "neutral" factors could be used to keep the appointments of the president lily white. How many blacks, for example, have had the opportunities to gain the particular kinds of experience or competencies that plausibly could be useful for the position in question. This, of course, is very much related to the racism that pervades the American socioeconomic structure. And the limited opportunities afforded blacks in the socioeconomic structure invariably limit the development of contacts with other influentials. The role of such neutral factors, especially past experiences and competence, is perhaps used more by whites to rationalize why blacks and other minorities do not gain such appointments than to justify any particular appointment that is made. The appointment of a black secretary of state, for example, would undergo much scrutiny and stimulate more opposition than would the appointment of a white person even though their qualifications were otherwise identical.

3. Very few blacks are appointed to key administrative positions, such as Executive Office of the president, cabinet, and sub-cabinet positions. And this seems to be the case regardless of the party in the White House. Only two blacks have ever served as members of the cabinet; the first of these appointments did not come until 1966 when President Johnson appointed Robert Weaver as secretary of housing and urban development. The second black cabinet officer was appointed in 1975 when President Ford named Attorney William Coleman as secretary of transportation. (President Johnson did appoint Thurgood Marshall as solicitor general, and later to the Supreme Court. And, of course, there have been a few other blacks appointed to judicial positions.) However, except as advisors on minority problems, black appointments have been so few that we continue to talk in terms of "firsts."

4. The structure of elections and representation in the House of Representatives makes it more likely that blacks would have more representation in the House than in the Senate. The concentration of blacks in particular congressional districts makes it more possible for potential black candidates to gain their party's nomination and to mount a viable election campaign. Financing a campaign in a single congressional district, for example, is much more within reach of potential black candidates at this stage of black economic and financial development. On the other hand, senators are elected on a statewide basis and chances of blacks getting necessary resources to launch effective campaigns for their party's nomination and in the subsequent general election are much more remote. The single exception is Senator Edward Brooke (R., Mass.) who was and is the only black person to serve in the U.S. Senate since Reconstruction. However, Brooke's political career as a Republican attorney general in Massachusetts and his policy position on questions salient to most blacks have not been in the mainstream of black politics. But neither is Brooke's constituency!

5. The structure and operation of the law-making process is such that those who propose new legislation have numerous procedural and political obstacles to overcome before they can achieve their ends. By the same token, those who oppose such new legislation are presented with many opportunities to impede and block its passage. Consider the necessity of gaining committee approval, the agreement of both houses, and the approval of the president (except that a two-thirds vote in both houses could override his veto). Consider moreover, other factors such as the operation of seniority and the **filibuster***. It is of course true, as

---

* Unlike the House of Representatives where debate is sharply limited, debate in the Senate is almost unlimited. Once gaining the floor, a senator has the right to talk (to filibuster) until stopping voluntarily. This permits a small group of senators to prevent voting on legislation with which they disagree.

one writer points out, that certain perceived obstacles such as the filibuster and the seniority system can also work for liberal ends.[9] In 1972, for example, civil rights supporters in the Senate successfully used the filibuster to defeat an antibusing bill designed to limit the authority of federal courts in desegregating urban schools. But mostly, as Table 8-2 shows, the filibuster has been used to block and impede passage of civil rights legislation. We should note, however, that a 1975 change in Senate rules now ostensibly makes it easier to end filibusters by requiring a three-fifths rather than a two-thirds vote of those present and voting to invoke cloture (limit debate).

It is also true that the seniority system appears to be losing some of its grip on social change. As old-line southern Democrats leave the scene, for example, their once dominant conservative control of committee

TABLE 8-2
Complete List of Cloture Votes Since Adoption of Rule 22

Following is a complete list through Feb. 6, 1974, of the 82 cloture votes taken since Rule 22 was adopted in 1917. Only 15 of these (shown in **boldface**) were successful. In the right-hand column is shown the vote necessary to invoke cloture under a proposed 3/5-majority vote. Nineteen additional cloture votes (shown in *italics*) would have been successful using the proposed change.

| | | | YEA VOTES NEEDED | |
ISSUE	DATE	VOTE	2/3 MAJORITY	3/5 MAJORITY
Versailles Treaty	Nov. 15,	1919	78–16	63	57
Emergency tariff	Feb. 2,	1921	36–35	48	43
Tariff bill	July 7,	1922	45–35	54	48
World Court	Jan. 25,	1926	68–26	63	57
Migratory birds	June 1,	1926	46–33	53	47
Branch banking	Feb. 15,	1927	65–18	56	50
Disabled officers	Feb. 26,	1927	51–36	58	52
Colorado River	Feb. 26,	1927	32–59	61	55
D.C. buildings	Feb. 28,	1927	52–31	56	50
Prohibition Bureau	Feb. 28,	1927	55–27	55	49
Banking Act	Jan. 19,	1933	58–30	59	53
Anti-lynching	Jan. 27,	1938	37–51	59	53
Anti-lynching	Feb. 16,	1938	42–46	59	53
Anti-poll tax	Nov. 23,	1942	37–41	52	47
Anti-poll tax	May 15,	1944	36–44	54	48
Fair Employment Practices Commission	Feb. 9,	1946	48–36	56	50

[9] Gary Orfield, *Congressional Power: Congress and Social Change* (New York: Harcourt Brace Jovanovich, Inc., 1975), esp. pp. 38–44.

ISSUE	DATE		VOTE	YEA VOTES NEEDED	
				2/3 MAJORITY	3/5 MAJORITY
British loan	May 7,	1946	41–41	55	49
Labor disputes	May 25,	1946	3–77	54	48
Anti-poll tax	July 31,	1946	39–33	48	43
FEPC	May 19,	1950	52–32	64*	58*
FEPC	July 12,	1950	55–33	64*	58*
Atomic Energy Act	July 26,	1954	44–42	64*	58*
Civil Rights Act	March 10,	1960	42–53	64	57
Amend Rule 22	Sept. 19,	1961	37–43	54	48
Literacy tests	May 9,	1962	43–53	64	58
Literacy tests	May 14,	1962	42–52	63	57
Comsat Act	Aug. 14,	1962	63–27	60	54
Amend Rule 22	Feb. 7,	1963	54–42	64	58
Civil Rights Act	June 10,	1964	71–29	67	60
Legislative reapportionment	Sept. 10,	1964	30–63	62	56
Voting Rights Act	May 25,	1965	70–30	67	60
Right-to-work repeal	Oct. 11,	1965	45–47	62	55
Right-to-work repeal	Feb. 8,	1966	51–48	66	59
Right-to-work repeal	Feb. 10,	1966	50–49	66	59
Civil Rights Act	Sept. 14,	1966	54–42	64	58
Civil Rights Act	Sept. 19,	1966	52–41	62	56
D.C. Home Rule	Oct. 10,	1966	41–37	52	47
Amend Rule 22	Jan. 24,	1967	53–46	66	59
Open Housing	Feb. 20,	1968	55–37	62	55
Open Housing	Feb. 26,	1968	56–36	62	55
Open Housing	March 1,	1968	59–35	63	57
Open Housing	March 4,	1968	65–32	65	58
Fortas nomination	Oct. 1,	1968	45–43	59	53
Amend Rule 22	Jan. 16,	1969	51–47	66	59
Amend Rule 22	Jan. 28,	1969	50–42	62	55
Electoral College	Sept. 17,	1970	54–36	60	54
Electoral College	Sept. 29,	1970	53–34	58	53
Supersonic transport	Dec. 19,	1970	43–48	61	55
Supersonic transport	Dec. 22,	1970	42–44	58	52
Amend Rule 22	Feb. 18,	1971	48–37	57	51
Anemd Rule 22	Feb. 23,	1971	50–36	58	52
Amend Rule 22	March 2,	1971	48–36	56	50
Amend Rule 22	March 9,	1971	55–39	63	57
Military Draft	June 23,	1971	65–27	62	55
Lockheed Loan	July 26,	1971	42–47	60	54
Lockheed Loan	July 28,	1971	59–39	66	59

* Between 1949 and 1959 the cloture rule required the affirmative vote of two-thirds of Senate membership rather than two-thirds of senators who voted.

TABLE 8-2 (continued)

ISSUE	DATE	VOTE	YEA VOTES NEEDED 2/3 MAJORITY	3/5 MAJORITY
Lockheed Loan	July 30,	1971	53–37	60	54
Military Draft	Sept. 21,	1971	61–30	61	55
Rehnquist nomination	Dec. 10,	1971	52–42	63	57
Equal Job Opportunity	Feb. 1,	1972	48–37	57	51
Equal Job Opportunity	Feb. 3,	1972	53–35	59	53
Equal Job Opportunity	Feb. 23,	1972	71–23	63	57
U.S.-Soviet Arms Pact	Sept. 14,	1972	76–15	61	55
Consumer Agency	Sept. 29,	1972	47–29	51	46
Consumer Agency	Oct. 3,	1972	55–32	58	53
Consumer Agency	Oct. 5,	1972	52–30	55	49
School Busing	Oct. 10,	1972	45–37	55	49
School Busing	Oct. 11,	1972	49–39	59	53
School Busing	Oct. 12,	1972	49–38	58	53
Voter Registration	April 30,	1973	56–31	58	53
Voter Registration	May 3,	1973	60–34	63	57
Voter Registration	May 9,	1973	67–32	66	59
Public Campaign Financing	Dec. 2,	1973	47–33	54	48
Public Campaign Financing	Dec. 3,	1973	49–39	59	53
Rhodesian Chrome Ore	Dec. 11,	1973	59–35	63	57
Rhodesian Chrome Ore	Dec. 13,	1973	62–33	64	57
Legal Services Program	Dec. 13,	1973	60–36	64	58
Legal Services Program	Dec. 14,	1973	56–29	57	51
Rhodesian Chrome Ore	Dec. 18,	1973	63–26	60	54
Legal Services Program	Jan. 30,	1974	68–29	65	58
Genocide Treaty	Feb. 5,	1974	55–36	61	55
Genocide Treaty	Feb. 6,	1974	55–38	62	56

SOURCE: Reprinted with permission from *Congressional Quarterly Weekly Report*, February 9, 1974, p. 317.

chairmanships is lessening. In addition, the quality and ideological outlook of southern Congress members on matters of race are changing if for no other reason than that their constituencies now include large numbers of black voters. But though traditionally opposed by blacks and liberals, seniority could conceivably work to their benefit. Thirteen of the 16 black members of Congress come from districts that have more than 50 percent black voters; one other (Barbara Jordan) comes from a district which is 42 percent black and 19 percent Spanish-American. (See Table 8-3.) While these large black constituencies might not necessarily con-

TABLE 8-3
Black Representatives and Seniority

Name	Elected	% Black in District	Committee	Seniority Rank
Burke, Yvonne (D., Cal., 37)*	1972	51	Appropriations	32 (37)**
Chisholm, Shirley (D., N.Y., 12)	1968	77	Education and Labor	14 (27)
Clay, William (D., Mo., 1)	1968	54	Education and Labor Post Ofc. & Civil Ser.	13 (27) 9 (19)
Collins, Cardiss (D., Ill., 7)	1973	55	Foreign Affairs Govt. Operations	19 (22) 17 (29)
Conyers, John (D., Mich., 1)	1964	70	Govt. Operations Judiciary	13 (29) 6 (23)
Dellums, Ronald (D., Calif., 7)	1970	26	Armed Services District of Columbia	19 (27) 4 (15)
Diggs, Charles (D., Mich., 13)	1954	66	District of Columbia Foreign Affairs	1 (15) (Chmn.) 6 (22)
Fauntroy, Walter (D., D.C.)	1970	71	District of Columbia Banking, Currency, & Housing	6 (15) 15 (29)
Ford, Harold (D., Tenn., 8)	1974	47	Banking, Currency, & Housing Veterans' Affairs	21 (29) 15 (19)

* Congressional districts are designated within states by number. For example, Representative Burke represents the 37th Congressional district of California; Representative Chisholm the 12th congressional district of New York, and so one.
** Total Democratic membership of committee.

TABLE 8-3 (continued)

NAME	ELECTED	% BLACK IN DISTRICT	COMMITTEE	SENIORITY Rank
Hawkins, Augustus (D., Calif., 21)	1962	54	Education and Labor House Administration	7 (27) 6 (17)
Jordan, Barbara (D., Tex., 18)	1972	42***	Govt. Operations Judiciary	23 (29) 14 (23)
Metcalfe, Ralph (D., Ill., 1)	1970	89	Interstate & Foreign Comm. Mer. Marine & Fisheries	16 (28) 12 (27)
Mitchell, Parren (D., Md., 7)	1970	74	Banking, Currency, & Housing Budget	14 (29) 9 (17)
Nix, Robert (D., Penn., 2)	1958	65	Foreign Affairs Post Ofc. & Civ. Serv.	7 (22) 4 (19)
Rangel, Charles (D., N.Y. 19)	1970	59	Ways and Means	18 (25)
Stokes, Louis (D., Ohio, 21)	1968	66	Appropriations Budget	24 (37) 14 (17)
Young, Andrew (D., Ga., 5)	1972	44	Rules	11 (11)

*** In addition, approximately 19 percent of the district is composed of Spanish-Americans.

SOURCES: Michael Barone et al., *The Almanac of American Politics* (Boston: Gambit, 1973), and *Congressional Directory, 1975.* Seniority rank calculated in accordance with *Congressional Directory, 1975.*

tinue to return the same black representatives, given what we know about the overwhelming success of incumbents in winning reelection, [10] it is plausible that in time a number of black representatives will gain seniority and thus stake a strong claim to committee chairmanships. However, it could also develop that seniority will become less a guarantee to committee chairmanships. The removal by House Democrats of three committee chairmen [11] as the 94th Congress opened in 1975 indicates that seniority cannot prevail in the face of a determined majority within a given party caucus. It would indeed be ironic if the influence of seniority diminishes about the very time that blacks gain in seniority. But as Table 8–3 demonstrates, the seniority status of blacks on important committees is such that this ironic situation, if it develops at all, is far in the future. And while this discussion of the filibuster and seniority system does illustrate how changes in the political landscape can bring about changes in the consequences of rules, that landscape has not changed sufficiently to overcome the stultifying effect of the rules. Indeed, on balance, the structure and nature of the law-making process as it operates today continue to favor those who wish to keep things as they are or who opt for incremental change. Those who desire more sweeping social change, the kind needed to elevate the status of blacks and other minorities, will still find the going very difficult.

6. From our discussion above, it follows that various resources both in and outside the Congress are needed to pass legislation. This is especially true of domestic public policy measures that would benefit the masses of blacks and minorities. Consider, for example, the resources needed to pass major civil rights legislation such as the Civil Rights Act of 1964. In this case there was strong support from the president, congressional leaders, and a large array of interest groups. Effective organization and communication among those supporting this legislation was also an indispensable resource. So too were the crisis situations brought about by civil rights demonstrations such as the 1963 March on Washington, D.C., and by violence such as the tragic assassination of civil rights leader Medgar Evers and the murder of four little black girls while attending Sunday School in a Birmingham church. These demonstrations, protests, and violence led President Kennedy to abandon his rather indirect approach to civil rights problems. Previously, the president had chosen to soft-pedal civil rights in hopes of gaining wider

---

[10] Charles Bullock, "House Careerists: Changing Patterns of Longevity and Attrition," *APSR* 66 (Dec. 1972), 1296. Also see *Congressional Record,* October 10, 1973, p. E6372.

[11] The House Democrats ousted Wright Patman (D., Texas) chairman of the House Banking and Currency Committee; W. R. Poage (D., Texas) chairman of the Agriculture Committee; and F. Edward Hebert (D., Louisiana) as chairman of the Armed Services Committee. See *Congressional Quarterly Weekly Report,* Vol. 33 (Jan. 25, 1975), p. 210.

support, especially from key southern congressional leaders, for other priorities. But by June 1963 the president began to take a more direct interest and assert leadership in pressing for civil rights legislation.

7. The role and position of the president is absolutely crucial to success in the legislative process. His weapons of influence make him by far the single most important elected official in government: his access and command of information resources; his instant command of free television and radio time for messages; his veto power over legislation, the threat of which may be more influential than its actual use; his administrative authority such as the enforcement or non-enforcement of particular policies; his powers of appointment; his control over the impoundment or release of funds; and the many other powers conferred upon him by the Congress or the Constitution, or assumed by him to be derived from these and other sources. Whereas in general Presidents Kennedy and Johnson used their powers to support civil rights interests, President Nixon used his authority to thwart or retard these interests. It is indeed the case that "the Presidency, the traditional defender of minority rights within the federal government, became [under Nixon] the principal hostile force."[12]

8. The greatest leverage that blacks have over a president is in influencing election outcomes. Given the structure of the electoral college and the concentration of blacks in states with large electoral votes, an overwhelming black vote in any of these states could prove decisive to a particular candidate. This fact is particularly important to Democratic party presidential expectations; the black electorate has contributed an increasing proportion of Democratic candidates' totals. According to a study published in 1972 this proportion rose from approximately 6 percent in the 1950's to almost 20 percent in 1968.[13] Nonetheless, once that leverage has been used and the election is over, there is almost no continuous black presence (influence) in the day-to-day operations of the presidency and his administration. To be sure, blacks can threaten to withhold or transfer support in subsequent elections. But the reality is that black options in our two-party presidential election system are severely limited. And their options between elections are even more limited. In short, access to and favorable attention from a president must come on the basis of election promises in exchange for election support, or from gaining positions of influence upon which a president must depend, or from a combination of these and other factors. So far at least, whatever influence blacks have on a president seems to rest almost

---

[12] Orfield, *Congressional Power*, p. 73.

[13] Robert Axelrod, "Where the Votes Come From: An Analysis of Electoral Coalitions 1952–1968," *APSR*, 66:1 (March 1972), 11–20.

entirely on election support. And as blacks well know, this has proven a slender reed indeed.

We now turn to a case study of the Congressional Black Caucus, an organized attempt of black members of Congress to promote the interests of blacks and other minorities.

From Protests to Politics: The Congressional Black Caucus

The Congressional Black Caucus is composed of all black members of the House of Representatives. The organization has its own staff and permanent office in Washington. Although only some six years old, the Caucus has already been the center of considerable controversy, ranging from attempts to define its own role and place in black politics to battling a president for recognition. In large measure, this discussion of the Congressional Black Caucus (CBC) centers around an article written by Alex Poinsett, senior staff editor of *Ebony* magazine. The article is reprinted below.* A concluding section attempts to update the article and to view the CBC within the framework of other matters discussed in this chapter.

THE BLACK CAUCUS: FIVE YEARS LATER

Alex Poinsett

I was attacked when I said that most of my colleagues in Congress are mediocre prima donnas who don't understand the level of human misery in this country. I don't think that was a demagogic statement. I think that was a true statement. But when I was attacked, I said okay, I'll back off that. I'll modify my statement. Congress is a mediocre institution that forces the need for mediocre prima donnas to develop.
—Rep. Ronald V. Dellums (D., Calif.)

---

* Reprinted by permission of *Ebony* Magazine, © 1973 by Johnson Publishing Company, Inc.

I've seen people come into this Congress feeling it was incumbent upon them to give everybody hell, talking about the wrongs and fancied wrongs that happen everyday. . . . They didn't correct a damn thing. . . . The legislation they sought to present to the House later on received little interest from any source. . . . In voicing your disapproval, you don't make your fellow member of Congress responsible for what you're condemning unless he is responsible. Nor do you condemn the whole white race.
—Rep. Robert N. C. Nix (D., Pa.)

Though they disagree sharply, Representatives Dellums and Nix are not at war with each other. Their markedly different views of Congress only reflect the rich diversity which distinguishes the 15 House members — all Democrats — who constitute the Congressional Black Caucus. Indeed, the two men are a study in contrasts. Dellums, a 37-year-old mystic temporarily employed as a politician, is into his second term. Nix, at 70, old enough to be Dellums' father and far less idealistic, is into his eighth. Dellums has been labeled a "radical extremist" bent on bringing the walls of the Establishment down. Nix has been dismissed as a conservative because of his long-standing opposition to confrontation politics. Dellums is a brilliant, compulsive talker who is so emotional he sat down in the middle of the floor and cried painful tears over the airplane death last December of his close friend and colleague, Rep. George Collins (D., Ill.). Less emotional, more deliberate in his conversational style, more tradition-bound in his approach to his work, Nix is a pipe stem chewer who sees cool, rational analysis as indispensable to the solving of social problems. While Dellums believes the Caucus can spearhead congressional reform, Nix strongly disagrees, pointing out that the Caucus is only 15 among 535 congressmen (House and Senate). Indeed, Nix has been called a "maverick" of the Caucus, since he seldom attends its meetings, believing his first obligation is to attend House sessions and meetings of the Foreign Affairs and the Post Office and Civil Service committees on which he serves. For all of their glaring differences in temperament and technique, Dellums and Nix have voting records which demonstrate unequivocally that both are dedicated — like their Caucus colleagues — to ending the oppression of black people.
    The "vibes" at once connecting and separating Dellums and Nix are a sampling of the Caucus which, after five years, is a beehive of confusion honeycombed with orderliness. If any general labeling of Caucus members is possible, it is that most defy labels of the traditional radical-moderate-conservative sort. Yet, because of similarities in their political thinking and activities, most Caucus members cluster into natural groupings of three. Off to the left are the sometimes rebellious, always charismatic Dellums, Shirley Chisholm (N.Y.) and John Conyers, Jr. (Mich.). Unusually unpredictable, they also tend to be unperturbed

about diplomatic niceties. "If we feel strongly about something," explains one member of this trio, "we're going to do it. Whenever things get hot in the Caucus, we're not afraid to say what we think. We don't bite our tongues when things need to be said." Thus it was Dellums who organized public hearings on U.S. war crimes in Southeast Asia following 1971 demonstrations by the Vietnam Veterans Against the War. It was Mrs. Chisholm who ran as a maverick candidate for the U.S. presidency. And it was Conyers who last year, along with Dellums, Chisholm and Representatives William F. Ryan (D., N.Y.) and Bella Abzug (D., N.Y.), introduced a resolution to impeach President Nixon because of his continued involvement in Southeast Asia.

Far more predictable, less volatile, more diplomatic in their general demeanor, Ralph Metcalfe (Ill.), Nix and Caucus Vice Chairman Augustus F. Hawkins (Cal.), are all situated off to the right in the Caucus. Shunning publicity, they prefer instead to attend their quiet, behind-the-scenes labors. As the oldest members of the Caucus, this trio perhaps displays the greatest respect for the venerable traditions of the House and perhaps are the least inclined to challenge those traditions. Hawkins declares: "Leadership belongs not to the loudest, not to those who beat on the drums or blow the trumpet, but to those who day in and day out, in all seasons, work for the practical realization of a better world — those who have the stamina to persist and to remain honest and dedicated, to those belongs the leadership."

If there is a left and a right in the Caucus, situated somewhere in the center are Louis Stokes (Ohio), William L. Clay (Mo.) and Walter E. Fauntroy (D.C.). "They're always taking the leadership role in terms of projecting the Caucus," explains a colleague. "Fauntroy in particular is great for drawing up lists of demands to people and groups. During the election campaign, he drew up a list of black demands for Senator George McGovern." As Caucus treasurer, Clay rode herd on its 1971 and 1972 fund raising dinners. His persistence helped the Caucus to net more than $144,000 out of the $200,000 gross the first year. Placing $20,000 in each of the five black banks in Los Angeles, St. Louis, Cleveland, Baltimore and Washington, he financed the Caucus' operating expenses with the remaining $44,000 and with contributions it later received which enabled the Caucus to spend $95,000 in 1971. Because it raised only about $50,000 in the midst of the election year's fierce competition for funds, Clay was obliged to use $60,000 of the Caucus' $100,000 cash reserve in 1972.

Perhaps the common thread weaving through a fourth Caucus trio, Charles C. Diggs (Mich.), Parren J. Mitchell (Md.), and Caucus secretary Charles B. Rangel (N.Y.), is that they neither can be lumped conveniently with the other groups nor do they form a natural grouping of their own. Once conservative enough to resist the Caucus designation as a

Black Caucus (it was originally "the Democratic Select Committee"), yet militant enough to resign in protest from the 1971 U.S. delegation to the United Nations because of U.S. support in Africa of racist South African and Portuguese regimes, Diggs has been described as a loner. Similarly, Mitchell is said to have "the uncanny ability to stand outside the pale of some of the confusion that sometimes occurs within the Caucus." Both he and Rangel have been described as "real diplomats," functioning as mediators and conciliators within the Caucus. Indeed, his colleagues regard Mitchell as the person who could be the Caucus' perennial "healer."

The final Caucus trio, Barbara Jordan (Tex.), Yvonne Brathwaite Burke (Cal.) and Andrew Young (Ga.), are freshmen who perhaps are too new to their work to be pigeonholed. Astute, diligent, Congresswoman Jordan has been described as "intimidating as a rural minister delivering a fire and brimstone sermon," because of her no-nonsense demeanor and her refusal to be part of the "in" crowd. Mrs. Burke, on the other hand, is less definitive than Miss Jordan, less assertive and less threatening. Yet she manages to be defiant and tough in a radically more subtle way as evidenced by her suave manner as a chairperson at last summer's Democratic National Convention. Meanwhile, Young exerts a cool, calming influence on Caucus meetings, sitting quietly, observing, but making insightful contributions. With their $42,500 annual salaries, yearly allowances of $170,000-plus for 16 staffers and office equipment, unlimited access to House hearings, a Congressional Library for research and a widely-read Congressional Record to publish their views, Caucus members are in command of resources heretofore unavailable to blacks, Young notes. Speaking out of his extensive experiences as a veteran of the hand-to-mouth days of the civil rights movement, he pointedly recounts his recent involvement in an Atlanta bus drivers strike in which settlement was delayed. "We got on the phone," Young recalls, "and the drivers got $1.5 million in back pay and a settlement. I have never been able to make a $1 million phone call before. In certain key situations, any member of this Caucus can pick up the phone and it can mean millions of dollars for the black community."

Young's thinking extends to Sen. Edward Brooke, the only black Republican in Congress and the only congressional black not a member of the Caucus. The Massachusetts law-maker has long been accused of being insensitive to black concerns because his constituency is only 2 percent black. But Young argues that the senator has never received public recognition for an important amendment he attached to the Housing and Urban Development Act of 1969. The Brooke amendment forbids local public housing authorities from charging tenants rent exceeding 25 percent of their adjusted incomes. Thus, for example, when Mayor Algernon J. Cooper of Prichard, Ala., was elected last fall, one of his first administrative acts was to enforce the Brooke amendment. HUD will refund $47,000 in rent overpayments to 79 public housing tenants in Prichard. The Brooke amendment, of course, is enforceable not only in that town but throughout the country.

The political and economic power wielded by Sen. Brooke and the Caucus grows out of the "Black Power" thrusts of the 1960's when blacks challenged America's church-school-university-labor union-professional-political bastions of institutional racism. Bursting on the national scene in January 1969, the Caucus sought to respond collectively to distress calls from citizens who, though living hundreds of miles from their congressional districts, saw them as Congressmen-at-Large, as national caseworkers for the nation's black, poor and disadvantaged.

"When we started the Caucus," recalls Chairman Stokes, "we had no idea that it would have the kind of impact on black America that it's had. All we were trying to demonstrate was that nine blacks, given the responsibility to be in the United States Congress, could come together to try to work on behalf of black people as best we knew how."

Unsure of its mission, the Caucus now served as national spokesman for blacks, now a national clearing house for black concerns, now a data collection agency, now a commission investigating the 1971 murders of Black Panthers in Chicago, probing brutal police repression at Jackson State College and Kent State University. And all the while the Caucus was turning down urgent requests to endorse black candidates for political offices around the country. Its major political undertaking, the one that projected it into the national consciousness, came to be its momentous confrontation with President Nixon regarding his conservative stance toward blacks.

For more than a year the White House had ignored a February 1970, Caucus request for an audience, claiming at one point: "Can't fit you in our calendar. Will get back to you soon." Yet, as Congressman Clay angrily complained, during the first 90 days after the Caucus request, President Nixon had met with 11 veteran and patriotic groups, with association executives, with the head nurse of a Vietnamese children's hospital and at numerous cocktail parties and state dinners. Clay noted that Nixon had travelled more than 35,000 miles in foreign countries but had ignored the suffering and deprivation in the nation's black ghettoes.

Still, the president refused a meeting. But a Caucus announcement that it would boycott his 1971 State of the Union Message prompted Nixon to send Sen. Brooke to beg the Caucus not to embarrass the president. When the Caucus boycotted the address anyway, despite internal opposition from Nix and its first chairman, Diggs, word leaked from the White House that a meeting would indeed be arranged "after a face-saving interval of about ten weeks."

Wide World Photos

Finally on the "Calendar." After months of trying, a request by the CBC for a meeting with President Nixon was finally honored. The meeting took place in the White House Cabinet room on March 25, 1971. Clockwise from lower right are: Reps. Parren J. Mitchell, Md.; Shirley Chisholm, N.Y.; Charles C. Diggs, Jr., Mich.; Nixon; Augustus F. Hawkins, Cal.; William Clay, Mo.; Ronald V. Dellums, Cal.; Robert Finch, HUD; Sec. George Romney; Walter Fauntroy, D.C.; Ralph H. Metcalfe and George W. Collins, Ill.; Robert N. C. Nix, Pa.; Clark MacGregor; John Conyers, Mich.; Louis Stokes, O.; and Charles B. Rangel, N.Y.

Thus, 13 months after its initial overtures, the Caucus confronted President Nixon with 61 recommendations assigning high priority to economic security and development but also addressing such important social problems as unstable and inequitable welfare programs, inadequate federal assistance to state and local governments, the flagging poverty program, poor child development services, civil rights, criminal justice and the drug problem. In many instances, the Nixon response amounted to, "we're working on it," or "this is what has been done in that regard." In short, much of his response did little more than rehash the administration's record, the very record the Caucus had come to criticize.

Three months after the abortive Caucus meeting with President Nixon, actor-producer Ossie Davis warned 2,800 guests at the Caucus' Washington fund-raising dinner that the time had come for rhetoric to take a back seat. His was an oblique allusion to the 1960's when rhetorical "revolutionaries" sprang up overnight, indulging in what Professor Matthew Holden aptly calls "a politics of collective psychiatry" which bolstered black self-esteem but did little to solve other pressing black problems. So now the time had come to produce. "It's not the man," Davis intoned, "it's the plan. It's not the rap, it's the map."

To develop a plan, the Caucus, between July 1971 and September 1972, held three hearings on "racism and repression in the military," "governmental lawlessness," and "racism in the media." The Caucus also conducted seven conferences on such subjects as "national health," "black enterprise." "education," and "Africa." It had intended to crystalize black thought throughout the nation by providing a national forum to explore solutions to black problems, but the Caucus was criticized for duplicating research already completed by several civil rights and social data gathering organizations. Meanwhile, a Caucus-sponsored Washington conference of black elected officials issued a call for a National Black Political Convention to be held in Gary, Ind., prior to the 1972 Republican and Democratic conventions, with Congressman Diggs as co-convenor along with Gary, Ind., Mayor Richard Hatcher and poet–political activist Imamu Amiri Baraka. But as the March 1972 date for the Gary Convention neared, the Caucus cooled on the idea, then finally voted not to participate as a body, although Rangel, Stokes, Fauntroy, Conyers, and Dellums joined Diggs in Gary.

Not only did the Caucus officially absent itself from Gary, it refused to endorse the 55-page Black Agenda of aspirations and demands drafted by the delegates. Instead, the Caucus issued a "Black Bill of Rights," reflecting its pragmatism about the sort of legislative agenda Congress might accept. Much more than that was at stake, however. Congressman Rangel explains:

> I went to the convention and what did I see except those forces that would want me out of office, using the convention as a vehicle to get some exposure. This is good! This is healthy! This indicates that at least the guy is on the right track — to get involved politically rather than just to stand around on a step ladder saying Rangel is no good. By the same token, I could not possibly allow the convention to select him as chairman and then bind me to whatever they want to do on the local level. I was asked the specific question at our Town Hall (New York) meeting: "Will you be bound by Gary?" I said, "Let's be realistic, my man. You do what you have to do . . . I will not be bound by your thing."

Such a stance toward the Gary convention generated controversy within the Caucus, already badly split over the presidential candidacy of Shirley Chisholm. Her decision had come at a time when other Caucus members were debating various political strategies for blacks, including the possibility of a black presidential candidate other than Mrs. Chisholm. So while Dellums and Mitchell supported the intrepid Brooklyn congresswoman, the Caucus as a body refused to endorse her and Rep. Clay remarked publicly: "I don't doubt her sincerity. I doubt her sanity."

These abrasive episodes revealed that contrary to unity statements by Caucus members, devisive personality clashes were erupting from occasional spasms of skepticism, suspicion, petty rivalry and jealousy which perhaps amounted to nothing more than the pain of Caucus growth from nine to 15 members in five years. In any case, Congressman Diggs had been appointed as the Caucus' first chairman primarily because of his seniority. But some of his colleagues came to consider him too conservative and too involved in outside interests and responsibilities to devote much time to his Caucus duties. Hence, the group abolished its seniority rule and replaced Diggs with Stokes.

One of the new chairman's first acts was to appoint Dellums chairman of a subcommittee to study where the Caucus had been, its current status, and where it ought to be going. The Caucus should abandon conferences and hearings before it, like so many white experts, studied blacks to death, the subcommittee reported. Instead of trying to be all things to all people, the Caucus should focus on the legislative process, the one specific area where it possessed the greatest expertise. In short, reported the subcommittee, the Caucus should provide a black perspective for any legislation that came through the House, especially through its committees. Thus, for example, as a member of the House Banking and Currency Committee, Congressman Mitchell would calculate the implications of, say, the Economic Stabilization Act for wages, prices and bank interest rates in the black community. Congressman Stokes on the powerful Appropriations Committee would, with hawkish intensity, monitor federal allocations for black concerns. And Chisholm, Clay and Hawkins on the Education and Labor Committee would provide a black input for its pending legislation.

Consistent with its legislative focus, the Caucus recently assembled more than 50 members of the House and Senate and representatives of more than 200 politically diverse groups from across the nation to develop a counter-strategy to President Nixon's $11 billion in budget cuts and impoundments allegedly designed to curb inflation by reducing or ending 115 "Great Society" programs. Established for the nation's 25 million poor (including one-third of black families), these programs have been branded by administration spokesmen as inefficient. Yet the massive inefficiency of, say, the Pentagon has not inspired plans for its dismantling.

Nixon's "New Federalism" shifts power from the federal government to the states and localities through a $6.1 billion general revenue sharing plan and $6.9 billion worth of special revenue sharing plans for education, manpower training, urban development and law enforcement. But Caucus members and many other blacks doubt that local and state officials can be trusted to distribute special revenue funds equitably. They see black problems as national in scope and therefore meriting national programs.

The most conspicuous of those programs slated to end this summer is the so-called "War on Poverty" administered by the Office of Economic Opportunity. While OEO is to be pieced out among a number of other federal agencies, its biggest piece — the 977 agencies of the Community Action Program — will be missing unless local and state governments elect to pay for them. Thus will the most effective representation for the affairs of the poor be eliminated. A House subcommittee headed by Congressman Hawkins has heard testimony suggesting that the junking of OEO may have a worse impact on the nation's poor than President Nixon apparently anticipates. And some witnesses have even predicted street riots for this summer.

That possibility has not stayed the president's hand, however. He has slapped an 18-month freeze on low-income housing and seven other programs in the Department of Housing and Urban Development, programs particularly beneficial to blacks. The biggest of the seven is the 24-year-old Urban Renewal Program, operating at just under $1 billion a year and Model Cities, a $600 million-a-year program for revitalizing decaying urban areas.

Nixon's $258 billion budget would replace 33 separate educational programs — many designed for the poor — with a $2.8 billion special revenue sharing plan allowing the states more voice in determining how the money should be spent. Once it becomes law, it may end once and for all any federal pretense at integrating the nation's schools.

Medicare, the federally financed health care program for the elderly, is another area in which President Nixon expects to make significant savings in the federal budget. He would charge patients 10 percent of the costs of their hospital stay starting on the second day. Under current law, patients pay $72 for the first day, nothing up to the 60th day and 25 percent of the costs afterwards. Since the average medicare patient is hospitalized for 13 days, the proposed budget would increase his costs to an estimated $200. And so, Congressman Conyers laments:

> We're really talking about life and death. People are going to die, because in Harlem they're cutting down the hypertension unit in the Harlem

Hospital. The unit is federally funded. That means that some old black folks are going to die. That's all. In other places it's not quite as dramatic as that, but it really relates to how long you're going to live if you're not eating regularly, if you're not working regularly. You're going to get caught up in the drug scene or try to do something illegal and you're going to get yourself sent to jail. Then you're going to WISH you were dead. . . .

Conyers and his Caucus colleagues believe Nixon's budget cuts may have awakened a host of sleeping Americans other than blacks. Congressman Young suggests that blacks suffer many of this society's problems first, because they are the furthest out on the fringes of this society. But the things that blacks suffer today, lower class whites will suffer tomorrow and middle class whites will suffer the day after tomorrow. Thus, as Young points out, when blacks first started complaining about the inferior quality of inner city schools, whites would not listen. But today everyone is aware that big city schools are bad — not just for blacks, but for whites as well. If whites had listened to black complaints about the dope addiction problem 25 years ago, by now the nation might have an effective solution. Only recentiy have whites become alarmed at dope addiction because of its rise in the suburbs and in the armed forces. For years blacks complained about discriminatory voter registration procedures. Now, finally, some whites are trying to reform voter registration laws.

Most Caucus members hope enough white farmers, bankers, real estate brokers, educators, suburbanites, etc. are being affected by Nixon's cutbacks to be moved to some sort of effective counteraction. For the cutback on housing will eliminate at least as many new middle income as low income housing. The freezing of funds for HUD water and sewer projects will most acutely affect suburban communities, particularly in new developments. Nixon's cutbacks will also grossly affect college students, university programs and hospital construction.

Congress, meanwhile, is considering bills by Senator Sam Ervin (D., N.C.), and Rep. George Mahon (D., Tex.) that would require the president to report to Congress if he impounds all or part of an appropriation. Whether these bills pass or not, most Caucus members believe Nixon's proposed budget is likely to undergo significant change in a Congress already alarmed by what it regards as the continued erosion of its power.

In his ineptness, in his insensitivity, in his desire to please the powers that be, Nixon may have, in his own uncanny way, unified the struggle for humaneness in this nation, suggests Congressman Dellums. He believes the president is moving against what Dellums calls America's "niggers." Since blacks are the oldest niggers in America, since they are at the very cutting edge of change, he believes they are peculiarly equipped to lead all the other new niggers who only recently have been discovering the niggerizing process. Thus is the Black Caucus a prophetic role in Congress, functioning as the spiritual, political and moral leader of America's niggers. Under Caucus leadership, perhaps all the niggers — the black ones, the brown ones, the yellow ones, the red ones, the white ones — may yet force this nation to fulfill its promise.

THE CBC: A FOLLOW-UP VIEW

The Poinsett article indicates that the CBC had decided to focus on legislation. This was indeed the direction of the Caucus, as is shown in workshops, speeches, and other activity in connection with its 1973 third annual fund-raising dinner. As Caucus Chairman Stokes put it, the primary purpose of the CBC is to "utilize the legislative process to help bring about full equality of opportunity in American society." The CBC, continued Stokes, is now at the point where it hopes to put "the black perspective into [all] legislation."

The 1973 dinner reflected additional evidence of this new legislative strategy.[14] Senator Edward Brooke, for example, made his first public display of unity with the CBC by attending and speaking at the dinner. And in his speech Brooke told the gathering that blacks must enter into broader coalitions and focus on economic rather than only racial issues. This "coalition" flavor was also symbolized by those who sat on the podium. Brooke was joined at the dinner by the new mayor of Los Angeles, Tom Bradley, who was guest of honor. In addition, several whites were also seated on the stage along with the widows of several well-known civil rights leaders: Martin Luther King, Jr., Whitney Young, Jr., Malcolm X, and Jackie Robinson. In short, seemingly everything about the dinner reflected the need for broader coalitions that would facilitate unity among blacks as well as promote cooperation with white allies.

In February 1974 Representative Charles Rangel (D., N.Y.) became the new chairman of CBC, replacing Stokes. Rangel cited the successful passage of "home rule" for the District of Columbia as evidence of the Caucus acting with a new "sophistication." He reemphasized that the CBC must limit itself to legislative concerns. Said Rangel:

I plan to present to the Caucus a legislative agenda that we can work on that will get us more realistic support rather than the spiritual support we have already.

We have no permanent friends, no permanent enemies; just permanent interests of black and minority constituents.[15]

---

[14] See *New York Times,* September 27, 1973, p. 13; September 30, 1973, p. 28; and October 1, 1973, pp. 1, 23.

[15] *New York Times,* March 18, 1974, p. 22.

In looking to the future Rangel indicated his intention to strengthen the CBC staff and to stimulate more participation from black elected officials in the national black convention movement. [16]

But perhaps the biggest challenge and opportunity facing the Caucus involves its relations and access to the new president, Gerald Ford. As a congressman from middle America (Grand Rapids, Michigan), Ford's record was far from sympathetic to the needs and goals of blacks. But, as president, Gerald Ford made the first move. [17] Within three days after assuming the presidency, Ford called Congressman Rangel directly indicating his desire to meet with the CBC. Rangel admitted that different interpretations had and would be made of the president's initiative in calling the meeting. But, said Rangel,

> Whatever interpretation you choose, both sides undeniably reaped benefits. Clearly, the President's initiation of the meeting just three days after taking office means he saw it in his own self-interest. Our quick acceptance reflected the majority view that we could only gain by making this effort at establishing communication with the new national administration.

The meeting between the president and the CBC took place on August 21. Although disappointed that the president's very first speech to the Congress indicated little if any sympathy for black concerns, the Caucus nevertheless decided "to give him the benefit of the doubt and approach the meeting in good faith as an effort to communicate." Accordingly, the CBC agreed "to meet the president halfway" and to structure its presentation for the meeting around "double digit inflation," the "domestic enemy number one" that the president had identified in his speech to Congress. Such emphasis, said Rangel, "did no violence to our own priorities, for it is the poor and minority communities that have suffered most because of runaway inflation." In keeping with the inflation theme, the CBC "warned" the president that budget cuts in such areas as housing, health, and education will be counterproductive, saying that "those who can least afford to lose federal aid will be hurt the most."

The Caucus also asked the president to appoint blacks and other minorities who would be "sensitive" to the needs of poor and minority communities "at every level of his administration." As to this request, the president responded that he "fully intended" to make such appointments. Rangel called this the "most important commitment" to come out of the meeting. Indeed, said the congressman, "the best and

---

[16] Ibid.

[17] The discussion is based on Representative Rangel's account of the meeting in "The President and The Black Caucus," *Focus* (September, 1974), Vol. 2, #11, pp. 4–5.

most lasting way to achieve [institutionalization of communication be-tween the executive branch and the CBC] is to have the type of executive agency appointees in this administration who will be sympathetic to the needs of the poor and minorities because of their ideological and philosophical commitment and, equally important, because of who they are." Overall, there appeared to be some optimism that the meeting would lead to improved relations between the CBC and "The Man" in the White House. But, as Rangel put it, that "optimism cannot be sustained unless it is fed by concrete accomplishment, and although we stand ready to work with the president if he proves his good will, we stand equally ready to oppose him if he does not."

Since the August 21 meeting the president has taken some actions that have undoubtedly caused the Caucus to be "less optimistic" about future relations with the president. For one thing, his "full and uncondi-tional" pardon of former President Nixon did nothing to convince blacks and other minorities that *all* men are *equal* under the law. Moreover, in an October 1974 news conference, the president served to provoke rather than quiet racial friction when he indicated sharp disagreement with "forced busing" (and a federal court order) at the very time that the Boston school situation was erupting in violence over the issue.[18] Con-sequently, given the situation, this attitude of the president toward "forced busing" greatly overshadowed his announced intention to en-force the law (the federal court decision). In any event, actions such as these are definitely not calculated to improve relations between the president and the CBC.

THE CBC IN PERSPECTIVE

In many ways the Congressional Black Caucus operates as an interest group. (See Chapter 7.) It certainly exhibits social solidarity — the need for people holding similar views "to enjoy the support, fellowship and solidarity of one another." The CBC also resembles the *expressive* interest groups, where people join to symbolize and express more effectively their values and opinions with respect to certain causes. It provides an excellent forum for the expression of opinion. In addition, the Caucus as interest group acts in a sense as a "Washington Lobby" for blacks and the poor, and has staff and funds to support these ends.

And just as with other groups, there are factors that affect the cohe-sion of the CBC. Consider, for example, those factors that tend to plague group unity. For one thing, each member operates from an independent power base (his or her district) and has an independent staff; this

---

[18] For an account of the Ford statement on the Boston situation and "forced busing" see, The *New York Times*, October 13, 1974, IV, p. 2, col. 1.

promotes independence from the Caucus as a group. In such a situation, for example, the CBC staff becomes of less importance to individual Caucus members who have their own staffs. As a consequence, these independent sources of strength, which accrue from the nature of the office itself, can and do lead to independence in action that could impair group unity.

On the other hand, however, there are strong factors that tend to promote group cohesion. Indeed, whether through a formal organization such as the CBC or not, the basic unity and cohesion of black members of Congress in legislative matters would seem to persist for some time. In this sense, the move of the CBC to concentrate (and restrict) its attention on legislative matters appears to be good strategy. To be sure, there is one overriding factor that promotes unity among black legislators: the similarities in the needs of their constituents invariably leads to similarities in policy positions. This is reflected well in the socioeconomic characteristics of the congressional districts from which Caucus members come.[19] For example, blacks constitute about 59 percent of the population in these districts. Median income for black Caucus districts is $7,666. However, somewhat more than 12 percent of the families in these districts live on incomes less than $3,000, well below the poverty line. Generally then, Caucus members represent the ghettos of the country. Almost all the districts include the "central city" areas with only a few having substantial surburban constituencies. Moreover, by and large, in the 1972 elections members from these districts won easily averaging somewhat over 78 percent of the vote. Undoubtedly, these common characteristics will serve to promote unity among black congressional members.

In addition, we suggest that the *force of blackness* in itself stimulates cohesion and identification among blacks in Congress. It remains as true today as it ever was that as long as blacks are disadvantaged as a group they must work as a group to remove those disadvantages. This might help to explain why the Congressional Black Caucus refused in 1975 to approve the application of a white member of Congress (Rep. Fortney H. Stark, Jr., D., Cal.) for membership in the Caucus. Indeed, in rejecting Stark's application, Caucus chairman Charles Rangel (D., N.Y.) stated that "the Caucus symbolizes black political development in this country. We feel that maintaining this symbolism," continued Rangel, " is critical at this juncture in our development."[20] Rangel and the CBC reasoned

---

[19] For a systematic and easily accessible profile on congressional districts see Barone et al., *The Almanac of American Politics* (Boston: Gambit, 1973). This volume also includes similar data on U.S. Senators.

[20] Quotes on the refusal of the Caucus to admit Rep. Stark are taken from Congressional Black Caucus *Press Release* dated June 19, 1975. Also see story, "Congress' Black Caucus Rejects White as Member," *The Washington Star*, June 19, 1975, p. A-13.

that just as the separate caucuses of Democrats and Republicans "have unique interests to protect and project and would not include non-party members in their respective groups, we too, have the same needs and concerns." Rangel then drove the point home. "The Black Caucus," he said, "is composed of seventeen House Members who share the common social, cultural and political experience of being black in America."[21] This latter point, it seems to us, vividly illuminates that the *force of blackness* remains a powerful (though not always articulated) influence enhancing black unity.

We may view the Congressional Black Caucus from yet another perspective. The change from "protests to politics" reflects a concern to increase black influence (power) in political institutions such as the Congress. The formation and continuing activities of the CBC symbolize this concern. A more tangible measure of increasing black political influence, however, relates to the number of blacks gaining seats in the Congress. In part, such an increase will depend upon whether those congressional districts that have significant black populations[22] can stimulate and put forth strong candidates and strong campaigns. The 1970 census shows there are 59 congressional districts that have 30 percent or more black populations. But as of 1974, only 16 of these 59 districts had black representatives.

But black influence in Congress depends on more than how many blacks happen to be members at any given time. As the dynamics of power in Congress now operates, it is not enough to gain membership in that body; one must be able to remain there for a long time. One needs to gain seniority. By doing so, one can normally become a committee chairman, and such positions give one crucial influence in the congressional power system. Obviously, however, one wishes to gain seniority (and eventually the chairmanship) on the right committee — that is, a committee that is important to the interests of the member's constituents. Of course, if one does not gain such an assignment initially, there is always the possibility of getting a preferable assignment later. But, as we have also seen, in changing from one committee to another, the member loses whatever seniority he had accumulated on the first committee.

The important question that arises here is how one gets the right committee assignment in the first place, or how one is able to gain such an assignment later. To a great extent, this depends upon the standing of the particular legislator with congressional leaders and with his colleagues. Moreover, such standing enhances or retards one's ability to build coalitions, and to gain sufficient support to enact legislation that is

---

[21] Ibid.

[22] For a detailed look at these districts — those having 30 percent or more black population — see Joint Center for Political Studies, *Guide to Black Politics '72* (Part II, the Republican National Convention, Washington, D.C., August 1, 1972), pp. 48-53.

important to him and to his constituents. To achieve standing, however, one has to conform to congressional norms. In general, this means giving proper deference to established procedures and rules, and recognizing the importance of bargaining, accommodation and compromise in the conduct of business. All this, of course, helps one to maintain good personal relations with colleagues and vice versa. In short, "don't push too far too fast," and above all "don't buck congressional leaders." The leaders, after all, achieved and maintain such positions because they followed the norms. And there are strong built-in temptations and pressures for others to do likewise.

Let us attempt to view this discussion of seniority and standing in terms of black influence in Congress and black politics generally. Consider the situation of black members of Congress. For the most part, these representatives come from **"safe" districts** — "safe" insofar as that a black will more likely than not be elected to represent the district. As the district becomes more "safe" in this sense, however, we might find an increasing competition between blacks as to what black can best represent the district. But, so far at least, black incumbents seem to follow the general incumbency pattern of being highly successful in reelection bids. This continued electoral success, however, could run into trouble. For example, while black representatives may be attempting to meet the needs of their constituents and may indeed have introduced measures and taken other actions toward this end, the fact is that these needs more often than not have not been met and are not being met. Thus the problems of the district remain. And the incumbent faces the not uncommon campaign charge of having done nothing about the situation. An important difference, of course, is that problems in heavily populated black districts, such as unemployment and poor housing, are highly visible and affect the everyday life of constituents. Under such circumstances, the black incumbent becomes increasingly susceptible to strong campaign challenges. This could pose a serious problem for black incumbents. As one of a few blacks in a collegial institution (House of Representatives) whose majority may not be especially sympathetic to his goals, it will be the rare occasion when a black incumbent can show a record of tangible accomplishments relative to meeting the problems of his district.

To appreciate the context in which black officials operate in a collegial institution requires a measure of sophistication (and a prolonged acceptance of the status quo) on the part of black voters which is perhaps unparalleled in American political history. No other group in America has been required to hold to such understanding and with such patient endurance for such a long period of time! Indeed, the problems that blacks face are by definition "controversial" in the context of American politics. Nonetheless, these problems are perceived by many blacks in terms of "non-negotiable demands" that must be met now, not later. But the bargaining, accommodation, and compromise needed to gain widespread support might lead the black congressman to temper these demands to get some type of legislation and to show some record of accomplishment. But in doing so the black legislator will more likely than not have to temper the rhetoric of his arguments that could provoke friction between him and his white colleagues. This could place severe strains on a black legislator. While perhaps understanding the necessity of compromise on substantive matters in terms of legislative strategy, he takes certain risks in compromising the rhetoric of his argument. Indeed such rhetoric might prove necessary to satisfy the long-term demands and desires of his constituents while simultaneously making present-day substantive compromises more palatable to them. And more important, it might be necessary for his political survival — that is, reelection, the one indispensable criterion for gaining influence in Congress. In any event, seniority and standing as matters now stand pose serious and persistent problems not only for black congressmen but for black politics generally. Of course it is true, as we discussed earlier in this chapter, that seniority can work to the advantage of blacks and civil rights interests. But as we have also seen, it is possible that in the future seniority may not be an automatic guarantee to a chairmanship. Under such circumstances standing and good personal relations with one's colleagues will undoubtedly take on added significance. It remains to be seen what the actual costs and benefits of such relations might be to the future of black politicians and black politics generally.

Topics for Discussion

1. The text states that "given the structure of presidential election politics, it would be most difficult for a black person to garner the necessary resources and overcome the other informal requirements to mount a viable presidential race." Do you agree with this assessment? Justify your position.

2. Before Watergate the trend was for liberals to support a strong presidency, while since Watergate there has been an attempt by liberals and conservatives alike to limit the powers of the president. Should presidential power be reduced? In what specific ways? Might this reduction threaten the separation of powers doctrine of the Constitution? If so, with what possible consequences? Is a strong Congress a realistic alternative to a strong president? Are there other alternatives? Discuss.

3. If a white person in Congress applies for membership in the Congressional Black Caucus (as has happened), should that person be admitted? Why or why not?

4. What are the advantages and disadvantages of the seniority rule for blacks and for the legislative process in general? Is the seniority system defensible and what alternatives are there to it? Discuss.

Suggested Readings

Berger, Raoul. *Impeachment: The Constitutional Problems.* Cambridge: Harvard University Press, 1973.

An historical and legal analysis of the constitutional provision relating to impeachment.

Berman, Daniel M. *A Bill Becomes a Law: Congress Enacts Civil Rights Legislation.* 2nd ed. New York: Macmillan Company, 1966.

Discusses the role and impact of congressional procedures that led to the passage of the Civil Rights Acts of 1960 and 1964.

Crouse, Timothy. *The Boys on the Bus.* New York: Random House, 1973.

A description of the 1972 presidential campaign and election.

Dymally, Mervyn, ed. *The Black Politician: His Struggle for Power.* Belmont, Calif.; North Scituate, Mass.: Duxbury Press, 1971.

Readings on black politics and political and legislative strategies.

Fenno, Richard. *The Power of the Purse.* Boston: Little, Brown, 1966.

A detailed analysis of the operation of the House Appropriations Committee.

Hargrove, Erwin C. *The Power of the Modern Presidency.* New York: Alfred A. Knopf, 1974.

A succinct discussion of the nature and powers of the presidential office.

Hinckley, Barbara. *The Seniority System in Congress.* Bloomington: Indiana University Press, 1971.

A study of the operation of congressional committees and the impact of the seniority rule.

Manley, John F. *The Politics of Finance.* Boston: Little, Brown, 1970.
A study of the House Committee on Ways and Means.

Moe, Ronald C., ed. *Congress and the President.* Pacific Palisades, Calif.: Goodyear Publishing Company, 1971.
A collection of readings that focus on various aspects of presidential–congressional relations.

Neustadt, Richard. *Presidential Power.* New York: John Wiley & Sons, 1960.
An examination of the sources and limitations of the political power of the president.

Orfield, Gary. *Congressional Power: Congress and Social Change.* New York: Harcourt Brace Jovanovich, 1975.
A study of the changing role of Congress in the development of public policy and social change.

Polsby, Nelson. *Congress and the Presidency.* 2nd ed. Englewood Cliffs, N.J.: Prentice-Hall, 1971.
An examination of the interaction between these two governmental branches.

Polsby, Nelson and Aaron Wildavsky. *Presidential Elections.* 3rd ed. New York: Charles Scribner's Sons, 1971.
A study of the strategies involved in presidential elections with an evaluation of possible reforms.

Thomas, Norman C., ed. *The Presidency in Contemporary Context.* New York: Dodd, Mead and Co., 1975.
A collection of readings that view the presidency in various contexts.

9

POLICY-MAKING AND THE NEED FOR POLITICAL RESOURCES

In the orderly process of government, success of an issue often depends on the skill of its advocates in understanding who holds the key to power on that issue, and how to approach that person in a friendly or persuasive manner. . . .

. . . Congress evidently gave little thought to the fact that if the poor people had the means to do things the right way — to hire a full-time lobbyist to touch the vital pressure points, to provide position papers, inserts for the Congressional Record, steaks and wine for the congressmen — they wouldn't be poor.

Nick Kotz, *Let Them Eat Promises: The Politics of Hunger in America**

The weakness of existing civil rights groups . . . was that they came to Washington once a year and talked to the Secretary of Labor or of HEW; the groups pushed for a big law once every three or four years, and forgot about the legislation once it was passed. No one remained to watch when agencies formulated guidelines or were slow to enforce the laws. Someone was needed in Washington "to run a monitoring operation at the federal level." . . .

From "The New Public Interest Lawyers"**

* © 1969 by Nick Kotz. Published by Prentice-Hall, Inc.
** Reprinted by permission of The Yale Law Journal Company and Fred B. Rothman & Company from *The Yale Law Journal*, Vol. 79, pp. 1081.

Introduction

The development of national policy is frequently complicated in appearance. The number of formal and informal actors is large.
Their various roles and interactions contribute to the complexity of the
process. In the preceding chapters we have discussed, in general terms,
both the formal and informal actors in the policy process. We have
reviewed, for example, the role of interest groups and the resources they
need and use to achieve their objectives in the political process. And we
have seen that black interest groups for the most part do not possess
many of these resources. Similarly, we have looked at the nature,
operation, and organization of political parties. Specific attention was
given to how political parties affect and are affected by attempts of
blacks to achieve their objectives.

We have also sketched, again in broad outline, the nature and importance of the president in the governmental process: his powers, roles,
influence, and in general the organization of the presidential office and
the administration. Similar broad sketches were made of Congress: its
organization and structure, its composition, and its legislative role. And
as with interest groups and parties, we gave special consideration to the
relation of the president and Congress to black hopes and black politics
generally. Overall then, these earlier chapters described generally the
various institutions and actors and their roles in the political system.

Our central purpose in this chapter is to view the interaction and
merging of these institutions and actors within the specific context of
national policy-making. We will look at the relative role and influence in
the policy process of such key actors as interest groups leaders and party
officials, the president and his chief advisers, members of Congress and
committee chairmen, and administrators and bureaucrats.

The Policy Process—An Overview

For our purposes here, the policy-making process is divided into four different phases:[1]
1. **Agenda**-Setting and Initiation
2. Initial Outcome: The Legislative Product
3. Secondary Outcome: Administration and Impact
4. Response, **Feedback,** and Future Prospects

---

[1] These phases represent a combination of ten functional activities of policy-making
presented in Charles O. Jones, *An Introduction to the Study of Public Policy* (Belmont, Cal.:
Duxbury Press, 1970).

Within this framework one finds an interconnected series of actions and interactions involving private and public, individuals, groups and institutions. Also included are the president and his apparatus comprising the institutionalized presidency, congressmen, the agencies and bureaus and the political parties, as well as the national news media.

We should emphasize that the process under discussion is not limited to a short period of time, say a single congressional term. It can take (and it has) a decade or more before an issue becomes a realistic part of the policy agenda. Sometimes it is even longer before specific policy results. Initiatives may fail but not be forgotten. Such was the case, for example, with the lengthy struggle for black civil and political equality. This example, and there are others that stimulated less public concern, illustrate one of the most criticized features of the policy process: it is slow to respond to demands. Neither the strong feelings surrounding a group's claims nor their presumed justice weigh quite so heavily in political decision-making as one might think. Despite the moral phrasing of the Constitution and the Bill of Rights, appeals to such ideas are of limited use in the political arena if the history of the civil rights struggle is any indication. Minority demands, such as those made by black Americans, mean a sharp break with practices which have matured during the course of American history. Adopting new programs or initiating new ways of dealing with continual problems may pose serious threats to existing social and political arrangements. Thus, policy-making can, especially when dealing with questions that affect the scope of political influence, engender dramatic confrontations within and outside government.

Another reason why some things don't get done, or are sometimes done very slowly, stems from congressional "sampling."[2] Since members of Congress cannot attend to every demand made of them, they pick and choose among the issues brought to them for action and decision. Sampling, however, implies the existence of bias; by definition some things are ignored. Constitutionally, both Congress and the president are required to do certain things at fixed times. Congress convenes on a firm date every year (January 3) unless changed by law. And because some legislation expires after a set time, the legislature must act promptly if those laws are to be continued in force. An example of this is the use of the "continuing resolution." This device has financial importance for government agencies whose fiscal year begins on July 1. If Congress has not completed its work on an appropriations bill, the continuing resolution "allows agencies to spend at the rate set for that agency in the previous year. . . . [O]r if only the House has passed the

---

    [2] Nelson W. Polsby, *Congress and the Presidency*, 2nd ed. (Englewood Cliffs, N.J.: Prentice-Hall, 1971), pp. 4–6.

appropriations bill, at whichever rate is lower, or, if both Senate and House have passed the bill, at whichever of those two rates is lower."[3]

To be sure, Congress can move with more than "deliberate speed" when the circumstances demand swift action. An acute, or crisis, situation presents a must-act condition; other business has to be postponed while elected officials deal with the crisis. A chronic problem of the body politic — for example, structural unemployment for some of the labor force — can be put aside.

We should add that while the president and the "institutionalized presidency," that is, the White House and Executive Office staffs, have a preeminent role in policy-making, members of Congress also may and do initiate legislation. Thus, the technique of sampling described above must also allow time for the many bills sponsored by the congressional membership. In addition, even though it is not explicitly included under sampling, the particular **ideology** (that is, the beliefs of committee chairmen in a policy area) will also influence what and how proposals are considered. This means that a president will try to avoid giving his policy proposals to a committee chairman who is known to be hostile to his intent. However, this searching for a receptive committee chairman may affect the content of the proposed legislation because the congressional policy system tends to be functionally specific in its organization.

Let us now examine the four policy phases. Although we believe these elements of the policy process are so closely connected that they can be combined, we see a number of patterned relationships.

Agenda Setting and Initation

National policy initiation has increasingly become the province of the presidency. Most modern presidents can reasonably expect to serve two terms (eight years) once elected to office.[4] However, they know that getting their programs through Congress takes time. A president's first term can be viewed then as a time to build a record on which to run for his second four years in office. Therefore, the first four years tend to be oriented toward accomplishing those things which can be done quickly. However, "quickly" is a relative term in the relations between president and Congress. The relationship between initiation and agenda-setting focuses upon the expanded role of the executive

---

[3] Richard F. Fenno, *The Power of the Purse: Appropriations Politics in Congress* (Boston: Little, Brown, 1966), p. 421.

[4] The eight year expectation does not apply to a successor president who, for whatever reason, completes an unexpired portion of the tenure of his predecessor in office.

branch as the initiator of legislation. Through communications such as State of the Union messages, budget messages, and specific program proposals, the president not only initiates policy but also makes an agenda for congressional consideration, debate and action. What the president wants is made clear, not left to the congressional imagination.

Since the administration of Franklin D. Roosevelt, presidents have also had another means of getting their message to the legislative branch. They have increasingly used the media, especially when there is a potentially strong opposition in Congress. In part, this is an educational technique to inform the public of proposed government actions. But it is also a device to create public support for the president's programs. For example, when former President Nixon wanted to halt court-ordered busing as a means to achieve school integration he went to the public via television. He told the listening public that lower federal courts:

> have gone too far; in some cases, beyond the requirements laid down by the Supreme Court in ordering massive busing to achieve racial balance. . . . There are many who believe that a constitutional amendment is the only way to deal with this problem. . . . But as an answer to the immediate problem . . . of stopping more busing now, the constitutional amendment approach has a fatal flaw — it takes too long. . . . And there's only one effective way to deal with the problem now. That is for Congress to act. That is why I am sending a special message to the Congress tomorrow urging immediate consideration and action. . . . [5]

It is, however, realistic to ask where the president's program originates. Certainly technical details are fleshed out by topical experts, both appointive and career officials. But the ideas for presidential programs may also originate in less formalized ways.

AGENDA SETTING AND ELECTORAL POLITICS

While somewhat vague and symbolic, campaign promises of a presidential candidate and united parties in mid-term elections may suggest potential agenda items for future legislative and executive attention. Electoral campaigns may show what the candidate(s) think about different issues.

Part of the explanation for the absence of clear policy and issue discussion during the campaigns is that getting elected is different from actually doing the job. And, quite naturally, a prospective president

---

[5] Quoted in Davis & Donaldson, *Blacks in the United States: A Geographic Perspective*, pp. 157–158.

doesn't want to commit himself too strongly before he takes office. In addition, if a candidate did take a firm position on a particular question, as Senator George McGovern did on the welfare issue against former President Nixon in 1972, he may find himself giving the opposition an exploitable issue to use against him.

Perhaps of greater importance, however, is that the campaigns are not designed for a discussion of the issues. Rather, they serve to attract, and make the candidate attractive to, the great middle of American politics. If the presidential hopeful gets too specific he is likely to alienate the middle ground. This is the condition which McGovern unwittingly created with his poorly thought out proposal to pay $1,000 to welfare recipients. On issues like welfare which have a high degree of ideological content, being specific entails risk. To the extent that a campaign tells us anything at all about the kinds of policies we might expect from a candidate if he is successful, it is by way of inference.

That is, assuming that the candidate is not a total unknown, his past political activity should give some evidence of what he will be like as president. Positions which he has previously taken on public issues can, if carefully studied, be reasonable indicators of future stances on similar or related issues.* This kind of presidential watching, however, requires an investment of time and energy which the general public does not make.

AGENDA SETTING AND INTEREST GROUPS

Certainly organized interest groups are involved in agenda setting through support of candidates likely to include their needs and wishes on an agenda for action. In American politics it is assumed that patience will at some future time be rewarded by positive government action in desired policy areas. While the denied group waits for these outcomes, it must also attempt to form **coalitions** with others. Such coalitions may require modification or even subordination of one group's goals in exchange for wider support. Sometimes the goals of the petitioning group can become the umbrella for the larger group. In either case, a broad base of support is often a necessary first step in getting the government to respond favorably to public demands.

Group formation and coalition building has been treated by many scholars as an important means by which the interests of *politically active*

---

* See, for example, James David Barber, *The Presidential Character: Predicting Performance in the White House* (Englewood Cliffs, N.J.: Prentice-Hall, 1972). A somewhat more accessible discussion of some of the points made here is contained in Nelson Polsby's "Our Quadrennial Drama," in his work *Political Promises: Essays and Commentary on American Politics* (New York: Oxford University Press, 1974), pp. 165–171.

publics are placed in the political marketplace.[6] More recently, there have been examples of small-sized interest groups placing their concerns on policy agendas without developing active wide-scale support. Small and less highly structured groups have been able to use the mass media to bring certain situations and viewpoints to public attention. Through use of the media such groups have activated third-party interests which may be "inconvenienced" by the publicity surrounding the issues in question. These third parties, then, may become concerned enough for their own self-interests to become active in seeking a political solution. The implication is clear that this tactic is more likely to be used by a relatively weak group. Third parties' resources are brought to bear on the agenda-setting process on behalf of a weak organization. Such political action tends to be issue-specific rather than broad and general. Moreover, its use seems to be limited so far to urban political systems rather than national. The restriction appears to result from the ad hoc character of these groups' formation. They are unable to sustain an active membership and effective leadership over time once the original demands are met.[7]

AGENDA SETTING AND DOMESTIC CRISES

Events such as war and energy shortage can bring issues rather quickly to the policy agenda. But the natural processes of American policy-making, especially on domestic concerns, tend to be characterized by slowness. This was noted by President Nixon in his speech on busing. This **incrementalism**, as it is frequently called, is closely related to the problem of providing funds for government activities.[8] In addition, we should keep in mind that the two-party system seldom reflects sharp differences on matters of public policy. The basic agreement on political values between Democrats and Republicans reinforces the incremental character of policy-making.

When a crisis situation develops it is difficult for the legislative and executive branches to respond. This is partly because their habitual patterns of response are oriented to regularities or the chronic problems

---

[6] See for example, David B. Truman, *The Governmental Process* (New York: Alfred A. Knopf, 1951); Robert H. Salisbury, *Interest Group Politics in America* (New York: Harper & Row, 1970); Earl B. Latham, *The Group Basis of Politics* (Ithaca, N.Y.: Cornell University Press, 1952); and Robert A. Dahl, *Preface to a Theory of Democracy* (Chicago: University of Chicago Press, 1956).

[7] Cf. Michael Lipsky, "Protest as a Political Resource," *APSR* 62:4 (December 1968), 1144-1158.

[8] Charles E. Lindblom discusses this feature of policy-making in his essay, "The Science of Muddling Through," *Public Administration Review*, 19 (Spring 1959), 79-88. Additional details on incrementalism can be found in Aaron B. Wildavsky, *The Politics of the Budgetary Process*, 2nd ed. (Boston: Little, Brown, 1974).

of the political system. The solution to critical problems will generally require an abrupt change in the way the public's business is handled by its officials. However, the nature of that change depends upon political choices made among competing definitions of the problem(s) to be addressed by government action. The timing of crises also contributes to the ways in which they are handled. Most situations defined as crises in political terms are in fact not wholly novel phenomena. That is, one can usually find its antecedents in some one or another chronic problem that has gone unattended. A chronic problem becomes a crisis, in this view, when some part of the public is concerned enough about it to want to act. Moreover, those most directly concerned must also be able to get others to share their concern. The issue, in other words, must have a "ripple effect" among the public.

Naturally, the media have an important part to play in the evolution of a crisis for they can enhance the "ripple effect." Direct political activity by individuals and groups in bringing the issues to the attention of legislators adds to the role of the media. Nontraditional forms of political behavior — for example, violence or mass protest demonstrations — help to foster a sense of crisis, especially if the issue is relatively specific. This specificity implies that possible solutions will be narrow in scope and impact. The tendency then is to define a crisis situation in its narrowest terms consistent with the key issue(s) of the crisis. If this is not possible, the attempt is to find a solution that is politically feasible and satisfactory to the petitioning group but that is, at the same time, not so broad that its scope and impact are likely to have effects within other policy arenas.

AGENDA SETTING AND THE IDEA WHOSE TIME HAS COME

Specific policy proposals may receive little support or interest when first introduced. With the sponsorship of skillful political actors in the legislative and/or executive branch such proposals gradually gain supporters. Many bills introduced by potential presidential candidates fit into this category; although such proposals may have little chance of current passage, they can help "build a record," induce interest group support, and perhaps garner media attention. There is a strong relationship between this "idea whose time has come" and the process described in the previous section. For example, the stage for the Model Cities program was created by several articles that appeared in national magazines. These articles emphasized the terrible conditions of the urban poor in the central city. There were pictures of the Watts riots in Los Angeles and other disturbances that occurred in the nation's cities. Consequently, in 1965, a letter and later a conversation between

Walter Reuther, president of the United Auto Workers, and President Johnson provided the catalyst to action. They proposed to concentrate federal programs in the center city and give the cities enough money to begin urban renewal programs. Jerome Cavanaugh, as Mayor of Detroit, in several conversations with Reuther had emphasized the need for a massive renewal program based on the existing Model Neighborhood in Detroit. President Johnson found the proposal to his liking. Consequently, the President formed a Task Force headed by then Professor Robert G. Wood of the Massachusetts Institute of Technology, later under-secretary of the Department of Housing and Urban Development.[9]

The Task Force was composed of academicians and federal officials who were unfamiliar with the problems confronting urban areas. Wood did possess some expertise in the field of urban renewal. Whether he understood the complicated "human" problems of the urban poor sufficiently to design an adequate program is another question. The Task Force included only one individual who could really represent the interest of the urban poor, of whom the majority were black. This was Whitney Young, president of the Urban League, an organization not known for aggressively championing black interests. To some extent, it may be argued that these interests were generally represented by the U.S. Conference of Mayors whose constituencies were increasingly made up of these groups. But, the president and Dr. Wood deliberately selected persons who had not been too strongly committed to or identified with any existing program such as those of OEO.

What did the Task Force propose? Why? The Task Force was strongly encouraged to develop new and innovative programs. In fact, Dr. Wood was given great latitude in terms of the type of proposals that could be submitted. But President Johnson also had some preferences. He instructed Dr. Wood and the Task Force to construct programs with the following characteristics: (1) that mayors and city councils were to have a principal role; (2) that social and physical planning should be coordinated; and (3) that racial integration and citizen participation were "desirable goals but would have to be played down in order to facilitate congressional passage."[10]

Initially, the Task Force had planned to propose that the program be enacted in only six or eight cities. However, they were aware of the congressional process. That is, the members of the Task Force were aware that congressional approval depended upon whether or not the

---

[9] Judson L. James, "Federalism and the Model Cities Experiment," *Publius* (Spring 1972).

[10] Ibid., p. 72.

congressmen's districts would benefit. With these instructions and considerations in mind, the Task Force set to work.

In January 1966, the Task Force formally presented its proposal which contained a number of "innovations." The innovations were fashioned so that they would be acceptable to Congress. The most drastic innovation was the concentration of resources in a defined neighborhood in a prescribed number of cities. The proposal also included a number of grant-in-aid programs that were to be coordinated by local officials and the neighborhood. The planning efforts were to be placed in a Community Development Agency which would link the mayor's office to the affected neighborhood. The bulk of the funds would come from existing programs and agencies.[11] This arrangement would supposedly satisfy the demand for participation as well as congressional concerns for official control. Indeed, the Task Force was very concerned about the proposal's fate in the Congress. The "re-programming" of existing appropriations would also satisfy those members of Congress who did not want to increase federal spending. As we shall see later in this chapter, the Task Force got a good deal of what it, and the president, wanted in the final legislation. Of course, though, some congressional modifications were included.

Initial Outcome: The Legislative Product

A convenient way to view the legislative phase of the policy process is in terms of coalition building. The sponsor or sponsors of proposals must build coalitions in both houses of Congress as well as in the relevant committees.

Several factors are important to policy coalitions. First, there are the *attitude and actions of the president.* Through White House staff and representatives of executive departments he lobbies for or against a bill at hearings, with individual legislators, and through the media. Tactics will largely depend on the partisan and ideological makeup of Congress. And naturally, if the bill is an administration bill, the president and his "helpers" will do all they can to help the measure along. Despite the absence of disciplined legislative parties, the president's policy position will usually be a major factor in defining the position of most members of both parties. It is also important to consider whether a president is working to pass or to defeat a bill on its merit, or whether he is trying to gain political advantage for electoral purposes. His tactics will vary ac-

---

[11] Ibid., p. 73.

cordingly. Compromises may be made in the former situation, but seldom in the latter. Thus, key members of Congress will try to find out the president's feelings on a particular measure before they commit themselves fully one way or the other.

Second, *department and agency bureaucrats* contribute to coalition construction. In many instances, these institutional representatives have a monopoly of information. How has a program worked? Its administrators have answers that are documented with mountains of supporting data. How will a new program work? Its technical authors can explain the prospects in exquisite detail. In other instances, bureaucrats use long-standing associations with individual legislators to rally support for proposals concerned with their agency. But there is little or no role for the public.

Coalition building in support of or in opposition to proposed legislation is also influenced by a third characteristic, the *committee structure* of Congress. Because the bulk of congressional work on bills is performed in committee and not on the floor of the House or Senate these smaller, functionally devised groups can significantly influence the final shape of the legislative product. For example, the policy areas of some committees are more conducive to "log-rolling" or **"pork-barrel"** tactics than others. That is, the issue being considered may have implications for some tangible interests of the members' constituencies. If the representatives are convinced that those interests will not be adversely affected by the **"marked-up" bill,** a strong committee coalition is likely when the bill is presented to the full House or Senate for debate and vote. If such a committee coalition is bipartisan, strictly partisan voting on the floor is unlikely. This is especially true when the subject matter is not of great interest to many of the legislators.

On the other hand, a committee whose policy areas are subject to ideological conflict — the House Labor Committee on Education is a good example — is less likely to arrive at a consensual coalition. Therefore, the House or Senate floor becomes the primary arena for coalition building on bills from such committees. Partisan and/or ideological differences are likely to be important factors. These differences will be revealed in the debate that precedes the final vote on the issue.

Similarly, it is important to note that the style of committee operation vis-à-vis House action will often determine whether much, little, or no bargaining and compromising goes on at the committee level. When a powerful committee chairman is determined to bring out a bill that will pass, committee activity is strongly oriented toward coalition formation — even though the subject matter itself may be controversial.

Fourth, *legislative parties* also affect congressional coalition building. There are several important variables: whether the White House and Congress are controlled by the same party, the relative strength of the majority and minority, the style and influence of party leadership, the amount of cohesiveness in each party, the role and clout of party subgroups such as the Democratic Study Group, and the anticipated closeness of the next election.

A fifth factor can be generally described as *constituency influence.* However, this does not mean only letters from home. Of course, constituents do include organized groups that serve as important referents — civil rights groups, labor unions, expressive associations, farmer organizations, associations of business and industry, and the like. Such organizations can influence legislators for several reasons. Their members or those they claim to represent may actually be an important segment of electoral constituencies and the organizations may be important to electoral success. Or the groups may simply share the legislator's own ideological leanings, a factor especially important for upwardly mobile representatives and senators. The coalition building role of such groups typically centers around two tactics: supporting tried-and-true friends and urging them to take more active roles in specific policy battles; and, shoring up others who might waver in certain instances.

Another important constituency influence is the legislator's perceptions of how the "folks back home" feel about a policy area. It seems likely that what is calculated is not what most voters feel about a particular bill, but what they feel about a given issue area. How this is calculated varies, but certainly communications from major supporters, party leaders and other key local individuals weigh heavily. Obviously, in many cases the legislator must realize that most of the home folks neither know nor care about the matter at hand!

In any given instance, one or more of these factors will be significant in developing congressional support for a policy proposal. In addition, several studies have indicated that certain policy decisions are more closely tied to presidential influence while others are related to party affiliation or constituency attitudes.[12]

This discussion has revealed the multiplicity of actors and some of their roles in making public policy. Although the general public's direct influence on this process is limited in most cases to letter writing, it is often remarked that their concerns are indirectly articulated through the "interest aggregation" function of the two major political parties. But, if some part of the public is not influential in the party's decisions, even indirect articulation loses much of its meaning. This has been the case with national policy that is relevant to black interests. The inability of

---

[12] See Aage Clausen, *How Congressmen Decide: A Policy Focus* (New York: St. Martin's Press, 1973), and Warren E. Miller and Donald E. Stokes, "Party Government and the Saliency of Congress," *Public Opinion Quarterly,* 26 (Winter 1962), and "Constituency Influence in Congress," *APSR,* 57:1 (March 1963).

black Americans to influence the policy-making process is another measure of their weakness in the political system.

In some respects the lack of influence can be viewed as a by-product of black urbanization. Many problems that affect the black minority most severely are related to their urban concentration. Therefore, we could expect that the way in which urban policy is handled would strongly affect black Americans. But, the American "love-hate" relationship with their large cities is further complicated by the addition of racial concerns. This condition is intensified because the potential for urbanization was not considered when Congress was initially organized. Cities, to the extent that they were considered at all by the founders, were the responsibilities of the states, not of the federal government.

Thus, despite the severe dislocations which urban populations suffered during the Depression, and the obvious implications of the general urbanization of the nation since the 1920's, Congress and the president gave little specific attention to urban affairs. That is, unlike agricultural interests, there was no committee specializing in the affairs of urban communities.[13] Not until the Kennedy administration was there an effort made to give urban policy questions an institutionalized status in the policy system. And, Kennedy's attempt to create a Department of Urban Affairs failed in part because some influential southerners in Congress saw it as having racial/civil rights implications to which they were opposed. The Johnson administration met with greater success. However, that success came at a high price. The creation of the Department of Housing and Urban Development with America's first black cabinet member as its head came after several years of violent urban political activity by blacks and extensive damage to some of the nation's largest cities. The passage of the Demonstration Cities Act (hereafter referred to by the more common name of Model Cities) gives us an opportunity to see the policy-making system in action.

MODEL CITIES: THE POLICY PROCESS IN ACTION

Model Cities was introduced as three separate bills in the House of Representatives. The bills were referred to the House Committee on Banking and Currency which was chaired by Wright Patman (D., Texas). Patman was a staunch supporter of the legislation. And, it is useful to indicate that Patman was also a long-time friend of President Johnson. From the president's point of view it made good political sense to have potentially controversial legislation considered not only by a

---

[13] For a useful discussion of this failure see Frederic N. Cleaveland, "Congress and Urban Problems," *Journal of Politics*, 28:2 (May 1966), 289–307; and also see the insightful study by Roscoe C. Martin, *Cities and the Federal System* (New York: Atherton, 1967).

supporter but also by a friend. That legislation of this type should be handled by a Committee on Banking and Currency may at first appear strange. However, in addition to its jurisdiction in the general area of banking and currency, and the Federal Reserve System, Patman's committee also oversaw matters of housing and home finance and urban redevelopment. Although the president and his Task Force conceived of the Model Cities program as something new, in terms of committee perceptions it was a variation of the urban renewal legislation with which the members were familiar. As such, it was likely that they would not think of the proposed legislation along the lines of novelty that its creators intended.[14]

The Model Cities legislation authorized participating cities the full array of available grants and urban aid in the fields of housing, urban renewal, transportation, welfare, economic opportunity, and related programs. In addition, the bill provided special grants amounting to 80 percent of the nonfederal cost of the programs included in the demonstration. It also included programs currently being financed under existing federal grant-in-aid programs and those proposed initially as part of the demonstration.

A second bill provided collateral programs for urban development. This was not a major concern in legislation submitted by the president. The third and final bill authorized federal assistance to finance and equip facilities for group medical and dental practices. It, too, was a minor segment of the Model Cities program.[15]

The three bills attracted a variety of supporters and opponents. The testimony of the groups' spokesmen indicated their concerns; but it also furnishes a basis for evaluating their roles and influence in the final legislative product.

The first individual to testify before the Committee was Dr. Robert E. Weaver, later to become Secretary of Housing and Urban Development, and the first black to hold a cabinet post. He impressed upon the committeemen the importance of the legislation in solving the physical, social, and economic problems confronting the nation's central cities. Weaver's comments went directly to the point of community involvement when he discussed the proposed eligibility criteria. Blight alone was insufficient. In addition to urban blight, the applicant would also be required to demonstrate that local officials and residents were able to work constructively together. Weaver stated:

---

[14] Cf. Aaron Wildavsky, "The Analysis of Issue Contexts in the Study of Decision Making," *Journal of Politics*, 24 (1962), 717–732, for a perceptive discussion of the influence of issue contexts and settings on the formation of public policy.

[15] U.S. Congress, House Committee on Banking and Currency, *Congressional Quarterly*, No. 9 (1966), p. 463.

The areas [must be] willing and able to bring together the public and private bodies whose joint action is necessary to solve their problems — willing to commit fully their energies and resources — willing to undertake actions which will have widespread and profound effects on the physical and social structures of the city.[16]

Unlike the Community Action Programs (CAP) of OEO which emphasized a dominant role for "the grassroots," the Model Cities program sought to create a less abrasive relationship between the lay public and elected officials.

Weaver also indicated that federal control would be limited; "this will be a local program."[17] He was attempting to gain the support of legislators and interest groups who had criticized the red tape in the administration of the poverty programs. Weaver continued, "All assistance under the program would be channelled into a demonstration agency established or designated by the local governing body to administer the program."[18] Despite the emphasis placed on local initiative, Weaver also indicated the likely nature of federal involvement. Undoubtedly, Weaver was aware of congressional doubts about urban officials' competence in handling large sums of money. He proposed that a federal coordinator be designated for each approved area; his function would be to provide liaison and coordination services.

Weaver was followed by spokesmen from the U.S. Conference of Mayors. The support of this body is easy to understand. Cities were in financial trouble and physically deteriorating because the suburban areas were attracting the commercial enterprises, the financially stable families, and other taxable entities. Their livelihoods and the viability of their cities depended upon how well they were able to deal with the complex problems. H. J. Addonizio, Mayor of Newark, endorsed the legislation in behalf of the U.S. Conference of Mayors.[19] The mayors strongly supported the idea of federal coordinators to provide liaison services in each approved project area. Surprisingly, however, they also urged that coordination be broadened by designating an assistant secretary or an assistant director for participating agencies. Mayor Addonizio was joined by several more colleagues before the Committee in support of the proposed legislation. Among these were Mayors Lindsay of New York City, Daley of Chicago, and Cavanaugh of Detroit.[20]

---

[16] Ibid., p. 493.

[17] Ibid., p. 494.

[18] Ibid., p. 495.

[19] Addonizio was later defeated in his bid for reelection by Kenneth Gibson, the first black mayor to emerge in the wake of the mid-sixties' urban violence.

[20] U.S. Congress, House Committee on Banking and Currency, *Congressional Quarterly*, No. 10 (1966), p. 563.

Organized labor, of course, had as a result of Reuther's active involvement supported the Model Cities proposal from its inception. Labor also had a self-interest in the program because it would increase the number of jobs available. The legislation called for an enormous amount of construction. Boris Shiskin, secretary of the AFL-CIO housing subcommittee, termed the bills "an important and auspicious step in the right direction."[21] But, he reminded the committee that the anticipated funding level was insufficient to deal adequately with the urban blight and the associated social and economic problems confronting the urban poor.[22]

Additional interest group support came from several groups directly involved in the nation's urban areas. The organizations and their representatives included: executive director of the Metropolitan Atlanta Region of the National Association of Housing and redevelopment officials; the president of the National Association of Home Builders; the president of the National Housing Conference; and the president of the National Farmers Union.[23] Each of these representatives tried to impress upon the Committee the importance of the legislation. They argued that the legislation provided programs that would greatly decrease the misery of the urban areas and their people.

Technical experts also testified in support of the program. Harold Wise, chairman of the National Legislative Committee of the American Institute of Planners (AIP), strongly endorsed the Model Cities proposals, but criticized their presentation as separate bills. He contended that the Demonstration Cities Act (H.R. 12341) and the Urban Development Act (H.R. 12939) could serve the needs of urban areas more adequately if they were consolidated under the same act. Wise felt that the administration was proposing two separate types of programs for two different constituencies — urban areas and growing suburban areas. Another to testify was Morris Ketchum Jr., president of the American Institute of Architects (AIA), who endorsed the "New Towns Provision." He argued very strongly for specifying high standards for design technology, including cost reduction techniques.

Both the AIP and the AIA saw potential gains for members of their respective professions. The architects naturally were interested in the jobs the program might provide. But they also saw Model Cities as an opportunity to introduce new concepts in housing design and construction techniques. The planners meanwhile saw the requirement for comprehensive planning as a vehicle that would put into practice their belief in integrated social and physical planning. And, there was a less obvious

---

[21] Ibid.

[22] Ibid., p. 564.

[23] Ibid.

dividend for the planners. They were a smaller and less prestigious group than the architects. The possibility of acquiring increased stature and influence through work in Model Cities programs was a consideration.

Although the administration had drawn the legislation in such a way as to gain support from several parts of the political spectrum, there was opposition. Indeed, some legislators believed that their constituents might sustain a loss if the legislation were to pass. For these critics of Model Cities it was essential for Congress to anticipate the "horrible" effects of the legislation. One of these groups was the National Association of Real Estate Boards (NAREB). This association has had a reputation for opposing the liberal viewpoint in housing and urban renewal matters. It had consistently opposed earlier housing acts and it opposed Model Cities.[24] The realtors argued that the proposal for another federal attempt that could further reduce local initiative. In their view the proponents of the legislation should:

> stop attempting to spoon feed the Congress and the [American] people in the area of federal assistance to whole communities. We should recognize that a gap in local initiative cannot be bridged by money alone.[25]

And, with a reference to traditional conservative thinking, the NAREB contended that the legislation was an "unwarranted intrusion of Government in the control of the future use of land . . . [which] would lead ultimately to the federalization of the nation's communities."[26]

The NAREB opposition was not based entirely upon its fear of federal domination, the unwise use of land, and the cities' lack of initiative to do their jobs. Its position also reflected a belief that its members might lose economically because of the federally sponsored housing.

James F. Steiners, spokesman for the Chambers of Commerce of the United States, opposed the measures on similar grounds. He also argued that the proponents of the program were assuming without real proof that the cities did not have adequate resources to solve their own problems. He was harshly critical of the liaison function as well. He foresaw a possibility that the federal coordinator would become a "commissar or czar who would possess vaguely defined powers."[27]

That part of the legislation which provided for federal monies to finance and equip facilities for group medical and dental practice in blighted areas was strongly opposed by the American Medical Association and the American Dental Association. The doctors argued that the

---

[24] Ibid.
[25] Ibid., No. 11, p. 605.
[26] Ibid.
[27] Ibid.

proposal was a weapon to put the individual practitioners out of business. Arguments which suggested that the urban poor received poor health and dental care were given only limited attention.

However, opposition to the Model Cities legislation was not that substantial. Nor were the arguments that the realtors and doctors presented persuasive to the Committee members. And, in any case the NAREB position was weakened by the enthusiastic participation of that industry in other federally assisted housing and urban renewal efforts. As for the medical profession, their almost traditional fears of socialized medicine as well as their expected opposing views carried little weight. The Committee on Banking and Currency was not studying medical legislation; it was considering problems of urban blight. It was an easy matter for the members of the Committee to focus their attention on questions of urban renewal and to downplay the possible implications for socialized health and dental services.[28] The Model Cities bill was accepted by Congress on the president's terms with two exceptions: the federal coordinator was eliminated and the funding level was reduced.

It is useful, then, to ask one final question about policy-making. Who benefits? But merely asking that question implies a larger number of related queries. One would like to know how a particular group or class of beneficiaries benefited from governmental actions. Answers to such questions are difficult to find, as we noted above. But there is usually some evidence available from which those who make such inquiries can develop reasonable inferences. The Model Cities program gives us an illustration of this point.

WHO BENEFITED?

Model Cities was expected to relieve the conditions of the urban poor, that is, blacks. It was purported to have been designed to enhance the quality of life within the central cities of metropolitan America. In fact, this was the first national program whose purpose was to deal with the social, economic, and health needs of the urban poor. It was the program that President Johnson viewed as giving meaning to the lives of the urban poor. But, what has really been the impact of the Model Cities program on the lives of the urban poor? Has it enhanced the quality of life in the center cities? Or has it worked toward strengthening the local government — that is, the mayor's position as a decision-maker?

---

[28] It should be stated, however, that similar arguments by the medical profession have been successfully used in opposing earlier efforts to develop national health care. Data from SRC election surveys for 1956-1971 suggest that public support was at a consistently high level over this 15-year period. Cf. Richard E. Dawson, *Public Opinion and Contemporary Disarray* (New York: Harper & Row, 1974).

The studies of the center city areas since the implementation of Model Cities have produced discouraging findings. They revealed that the urban poor are still living under conditions that were prevalent before the enactment of Model Cities.[29] A study conducted by the National Urban Coalition discovered that the conditions reported in the Kerner Report were still present in the urban areas. The study indicated that the quality of life had not been improved in the cities investigated. In fact, the study revealed that the quality of life had really changed for the worse: (1) housing is still the national scandal it was then; (2) the rates of crime and unemployment and disease and heroin addiction are higher; (3) welfare rolls are larger; and (4) relations between minority communities and the police are just as hostile. One change for the better was the more positive attitude blacks and the urban poor gained of themselves. This is not necessarily connected with Model Cities.[30] Some community activists and planners, however, criticized what they saw as the most detrimental aspects of the program: (1) breaking up ethnic neighborhoods — destroying a sense of community, and (2) the forced relocation of the urban poor without adequate provisions for new housing.[31] Similar criticisms were also made of the urban renewal programs that had preceded Model Cities by more than a decade. There was no effective answer to these criticisms.

Some observers have taken the view that the federal government simply cannot correct some of the urban problems which plague American life.[32] And not all of those who take this position can be dismissed as conservatives. The politically active among urban blacks have increasingly blamed the government for the failures (real and imagined) of programs like Model Cities. However, passage of a bill by Congress does not end the policy process. Indeed, as we shall see in the following section the congressional action sets in motion a wide range of activities by other parts of government.

Secondary Outcome: Administration and Impact

The impact of legislation approved by Congress can be viewed in terms of the following questions:

1. Does the act actually allocate or reallocate resources to certain groups or individuals?

---

[29] See "National Survey of Housing Abandonment," conducted by Center for Community Change, National Urban League, April, 1971; George J. Washnis, "An Overview of the Program's Progress," in *Model Cities Service Center Bulletin,* 2, No. 9 (June 1971); and "State of the Cities," by the National Urban Coalition, 1972.

[30] "State of the Cities" by National Urban Coalition, 1972.

[31] Ibid., p. 9.

[32] See, for example, Edward Banfield, *The Unheavenly City* (Boston: Little, Brown, 1971).

2. If so, who gets what benefits and who pays what costs?
3. Does the act place regulations on individuals or groups?
4. If so, who is to enforce these regulations? With what sanctions?
5. Does the bill delegate authority to make allocations or regulations? If so, to whom?

Unless a policy is self-executing, or the guidelines as to "who gets how much of what" are unusually clear and explicit, there will be some administrative discretion in **implementation.** To discover the actual impact that a program has on a target population or problem area, several features of administration should be considered.

To begin with, who is given administrative authority? An old-line agency, an agency upgraded for the task, or a newly created structure? For both the War on Poverty and Model Cities programs, new agencies were developed: the Office of Economic Opportunity for the former and a new department, Housing and Urban Development, for the latter.[33] The creation of new agencies may arouse jealousies in the older agencies which heretofore have had responsibility in the particular policy area. For OEO and Model Cities this problem was compounded by the emergence of interagency conflict around President Johnson's desire that federal efforts in the cities be coordinated. This meshing of sometimes competing energies and interests does not just happen, it has to be made to happen. And if the president or someone with his proxy isn't there to see it through, coordination is unlikely to become fact.

Second, if a new administrative structure is created, will it be visible and thus vulnerable to political attacks?[34] If so, can such attacks affect the allocation or regulatory function? The staff of a new administration is also important: recruitment patterns, political ties, past experience in similar policy areas, and possible links to clientele groups.

Third, changes in administrative practices and orientations over time greatly affect the impact of policy. The concept of life cycles of regulatory commissions is one important pattern to be considered. This phenomenon might well apply to structures created to deal with areas such as civil rights, environmental protection and product safety. Agencies can be and are "captured" by clientele groups, even by those that they are supposed to regulate. In fact, administrator and client can become so closely tied that it is often difficult to distinguish precisely who is making administrative decisions.[35]

---

[33] Actually the Department of Housing and Urban Development was simply given this function. It had been created in the administration of former President John F. Kennedy. Model Cities was its first "new" activity.

[34] Matthew Holden has suggested that political attacks may not all be of a partisan type. Interagency rivalries may also lead to conflicts which he calls "imperialism"; see his essay, "Imperialism in Bureaucracy," *APSR* 60 (December 1966):943-951.

[35] See Francis E. Rourke, *Bureaucracy, Politics and Public Policy* (Boston: Little, Brown, 1969), pp. 11-24, and Grant McConnell, *Private Power and American Democracy* (New York:

Fourth, just as it is possible for an agency to be "captured" by its clientele, so too can a similar "capture" be made by a legislator whose committee works in that particular functional area. The relationships developed between administrators and members of Congress can affect future funding and thus lead to expansion or reduction of program benefits and/or program scope.[36]

Fifth, if administrative structures have discretion in establishing program guidelines, setting standards of eligibility for program participation or approving funding of projects at state and local levels, what criteria are used for making such decisions? It is quite possible that such discretion can lead to results different from those envisioned by sponsors and supporters of original legislation. Yet many such decisions go unchallenged. This may well be because many congressional coalitions can be built only for statements of general intent and would break down if specific allocations were involved.

Sixth, administrative functions may be diffused through various levels of bureaucratic structures. Until very recently, all of the categorical assistance programs were administered in part at the federal level and in part at the local or county level. Such dispersion of administrative discretion created hundreds of welfare "systems." Under such a situation, the impact of policy on a national basis cannot be accurately assessed.

Response, Feedback and Future Prospects

This phase of the policy process theoretically leads back to the beginning of the cycle, assuming first that adoption of a policy has some kind of impact and second that someone notices it. Responses ideally should come from those persons or groups to be affected by a specific program. However, if those targets are unorganized and without access to political actors or public attention, their pleasure or displeasure with program results may be unnoticed. While young men from low-income families were being drafted in greater proportions and receiving fewer deferments than youths of higher socioeconomic status, there was no available feedback route for complaints about this feature of the Selective Service System.[37] However, when large numbers of

---

Albert A. Knopf, 1966); see also Philip Selznick, *TVA and the Grass Roots* (New York: Harper & Row, 1966).

[36] For a discussion of this phenomenon see Wildavsky, *The Politics of the Budgetary Process.*

[37] See James W. Davis and Kenneth M. Dolbeare, *Little Groups of Neighbors: The Selective Service System* (Chicago: Markham Publishing Company, 1968).

middle and upper class youths began attacking the draft as part of the Vietnam War protests, this response to an established policy was attended to by both political actors and the national media.

Since few national programs are systematically evaluated in terms of how much change is produced in target populations or whether specific governmental actions actually "solve problems," it seems that much of the content of response is quite subjective in nature. At best, praise or disappointment will often be registered by leaders, real or self-appointed, of target groups. Nevertheless, how leaders with ties to policy actors respond can have an influence on the future of a given policy. Equally important can be the response of persons or groups affected by an unplanned consequence of a program. The reaction to community action registered by local elected officials was important in modifying OEO programs and activities, such as the Green Amendments of 1966 which gave elected officials a stronger voice in the use of these federal funds. In turn, these modifications were made part of the Model Cities legislation, as we have seen.

Because many programs require the creation of extensive administrative networks, they may also create new constituent and clientele groups with an interest in program maintenance. While part of their feedback may entail suggestions for improvement, it is also safe to predict that their overall response will be positive. Thus policies that create a significant number of administrative units more or less create support groups for the future. We should also note the importance to future modifications, increments or terminations of specific policies to the responses of original sponsors, supporters and opponents.

Of course presidents, legislators, and even "experts," like other mortals, often see what they want to see. They too can be seduced by symbolic reassurances. However, if association with a certain policy has aided one of these actors politically, it is likely that the actor will wish to continue this association if expansion or modification appears promising. If opponents feel that the program has not produced the dire consequence they predicted, or if their reference groups no longer care very much about the issue, they may accept incremental expansion.

One of the more troublesome situations in the policy process stems from the recognition by participants in the process that they have sponsored and carried through programs which are not fulfilling their promises. This seems to be the current dilemma of many critics concerning many of our current social programs. While negative responses and feedback are easy to find, new policy approaches to chronic problems are slow to emerge. And, we recognize that radical proposals are not likely to be accepted quickly, though they may be at some future time. Perhaps this is simply another indication that there are time lags at all points in the policy process. Or perhaps it substantiates the notion that there is "periodicity" to policy actions which expand the role of government.[38]

In one sense, the Model Cities program, like the War on Poverty which preceded it, is unique. The policy process does not ordinarily move with such speed. If, however, the political climate is supportive — that is, if Congress and the president both perceive broad support for initiatives in a given issue area — the likelihood of political obstacles being raised is lessened.

It is also significant to note that there was little evidence of specific black activity around this legislation. This absence reveals a consistent weakness in black attempts to seek beneficial changes through policy-making. For the policy process is preeminently a set of political actions in which knowledge and votes count heavily. The two major organizations of black interests had little effective expertise in the policy issue areas of housing and poverty. Even more important, however, was the absence of black elected officials at the national level who might have been involved in the decision-making on the Model Cities Program. Thus, one of the priority items on the black political agenda became electoral politics; the objective of course was to put blacks in office. But, there too the black citizen was at a disadvantage. Thus from a black perspective we must ask if the policy accomplishments represent symbolic or substantive policy gains in the absence of desirable changes in other areas. While the Model Cities case was unusual in regard to the speed of governmental action, it is instructive to recall the small direct role played by blacks in its initiation and formulation, unless we take the position that the legislation was a direct outgrowth of black political violence in the cities. But, as we have noted earlier, that political activity was unique. Moreover, it is not the type of political effort which can be employed on a long-term basis. However, the lack of institutionalized actors makes black involvement in political agenda setting a difficult undertaking.

The NAACP, the major black interest group, has until recently committed most of its limited resources to litigation and legislation in the areas of civil rights and education. The Urban League, on the other hand, seldom takes an active political role, in part because of its habitual preference for private negotiations and undoubtedly also because of prohibitions against lobbying by tax-exempt groups. The Leadership Conference on Civil Rights has been just that, concerned with the passage of civil rights legislation.

Although there has been progress in this area in the last decade these groups have reason to believe blacks remain vulnerable. An example is the Nixon administration's efforts to weaken the provisions of the Voting

---

[38] See James Sundquist, *Politics and Policy* (Washington, D.C.: The Brookings Institution, 1968).

Rights Act. Consequently, they have chosen to continue their efforts in the civil rights field. In view of limited political resources this appears to be a rational strategy. Black influence on policy through the bureaucracy is also limited because of their small numbers of high level administrative posts and their disproportionate numbers at low levels of the administrative structure. In time, perhaps, black bureaucratic influence may grow in salient policy areas — housing and welfare, for example — because these parts of the administrative structure have the largest numbers of black employees. The legislative outcomes may be most susceptible to black influence if the Congressional Black Caucus can continue to grow. Again, however, the small size of the Caucus may be a detriment aggravated by the complexity of the policy process. This latter problem can only be overcome with time which black legislators and other officials must devote to learning. Some efforts in this direction are being made through the attempts of the Caucus to develop a cohesive policy position of black concerns. At the same time, it should be recognized that given the numerical minority status of the Caucus members, they must be able to forge coalitions with members of the majority if they are to have any hopes for success. The outcomes of these efforts will be somewhere in the future.

In the meantime, the higher levels of political participation among blacks does imply that the feedback mechanisms of the policy system will contain more politically relevant information from that section of the population. But the pervasive levels of low educational attainment in most black communities will continue to constrain the effectiveness of black Americans in the policy process. For black legislators, like their white colleagues, need technical and expert information on policy questions. The educational inequalities which we discussed in an earlier chapter, compounded by the absence of viable alternative resources generally distributed among black citizens, impose limits upon the ability of black legislators to compete in forming the policy agenda. The inability of blacks to affect significantly the policy process is further evidence of their weakness in the nation's political life. Admittedly, corrective actions to overcome these deficiencies will take time, but the question is how much time.[39]

Topics for Discussion

1. Why is there little systematic policy *planning* in government? How could planning be encouraged and improved?

---

[39] One study specifically addresses these weaknesses of blacks; see Harold L. Wolman, Norman C. Thomas, "Black Interests, Black Groups and Black Influence in the Federal Policy Process: The Cases of Housing and Education," *Journal of Politics*, 32 (1970), 875-897.

2. Because of the complex nature of modern society, public policies have many unanticipated consequences. Give some examples of past legislation and suggest ways in which their consequences might have been identified in advance.

3. What advice would you give to a member of the Congressional Black Caucus with regard to strengthening the black policy-making role?

Suggested Readings

Allensworth, Donald. *Public Administration: The Execution of Public Policy.* Philadelphia: Lippincott, 1973.

A study of the problems of implementing congressional legislation.

Blumenthal, Richard. "The Bureaucracy: Antipoverty and the Community Action Program." In Allen P. Sindler, ed., *American Political Institutions and Public Policy: Five Contemporary Studies.* Boston: Little, Brown, 1969.

A study of the in-fighting between agencies over administration of the resources of the Community Action Program.

Braybrooke, David and Charles Lindblom. *A Strategy of Decision.* New York: Free Press, 1963.

The classic formulation of the idea of incremental decision processes in government.

Clausen, Aage. *How Congressmen Decide: A Policy Focus.* New York: St. Martin's Press, 1973.

A study of the forces and motives which influence the behavior of congressmen in the legislative role.

Martin, Roscoe C. *Cities and the Federal System.* New York: Atherton, 1967.

An examination of the role of the federal government in the political and policy processes of local governments.

Moynihan, Daniel P. *Maximum Feasible Misunderstanding.* New York: Free Press, 1969.

A description and analysis of the problems plaguing the implementation of public policy decisions during the Johnson years.

Sundquist, James. *Politics and Policy*. Washington: Brookings, 1968.

A comparative study of the interplay between congressional and executive politics and policy formulation during the Eisenhower, Kennedy and Johnson administrations.

10

THE PROBLEM RESTATED

I say emphatically, the black politician is a national necessity. He is the last great white hope for peace in this land, where race has played such a dominant role in history. He must be supported by both whites and blacks while the majority of black people are still unresponsive to the entreaties of the black revolutionaries now compaigning throughout the land. The visible distribution and sharing of power with the black politicians is not only right and proper but such action also serves to neutralize the influence of the extremist.

Most people who argue that violence is not the way to achieve racial justice in America and that those who employ it as a weapon to produce change must be detected, immediately apprehended, and dealt with firmly. If this is so, why is it that those who exercise power almost always wait for violence before constructive action is taken and improved programs instituted?

Gerald A. Lamb*

In far too many local Urban Leagues (and other local organizations) I hear leaders and officials talk about the apathy of black people, particularly their political apathy. To those of you who might agree that apathy does indeed exist, I retort with the words of Eldridge Cleaver: "Today is an era of mass awareness, when the smallest man on

---

* Reprinted with permission from Gerald Lamb, "The Uncommon Man" in Mervyn M. Dymally, ed. *The Black Politician: His Struggle for Power* (Scituate, Mass.: Duxbury Press, 1971). (At the time of the article from which the above quotes were taken Mr. Lamb was State Treaturer of Connecticut.)

the street is in rebellion against the system which has denied him life and which he has come to understand robs him of dignity and self-respect." I suggest to you that the "mass awareness" of that "smallest man on the street" leads him to the active — not passive but active — act of staying away from the polls. And he will continue to stay away until those of us in politics can provide some positive reasons for positive actions on his part.

Shirley Chisholm, United States Congresswoman (D., New York)*

Because of the black man's situation, which is radical by any definition, and because of the nature of American politics, which is moderate to conservative by any definition, the black man in America has been condemned to seek radical ends within a political framework which was designed to prevent sudden and radical social and economic changes.

For almost one hundred years now, the black outsiders of America have been squirming within the halters of this maddening dilemma. During this period, some representatives of the outsiders in the councils of the insiders have made striking gains *as individuals*. But black people as a group have not been able to change their status and their social and economic conditions with political instruments. And the question we must grapple with now is whether it will ever be possible to achieve fundamental social and economic change by the practice of politics as defined by the insiders.

Mervyn M. Dymally, "The Black Outsider and the American Political System"**

---

* Reprinted with permission from Shirley Chisholm, "Ghetto Power in Action: The Value of Positive Action" in Mervyn M. Dymally, ed., *The Black Politician: His Struggle for Power*.

** Second Part, in Mervyn M. Dymally, ed., *The Black Politician: His Struggle for Power*, (Scituate, Mass.: Duxbury Press, 1971), p. 118. Reprinted with permission.

Introduction

Americans have faced and coped with many problems. But the problem of race is as much the "American Dilemma" today as when Gunnar Myrdal wrote his study some thirty years ago. To be sure, some progress has been made. Supreme Court decisions and various legislative enactments symbolize this progress. Nonetheless, blacks in this country still do not fully enjoy the privileges and benefits of American society as do white Americans.

We refuse to debate political analysts such as the Scammons and Wattenbergs who resort to "statistics" to support their claim that a majority of blacks are now in the "middle class."[1] Rather we merely suggest that "statistics" can be used to support various positions; in any event, "statistics" do not tell the full story. Information reporting systems — including the Census Bureau — are not geared to find (or count) many of those people whose inclusion might lead to different interpretations.[2] We refer to blacks and others who are without homes, jobs, money, and education.

But even with good "statistics" it remains difficult to describe the quality of life in black America without actually observing (and we daresay experiencing) how blacks live (survive) in this country. One must consider firsthand, for example, the familiar patterns of employment, housing, education, and public services that generally exist in black communities. Only then can one *really* gain an appreciation of the difference that color and race have made and continue to make in allocating values in the American political system.

This concluding chapter examines *the problem* both from a broad, general perspective and from more systematic, topical perspectives.

The Problem in General Perspective

THE TURBULENT SIXTIES

By the end of the past decade, blacks had made some significant political gains. Political participation was no longer a denied activity. Large numbers of black Americans had been elected to political offices. Political violence, which had been such a prominent feature of

---

[1] See Ben J. Wattenberg and Richard Scammon, "Black Progress and Liberal Rhetoric," *Commentary* 55 (April 1973).

[2] See discussion on the effect of the 1970 census undercount on revenue sharing in Robert P. Strauss and Peter B. Harkins, *The 1970 Census Undercount and Revenue Sharing: Effect on Allocations in New Jersey and Virginia* (Joint Center for Political Studies, June 1974). See especially Appendix 4, "Correspondence."

black politics between 1964 and 1968, was rejected by the majority of blacks after Martin Luther King's death in 1968. In addition, the hardline stance adopted by former President Nixon during his campaign and the actions of his administration while in office very likely raised the costs of violence to unacceptable levels. But it is just as important to recognize that blacks did not believe political violence was a useful long-range strategy. Most of the research on the perceptions of violence among blacks suggests that it had instrumental value as a dramatic form of political expression.

Similarly, blacks used other less destructive forms of political expression. The use of the language of the "streets," especially obscenity, was found to be successful in the confrontationist politics of the urban activist. Indeed, the so-called respectable leaders in black communities frequently accepted the existence of a political division of labor between themselves and the activists. The activists, using an expressive style in language and behavior, were regarded as "shock troops." Bargaining on the issues of the political agenda of blacks quite often was the responsibility of the quiet voices. This division of labor implied, however, that some fundamental agreement on goals and objectives had been reached beforehand. There was some degree of sense of political community among the activists and the more moderate parts of the black community. Without it, the candidacies of men like Carl Stokes, Kenneth Gibson and Richard Hatcher for mayoralty seats, or Ronald Dellums, John Conyers, and Andrew Young for congressional seats would not have been possible. Violence as a political instrument was rejected. But the willingness to employ it for desired ends was not totally absent. Political allegiance or belief in the system's ability to respond to grievances was an essential fact in the turn from violence and protests to more traditional forms of political action.

But traditional political action is slow to produce the kinds of outcomes in policy which would relieve some of the most oppressive burdens of the black American. There is also the little noted fact that after civil rights victories are achieved, the capacity of the government as government to initiate improving programs and politics is limited. In addition, gains made with government assistance can be undermined by strategies of *benign neglect.* In a private memorandum to then President Nixon, Daniel Moynihan recommended just such an approach. Said Moynihan:

> The time may have come when the issue of race could benefit from a period of "benign neglect." The subject has been too much talked about. The forum has been too much taken over by hysterics, paranoids, and boodlers on all sides. We may need a period in which Negro progress continues and racial rhetoric fades.[3]

---

[3] Reprinted in San Francisco *Sunday Examiner and Chronicle,* March 8, 1970, p. 24.

Moynihan went further in his advice to the president in saying:

> . . . social alienation among the black lower classes is matched, and probably enhanced, by a virulent form of anti-white feeling among portions of the large and prospering black middle class. It would be difficult to overestimate the degree to which young, well-educated blacks detest white America.

Animosity toward white America in 1970, however, should hardly come as a surprise. The point had been made earlier, for example, when the Kerner Commission made its famous "two societies, one black–one white" observation. To those whites, of whom we take Moynihan to be rather representative, who find middle class and sophisticated black detestation of white America unsettling, one can only ask what they expect in its stead. Indeed, one of the most significant results from black political assertiveness was the cathartic release of this long-standing bitterness. That these feelings should be most strongly held among members of a relatively successful stratum of black society could have been anticipated. It was precisely the educated and achieving blacks who were able to most keenly feel the effects of *the problem* as we have defined it here.

What we had during the sixties in some ways resembled the situation of England after 1815 when "'mass unrest . . . was simply a spontaneous response to intolerable conditions, which was then used as a threat by the Reform leaders — but was not really controllable by them."[4] Similarly, black leaders in the civil rights movement and those who sought programmatic initiatives from government could not *control* the urban outbursts. But the outbursts could be used to support demands for tangible responses. And further emphasis on the need for tangible responses was implicit in the degree to which middle-class blacks gave tacit approval to political violence, although they generally refrained from direct participation.[5]

---

[4] G. Bingham Powell, Jr., "Incremental Decentralization: The British Reform Act of 1832," in Gabriel A. Almond, Scott C. Flanagan, Robert J. Mundt, eds., *Crisis, Choice and Change: Historical Studies of Political Development* (Boston: Little, Brown, 1973), p. 119.

[5] Who rioted and how blacks interpreted the violence of the sixties are vexing questions. A number of officials and some scholarly analysts concluded that the rioters were primarily "riff raff" and enjoyed little support in their communities. For examples of this view see the report of the McCone Commission after the Watts Riots of 1965, entitled *Violence in the City — An End or a Beginning? A Report by the Governor's Commission on the Los Angeles Riots, 1965* (Sacramento, California); and also see Edward Banfield, "Rioting Mainly for Fun and Profit," in James Q. Wilson, ed., *The Metropolitan Enigma* (Cambridge: Harvard University Press, 1968). Challenging the "riff raff" theory is the *Report of the National Advisory Committee on Civil Disorders* (Washington, D.C.: U.S. Government Printing Office, 1968); and also see Nathan Cohen, ed., *The Los Angeles Riots* (New York: Praeger, 1970).

The quieting of black protesters since the 1968 elections may also be related to a black belief that the activist posture that they prefer in the government was likely to be brought about by the black congressional victories. But there had also emerged a strong and more secure sense of racial self-confidence. Black Americans had, by the middle sixties, begun to reject stereotypic images of themselves. In addition, it was no longer necessary to look to the black church for leadership. Nor was the wider society's definition of a black "leader" definitive.[6] In any event, by 1970 there was a diverse collection of individuals and organizations to whom black Americans gave their respect.

The opinions of black Americans reveal a clear pattern of cynicism about government. To some extent political cynicism is always a normal facet of the political process. Dissatisfaction with government actions in issue areas of interest to blacks has led to steady decline in their evaluation of government. Although policy dissatisfactions may reflect, in some cases, specific policy defeats, for the black community the dissatisfactions are cumulative. Moreover, the setbacks have often come in ways which reduced or appeared to threaten prior gains. This seemed to be the case, for example, with the Nixon administration's proposals to modify the Voting Rights Act of 1965.

The VRA in effect suspended the use of literacy tests or similar devices. It also authorized the use of federal supervision of election procedures in some areas of the country, primarily the South.[7] But in stating the administration's position on a proposed five-year extension of the Act, Attorney General John Mitchell argued that the Nixon administration could not support the extension of legislation that was essentially regional in character. To overcome such defects, the administration proposed that several deletions be made in the existing Act. What concerned civil rights forces most was the suggestion that the affected areas (in the South) no longer be required to get Justice Department approval prior to making changes in their voting laws. Supporters of the Act viewed this as a "sophisticated but deadly way to void the 1965 Act, diluting its impact on areas where discrimination was most prevalent. . . ."[8] In some ways the position resembled that adopted at the time when federal troops were removed from the South to end Reconstruction. Indeed, many of the Republicans who supported the adminis-

---

[6] Interestingly, Moynihan also suggested to President Nixon that the administration should try to make a black spokesman out of Jerome Holland, Ambassador to Nigeria, a man who was not widely known to the mass of blacks. Moynihan was thinking of someone who could appeal to the black "silent majority." He did not indicate in his memorandum how this could be accomplished, nor did he define the silent majority to which he referred.

[7] *Congressional Quarterly* (January 23, 1970), 237.

[8] Ibid.

tration's position, like then Congressman Gerald Ford, "urged approval of the Administration bill saying that the purpose of such 'discriminatory legislation' [the 1965 Act] had been accomplished and that the South should not continue to be punished for actions since remedied."[9]

Persistent signs of black dissatisfaction have been evident, however, since the violent protests and demonstrations ceased in 1968. Parenthetically, we might note that a number of blacks saw the police violence during the Democratic Convention at Chicago that year as a demonstration of the kind of response which they could expect if they had pursued political violence. At the same time, there were some in the black communities who adopted an "I told you so" attitude when whites criticized the behavior of the Chicago police. For them this was but an example of the "police brutality" which triggered several of the black rebellions. Thus, Reverend Jesse Jackson, one of the new black spokesmen after King's assassination, remarked to a *Time Magazine* reporter:

> Our experience with the hot summers is that it was a bit futile, given the Man's military superiority. . . . There is no more shock value in riots. The Man is ready for that too.[10]

Whitney Young also commented on the lack of black resources to carry on a sustained violent conflict:

> It's completely out of the question. To have war you've got to have some reasonable balance in the forces. Otherwise, you have a massacre. We're back with Nat Turner [an ex-slave who led a short-lived, but bloody revolt against white slave owners] again. That's not war, that's suicide. You're going to have sensation-seeking media who will play up those incidents and that rhetoric and make it seem as though they represent more people than they really do. This doesn't mean that the black people are not angry, bitter and enraged, and wouldn't like to kill some white people. But in terms of organized war, it's out of the question.

No one, it seemed, wanted to return to the *politics of the streets*. But there was still dissatisfaction among black Americans. The rebellions did not include interpersonal violence. Yet they can be viewed as attacks on the most accessible manifestations of the system's oppressive character: the institution of private property which occupies an almost sacred niche in the hierarchy of the nation's political values. Destruction of property was a dramatic expression of black political grievances. For the participants, as well as for many onlookers, the violence drew national and

---

[9] Ibid.
[10] "Black American 1970," *Time Magazine* (April 6, 1970), p. 15.

Wide World Photos

"Frustration and Defiance: Shoe vs. Guns." An incident in the July 1967 Detroit rebellions: an unidentified black man hurls a shoe at police who have sealed off the troubled area of the city.

international attention to the scope of discontent in the nation's black communities.

The most extreme black political violence during the sixties was primarily an urban phenomenon. But it was actually a part of the nationalized activism initiated by the nonviolent mass protests. It should be kept in mind that these earlier protests were also urban-centered. The nationalization of the conflict was made possible partly by salience and drama and also by the detailed coverage of the media.

Moreover, the civil rights protests which began in Birmingham did not end when blacks won the right to sit where they pleased on public transportation. The Montgomery bus boycott which launched the spectacular career of the Rev. Dr. Martin Luther King, Jr. was a stage in the political struggle for black *citizenship* that began before the Civil War. The

Wide World Photos

A Sober Reminder. The scars of urban violence remain as a constant and sober reminder of what needs to be done. This photograph, taken in 1974, shows a black woman on Springfield Avenue in Newark, N.J., center of that city's 1967 violence.

civil rights phase culminated in the massive demonstration in Washington, D.C., in August 1963. At the forefront of this demonstration with Dr. King was A. Philip Randolph whose proposal for an earlier march on the Capitol was called off some twenty years earlier. But, in the midst of this uncommon example of public concern over the question of black civil rights, changes in the nature of black political action were emerging. A newer and younger group of black political activists, primarily from the Student Non-Violence Coordinating Committee (SNCC) had begun to take a less moderate, nationalist stance toward American society, its institutions and political processes.[11]

---

[11] The significance of SNCC on later black political developments has not been carefully studied. For a critical view on the nationalism and hostility of the organization to white involvement in the black struggle see Benjamin Muse, *The American Negro Revolution*. Also see the treatment in Hanes Walton, Jr., *Black Politics* (Philadelphia: Lippincott, 1972), pp. 156–60; and Harry Holloway, *The Politics of the Southern Negro* (New York: Random House, 1969).

Antiwhite hostility and harsh criticisms of the various institutions of society were increasingly prominent features of black political protest after 1963. For some blacks hostility was an outgrowth of President Kennedy's assassination. Perhaps of even greater importance were the murders of four black children in the bombing of a black church in Birmingham in the spring prior to the March on Washington. However, it was also apparent that the demonstrations caused few changes in the daily lives of blacks in the rural South or in the northern ghettoes. Blacks began to ask more searching questions about themselves, the society in which they lived, and their place in it.

And, there was a subtle though important change in the black middle class. The civil rights protests were for many of this class their first experience in active political participation. Initially, with its religious character, these protests had the respectability that the black middle class valued. Middle class involvement helped to demonstrate a racial solidarity that was lacking in earlier black movements. One consequence of black solidarity was the "white backlash." While not anticipated, this effect could have been predicted from historical experience.

The backlash which followed the gains of the early sixties again revealed white ambivalence toward the need to do more to meet black demands for social justice and full participation in national life. It was difficult for black Americans to develop a sense of belonging in the face of shifting white opinion. White opposition to black demands was often couched in terms of a dislike of government's supportive efforts. Nevertheless, underlying this view was a strong belief, especially among lower and lower middle class white America, that somehow blacks were moving too fast. Moreover, the inevitable comparisons were drawn by which these white Americans could maintain that the government was not especially concerned about *their* well-being.

By 1964 white backlash became a campaign issue for Senator Goldwater, the Republican candidate. It did him little good because his hawkish views on the Vietnam war drove many potential supporters away. Lyndon Johnson, the Democratic victor in 1964, pushed ahead with the programs of the "Great Society." The War on Poverty (the domestic phase of these programs) was intended to address poverty regardless of race. However, it was regarded by many whites as principally a response to urban blacks. The problems of poverty were most dramatically and depressingly apparent in the cities. And, because the poor in large urban centers were disproportionately black, it was an easy matter to infer that the war had only one "theater of operations."

Even more unsettling to national opinion were the efforts made by blacks to convert government-financed community action programs into vehicles of political action against local government institutions. These conflicts also became nationalized; most urban bureaucracies were targets of direct action protests until the late sixties. As if this turmoil weren't enough, the black rebellions and "long, hot summers" of the big cities began barely a year after the War on Poverty's efforts were initiated. However, in spite of the turmoil and hostile white opinion, the anti-poverty effort led to increased black representation in urban bureaucracies. This effect, combined with the surge in traditional modes of political participation, has created urban political bases for black political activity.

To be sure, many of the problems of blacks remain. It is still difficult to get housing; there is deterioration in the cities and resistance to integration in the suburbs. Inner-city schools continue to present seemingly insoluble educational programs. Unemployment in the ghettos far exceeds the national average. Also, the fiscal condition of the central city remains precarious, and its influence in metropolitan regions continues to decline. For these and other reasons, many investigators are not hopeful about the potential for black political power based on the central city.[12] One problem appears to be that just as blacks begin to acquire some measure of political resources, the pressures for local, area-wide government organizations gained strength. And, at first blush, many blacks understandably view proposals for metropolitan cooperation or metropolitan government as a way to threaten their emerging, albeit meager, store of political power. Indeed, black Americans are principally big-city residents. And from the evidence at hand they are likely to remain so. White suburban walls still pose formidable barriers and severely restrict the quality of life in the central city.[13]

THE UNCERTAIN SEVENTIES

The turbulence and dissatisfaction of the seventies have led to some significant declines in black trust in the government. Perhaps equally or even more serious for the future is the widespread black belief that white Americans don't really care what happens to black people.[14] (See Table 2-9 in Chapter 2 which shows the interper-

---

[12] One of the earliest statements of this view is contained in Francis Fox Piven and Richard A. Cloward, "Black Control of Cities," *The New Republic* (September 30 and October 7, 1967); and also see H. Paul Friesma, "Black Control of Central Cities: The Hollow Prize," *Journal of the American Institute of Planners* (March 1969), pp. 75–79 for a similarly pessimistic assessment; further insight into this problem can be gained from the study of city-county consolidation in Jacksonville, Florida: see Lee Sloan and Robert M. French, "Black Rule in the Urban South?" *Trans Action* 9:1–2 (November 12, 1971), 29–34.

[13] Cf. Bennett Harrison, *Urban Economic Development: Suburbanization, Minority Opportunity, and the Condition of the Central City* (Washington, D.C.: Urban Institute, 1974).

[14] The ambivalence of whites toward black progress is cogently presented in Louis Harris, *The Anguish of Change* (New York: Norton, 1974). Earlier studies make essentially the same point. The most detailed of these works is, of course, the *Report of the Kerner Commission*. This investigation starkly revealed the two-societies character of American life. Thus, in a sense, the later study by Harris shows the degree to which problems which were identified after the black rebellions remained unresolved.

sonal aspects of this black-white dilemma.) More serious perhaps is a point which we made earlier but which bears repeating: while a majority of whites indicate that they want to see equality for blacks become a reality, they are unsure about when and how this should come about.

In addition, large numbers of whites, according to Louis Harris, entertained the belief that "blacks were asking for more than they were ready for." [15] It was as if the white majority wanted black Americans to pass through some form of tutelage, comparable to that of some of the former African colonial territories. [16] But the black American is no longer willing to accept such a role. It would be a retrogressive step to the kind of blatant second-class citizenship status that existed prior to the *Brown* decision in 1954. The willingness to engage in political combat is one of the most significant legacies of the turbulent sixties. Blacks now believe that the only way to overcome the social, political and economic deficiencies is to press. This means using all of the resources that are available to them, including if necessary the unconventional political style of the sixties.

One question has not been specifically examined here thus far. What have been the consequences of the political changes since the start of the civil rights demonstrations in the late 1950's? Because there was a good deal of hostility toward the system expressed during the rebellions, it has often been assumed that this represented a substantial withdrawal of black support for the government. There is some evidence to support this view. [17]

But the level of support that a group of people gives to the political regime seems to be different from that which is given to the government as an abstraction. Moreover — and this seems to be the case with blacks — it is likely that support for particular institutions within the government may be sufficient to maintain overall loyalty. For example, the demands for civil equality for blacks have usually found some favor with the presidents since Franklin Roosevelt and with the Supreme Courts since 1954. At the same time, however, the decentralized character of the American political system has provided numerous instances in which black feelings of political cynicism, distrust, and disaffection have resulted from local actions. [18] Most important, however, is that despite the stated dissatisfactions of black Americans, the kinds of political

---

[15] Harris, *The Anguish of Change*, p. 235.

[16] Cf. Rupert Emerson, *From Empire to Nation* (Cambridge: Harvard University Press, 1960).

[17] Since the rebellions several studies have appeared which treat this topic. A useful collection of essays may be found in Charles S. Bullock, III, and Harrell R. Rodgers, Jr., eds., *Black Political Attitudes: Implications for Political Support* (Chicago: Markham, 1972).

[18] Cf. H. Edward Ransford, "Isolation, Powerlessness and Violence: A Study of Attitudes and Participation in the Watts Riot," *American Journal of Sociology* 73 (1968), 581–91; and also see the discussion in David Easton, *A Systems Analysis of Political Life* (New York: John Wiley & Sons, 1965).

behavior which they adopted following the violent activism were essentially traditional. The rhetorical flourishes about the creation of a new political system were only words, if we are to judge from the evidence of the past several years. Nor, as we have suggested earlier, should one conclude that the low levels of formal black participation through voting necessarily indicate declining political support. The explanation for this failure to participate may reflect a much more careful assessment of the value of the vote.

Yet it is still true that black support for the political system has shown a continual decline since the mid-sixties. Notice, for example, the abrupt shift in black trust in government compared with a similarly abrupt change in attitudes toward the Vietnam war. (See Figure 10-1.) It should be noted that the high point for both issues (for blacks) comes in 1966. This was at the time when the War on Poverty was stimulating the greatest amount of improvement for black problems. Another indication of declining black confidence in several aspects of the political process can be seen in Figure 10-2. There is a steady decline between 1964 and 1972 in the level of confidence in legislators. This includes those years in which blacks had begun to make some gains in black congressional representation. Perhaps these gains were too little and too late to alter a decline which had already been set in motion. This would seem to be a reasonable interpretation since the decline was also apparent in the results shown for 1964.

Still, there are those who maintain that if blacks were only to exercise their franchise in sufficient numbers and engage in a broad range of "bootstrap" activities, the extent of the problems about which they complain would be significantly reduced. After major national elections there is always some interest in the size of the black vote. And, when the predictably low turnout figures are produced, many "liberal" Americans who should know better sadly shake their heads with an attitude of "I told you so."

As mentioned above, this *refusal* to participate may very well reflect a more careful (and negative) assessment of the value of the vote. After all, there is reason to believe that voting will produce desired outcomes in public policy. This notion is instilled in the public schools; it is part of the political socialization function of schools. There, the civics curriculum does not address the complexities of policy-making, nor does it analyze the workings of the political process as a general phenomenon. Political linkages between the black American and the system seem to be based upon symbols and rituals to a greater extent than one would find among white citizens. The schools can perform the basic *Americanization* of black children, such that a primitive attachment would develop. Yet they do not appear to have been able to forge the kinds of linkages between blacks and the polity. These linkages come from a feeling of

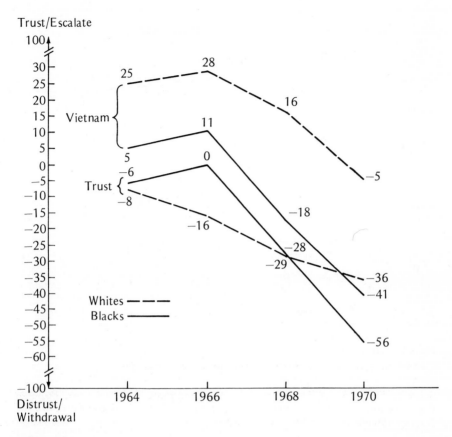

FIGURE 10-1
**Indices of Trust in Government and Support for Withdrawal from Vietnam,
1964-1970**

SOURCE: Arthur H. Miller, "Political Issues and Trust in Government: 1964–
1970." Reprinted with permission from *American Political Science Review* 68:3
(Sept., 1974), p. 959.

power and control over one's destiny as expressed in satisfactions produced by government policies. A sense of efficacy has not developed among black Americans. Yet blacks do consider themselves to
be Americans. This is simply a gross attachment. And, as David Easton
pointed out, "the peculiar characteristic of this attachment is that it is not
conditional upon specific returns at any moment."[19] However, during

---

[19] Ibid., p. 272.

Confidence

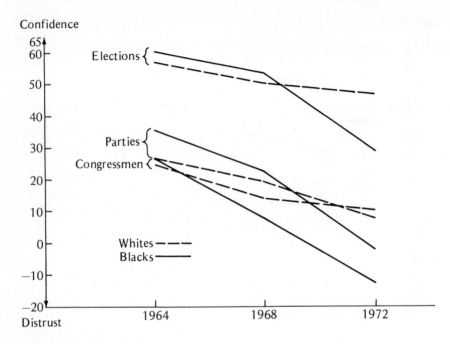

FIGURE 10-2
Confidence in Leaders, Parties, and Elections, 1964–1972

SOURCE: Arthur H. Miller, "Rejoinder to 'Comment by Jack Citrin: Political Discontent of Ritualism.'" Reprinted with permission from *American Political Science Review* 68:3 (Sept. 1974), p. 990.

certain periods, as for example during World War II, the tenuous nature of this kind of attachment is steadily revealed.[20]

In any event perhaps it is out of the growing sense of unity and political effectiveness among black Americans that one can seek to explain their declining trust in government. But there have been few periods of growth in trust among blacks. (See Figure 10-3.) The most precipitous decline, as we have stated elsewhere, set in with the election of a Republican president in 1968. Yet that seems merely to have continued a trend that began earlier. Clearly, the Watergate scandals had impact on black views. But the magnitude of that impact was not as

---

[20] Black morale at the beginning of World War II was low. The New Deal had improved things to some extent, but the system of rigid discrimination had been breached hardly at all by these policies. Moreover, blacks remembered their high hopes for democracy at the time of World War I. "Most Negroes," says, Richard Dalfiume,

succumbed to the "close ranks" strategy announced by . . . DuBois, who advocated [subordinating] racial grievances in order to give full support to winning the war.

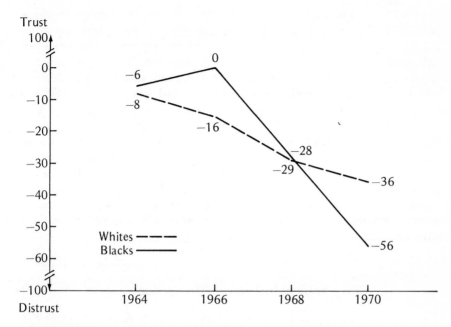

FIGURE 10-3
Index of Trust in Government By Race, 1964–1970

Source: Arthur H. Miller, "Political Issues and Trust in Government: 1964–1970." Reprinted with permission from *American Political Science Review* 68:3 (Sept., 1974), p. 955.

great among blacks as among the white citizens. (Note the change in white trust in government between 1972 and 1973.)

For blacks, however, the traditional institutions of government simply had lost what degree of credibility they once had. Only the Su-

---

But the image of a new democratic order was smashed by the race riots [and] lynchings. . . . The result was a mass trauma, and a series of movements among Negroes in the 1920's which were characterized by a desire to withdraw from a white society which wanted little to do with them. When the war crisis of the 1940's came along, the bitter memories of World War I were recalled with the result that there was a built-in cynicism among Negroes toward the democratic slogans of the new war.

Richard M. Dalfiume, "The 'Forgotten Years' of the Negro Revolution," *The Journal of American History*, 5:1 (June 1968), 92–93; also see the sources cited in that essay. Of course, the black movements to withdraw are best represented by the activities of Marcus Garvey, a Jamaican black and not a black American. There are two quite useful works on Garvey and the United Negro Improvement Association (U.N.I.A.) which he led to short-lived prominence; Edmund D. Cronon, *Black Moses: The Story of Marcus Garvey and the United Negro Improvement Association* (Madison, Wisc.: University of Wisconsin Press, 1955); and Theodore G. Vincent, *Black Power and the Garvey Movement* (Berkeley, Cal.: Ramparts, n.d.).

preme Court has managed to maintain a favorable position in black political judgment. And, despite the presence of the "strict constructionists" appointed by President Nixon, black and white assessment of this institution are wide apart. But blacks continue to trust the court. It would appear that black Americans have shed some of the idealism which characterized their political attitudes and actions during the civil rights era. They have taken on a more pragmatic approach to the use of the political machinery which is available to them. And, though they have a wariness which stems from long acquaintance with the system, black Americans appear to be willing to give the black political leaders a chance to make the political process work for their interests. But, as we discuss later in this chapter, this "willingness" imposes a heavy responsibility on black political leaders. Perhaps even more so, it imposes a heavy responsibility on white political leaders if future policy conflicts involving race are to be resolved peacefully.

The Problem in Topical Perspective

PROBLEMS OF AN IDENTIFIABLE MINORITY

The biggest problem that black Americans face is that they are in a country that has historically oppressed black people because they are *black*. Not only is slavery the most sordid story in American history, but it ranks as one of the most sordid stories in human history. The vestiges of slavery were deeply engrained in American society. *Dred Scott* and *Plessy* v. *Ferguson* show the depth of its penetration in our constitutional and legal fabric. And despite court decisions and congressional legislation of the 1950's and 1960's, Americans have continued to find ways to perpetuate inequities toward blacks. Witness the enactment of rigid housing codes and zoning regulations for the purpose of "protecting" residential areas *from blacks!* Witness recent court decisions and legislation that have been ushered in under the name of "law and order." Witness, moreover, the great amount of discretion that characterizes the work of legal officials — policemen, prosecutors, and judges, the overwhelming majority of whom are whites. And there are other examples.

However, the point here is not that these and other cases are anti-black. Superficially, they are quite neutral. But being neutral in a context that was never "color-blind" is hardly neutrality. Indeed, legal neutrality can be and has been used to discriminate against certain people and to favor others. Because blacks have been and are a "despised minority" they suffered the brunt of these neutral, legal methods. And while it might be difficult to prove *legally* racial discrimination in specific cases, the outcomes of many such cases over time leaves little doubt as to how blacks remain *legally* disadvantaged.[21]

Of course, that blacks are still legally disadvantaged is but a reflection of similar disadvantages they encounter in the political and socio-economic realms. For example, black political power, though increasing, is still quite limited. And that limitation will remain as long as race retains its salience in voting and elections. The same holds true with respect to jobs, educational opportunity, and economic advancement. Whether race continues to occupy a central place in American life is indeed, as Mathew Holden put it, "The White Man's Burden."[22]

The white majority, throughout the history of this nation, has treated blacks as a group. Consequently, they have reacted (and acted) as a group. Given the history of race relations in America, can anyone really expect blacks to do otherwise? Indeed even those blacks who "have it made," so to speak, "can never be sure." Education, money, social status notwithstanding have *seldom* bought for blacks the position they have bought for whites. And they have *never* bought for blacks the peace of mind that they have bought for whites. That they have not done so is due to one reason and one reason alone — that of color. Blacks who are at present "on top" can never forget that when and if, for whatever reasons, they should no longer maintain their status or job, they too are subject to the same rebuffs and maltreatment as blacks generally.[23] This is the *single most* important reason why many blacks who "have it made" *find* ways to identify with the "brothers" who have been less successful. In short, the uncertain status of blacks as a group makes for an uncertain status for individual blacks regardless of their qualifications or success.[24] Or put another way, the success of individual blacks is tied more to the status of blacks as a whole than many white Americans (and some successful blacks as well) might care to admit or recognize. That individual status might be closely related to group status is nothing new. But when skin color becomes *the* major determinant of individual status and achievement, as it has throughout American history, the differences between the problem of blacks and those of other groups become manifest.

---

[21] For an empirical analysis of this and related questions, see Nolan Jones, "Differential Legal Treatment Between Whites and Blacks as a Function of Social Context," Ph.D. Thesis, Washington University, 1975.

[22] See generally, Matthew Holden, *The White Man's Burden* (New York: Chandler Publishing Co., 1973).

[23] A bitter, but lucid statement of this prospect is contained in Alex Haley, *The Autobiography of Malcolm X* (New York: Grove Press, 1966).

[24] And, of course, white Americans are unaware of the demeaning message which is conveyed when they single out yet another black "first." The attempt to create role models for the black American serves only to remind him/her of the group's tenuous hold on a place in the society.

SYSTEM BIASES

The nature of the American political system, as discussed in Chapter 3, illuminates certain built-in biases that make resolution of *the problem* more difficult. Consider certain formal structural features of the governing system: separation of powers, checks and balances, bicameralism, federalism, and so on. These features provide great advantage for those who are against change and who wish to maintain the status quo. They favor incremental and marginal change and pose formidable obstacles to decisive, fundamental change. With federalism, for example, even those who succeed in enacting policies at the national level often find their expected benefits frustrated (or obliterated altogether) once they reach the state and local levels.[25]

Still further, consider the impact of majority rule. Majority rule is considered the most expedient and appropriate way of making decisions in democratic government. Nonetheless it poses dilemmas for a long-term oppressed minority group which seeks to improve its status through the system. By its very terms majority rule means compromise and coalition politics. This applies in just about every arena of American politics: elections, courts, legislatures. Yet, under majority rule politics, blacks are expected to accept (and even *understand*) that "we (coalition-builders) cannot at this time grant you *all* the rights that other Americans (whites) enjoy; we can only grant some, but remember that some is better than what you have now." Is this not in effect what blacks have been told for more than 100 years and are still being told today? Does this not call for a patience, understanding, and sophistication far beyond that which has been asked of any group of Americans? Nonetheless, this has been the operational effect of majority rule in attempts to solve problems facing blacks.

But should blacks in the 1970's accede to and accept a majority rule on matters that go to the very essential value and dignity of persons as individuals? Is not there a *substance* as well as *process* of democracy? The riots of the 1960's, if nothing more, reflected the frustration that many blacks felt and still feel over these very questions. Nonetheless, success in the American political system puts a premium on majority rule. Consequently the determination of even the most fundamental and elemental rights of blacks remains at the mercy (and whim) of majority

---

[25] See, for example, Harold Seidman, *Politics, Position, and Power: The Dynamics of Federal Organization* (New York: Oxford University Press, 1970) esp. ch. 5 on "Cooperative Federalism." Also see Jeffrey L. Pressman and Aaron Wildavsky, *Implementation: How Great Expectations in Washington Are Dashed in Oakland* (Berkeley: University of California Press, 1973); Michael D. Reagan, *The New Federalism* (New York: Oxford University Press, 1972); and Alan K. Campbell, ed., *The States and the Urban Crisis* (Englewood Cliffs, N.J.: Prentice-Hall, Inc., 1970).

rule–coalition–compromise politics. We should remember, however, that majority rule as a principle of democratic government is designed to operate in situations in which basic and fundamental rights are *already* safeguarded and are not at issue.

But principle is one thing and practice another. The basic rights of black Americans (such as the right to vote) continue to be *negotiated* through majority rule politics. And the limited gains which are possible through majority rule politics depend in large measure on having the *resources* necessary to build majorities, to forge coalitions, to exact compromises. Here, too, as we have pointed out earlier, black Americans are at a disadvantage. Blacks simply do not have, except in isolated instances, the combination of resources (money, numbers, position, status) needed to prevail in their objectives. Nor has there been sufficient time or incentives for blacks to develop the infrastructure which could support long term political action. Similarly, the same weakness may help to explain the short-lived experience with political violence in an attempt to redress the power imbalance.

The "rules of the game" affect all kinds of groups and all types of people who attempt to achieve all types of policy objectives. But they impose special hardships on blacks and other minority groups. For it is these groups whose political demands imply fundamental, structural change in the distribution of resources in the political system. Without such resources blacks and other minorities are at a disadvantage as they begin the "game" of politics. This is a reality that can no longer be ignored. And black elected officials bear a particularly heavy burden and responsibility to see that it is not ignored. To this matter we now turn.

BLACKS AND PUBLIC POLICY: PROBLEMS AND PROMISES

Our discussion of the American political system clearly demonstrates that effecting changes in public policy is a complex, difficult task. This is especially the case when dealing with controversial issues. And, in American society issues affecting blacks are by definition highly controversial. As a result, system biases become even more potent obstacles. Thus, those who oppose such changes have a number of built-in "advantages" to bolster their opposition. Alternatively, those who seek such policy changes need enormous resources to overcome these biases. But, as we have seen, changes in public policy do not guarantee changes in practice. Consequently, especially in highly controversial policy areas, a constant and continued presence is required to see that policy implementation follows policy enactment. This explains, in large measure, why many policies ostensibly enacted to support the interests of blacks (and the poor) are so difficult to put into practice.

Similarly, it explains the tenuousness and fragility of policies that affect blacks. It is difficult enough to harness the resources (and coalitions) necessary for success at the policy enactment stage. It is even more difficult (and quite a different matter) to maintain the resources (and coalitions) necessary for success at the policy implementation stage. Some vivid examples include such policies as those embodied in *Brown* v. *Board of Education* (1954), the Civil Rights Act of 1964, and the Voting Rights Act of 1965. The VRA, as pointed out earlier, especially illustrates the tenuousness of policy enactments that affect blacks; by its very terms the Act must be renewed or extended at stated intervals. Consequently, many of the original battles over guaranteeing black voting rights are subject to renewal with no guarantee that the original outcomes will be the same or even strengthened; they could be weakened.

This is the type of political context and terrain in which black politicians and black leaders must operate. And as suggested earlier, we believe that a heavy educational and moral responsibility rests on the shoulders of such black leaders "to tell it like it is." To do otherwise, they might find themselves in an almost intractable and impossible bind. On the one hand, there certainly were and are sound and practical reasons for black leaders to support the move "from protests to politics." On the other hand, there were and are similar reasons why black followers should expect changes to flow from these widely publicized electoral victories. Take, for example, the case of black mayors. Much celebration and hope have accompanied the ever increasing number of these black chief executives. And while this turn of events definitely engenders a cautious optimism, it simultaneously requires a cautious realism. Let us take a closer look at the situation.

Black mayors — such as Thomas Bradley in Los Angeles, Maynard Jackson in Atlanta, Kenneth Gibson in Newark — must not only be concerned with running the city, they must also be concerned that black constituencies expect them to do something about *black* problems. And it matters not that blacks constitute less than a majority of the city's population: the fact remains that the overwhelming support by blacks for black candidates indicates that blacks expect more from black than from white candidates. Nonetheless, it is frequently the case that doing anything about black problems depends upon the mayor's ability to solve citywide problems. And increasingly we have come to accept that the resources at the local level are not adequate to cope with these problems. Consequently, unless major changes occur (for example, massive federal aid programs) there is little reason to believe that black mayors will meet with any more success than their white predecessors.

In describing his second term in office, former Mayor Carl Stokes points out some of the problems which beset the black political executive:

Politics requires that a man compromise with existing conditions. But the problems in Cleveland and the other large cities of this country can no longer afford the luxury of compromise with those who want to keep the system running as it is. For four years in Cleveland, those who did want to keep the system running in the same old way knew they had to fight me and beat me. Civic leaders, especially newspaper editors, were constantly wringing their hands and prattling about the evils of confrontation politics and the need to avoid conflict. Problems, they said, cannot be solved in an atmosphere of conflict. Problems come from conflict. Our problems were born of the age-old conflict between the haves and the have-nots. They were exacerbated by a city government that was resistant to change and people who refused to respond to overall city problems.[26]

The Stokes approach was direct and destined to failure, and he knew it. "I took the power of the mayor's office and a solid constituency," he said, "and went head on against those who didn't want the poor in their neighborhood, didn't want the blacks in their neighborhood, were determined to exclude blacks from jobs and new economic opportunities. But," Stokes continued,

I knew I couldn't survive. And when I talk about going against those in power, I don't mean just the newspapers and the business and industrial concerns; I also mean those who are in possession, the middle-class people who have the jobs, who live in the neighborhoods with the nice decent housing and the recreational areas that are well maintained. I am talking about the people who have and who are not willing to give up what they have. You have to make them give it up. You are asking for a struggle. Out of that struggle the cutting edge has to be blunted . . . even sacrificed. That's what happened to Carl Stokes in Cleveland. I accept it. I'll go on to the next thing and let someone who is constituted differently from me come back one day and begin the process again. Someone will come.[27]

Whether that "someone will come" remains an open question. Nonetheless, we suggest that the problems which Carl Stokes, a black mayor, faced are similar to the problems that face black elected officials generally.

A Concluding Note

The Bicentennial celebration might prove a festive occasion for some but it might not prove so for others, especially blacks and other minorities. The practices of American society simply have not lived up to

---

[26] Carl Stokes, *Promises of Power* (New York: Simon and Schuster, 1974), p. 245.
[27] Ibid., p. 252.

the lofty ideals it espouses and transmits from generation to generation. What black people seek is a better fit between these ideals and the realities of their daily life. Mostly, however, the structure and patterns of American politics seriously impede the attainment of this objective. This does indeed raise the question as "to what extent does an oppressed minority have any control over its fortunes through democratic politics."[28] But so far at least, the black experience in American democratic politics does not allow us to view this question with much optimism.

Topics for Discussion

1. Do you feel that problems facing blacks can be solved through "politics" as the American political system presently operates? Would you suggest alterations or changes in the system that might enhance prospects for overcoming such problems? Do you think these alterations or changes can be brought about? Why or why not?

2. Whatever else may be said, protests (marches, demonstrations, and violence) called attention to and spurred action on problems facing black Americans. In due time, however, blacks turned from "protests" to "politics." Do you think this was a wise move? Why or why not? Under what circumstances, if any, should blacks turn from "politics" to "protests"? What would be the costs and benefits of such strategy? Are there alternative strategies? What are they? How effective might these strategies prove in terms of overcoming problems that face blacks and other minorities?

3. There are several competing views that attempt to explain and, in some instances, justify the status of blacks in the American political system. Let us consider two such competing views. One view holds that blacks are responsible for their low status because they fail or neglect to use fully the political resources available to them. Another view holds that the political system operates to disadvantage blacks through such institutional structures as separation of powers, federalism, political parties, and majority rule. These institutional structures and the basic political ethos together form public policy to impede black progress. Discuss the pros and cons of both views. Be certain to cite examples to support your position.

---

[28] William R. Keech, Review of *Black Political Parties: An Historical and Political Analysis* by Hanes Walton, Jr., in *American Political Science Review*, Vol. 68, p. 1342 (September, 1974).

4. Is black control of central cities a myth or reality? What factors did or should you consider in answering this question? How might movements promoting metropolitanwide government affect black political power in central cities? In short, what are the costs and benefits of metropolitan government for black politics and minority politics generally?

5. Have the civil rights movement and the resulting legislative and administrative policies and programs improved the everyday lot of the masses of black people? In short, who benefited from this activity? Why? Discuss thoroughly.

Suggested Readings

Aberbach, Joel and Jack L. Walter. *Race in the City*. Boston: Little, Brown, 1973.

Views contemporary urban problems on basis of case study of changing black and white attitudes toward government and politics in Detroit following the 1967 riots through 1971.

Bullock, Charles S. III, and Harrell R. Rodgers, Jr., eds. *Black Political Attitudes: Implications for Political Support*. Chicago: Markham, 1972.

A collection of essays focusing on black political attitudes toward various facets of the governmental system.

Bullock, Charles S. III, and Harrell R. Rodgers, Jr., eds. *Law and Social Change: Civil Rights Laws and Their Consequences*. New York: McGraw-Hill, 1972.

Discusses the effect of law in bringing about social change in various areas, e.g., education, voting, employment.

Burns, James M. *Uncommon Sense*. New York: Harper & Row, 1972.

A critique of the American political system with proposals to "transform" not "patch up" the system.

French, Robert M. and Lee Sloan. "Black Rule in the Urban South." *Trans-Action*, Vol. 9 (1971), p. 29.

Concentrates on the political implications of metropolitan government for blacks.

Friesma, Paul. "Black Control of Central Cities: The Hollow Prize." *Journal of the American Institute of Planners* (March, 1969), pp. 75-79.

A pessimistic interpretation of importance of black control of central cities.

Harris, Louis. *The Anguish of Change.* New York: Norton, 1973.
An interpretation of American public opinion from 1960 through 1973 over a range of topics, including a succinct discussion (ch. 13) of attitudes of blacks and whites toward each other.

Holden, Matthew, Jr. *The White Man's Burden.* New York: Chandler Publishing Company, 1973.
An analysis of racial politics focusing on proposals for achieving social peace in the United States.

Jones, Mack. "Black Officeholders in Local Government of the South: An Overview." (Paper prepared for delivery at the Annual Meeting of the American Political Science Association, 1970.)

Jones, Nolan. "Differential Legal Treatment Between Whites and Blacks as a Function of Social Context." Unpublished Ph.D. Thesis, Washington University, 1975.
Compares and contrasts legal treatment of blacks and whites in three St. Louis area communities as a function of social context.

Lowi, Theodore. *The End of Liberalism.* New York: Norton, 1969.
A critical assessment of the modern liberal state with an argument for an alternative ideology — "juridical democracy."

Morris, Lorenzo. "The Impact of Culture on Political Participation." Dissertation, University of Chicago, 1974.

Patterson, Ernest. *Black City Politics.* New York: Dodd, Mead & Co., 1974.
A detailed study of the role of blacks in St. Louis politics leads the author to a searing commentary on the position of blacks in big city politics in relation to how blacks perceive the legitimacy of the political system.

Ransford, Edward H. "Isolation, Powerlessness and Violence: A Study of Attitudes and Participation in Watts Riot." *American Journal of Sociology,* 73, (1968).

Stokes, Carl. *Promises of Power.* New York: Simon and Schuster, 1974.
An autobiography that illuminates the political impact of a black mayor.

THE CONSTITUTION OF THE

UNITED STATES OF AMERICA

We the people of the United States, in order to form a more perfect Union, establish Justice, insure domestic Tranquility, provide for the common defence, promote the general Welfare, and secure the Blessing of Liberty to ourselves and our Posterity, do ordain and establish this Constitution for the United States of America.

Article I

Section 1. All legislative Powers herein granted shall be vested in a Congress of the United States, which shall consist of a Senate and House of Representatives.

Section 2. The House of Representatives shall be composed of Members chosen every second Year by the People of the several States, and the Electors in each State shall have the Qualifications requisite for Electors of the most numerous Branch of the State Legislature.

No Person shall be a Representative who shall not have attained to the Age of twenty-five Years, and been seven Years a Citizen of the United States, and who shall not, when elected, be an Inhabitant of that State in which he shall be chosen.

Representatives and direct Taxes shall be apportioned among the several States which may be included within this Union, according to their respective Numbers, which shall be determined by adding to the whole Number of free Persons, including those bound to Service for a Term of Years, and excluding Indians not taxed, three fifths of all other persons. The actual Enumeration shall be made within three Years after the first Meeting of the Congress of the United States, and within every subsequent Term of ten Years, in such Manner as they shall by Law direct. The Number of Representatives shall not exceed one for every thirty Thousand, but each State shall have at Least one Representative; and until such enumeration shall be made, the State of New Hampshire shall be entitled to chuse three, Massachusetts eight, Rhode Island and Providence Plantations one, Connecticut five, New York six, New Jersey four, Pennsylvania eight, Delaware one, Maryland six, Virginia ten, North Carolina five, South Carolina five, and Georgia three.

When vacancies happen in the Representation from any State, the Executive Authority thereof shall issue Writs of Election to fill such Vacancies.

355

The House of Representatives shall chuse their Speaker and other Officers; and shall have the sole Power of Impeachment.

Section 3. The Senate of the United States shall be composed of two Senators from each State, chosen by the Legislature thereof, for six Years; and each Senator shall have one Vote.

Immediately after they shall be assembled in Consequence of the first Election, they shall be divided as equally as may be into three Classes. The Seats of the Senators of the first Class shall be vacated at the Expiration of the Second Year, of the second Class at the Expiration of the fourth Year, and of the third Class at the Expiration of the sixth Year, so that one third may be chosen every second Year; and if Vacancies happen by Resignation, or otherwise, during the Recess of the Legislature of any State, the Executive therefore may make temporary Appointments until the next Meeting of the Legislature, which shall then fill such Vacancies.

No Person shall be a Senator who shall not have attained to the Age of thirty Years, and been nine Years a Citizen of the United States, and who shall not, when elected, be an Inhabitant of that State for which he shall be chosen.

The Vice President of the United States shall be President of the Senate, but shall have no Vote, unless they be equally divided.

The Senate shall chuse their other Officers, and also a President pro tempore, in the Absence of the Vice President, or when he shall exercise the Office of President of the United States.

The Senate shall have the sole Power to try all Impeachments. When sitting for that Purpose, they shall be on Oath or affirmation. When the President of the United States is tried, the Chief Justice shall preside: And no Person shall be convicted without the Concurrence of two thirds of the Members present.

Judgment in Cases of Impeachment shall not extend further than to removal from Office, and disqualification to hold and enjoy any Office of honor, Trust, or Profit under the United States: but the Party convicted shall nevertheless be liable and subject to Indictment, Trial, Judgment, and Punishment, according to Law.

Section 4. The Times, Places and Manner of holding Elections for Senators and Representatives, shall be prescribed in each State by the Legislature thereof; but the Congress may at any time by Law make or alter such Regulations, except as to the Places of chusing Senators.

The Congress shall assemble at least once in every Year, and such Meeting shall be on the first Monday in December, unless they shall by Law appoint a different Day.

Section 5. Each House shall be the Judge of the Elections, Returns and Qualifications of its own Members, and a Majority of each shall constitute a Quorum to do Business; but a smaller Number may adjourn from day to day, and may be authorized to compel the Attendance of absent Members, in such Manner, and under such Penalties as each House may provide.

Each House may determine the Rules of its Proceedings, punish its Members for disorderly Behavior, and, with the Concurrence of two thirds, expel a Member.

Each House shall keep a Journal of its Proceedings and from time to time publish the same, excepting such Parts as may in their Judgment require Secrecy; and the Yeas and Nays of the Members of either House on any question shall, at the Desire of one fifth of those Present, be entered on the Journal.

Neither House, during the Session of Congress, shall without the Consent of the other, adjourn for more than three days, nor to any other Place than that in which the two Houses shall be sitting.

Section 6. The Senators and Representatives shall receive a Compensation for their Services, to be ascertained by Law, and paid out of the Treasury of the United States. They shall in all Cases, except Treason, Felony, and Breach of the peace, be privileged from Arrest during their Attendance at the Session of their respective Houses, and in going to and returning from the same; and for any Speech or Debate in either House, they shall not be questioned in any other Place.

No Senator or Represenative shall, during the Time for which he was elected, be appointed to any civil Office under the Authority of the United States, which shall have been created, or the Emoluments whereof shall have been encreased during such time; and no Person holding any Office under the United States, shall be a Member of either House during his Continuance in Office.

Section 7. All Bills for raising Revenue shall originate in the House of Representatives; but the Senate may propose or concur with Amendments as on other Bills.

Every Bill which shall have passed the House of Representatives and the Senate, shall, before it become a Law, be presented to the President of the United States; If he approve he shall sign it, but if not he shall return it, with his Objections to that House in which it shall have originated, who shall enter the Objections at large on their Journal, and proceed to reconsider it. If after such Reconsideration two thirds of that House shall agree to pass the Bill it shall be sent, together with the Objections, to the other House, by which it shall likewise be reconsidered, and if approved by two thirds of that House, it shall become a Law. But in all such Cases the Votes of both Houses shall be determined by Yeas and Nays, and the Names of the Persons voting for and against the Bill shall be entered on the Journal of each House respectively. If any Bill shall not be returned by the President within ten Days (Sundays excepted) after it shall have been presented to him, the Same shall be a Law, in like Manner as if he had signed it, unless the Congress by their Adjournment prevent its Return, in which Case it shall not be a Law.

Every Order, Resolution, or Vote to which the Concurrence of the Senate and House of Representatives may be necessary (except on a question of Adjournment) shall be presented to the President of the United States: and before the Same shall take Effect, shall be approved by him, or being disapproved by him, shall be repassed by two thirds of the Senate and House of Representatives, according to the Rules and Limitations prescribed in the Case of a Bill.

Section 8. The Congress shall have Power To lay and collect Taxes, Duties, Imposts and Excises, to pay the Debts and provide for the common Defence and general Welfare of the United States; but all Duties, Imposts and Excises shall be uniform throughout the United States;

To borrow money on the credit of the United States;

To regulate Commerce with foreign Nations, and among the several States, and with the Indian Tribes;

To establish an uniform Rule of Naturalization, and uniform Laws on the subject of Bankruptcies throughout the United States;

To coin Money, regulate the Value thereof, and of foreign Coin, and fix the Standard of Weights and Measures;

To provide for the Punishment of counterfeiting the Securities and current Coin of the United States;

To Establish Post Offices and Post Roads;

To promote the Progress of Science and useful Arts, by securing for limited Times to Authors and Inventors the exclusive Right to their respective Writings and Discoveries;

To constitute Tribunals inferior to the supreme Court;

To define and punish Piracies and Felonies committed on the high Seas, and Offenses against the Law of Nations:

To declare War, grant Letters of Marque and Reprisal, and make Rules concerning Captures on Land and Water;

To raise and support Armies, but no Appropriation of Money to that Use shall be for a longer Term than two Years;

To provide and maintain a Navy;

To make Rules for the Government and Regulation of the land and naval Forces;

To provide for calling forth the Militia to execute the Laws of the Union, suppress Insurrections and repel Invasions;

To provide for organizing, arming, and disciplining, the Militia, and for governing such Part of them as may be employed in the Service of the United States, reserving to the States respectively, the Appointment of the Officers, and the Authority of training the Militia according to the discipline prescribed by Congress;

To exercise exclusive Legislation in all Cases whatsoever, over such District (not exceeding ten Miles square) as may, by Cession of particular States, and the Acceptance of Congress, become the Seat of the Government of the United States, and to exercise like Authority over all Places purchased by the Consent of the Legislature of the State in which the Same shall be, for the Erection of Forts, Magazines, Arsenals, dock-Yards, and other needful Buildings; — And

To make all Laws which shall be necessary and proper for carrying into Execution the foregoing Powers, and all other Powers vested by this Constitution in the Government of the United States, or in any Department or Officer thereof.

Section 9. The Migration or Importation of Such Persons as any of the States now existing shall think proper to admit, shall not be prohibited by the Congress prior to the Year one thousand eight hundred and eight, but a Tax or duty may be imposed on such Importation, not exceeding ten dollars for each Person.

The privilege of the Writ of Habeas Corpus shall not be suspended, unless when in Cases of Rebellion or Invasion the public Safety may require it.

No Bill of Attainder or ex post facto Law shall be passed.

No Capitation, or other direct, Tax shall be laid, unless in Proportion to the Census or Enumeration herein before directed to be taken.

No Tax or Duty shall be laid on Articles exported from any State.

No Preference shall be given by any Regulation of Commerce or Revenue to the Ports of one State over those of another: nor shall Vessels bound to, or from, one State be obliged to enter, clear, or pay Duties in another.

No money shall be drawn from the Treasury, but in Consequence of Appropriations made by Law; and a regular Statement and Account of the Receipts and Expenditures of all public Money shall be published from time to time.

No Title of Nobility shall be granted by the United States: And no Person holding any Office of Profit or Trust under them, shall, without the Consent of the Congress, accept of any present, Emolument, Office, or Title, of any kind whatever, from any King, Prince, or foreign State.

Section 10. No State shall enter into any Treaty, Alliance, or Confederation; grant Letters of Marque and Reprisal; coin Money; emit Bills of Credit; make any Thing but gold and silver Coin a Tender in Payment of Debts; pass any Bill of Attainder, ex post facto Law, or Law impairing the Obligation of Contracts, or grant any Title of Nobility.

No State shall, without the Consent of the Congress, lay any Imposts or Duties on Imports or Exports, except what may be absolutely necessary for executing its inspection Laws; and the net Produce of all Duties and Imposts, laid by any State on Imports or Exports, shall be for the Use of the Treasury of the United States; and all such Laws shall be subject to the Revision and Controul of the Congress.

No State shall, without the Consent of Congress, lay any Duty of Tonnage, keep Troops, or Ships of War in time of Peace, enter into any Agreement or Compact with another State, or with a foreign Power, or engage in War, unless actually invaded, or in such imminent Danger as will not admit of delay.

Article II

Section 1. The executive Power shall be vested in a President of the United States of America. He shall hold his Office during the Term of four Years, and, together with the Vice President, chosen for the same Term, be elected, as follows:

Each State shall appoint, in such Manner as the Legislature thereof may direct, a Number of Electors, equal to the whole Number of Senators and Representatives to which the State may be entitled in the Congress; but no Senator or Representative, or Person holding an Office of Trust or Profit under the United States, shall be appointed an Elector.

The Electors shall meet in their respective States, and vote by Ballot for two Persons, of whom one at least shall not be an Inhabitant of the same State with themselves. And they shall make a List of all the Persons voted for, and of the Number of Votes for each; which List they shall sign and certify, and transmit sealed to the Seat of the Government of the United States, directed to the President of the Senate. The President of the Senate shall, in the Presence of the Senate and House of Representatives, open all the Certificates, and the Votes shall then be counted. The Person having the greatest Number of Votes shall be the President, if such Number be a Majority of the whole Number of Electors appointed; and if there be more than one who have such Majority, and have an equal Number of Votes, then the House of Representatives shall immediately chuse by Ballot one of them for President; and if no Person have a Majority, then from the five highest on the List the said House shall in like Manner chuse the President. But in chusing the President, the Votes shall be taken by States the Representation from each State having one Vote; A quorum for this Purpose shall consist of a Member or Members from two thirds of the States, and a Majority of all the States shall be necessary to a Choice. In every Case, after the Choice of the President, the Person having the greater Number of Votes of the Electors shall be the Vice President. But if there should remain two or more who have equal Votes, the Senate shall chuse from them by Ballot the Vice President.

The Congress may determine the Time of chusing the Electors, and the Day on which they shall give their Votes; which Day shall be the same throughout the United States.

No person except a natural born Citizen, or a Citizen of the United States, at the time of the Adoption of this Constitution, shall be eligible to the Office of President; neither shall any Person be eligible to that Office who shall not have attained to the Age of thirty-five Years, and been fourteen Years a Resident within the United States.

In case of the removal of the President from Office, or of his Death, Resignation or Inability to discharge the Powers and Duties of the said Office, the Same shall devolve on the Vice President, and the Congress may by Law provide for the Case of Removal, Death, Resignation or Inability, both of the President and Vice President, declaring what Officer shall then act as President, and such Officer shall act accordingly, until the Disability be removed, or a President shall be elected.

The President shall, at stated Times, receive for his Services, a Compensation, which shall neither be increased nor diminished during the Period for which he shall have been elected, and he shall not receive within that Period any other Emolument from the United States, or any of them.

Before he enter on the Execution of his Office, he shall take the following Oath or Affirmation: "I do solemnly swear (or affirm) that I will faithfully execute the Office of President of the United States, and will to the best of my Ability, preserve, protect and defend the Constitution of the United States."

Section 2. The President shall be Commander in Chief of the Army and Navy of the United States, and of the militia of the several States, when called into the actual Service of the United States; he may require the Opinion, in writing, of the principal Officer in each of the Executive Departments, upon any Subject relating to the Duties of their respective Offices, and he shall have Power to grant Reprieves and Pardons for Offenses against the United States, except in Cases of Impeachment.

He shall have Power, by and with the Advice and Consent of the Senate to make Treaties, provided two thirds of the Senators present concur; and he shall nominate, and by and with the Advice and Consent of the Senate, shall appoint Ambassadors, other public Ministers and Consuls, Judges of the supreme Court, and all other Officers of the United States, whose Appointments are not herein otherwise provided for, and which shall be established by Law; but the Congress may by Law vest the Appointment of such inferior Officers, as they think proper, in the President alone, in the Courts of Law, or in the Heads of Departments.

The President shall have Power to fill up all Vacancies that may happen during the Recess of the Senate, by granting Commissions which shall expire at the End of their next Session.

Section 3. He shall from time to time give to the Congress Information of the State of the Union, and recommend to their Consideration such Measures as he shall judge necessary and expedient; he may, on extraordinary Occasions, convene both Houses, or either of them, and in Case of Disagreement between them, with Respect to the Time of Adjournment, he may adjourn them to such Time as he shall think proper; he shall receive Ambassadors and other public Ministers; he shall take Care that the Laws be faithfully executed, and shall Commission all the Officers of the United States.

Section 4. The President, Vice President and all civil Officers of the United States, shall be removed from Office on Impeachment for, and Conviction of, Treason, Bribery, or other high Crimes and Misdemeanors.

Article III

Section 1. The judicial Power of the United States, shall be vested in one supreme Court, and in such inferior Courts as the Congress may from time to time ordain and establish. The Judges, both of the supreme and inferior Courts, shall hold their Offices during good Behaviour, and shall, at stated Times, receive for their Services a Compensation, which shall not be diminished during their Continuance in Office.

Section 2. The judicial Power shall extend to all Cases, in Law and Equity, arising under this Constitution, the Laws of the United States, and Treaties made, or which shall be made, under their Authority; — to all Cases affecting Ambassadors, other public Ministers and Consuls; — to all Cases of admiralty and maritime Jurisdiction; — to Controversies to which the United States shall be a Party; — to Controversies between two or more States; — between a State and Citizens of another State; — between Citizens of different States; — between Citizens of the same State claiming Lands under the Grants of different States, and between a State, or the Citizens thereof, and foreign States, Citizens or Subjects.

In all Cases affecting Ambassadors, other public Ministers and Consuls, and those in which a State shall be a Party, the supreme Court shall have original Jurisdiction. In all the other Cases before mentioned, the supreme Court shall have appellate Jurisdiction, both as to Law and Fact, with such Exceptions, and under such Regulations as the Congress shall make.

The trial of all Crimes, except in Cases of Impeachment, shall be by Jury; and such Trial shall be held in the State where the said Crimes shall have been committed; but when not committed within any State, the Trial shall be at such Place or Places as the Congress may by Law have directed.

Section 3. Treason against the United States, shall consist only in levying War against them, or, in adhering to their Enemies, giving them Aid and Comfort. No Person shall be convicted of Treason unless on the Testimony of two Witnesses to the same overt Act, or on Confession in open Court.

The Congress shall have Power to declare the Punishment of Treason, but no Attainder of Treason shall work Corruption of Blood, or Forfeiture except during the Life of the Person attained.

Article IV

Section 1. Full Faith and Credit shall be given in each State to the public Acts, Records, and judicial Proceedings of every other State. And the Congress may by general Laws prescribe the Manner in which such Acts, Records and Proceedings shall be proved, and the Effect thereof.

Section 2. The Citizens of each State shall be entitled to all Privileges and Immunities of Citizens in the several States.

A Person charged in any State with Treason, Felony, or other Crime, who shall flee from Justice, and be found in another State, shall on demand of the executive Authority of the State from which he fled, be delivered up, to be removed to the State having Jurisdiction of the Crime.

No Person held to Service or Labour in one State, under the Laws thereof, escaping into another, shall, in Consequence of any Law or Regulation therein, be discharged from such Service or Labour, but shall be delivered up on Claim of the Party to whom such Service or Labour may be due.

Section 3. [1] New States may be admitted by Congress into this Union; but no new State shall be formed or erected within the Jurisdiction of any other State; nor any State be formed by the Junction of two or more States, or Parts of States, without the Consent of the Legislatures of the States concerned as well as of the Congress.

The Congress shall have Power to dispose of and make all needful Rules and Regulations respecting the Territory or other Property belonging to the United States; and nothing in this Constitution shall be so construed as to Prejudice any Claims of the United States, or of any particular State.

Section 4. The United States shall guarantee to every State in this Union a Republican Form of Government, and shall protect each of them against Invasion; and on Application of the Legislature, or of the Executive (when the Legislature cannot be convened) against domestic Violence.

Article V

The Congress, whenever two thirds of both Houses shall deem it necessary, shall propose Amendments to this Constitution, or, on the Application of the Legislatures of two thirds of the several States, shall call a Convention for proposed Amendments, which, in either Case, shall be valid to all Intents and Purposes, as part of this Constitution, when ratified by the Legislatures of three fourths of the several States, or by Conventions in three fourths thereof, as the one or the other Mode of Ratification may be proposed by the Congress; Provided that no Amendment which may be made prior to the Year One thousand eight hundred and eight shall in any Manner affect the first and fourth Clauses in the Ninth Section of the first Article; and that no State, without its Consent, shall be deprived of its equal Suffrage in the Senate.

Article VI

All Debts contracted and Engagements entered into, before the Adoption of this Constitution shall be as valid against the United States under this Constitution, as under the Confederation.

This Constitution, and the Laws of the United States which shall be made in Pursuance thereof; and all Treaties made, or which shall be made, under the Authority of the United States, shall be the supreme Law of the Land; and the Judges in every State shall be bound thereby, any Thing in the Constitution or Laws of any State to the Contrary notwithstanding.

The Senators and Representatives before mentioned, and the Members of the several State Legislatures, and all executive and judicial Officers, both of the United States and of the several States, shall be bound by Oath or Affirmation, to support this Constitution; but no religious Test shall ever be required as a Qualification to any Office or public Trust under the United States.

Article VII

The Ratification of the Conventions of nine States shall be sufficient for the Establishment of this Constitution between the States so ratifying the Same.

ARTICLES IN ADDITION TO, AND AMENDMENT OF, THE CONSTITUTION OF THE UNITED STATES OF AMERICA, PROPOSED BY CONGRESS, AND RATIFIED BY THE LEGISLATURES OF SEVERAL STATES PURSUANT TO THE FIFTH ARTICLE OF THE ORIGINAL CONSTITUTION.

Amendment I [1791]

Congress shall make no law respecting an establishment of religion, or prohibiting the free exercise thereof; or abridging the freedom of speech, or of the press; or the right of the people peaceably to assemble, and to petition the Government for a redress of grievances.

Amendment II [1791]

A well regulated Militia, being necessary to the security of a free State, the right of the people to keep and bear Arms, shall not be infringed.

Amendment III [1791]

No Soldier shall, in time of peace be quartered in any house, without the consent of the Owner, nor in time of war, but in a manner to be prescribed by law.

Amendment IV [1791]

The right of the people to be secure in their persons, houses, papers, and effects, against unreasonable searches and seizures, shall not be violated, and no Warrants shall issue, but upon probable cause, supported by Oath or affirmation, and particularly describing the place to be searched, and the persons or things to be seized.

Amendment V [1791]

No person shall be held to answer for a capital, or otherwise infamous crime, unless on a presentment or indictment of a Grand Jury, except in cases arising in the land or naval forces, or in the Militia, when in actual service in time of War or public danger; nor shall any person be subject for the same offence to be twice put in jeopardy of life or limb; nor shall be compelled in any criminal case to be a witness against himself, nor be deprived of life, liberty, or property, without due process of law; nor shall private property be taken for public use, without just compensation.

Amendment VI [1791]

In all criminal prosecutions, the accused shall enjoy the right to a speedy and public trial, by an impartial jury of the State and district wherein the crime shall have been committed, which district shall have been previously ascertained by law, and to be informed of the nature and cause of the accusation; to be confronted with the witnesses against him; to have compulsory process for obtaining witnesses in his favor, and to have the Assistance of Counsel for his defence.

Amendment VII [1791]

In Suits at common law, where the value in controversy shall exceed twenty dollars, the right of trial by jury shall be preserved, and no fact tried by jury, shall be otherwise re-examined in any Court of the United States, than according to the rules of the common law.

Amendment VIII [1791]

Excessive bail shall not be required, nor excessive fines imposed, nor cruel and unusual punishments inflicted.

Amendment IX [1791]

The enumeration in the Constitution, of certain rights, shall not be construed to deny or disparage others retained by the people.

Amendment X [1791]

The powers not delegated to the United States by the Constitution, nor prohibited by it to the States, are reserved to the States respectively, or to the people.

Amendment XI [1798]

The Judicial power of the United States shall not be construed to extend to any suit in law or equity, commenced or prosecuted against one of the United States by Citizens of another State, or by Citizens or Subjects of any Foreign State.

Amendment XII [1804]

The Electors shall meet in their respective states and vote by ballot for President and Vice-President, one of whom, at least, shall not be an inhabitant of the same state with themselves; they shall name in their ballots the person voted for as President, and in distinct ballots the person voted for as Vice-President, and they shall make distinct lists of all persons voted for as President, and all persons voted for as Vice-President, and of the number of votes for each, which lists they shall sign and certify, and transmit sealed to the seat of the government of the United States, directed to the President of the Senate; — The President of the Senate shall, in the presence of the Senate and House of Representatives, open all the certificates and the votes shall then be counted; — The person having the greatest number of votes for President, shall be the President, if such number be a majority of the whole number of Electors appointed; and if no person have such majority, then from the persons having the highest numbers not exceeding three on the list of those voted for as President, the House of Representatives shall choose immediately, by ballot, the President. But in choosing the President, the votes shall be taken by states, the representation from each state having one vote; a quorum for this purpose shall consist of a member or members from two-thirds of the states, and a majority of all the states shall be necessary to a choice. And if the House of Representatives shall not choose a President whenever the right of choice shall devolve upon them before the fourth day of March next following, then the Vice-President shall act as President, as in the case of the death or other constitutional disability of the President. — The person having the greatest number of votes as Vice-President, shall be the Vice-President, if such number be a majority of the whole number of Electors appointed, and if no person have a majority, then from the two highest numbers on the list, the Senate shall choose the Vice-President; a quorum for the purpose shall consist of two-thirds of the whole number of Senators, and a majority of the whole number shall be necessary to a choice. But no person constitutionally ineligible to the office of President shall be eligible to that of Vice-President of the United States.

Amendment XIII [1865]

Section 1. Neither slavery nor involuntary servitude, except as a punishment for crime whereof the party shall have been duly convicted, shall exist within the United States, or any place subject to their jurisdiction.

Section 2. Congress shall have power to enforce this article by appropriate legislation.

Amendment XIV [1868]

Section 1. All persons born or naturalized in the United States, and subject to the jurisdiction thereof, are citizens of the United States and of the State wherein they reside. No State shall make or enforce any law which shall abridge the privileges or immunities of citizens of the United States; nor shall any State deprive any person of life, liberty, or property, without due process of law; nor deny to any person within its jurisdiction the equal protection of the laws.

Section 2. Representatives shall be apportioned among the several States according to their respective numbers, counting the whole number of persons in each State, excluding Indians not taxed. But when the right to vote at any election for the choice of electors for President and Vice President of the United States, Representatives in Congress, the Executive and Judicial offices of a State, or the members of the Legislature thereof, is denied to any of the male inhabitants of such State, being twenty-one years of age, and citizens of the United

States, or in any way abridged, except for participation in rebellion, or other crime, the basis of representation therein shall be reduced in the proportion which the number of such male citizens shall bear to the whole number of male citizens twenty-one years of age in such State.

Section 3. No person shall be a Senator or Representative in Congress, or elector of President and Vice President, or hold any office, civil or military, under the United States, or under any State, who having previously taken an oath, as a member of Congress, or as an officer of the United States, or as a member of any State legislature, or as an executive or judicial officer of any State, to support the Constitution of the United States, shall have engaged in insurrection or rebellion against the same, or given aid or comfort to the enemies thereof. But Congress may by vote of two-thirds of each House, remove such disability.

Section 4. The validity of the public debt of the United States, authorized by law, including debts incurred for payment of pensions and bounties for services in suppressing insurrection or rebellion, shall not be questioned. But neither the United States nor any State shall assume to pay any debt or obligation incurred in aid of insurrection or rebellion against the United States, or any claim for the loss or emancipation of any slave; but all such debts, obligations and claims shall be held illegal and void.

Section 5. The Congress shall have power to enforce, by appropriate legislation, the provisions of this article.

Amendment XV [1870]

Section 1. The right of citizens of the United States to vote shall not be denied or abridged by the United States or by any State on account of race, color, or previous condition of servitude.

Section 2. The Congress shall have power to enforce this article by appropriate legislation.

Amendment XVI [1913]

The Congress shall have power to lay and collect taxes on incomes, from whatever source derived, without apportionment among the several States, and without regard to any census or enumeration.

Amendment XVII [1913]

The Senate of the United States shall be composed of two Senators from each State, elected by the people thereof, for six years; and each Senator shall have one vote. The electors in each State shall have the qualifications requisite for electors of the most numerous branch of the State legislatures.

When vacancies happen in the representation of any State in the Senate, the executive authority of such State shall issue writs of election to fill such vacancies: *Provided,* That the legislature of any State may empower the executive thereof to make temporary appointments until the people fill the vacancies by election as the legislature may direct.

This amendment shall not be so construed as to affect the election or term of any Senator chosen before it becomes valid as part of the Constitution.

Amendment XVIII [1919]

Section 1. After one year from the ratification of this article the manufacture, sale, or transportation of intoxicating liquors within, the importation thereof into, or the exportation thereof from the United States and all territory subject to the jurisdiction thereof for beverage purposes is hereby prohibited.

Section 2. The Congress and the several States shall have concurrent power to enforce this article by appropriate legislation.

Section 3. This article shall be inoperative unless it shall have been ratified as an amendment to the Constitution by the legislatures of the several States, as provided in the Constitution, within seven years from the date of the submission hereof to the States by the Congress.

Amendment XIX [1920]

The right of citizens of the United States to vote shall not be denied or abridged by the United States or by any State on account of sex.

Congress shall have power to enforce this article by appropriate legislation.

Amendment XX [1933]

Section 1. The terms of the President and Vice President shall end at noon on the 20th day of January, and the terms of Senators and Representatives at noon on the 3d day of January, of the years in which such terms would have ended if this article had not been ratified; and the terms of their successors shall then begin.

Section 2. The Congress shall assemble at least once in every year, and such meeting shall begin at noon on the 3d day of January, unless they shall by law appoint a different day.

Section 3. If, at the time fixed for the beginning of the term of the President, the President elect shall have died, the Vice President elect shall become President. If the President shall not have been chosen before the time fixed for the beginning of his term, or if the President elect shall have failed to qualify, then the Vice President elect shall act as President until a President shall have qualified; and the Congress may by law provide for the case wherein neither a President elect nor a Vice President elect shall have qualified, declaring who shall then act as President, or the manner in which one who is to act shall be selected, and such person shall act accordingly until a President or Vice President shall have qualified.

Section 4. The Congress may by law provide for the case of the death of any of the persons from whom the House of Representatives may choose a President whenever the right of choice shall have devolved upon them, and for the case of the death of any of the persons from whom the Senate may choose a Vice President whenever the right of choice shall have devolved upon them.

Section 5. Sections 1 and 2 shall take effect on the 15th day of October following the ratification of this article.

Section 6. This article shall be inoperative unless it shall have been ratified as an amendment to the Constitution by the legislatures of three-fourths of the several States within seven years from the date of its submission.

Amendment XXI [1933]

Section 1. The eighteenth article of amendment to the Constitution of the United States is hereby repealed.

Section 2. The transportation or importation into any State, Territory, or possession of the United States for delivery or use therein of intoxicating liquors, in violation of the laws thereof, is hereby prohibited.

Section 3. This article shall be inoperative unless it shall have been ratified as an amendment to the Constitution by conventions in the several States, as provided in the Constitution, within seven years from the date of the submission hereof to the States by the Congress.

Amendment XXII [1951]

Section 1. No person shall be elected to the office of the President more than twice, and no person who has held the office of President, or acted as President, for more than two years of a term to which some other person was elected President shall be elected to the office of President more than once. But this Article shall not apply to any person holding the office of President when this Article was proposed by the Congress, and shall not prevent any person who may be holding the office of President, or acting as President, during the term within which this Article becomes operative from holding the office of President or acting as President during the remainder of such term.

Section 2. This article shall be inoperative unless it shall have been ratified as an amendment to the Constitution by the legislatures of three-fourths of the several States within seven years from the date of its submission to the States by the Congress.

Amendment XXIII [1961]

Section 1. The District constituting the seat of Government of the United States shall appoint in such manner as the Congress may direct:

A number of electors of President and Vice President equal to the whole number of Senators and Representatives in Congress to which the District would be entitled if it were a State, but in no event more than the least populous state; they shall be in addition to those appointed by the states, but they shall be considered, for the purposes of the election of President and Vice President, to be electors appointed by a state; and they shall meet in the District and perform such duties as provided by the twelfth article of amendment.

Section 2. The Congress shall have power to enforce this article by appropriate legislation.

Amendment XXIV [1964]

Section 1. The right of citizens of the United States to vote in any primary or other election for President or Vice President, for electors for President or Vice President, or for Senator or Representatives in Congress, shall not be denied or abridged by the United States or any State by reason of failure to pay any poll tax or other tax.

Section 2. The Congress shall have power to enforce this article by appropriate legislation.

Amendment XXV [1967]

Section 1. In case of the removal of the President from office or of his death or resignation, the Vice President shall become President.

Section 2. Whenever there is a vacancy in the office of the Vice President, the President shall nominate a Vice President who shall take office upon confirmation by a majority vote of both Houses of Congress.

Section 3. Whenever the President transmits to the President pro tempore of the Senate and the Speaker of the House of Representatives his written declaration that he is unable to discharge the powers and duties of his office, and until he transmits to them a written declaration to the contrary, such powers and duties shall be discharged by the Vice President as Acting President.

Section 4. Whenever the Vice President and a majority of either the principle officers of the executive departments or of such other body as Congress may by law provide, transmit to the President pro tempore of the Senate and the Speaker of the House of Representatives their written declaration that the President is unable to discharge the powers and duties of his office, the Vice President shall immediately assume the powers and duties of the office as Acting President.

Thereafter, when the President transmits to the President pro tempore of the Senate and the Speaker of the House of Representatives his written declaration that no inability exists, he shall resume the powers and duties of his office unless the Vice President and a majority of either the principal officers of the executive department or of such other body as Congress may by law provide, transmit within four days to the President pro tempore of the Senate and the Speaker of the House of Representatives their written declaration and the President is unable to discharge the powers and duties of his office. Thereupon Congress shall decide the issue, assembling within forty-eight hours for that purpose if not in session. If the Congress, within twenty-one days after receipt of the latter written declaration, or, if Congress is not in session, within twenty-one days after Congress is required to assemble, determines by two-thirds vote of both Houses that the President is unable to discharge the powers and duties of his office, the Vice President shall continue to discharge the same as Acting President; otherwise, the President shall resume the powers and duties of his office.

Amendment XXVI [1971]

Section 1. The right of citizens of the United States, who are eighteen years of age or older, to vote shall not be denied or abridged by the United States or any State on account of age.

Section 2. The Congress shall have the power to enforce this article by appropriate legislation.

GLOSSARY

Agenda: A list of items of business to be considered during a legislative session, committee meeting, and so on.

Ambivalence: The simultaneous belief in opposing or contradictory feelings and attitudes.

Amicus curiae briefs: A legal document presented to the Supreme Court by a party not directly involved in the controversy itself with the intention of providing the Court with additional information and/or influencing the Court's decision to favor a specified interest.

Appellate jurisdiction: The authority of a superior court to review rulings of a lower or inferior court.

"Benign neglect": A suggestion to allow racial tensions to ease, interpreted as a plot to abandon the civil rights movement. The phrase originated in a 1970 memo from Daniel P. Moynihan, Urban Affairs Advisor to President Nixon.

Bicameral: Having two houses or chambers.

Briefs: Formal outlines of lawyers' arguments for a case that set forth the main contentions with supporting statements or evidence.

Bureaucracy: A large, public organization, characterized by specialization of functions, adherence to fixed rules, and a hierarchical authority structure.

Caucus: A meeting of members of a legislative body who belong to the same party. Caucuses are held for various purposes such as the election or nomination of party leaders, the discussion of the legislative calendar, and the discussion of party policy.

Checks and balances: A system designed to regulate the mutual relations between the several constituent parts of the government, thereby preventing the abusive use of governmental power. The system, recognizing the principle of separation of powers, seeks to protect each branch of government against each other (and the people against all) by requiring the approval by one department of certain acts of another.

Civil litigation: The process by which the courts are used to settle private disputes. A civil case may also involve a dispute between a government and an individual. Civil cases arise in such areas as banking, contracts, torts, and workmen's compensation.

Civil War Amendments: The Thirteenth, Fourteenth, and Fifteenth Amendments to the federal Constitution, all of which were adopted within a few years after the Civil War. The Thirteenth Amendment provides for the abolition of slavery. The Fourteenth includes due process and equal protection clauses. The Fifteenth provides that no citizen of the U.S. shall have the right to vote denied or abridged on account of race, color, or previous condition of servitude, and it gives the Congress power to enforce the article by appropriate legislation.

Class: A group of individuals often differentiated by similar employment types, level of education, or income, who share common social or economic status.

Class system: The organization of society into vertical groupings based on social, economic, and/or political criteria.

Coalition: An alliance of differing political interests which seeks to form an effective majority on a matter of common concern.

Compliance: The extent to which a court decision is followed, obeyed, evaded, or ignored.

Constitutional courts: Courts that exercise judicial power pursuant to Article III. Federal constitutional courts of general jurisdiction include the Supreme Court, courts of appeal, and district courts. Congress has also created constitutional courts of special jurisdiction such as the court of claims. Judges on constitutional courts — or Article III courts as they are sometimes called — have life tenure pending "good behavior."

Criminal law: That part of the legal order which concerns itself with the treatment and punishment of crime. Criminal law establishes rules of conduct and provides for sanctions against those who violate those prescribed rules.

Decisive, fundamental change: Alteration of the status quo by an abrupt reversal of previous policy.

De facto/de jure: According to reality (de facto) as opposed to the way things are defined according to the law (de jure).

De jure segregation: Racial segregation that occurs with the sanction of the law.

Democracy: A philosophy of social and political organization, which gives to individuals a maximum of freedom and a maximum of responsibility. Generally, democracy requires institutions through which individuals are at least periodically given an opportunity to exercise their choice with regard to leaders, political policies, and programs.

Depression: One of the several phases of the business cycle marked by business stagnation, low prices, and mass unemployment.

"Educative" function: The process of modifying societal norms as a function of law, as for example, through judicial decisions.

Electioneering: The process of seeking to influence election outcomes by supporting candidates who are favorably disposed to one's goals or interests.

Electoral college: The name given to those persons elected from each state to cast the electoral votes of that state for the president and vice president. Each state has electoral votes equal to its total number of senators and representatives in Congress.

Elites: Groups whose control of political resources allows them to exert unusual influence in the political process.

En banc: A situation in which all members of a U.S. court of appeals in a particular circuit convene to hear and decide a case together.

Executive Office of the President: A group of agencies operating directly under the president including, for example, the White House Office, the National

Security Council, the Central Intelligence Agency, the Council of Economic Advisors.

Expressive interest groups: Those interest groups which are formed for the purpose of allowing the membership to express their opinions on particular issues, without necessarily effecting any change in governmental policy.

Federalism: A system of government in which power is divided between a central government and subunits.

Feedback: Assessment of policy outcomes that are channelled through the legislative process to modify policies or implementation techniques.

Filibuster: The practice in a legislative body of talking and debating a bill at great length in an effort to modify the bill significantly or prevent it from being acted upon finally.

Floor leaders: Party members who are designated as leaders on the floor of a legislative body. They try to maintain party solidarity, carry out the party program, and indicate who will speak on certain measures.

Gerrymandering: The designation of legislative district lines of demarcation with the intent of favoring certain partisan, factional, or racial interests.

Grandfather clause: A clause contained in several post-Civil War suffrage laws of southern states, which waived literacy and property requirements for persons who had voted or whose progenitors had voted prior to 1867, keeping the franchise for illiterate whites. The clause was declared unconstitutional by the Supreme Court in 1915.

Hearings: A formal session of a legislative committee in which witnesses present testimony on matters under consideration by the committee.

Hobbesian: Characteristic of Thomas Hobbes, a Middle Ages philosopher who believed that absolute government was necessary to control the inevitable selfishness of humans.

Ideology: A set of ideas about the social and political system, especially the form and role of government.

Impeachment: A formal accusation against a public official by a legislative body. The Constitution provides that the House of Representatives shall have the power by a majority vote to impeach the president, vice president and all civil officers of the United States on the grounds of treason, bribery, or other high crimes and misdemeanors.

Implementation: The actual carrying out of a policy through bureaucratic channels.

Incremental and marginal change: Gradual alteration of the status quo by a series of slight policy changes.

Incrementalism: A series of small and gradual shifts in policy and politics, usually of a remedial nature.

Individualism: A doctrine which holds that the chief end of society is the promotion of individual welfare, the recognition of the dignity of humans, and the moral obligation of the state to help individuals to achieve their highest capability. Individualism may also carry certain economic connotations, that is, laissez faire.

Industrialization: The process of producing goods and services utilizing inanimate sources of energy, machines, and specialized scientific skills.

Interest group: An organized group of people seeking to use its influence to promote a common interest. Political interest groups seek to influence parties, legislators, administrators, and courts.

Judicial activism: A concept of the judicial role, in which some judges aggressively pursue their jobs from the perspective that they are effecting public policy through their decisions.

Judicial review: The review by courts of legislative statutes and executive or administrative acts to determine whether or not such acts are consistent with a written constitution or are in excess of powers granted by it.

Judicial self-restraint: A concept of the judicial role in which some judges perceive their function to be that of interpreting and applying the "law," and reach their decisions without regard for the policy implications.

Legalism: A concept or value intrinsic in the American political system which asserts the need for formal rules, laws, statutes, ordinances, and constitutions in order to govern.

Legal system: The interdependent roles and functions of various participants in the legal process, such as judges, prosecutors, lawyers, police, and so on.

Legitimization: The process by which a political system engenders and maintains the belief that existing political institutions are the most beneficial and appropriate ones for the society.

Limited government: The pattern of government characterized by institutionalized restraints on the use of political power.

Lobbying: The practice of attempting to influence the form and content of policies emanating from the legislature, the office of the executive, or the judiciary.

Majority rule: A principle of democratic politics, resting on the weight of superior numbers, that the decisions arrived at by a majority of those voting should be binding upon all.

"Marked up" bill: Potential legislation whose enacted form is much different from its appearance when it began to move through congressional committees.

Material benefits: The tangible rewards given to group members in exchange for their continued support for the group leadership. These benefits may be very small — insurance, coffee breaks — or very substantial — better wages, special tax advantages.

Metropolitan government: The consolidation of a central city and some or all of the outlying suburbs, usually the county or counties, into a single governmental unit.

"Middle class": A fluid heterogeneous socioeconomic grouping, composed principally of business and professional people, bureaucrats, and some farmers and skilled workers who share common social characteristics and values.

Multimember district: An electoral district from which two or more legislators are chosen.

National ghetto system: A concept describing the heavy concentration of blacks in the central city areas with possible political control as a result of whites' emigrating to suburbia.

Nationalism: Loyalty and devotion to a nation, a sense of national consciousness.

National nominating convention: A meeting of members of a political party to nominate candidates for the presidency and vice presidency, adopt a party platform, and conduct the general business of the party. The national nominating conventions meet every four years, several months prior to the November presidential election.

Nonpartisan elections: Elections in which the ballots contain no political party designations.

Oral arguments: Oral presentation by the lawyers of a case before the Supreme Court after briefs and other pertinent materials have been filed with the justices. The maximum time allowed for such arguments is generally one hour for each party during which justices may ask questions or request additional information pertaining to the case.

Original jurisdiction: The authority of a court to hear a case for the first time.

Overlapping membership: A group theory concept referring to the fact that people may belong to several or many different groups with different interests at the same time.

Patronage system: The appointment to government jobs on a basis other than merit.

Political cynicism: The attitude of being distrustful of human nature and motives in politics.

Political machine: A political organization which is relatively efficient and has a successful record of winning public office for its candidates. The distinguishing characteristic of a machine is its high degree of organization and effectiveness.

Political socialization: The process by which individuals learn appropriate behavioral norms and the values of the political system.

Political symbol: An object, word, or action, usually stressing participation, responsiveness of government, danger, complexity, and so forth, which repeatedly produces a response on the part of political spectators.

Political system: The concept referring to all political activities (interest groups, voters, courts, legislatures, and so on) within a society. The political system reflects a framework of interdependence of activities and a definite boundary separating the public sector from other sectors.

Poll tax: A tax levied in some of the southern states, or a charge imposed on everyone who voted in an election, for the unofficial purpose of discouraging poorer citizens, especially blacks, from voting. The poll tax was outlawed by the Twenty-fourth amendment.

Popular sovereignty: The principle which asserts that the people possess the ultimate political authority and can use that authority to abolish, create, or perpetuate government.

Pork-barrel legislation: Legislation appropriations funds for local projects not critically needed; members of Congress tacitly agree not to question strongly each other's pet projects.

Poverty level: Poverty is a relative concept used to indicate a general lack of money or material possessions. The federal government establishes a poverty level or threshold that ranges from $2,010 for a single person living in a metropolitan area to $6,468 for a family of seven. By this definition, 12.6 percent of Americans in 1970 were below the poverty level.

Power élite: A person, or groups of persons, who exercises dominance or control in the formulation and implementation of major economic, social, and political decisions at the local or national level.

Presidential primaries: A nominating procedure employed by several states which enables voters to participate in the selection of their party's presidential nominee, usually by the election of delegates to the nominating convention.

Presidential roles: The many expectations placed upon the person who occupies the office of president. For example, he is expected to be the Chief of State, Chief Executive, Commander-in-Chief, Chief Diplomat, Chief of his Party, and World Leader.

Private action: A doctrine developed by courts to describe actions taken by individuals which presumably were beyond the purview of the Constitution. (See "State action".)

Reapportionment: Legislation altering district shapes and sizes in order to change the district's constituency.

Remand: The sending of a case to a lower court from a superior court.

Representative government: A government in which representatives are elected by the people to make decisions.

"Rules of the game": Widely held interests or values which are a part of many established patterns of behavior in a society. The "rules" are informal norms shared and adhered to by a large majority of the members of a group.

Safe district: A district where party control is sufficiently strong to prevent serious competition by the opposing party.

Selection variables: The factors which influence the consideration of a particular individual for an office, such as the variables involved in the nomination of a person to the Supreme Court.

Seniority: The tradition widely observed in the United States Congress, as well as in state legislatures, of assigning committee positions, office space, and symbols of authority on the basis of length of service in the legislative chamber.

Separation of powers: A principle in the American political system whereby power and duties are delegated and distributed among the three branches of government — legislative, executive, and judicial.

Single-member district: An electoral district which returns one member chosen by a plurality of the votes cast in an election to a legislative body, such as the Congress or a state legislature.

Social solidarity: A reward of group membership which fulfills the needs of people who hold similar views to enjoy the mutual support and fellowship of each other.

Standing committees: The permanent and officially established committees of a legislative body, which are given authority over certain kinds of legislation.

State action: A doctrine developed by courts to indicate that actions of a state — laws or administrative regulations — that deprive persons of certain rights, such as those of the Fourteenth Amendment, constitute "state action" and are hence unconstitutional. This is to be distinguished from "private action," which has for some time been interpreted by the Supreme Court as being immune from such constitutional restrictions. Recent court decisions, however, indicate that the "state/private" action distinction is posing less of a barrier for the constitutional protection of minority rights.

"State of the Union" address: An annual message from the president to Congress which is customarily delivered early in each session. The Constitution directs the president to inform the Congress on the state of the nation and to recommend measures for Congress' consideration.

Statutory interpretation: The meaning that a court gives to a legislative act.

Stereotype: A set of attitudes about other individuals which simplify and reduce reality, often to a highly distorted and inaccurate form.

Stratification: The distribution of society into varying classes, resulting in differentiation among individuals in terms of their status, power, and privileges in the society.

"Strict constructionist": Justices who perceive their roles as merely to interpret the Constitution to the letter without interjecting their personal policy objectives, or who limit themselves to the narrow constitutional and legal questions of a case.

Structural unemployment: Unemployment caused by an individual's lack of skills or mobility rather than by poor economic conditions. Increasing the money supply will have only limited impact on structurally unemployed individuals.

Suburbanization: The movement of people usually from high density cities to low density housing outside the governmental boundaries of the cities.

"Suspect" classification: Certain classifications or ways of categorizing people by government require "strict judicial scrutiny." Classifications based on race or national origin, for example, are "odious to our system" and are "inherently suspect."

Symbolic benefits: Rewards offered in the form of a token response to particular demands. Symbolic benefits are usually given to imply that a more meaningful response will be forthcoming.

Three-fifths compromise: A decision of the Convention of 1787 which provided that in estimating a state's population for representation in Congress and apportioning direct taxes, only three-fifths of the total number of slaves were to be counted. The decision was a compromise between southern and northern states.

Two party system: Two major political parties dominate in the electoral process and, hence, in the allocation of political positions (elective and appointive) within all levels and organs of government.

Underemployment: The incidence where individuals are employed at jobs at less than their capacity.

Urban: The term used to describe an area of high population density.

Veto: The act of an executive returning to a legislature unsigned and with stated objections a bill which has passed the legislature and which requires the executive's approval before it can become law. Under the Constitution, a vote of two-thirds of those present and voting in both the House and Senate is necessary to override the president's veto and make the bill a law.

White primary: The name given to the primary elections held in several southern states from which blacks were excluded on the basis that the party was a voluntary organization competent to determine its own membership. White primaries were declared unconstitutional by the Supreme Court in 1944.

Writ of mandamus: A formal written order issued by a superior court directed to a public officer, corporation, or individual to compel the performance of an act. It may be applied to ministerial but not to discretionary duties.

INDEX

Items in boldface designate words that are included in the glossary.

Abernathy, Ralph, 223
Ad Hoc Council on Civil Rights Leadership, 225-226
Almond, Gabriel, 104-105
American Bar Association, 146-148
American political values
  black support of, 88
  conflict and compromise, 74-75
  individualism, 70-72
  legalism, 73-74
  majority rule, 72-73
  middle class position, 79
Americanization of black children, 342
Amicus curiae brief, 214

Baker v. *Carr,* 122
Benign neglect, 39-40, 333-334
Bicentenniel, 351
Black affluence, 51-55
Black attitudes
  antiwhite, 339
  in the 1970's, 341-346
  support of the government, 342, 344-346
  view of violence after 1968, 65, 67, 335
Black clergy, 97-98
Black codes, 94
Black élite, 102-104
Black interest groups (*See also* Interest groups)
  and civil rights, 215
  coalition building, 223-229
  staff and money, 255-256
Black leaders, 350

Black mayors, 8, 350
  (*See also* individual names)
Black middle class, 40, 339
Black Muslims, 220
Black party identification, 253
Black political appointments, 9-10
Black political coalition, 229-234
Black political conventions, 253
Black political organizations, 107-109
Black political participation, 195-196
Black population
  big city oriented, 2
  by states, 4-6
  in selected cities, 7
Black power, 44, 221, 223
Black social position, 347
Black voter participation, 129-131, 342
Black women, 39
Black v. white attitudes
  faith in the political system, 64
  towards integration, 58-59, 63
Blacks as congressional committee chairmen, 269
Blacks in Congress, 270-273
Blacks and organized labor, 256
Blacks and political expression, 333
Blacks and public policy, 349-351
Bradley, Thomas, 8
Brooke, Edward, 288-289, 295
Brown v. *Board of Education,* 19, 172
Bunche, Ralph, 108
Burger Court (*See also* individual decisions)
  effects on black Americans, 192-195
  busing, 182-185

compared to Warren Court, 167
criminal defendants, 189-191
impact on lower courts, 197-198
integration of public facilities, 180
jury verdicts, 190-191
legislative apportionment, 179
poverty law, 185-189
school integration, 177-178, 181
Burger, Warren E., 194-195
Busing, 46, 178, 179, 182-185, 246

Carmichael, Stokely, 221
Campaigns, 308-309
Census Bureau, 332
Chairmen of congressional commit-
tees, 268-270
Chicago political machine, 269
Chisholm, Shirley, 292
Checks and balances, 77
Civic duty, 84
Civil Rights Act of 1875, 15
Civil Rights Act of 1964, 229
Civil Rights Cases, 16, 168
Civil Rights Movement, 216-235
Civil War Amendments, 15
Class insecurity, 55-57
Class system in America, 80
Cloture votes, 278-280
Coleman Report, 43-44
Coleman, William, 277
Compliance with court decisions,
200-202
Compromise, 74-75
Congress
  black candidates, 277
  committee chairmen, 268-270
  filibuster, 277-278
  floor leader, 275
  legislative process, 275
  organization, 266-268
  policy-making, 322-323
  seniority, 278, 280-283
Congress of Racial Equality (CORE),
109, 221-223
Congressional Black Caucus
  cohesion, 298
  creation, 289
  divisions within, 292
  future of, 296-297
  as an interest group, 297
  legislative strategy, 292-293
  membership, 118, 120, 286-288

and President Ford, 296
and President Nixon, 289-291, 294
Courts (*See also* Burger Court, Federal
courts, Supreme Court, Warren Court)
  judicial review, 135
  policy-making, 166-167
  statutory interpretation, 138-139
Criminal defendants, 175, 189-191

Dahl, Robert, 198
Dawson, William L., 269, 273
De facto segregation, 178
DeFunis v. *Odegaard*, 141-142
De jure segregation, 178
Dellums, Ronald, 118, 120, 285-286
Democratic party and blacks, 244,
246-252
Democratic party convention, 250
Depression, the, and racism, 17-18, 31
Detroit metropolitan busing plan,
182-185
Diggs, Charles, 269
Discrimination in employment, 32
Dred Scott case, 12-15
Dual labor market, 34
DuBois, W. E. B., 107
Dye, Thomas, 42, 52

Easton, David, 343
Economic inequality, 28-29
Education (*See also* Schools and educa-
tion)
  school finance, 186-187
  segregation, 168-170, 172
Eisenhower, Dwight D., 243
Elected black officials, 9, 113-120
European immigrants, 29-30
Evers, Medgar, 225
Executive Office of the President, 265
Expressive interest groups, 208

Fair Employment Practices, 39
Family structure, 27
Federal courts (*See also* Supreme
Court)
  selection of judges, 151-152
  structure, 150-151
Federalism, 76
Federal Regulation of Lobbying Act,
212
Filibuster, 277-278
Ford, Gerald, 244, 296

Fourteenth Amendment, 16
Freedom rides, 110

Gary Convention, 291
Gerrymandering, 180
Ghettoes, 49
Gibson, Kenneth, 8
Government employment of blacks, 123–127
Grandfather clause, 170

Harlan, John Marshall, 17
Harris v. *New York*, 189–190
Hatcher, Richard, 8
Hayes-Tilden election, 15
Holden, Mathew, 347
Hoover, Herbert, 243
Housing, 186
  black home ownership, 47, 51, 58
  discrimination practices, 17–18, 48, 173–174
  and education, 47
  federally insured mortgages, 48
  suburbanization, 49–51
Housing and Urban Development, Department of (HUD), 316
Hunter, Floyd, 79

Impact of court decisions, 200–202
Income for blacks
  by family, 39–40
  city and suburban figures, 51
  median family income, 34–36
  since World War II, 33
Incrementalism, 310
Individualism, 70–72
Insecurity, 51–57
Interest groups
  black groups, 215
  Civil Rights Movement, 216–235
  electioneering, 211
  litigation, 214
  lobbying, 212–214
  and Model Cities, 319–320
  nature of, 207–209
  perceived power of, 80–83
  and policy-making, 309–310
  and public opinion, 211
  resources and influence, 209–211
  violence, 215

Jackson, Jesse, 240, 336
Jackson, Maynard, 8, 123

Jim Crow laws, 94
Johnson v. *Louisiana*, 190
Jones, Mack, 196
Jones v. *Mayer*, 174
Judges
  blacks, 155–159
  political role, 149
  socioeconomic characteristics, 154–155
Judicial activism, 159–160
Judicial review, 135
Judicial selection, 146–148, 150–153
Judicial self-restraint, 159–160
Jury verdicts, 190–191

Kansas City mini-convention, 250
Kennedy, John F., 124–125, 283–284
Kerner Commission Report, 57–58, 334
Keyes v. *School District No. 1*, 178
King, Martin Luther, 13
  moderate position, 233–234
  and the NAACP, 225
  and SCLC, 222–223
  and Stokely Carmichael, 231
Ku Klux Klan (KKK), 94

Law and order, 10, 189–191, 236
Law schools
  admission to, 141–142
  institutional racism, 143–144
Lawyers
  American Bar Association, 146–148
  bar admission, 144–145
  and the legal process, 139–140
  and the legal profession, 140
  nature of practice, 145–148
Legalism, 73–74
Limited government, 75
Lobbying, 212–214
  (*See also* Interest groups)

Majority rule, 72–73, 348–349
Malcolm X, 220
Marbury v. *Madison*, 135–138
March on Washington, 113, 226
Marshall, Thurgood, 180, 184–185, 187
Maxwell Case, the, 52–55
McGovern-Fraser Commission, 248
McKissick, Floyd, 221
McLaurin v. *Oklahoma*, 170
Melting pot thesis, 28
Meredith, James, 232

Middle class blacks, 55–57, 102, 105, 128
Militant blacks, 113
Military discrimination, 32
Milliken v. *Bradley*, 183–185
Mills, C. Wright, 79
Miranda v. *Arizona*, 189–190
Missouri ex rel Gaines v. *Canada*, 169
Mitchell, John, 335
Model Cities, 311–312, 316–322
Moynihan, Daniel P., 27, 39–40, 333–334
Moose Lodge No. 107 v. *Irvis*, 181–182
Muhammad, Elijah, 220
Murphy, Walter, 160–161
Myrdal, Gunnar, 18

National Association for the Advancement of Colored People (NAACP)
    activities of, 107–109
    creation of, 19
    Legal Defense staff, 167
    litigation, 19–20, 214
    and the Urban League, 219–220
National Association of Real Estate Boards, 320
National Bar Association, 148
National ghetto system, 2
Nationalization of race issue, 19–20
New Deal, 31, 33
Nix, Robert N., 286
Nixon, Richard M.
    benign neglect, 41–42
    black voters, 244, 333–336
    busing, 308
    Congressional Black Caucus, 289–291, 294
    court appointments, 171
    law and order, 190
    trust in government, 11

O'Boyle, Archbishop, 226–227
Office of Economic Opportunity (OEO), 318, 323, 325
Operation PUSH, 240
Organized labor and blacks, 30, 256, 319

Peltason, Jack, 160
Piore, Michael, 34–35
Plessy v. *Ferguson*, 16, 168
Poinsett, Alex, 285

Political education of blacks, 31–35, 96–97
Political machines and blacks, 100–101, 269
Political participation, 10
Political parties (*See also* Democratic party and Republican party)
    federalism, 241
    platforms, 246–247
    two-party system, 240–242
Political resources, 92–93
Political socialization, 28, 88
Political status of blacks, 9–11
Poll tax, 170
Popular sovereignty, 75
Pork-barrel, 314
Poverty, 8
    economic inequality, 28–29
    explanation of, 26–28
Poverty law, 175–176, 185–189
Powell, Adam Clayton, 269, 273–274
Power élite, 79–80, 83–84
President
    as administrator, 265–266
    blacks as candidates, 276
    blacks in the cabinet, 277
    as civil rights leader, 284
    election of, 263–264
    roles of, 263
Private clubs and blacks, 181–182
Protest, political, 10, 32
    (*See also* Violence)
Protestant ethic, 72
Public policy-making process
    agenda and initiation, 307–313
    coalition building, 313–316
    constituency influence, 315
    crisis, 310–311
    overview, 305–307
    response to, 324–325
Public schools (*See* Schools and education)

Quality of life in cities, 322

Racial stereotypes, 29
Racism in America, 346, 348–349
    (*See also* White attitudes toward blacks)
Randolph, A. Philip, 32, 224, 230
Rangel, Charles, 295–296
Reapportionment, 122–123
Reconstruction, 94

Regulatory commissions, 323–324
Reitman v. *Mulkey*, 173–174
Representative government, 75–76
Republican party and blacks, 242–244
Restrictive covenants, 48
Reuther, Walter, 226
Reverse migration, 2, 8
Roosevelt, Franklin D., 17, 31, 33
Roosevelt, Theodore, 99
Rustin, Bayard, 224

Safe legislative districts, 300
Salisbury, Robert, 208
Sampling, 306
Samuelson, Paul, 36
San Antonio Independent School District v. *Rodriguez*, 186–187
Schools and education
    black students enrolled, 44
    Coleman Report, 43–44
    de facto and de jure segregation, 43
    integration, 181
    separate but equal, 16, 42
    socialization, 96, 342
    violence, 46
Selective Service System, 324–325
Seniority system in Congress, 268, 278, 280–283
Separate but equal, 16, 42
Separation of powers, 76–77
Shelley v. *Kraemer*, 49
Sit-ins, 110
Skolnick, James, 58
Slavery, 27–29, 346
Smith v. *Allwright*, 170
Sorauf, Frank, 78
South
    black migration, 2, 30
    black population, 4–6
Southern Christian Leadership Conference (SCLC), 109, 223–224
Spear, Allan, 30
State population by race, 4–6
Stratification system, 56
Status quo preservation, 77–78
Stokes, Carl, 8, 120–123, 350–351
Structural unemployment, 36
Student Nonviolent Coordinating Committee (SNCC), 109, 220–221
Suburbanization
    and blacks, 49
    and white migration, 2–3

Supreme Court (*See also* Burger Court, Warren Court, and individual cases)
    black support of, 346
    Civil Rights Act of 1875, 15
    Civil Rights Cases, 16
    compliance with decisions, 200–202
    constitutionalizing racism, 168–170
    Dred Scott case, 12, 15
    and racial discrimination, 172–175
    segregation in education, 168–170
    selection of justices, 153
    weakness on racial justice, 199
Swann v. *Charlotte-Mecklenberg Board of Education*, 178–179
Sweatt v. *Painter*, 169

Taney, Roger, 12
Three-fifths compromise, 12
Truman administration, 19, 39
Trust in government, 11
Two party system, 78

Unemployment, 8, 36–38
Upper class blacks, 102–104
Urban League, 107, 219
Urbanization and blacks, 2–3, 8, 100–102

Violence, 57, 65, 67, 333
Voting by blacks, 92–94
    Democratic party support, 106
    low turnout, 93–96
    participation, 84–85
    Reconstruction, effect of, 94
    urban concentration, 118
    white primary, 170
Voting Rights Act of 1965, 230, 335

Warren Court (*See also* individual decisions)
    compared to Burger Court, 167, 191–192, 197–199
    criminal defendants, 175
    major issues confronted, 193
    political leadership, 198
    poverty law, 175–176
    racial discrimination, 172–175
Washington, Booker T., 96, 99
Watergate scandal, 265, 344
Weaver, Robert E., 277, 317–318
Welfare recipients' rights, 187–188

White attitudes toward blacks
  backlash, 339–341
  hostility, 62
  general feelings, 111–112
  racial solidarity, 57
White v. black attitudes, 62–63
White flight, 8, 43
White House Conference on Civil
Rights (1966), 231
White primary, 170
White, Walter, 32
Whitcomb v. *Chavis*, 179
Wilkins, Roy, 220, 225, 232

Wilson, James Q., 104–106
Women, black, 39
Woods, Robert G., 312
World War I
  effects on blacks, 30–31
  and racism, 19
Wright v. *Council of the City of Emporia*, 181
Wyman v. *James*, 187–188

Young, Coleman, 8
Young, Whitney M., 219, 336

DATE DUE	
MAR 0 9 1999	
MAR 1 7 1999	
APR 1 2 1999	
MAR 1 6 2000	
MAY 1 0 2001	